Apparel Production Terms and Processes

2nd Edition

Janace E. Bubonia

Texas Christian University

Fairchild Books

An imprint of Bloomsbury Publishing Inc

BLOOMSBURY

NEW YORK · LONDON · OXFORD · NEW DELHI · SYDNEY

Fairchild Books

An imprint of Bloomsbury Publishing Inc

1385 Broadway	50 Bedford Square
New York	London
NY 10018	WC1B 3DP
USA	UK

www.bloomsbury.com

**FAIRCHILD BOOKS, BLOOMSBURY and the Diana logo
are trademarks of Bloomsbury Publishing Plc**

First edition published 2012

This edition first published 2017

Library of Congress Cataloging-in-Publication Data
Names: Bubonia, Janace E., author.
Title: Apparel production terms and processes / Janace E. Bubonia, Ph.D.,
Texas Christian University.
Description: 2nd edition. | New York, NY, USA : Fairchild Books, an imprint of Bloomsbury
Publishing Inc., 2017.
Identifiers: LCCN 2016028510| ISBN 9781501315572 | ISBN 9781501315589 (ePDF)
Subjects: LCSH: Clothing trade—Terminology. | Fashion—Terminology. | Clothing factories—
Equipment and supplies—Terminology. | Dressmaking materials—Terminology.
Classification: LCC TT494 .B83 2017 | DDC 687.01/4--dc23 LC record available
at https://lccn.loc.gov/2016028510

ISBN:	PB:	978-1-5013-1557-2
	ePDF:	978-1-5013-1558-9

Cover design: Liron Gilenberg www.ironicitalics.com
Cover Images: Courtesy of Janace Bubonia

Typeset by Lachina
Printed and bound in the United States of America

CONTENTS

EXTENDED CONTENTS

PREFACE

The apparel industry's global supply chain is dynamic and is continuously evolving due to advances in technology and communications that are changing the way products are developed, produced, and distributed. These advances continually prompt revisions to existing terms and produce a need for new vocabulary. *Apparel Production Terms and Processes* is a reference for educators, students, industry professionals, and consumers interested in learning more about terminology and materials used in the mass production of apparel products. It is important to note that this edition is not a resource for couture or home sewing terminology and techniques, as garments resulting from these classifications do not utilize mass production techniques.

ORGANIZATION OF THE TEXT

This new edition is divided into four parts: Part One, "Apparel Production Overview"; Part Two, "Raw Materials and Component Parts"; Part Three, "Design Development and Product Specifications"; and Part Four, "Production and Quality Control." Parts and chapters are presented in a progression that relates to the flow of the production process or the route of the garment from its origin through development to completion. Terms are grouped according to subject by use or application. Each part opens with a graphic to illustrate the processes and a brief summary of the chapters contained within and how they relate to one another. Chapters open with a brief introduction followed by terms that are listed alphabetically, in some cases alphabetically under general headings, or in logical order of process. For items that go by more than one name, alternate terms are given—for example, **Decorative Elastic** (**Fancy Elastic**). Terms are defined and illustrated with photographs or drawings for clarification where applicable. Photographs, illustrations, and tables accompany the definitions to reinforce the written descriptions and provide visual recognition. Lists of use or examples follow many definitions to provide the reader with an easy way to assimilate the facts. Due to space limitations, some judgment regarding information to be included within each chapter was required. If a particular definition contains another entry term that may further help the reader grasp the definition, that other entry term is indicated in italics.

NEW TO THIS EDITION

There are several new additions to this book. A new chapter on sizing and fit provides the reader with a stronger understanding of how sizing of garments and fit are determined, corrected, and managed. New labeling and safety regulations include international requirements for compliance in order for products to enter into commerce. In addition, ISO stitch and seam classifications are integrated alongside ASTM International standards to provide awareness of the parallels between the two. Inspection is now featured as an important aspect relating to the quality of apparel items as well as new technologies and terminologies incorporated throughout the book.

The industry resource guide has been updated at the end of the book to provide a means for contact and gathering additional information. This guide is divided into categories that follow the organization of content within the book. Metric conversion tables have also been included to provide quick access to common calculations. An index with the most frequently used ASTM and ISO stitch and seam classifications for apparel and an alphabetical cross-referenced index at the end of the book will help the reader to locate specific terms.

APPAREL PRODUCTION TERMS AND PROCESSES STUDiO™

Fairchild Books has a long history of excellence in textbook publishing for fashion education. Our new online STUDIOS are specially developed to complement this book with rich media ancillaries that students can adapt to their visual learning styles. *Apparel Production Terms and Processes STUDIO* features online self-quizzes with scored results and personalized study tips and flashcards with terms/definitions and image identification to help students master concepts and improve grades. It also offers visual analysis exercises, specification sheets, and defect activities that ask readers to determine the rating category for various garment defects (i.e., critical, major, or minor).

STUDIO access cards are offered free with new book purchases and also sold separately through Bloomsbury Fashion Central (www.BloomsburyFashionCentral.com).

INSTRUCTOR'S RESOURCES

The second edition of *Apparel Production Terms and Processes* offers an all new instructor's guide that provides sample syllabi, teaching strategies for a range of courses, video links, sample activities and projects, and learning outcomes for each chapter. A quiz bank and test questions are available to instructors, as well as an image bank of selected photos for instructors to integrate into lecture materials.

ACKNOWLEDGMENTS

Thank you to everyone who made this new edition a reality. To the staff of Fairchild Books, including Senior Acquisitions Editor Amanda Breccia, Development Editor Amy Butler, Art Development Editor Edie Weinberg, and Photo Researcher Gail Henry.

Thank you to the following reviewers, selected by Fairchild Books, for your valuable comments: Anne Marie Allen, Fashion Institute of Design and Merchandising (FIDM); Desirae Allen, Johnson and Wales University; Su-Jeong Hwang Shin, Texas Tech University; Diane Limbaugh, Oklahoma State University; Luz Pascal, Fashion Institute of Technology (FIT); Emily Pascoe, Montclair State University; and Mary Simpson, Baylor University.

To companies and industry professionals, thank you for your willingness to provide material samples and images to reinforce the understanding of fashion production concepts and terms.

To the Dean of the College of Fine Arts and the faculty and staff in the Department of Interior Design and Fashion Merchandising, thank you for your encouragement and support during the preparation of this new edition.

Thank you to my loved ones and close friends for your inspiring words, unwavering support, and endless encouragement during the development of this book.

I would also like to convey my sincere appreciation to the readers of the past edition, whose support and acceptance led to this new edition.

The Publisher wishes to gratefully acknowledge and thank the editorial team involved in the publication of this book:

Senior Acquisitions Editor: Amanda Breccia
Development Editor: Amy Butler
Assistant Editor: Kiley Kudrna
Art Development Editor: Edie Weinberg
Photo Researcher: Gail Henry
Production Manager: Claire Cooper
Project Manager: Chris Black, Lachina

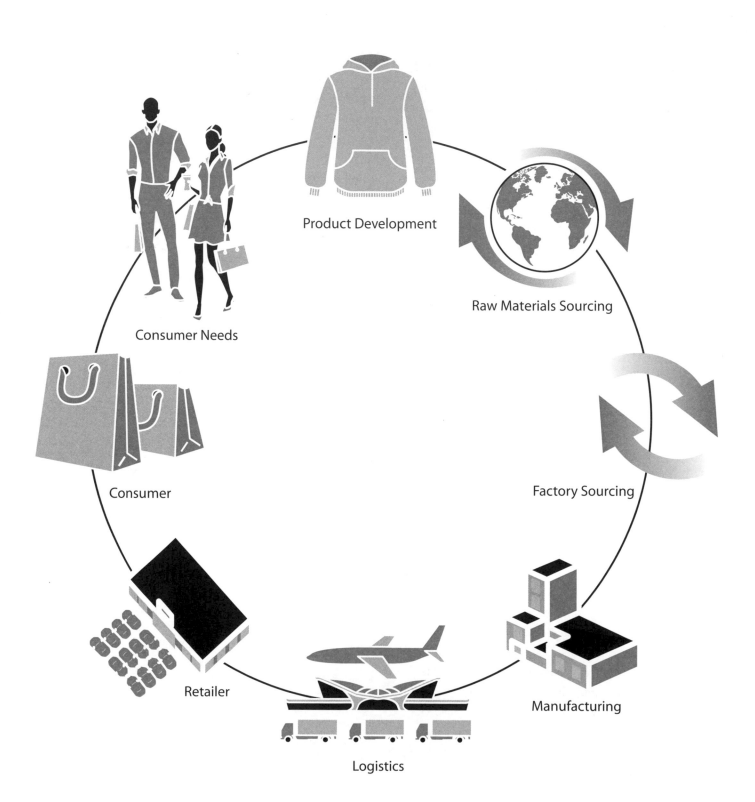

Product Development

Raw Materials Sourcing

Factory Sourcing

Manufacturing

Logistics

Retailer

Consumer

Consumer Needs

Apparel Production Overview

The business of apparel production is fast paced, complex, and ever changing. As consumer demand grows for products to enter the marketplace at a rapid pace, it is pressuring supply chains to be agile and run as lean as possible. Technology is allowing companies to meet customer demand for fashion products by utilizing systems for increasing efficiency along the supply chain. Part One of this book will provide an overview of the various components that comprise the global supply chain. A brief history of the development of the apparel industry will reveal its evolution and technological advancements. The North American classification system for the apparel supply chain is outlined to increase understanding of the organization of the apparel industry. In addition, brand categories, price classifications, and apparel product categories will be discussed.

CHAPTER 1

The Global Scope of Apparel Production

Apparel products are manufactured all around the world. Global sourcing trends show continuous growth in apparel production among developing countries and those that are evolving.

THE GLOBAL SUPPLY CHAIN

Apparel production is a labor-intensive process by which raw materials are converted into finished saleable garments. The apparel and textiles industry is one of the most active international trade sectors. "The global fashion apparel industry is one of the most important sectors of the economy in terms of investment, revenue, trade and employment generation all over the world," as reported by fashionproducts.com, the fashion industry manufacturers and wholesale suppliers directory. Advances in technology and global trade have made production more efficient and cost-effective for many companies today. The **global supply chain** for the apparel industry is composed of

- Fiber producers, textile plants, and findings manufacturers
- Apparel manufacturers
- Distributors and transporters of fashion goods
- Retailers including brick-and-mortar stores, catalogues, television shopping networks, and the internet
- End consumers who purchase fashion products

Sewing operators in an apparel manufacturing plant

Prior to mechanized textile manufacturing, which began during the eighteenth century, **craft style production** was the norm. People purchased raw materials for the purpose of weaving and sewing textile products by hand in their homes. During this time, India produced and exported very fine fabrics that were highly desired. Textile designs from China, Japan, and India influenced Western cultures. European manufacturers began copying and producing textiles in Asian styles. England in particular was producing sophisticated patterned fabrics that were quite elaborate, which made them more expensive than those imported from India. The labor-intensive task of weaving these fabrics by hand made it difficult for England to compete with lower-priced goods imported from India.

First Industrial Revolution

The development of and improvements in coal-, iron-, and steam-driven mechanisms in eighteenth-century England resulted in an **industrial revolution**. Technological advances in textile machinery and the creation of mills and factories gave way to the development of mass-produced textile goods at competitive prices. The first textile invention of note during this time was the flying shuttle, which significantly improved weaving speeds by using a mechanically driven shuttle to increase fabric output while reducing labor costs. As a result of increasing weaving speeds, demand for the production of spun yarns grew. From 1764 to 1785 numerous inventions led to advances in spinning of yarns and weaving. Eli Whitney revolutionized the industry with his cotton gin that mechanized cleaning and separation of fibers. During this time cotton was the most widely used fiber for textile

Spinning of yarn by hand

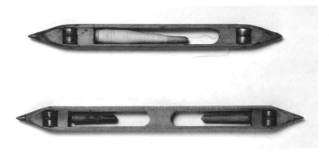

Flying shuttles for weaving

Yarns being created on a spinning Jenny

Lockstitch sewing machine

goods. The chain-stitch and lockstitch sewing machines allowed for mechanized sewing. These inventions were followed by the first commercially produced paper patterns for apparel and the addition of the first synthetic dyes and fibers. Inventions that revolutionized the textiles industry during the first industrial revolution are outlined in Table 1.1.

■ Second Industrial Revolution

The **second industrial revolution** began in 1870 and was centered on chemicals, electricity, and steel. Some scholars credit this period as a phase of the first industrial revolution. In 1872 factory-style production was becoming more efficient through inventions powered by steam and electricity, such as cutting machines that allowed for multiple layers of fabric to be cut simultaneously. During the second industrial revolution, inventors made great advances in commercial production of the synthetic fiber rayon and viscose rayon. Increased production of textile goods made

TABLE 1.1

Textiles Industry Inventions of the First Industrial Revolution

Date	Inventor	Invention
1733	John Kay	Flying shuttle, increased weaving speed
1764	James Hargreaves	Spinning Jenny, an improved spinning wheel
1764	Richard Arkwright	Water frame, the first water-powered spinning frame, which produced stronger yarns
1779	Samuel Crompton	Spinning mule, allowed for different types of yarns to be produced
1785	Edmund Cartwright	Patented power loom, driven by steam, allowed for yarns to be woven into fabric
1790	Richard Arkwright	Opened steam-powered textile factory in England
1792	Eli Whitney	Cotton gin, mechanized the cleaning of cotton by separating the fibers from the seeds
1804	Joseph Marie Jacquard	Jacquard loom attachment, allowed for complex woven designs to be created on a loom
1813	William Horrocks	Variable speed batton, an improved power loom
1830	Barthelemy Thimonnier	Chain-stitch sewing machine, allowed for mechanized sewing
1844	John Mercer	Mercerized cotton
1846	Elias Howe	Lockstitch sewing machine, provided better-quality stitches and seams
1849	Walter Hunt	Safety pin
1851	Isaac Singer	Improved and patented lockstitch sewing machine with presser foot and treadle for hands-free sewing
1855	George Audemars	Artificial silk rayon filaments
1856	Sir William Henry Perkin	First synthetic aniline dye, providing the ability to dye fabric bright colors
1858	Ellen Demorest	First paper patterns for dresses
1863	Ebenezer Butterick	Patent for first proportionally sized paper patterns for apparel

(Bellis, 2009a; Swicofil AG Textile Services, n.d.; Tortora & Marcketti, 2015)

TABLE 1.2

Textiles Industry Inventions of the Second Industrial Revolution

Date	Inventor	Invention
1872	Unknown	Steam-powered cutting machine, allowed simultaneous cutting of multiple layers of fabric
1872	Aaron Montgomery Ward	First mail-order catalogue
1874	Charles Goodyear, Jr.	Shoe welt stitching machine
1884	Hilaire de Berniguad, the Count of Chardonnay	First commercial synthetic fiber, Chardonnay silk made from rayon fibers
1890	Unknown	Electric cutting machine
1893	Sears, Roebuck, and Co.	Another mail-order catalogue
1893	Whitcomb Judson	Zipper
1894	Frederick Winslow Taylor	Scientific management, efficient assembly-line production in factories
1891/2	Charles Frederick Cross, Edward John Bevan, and Clayton Beadle	Viscose rayon process. First commercial production of viscose rayon by Courtaulds Fibers, 1905

(Bellis, 2009a; Swicofil AG Textile Services, n.d.; Tortora & Marcketti, 2015)

way for new outlets to sell goods. In 1894 Frederick Winslow Taylor revolutionized assembly-line production by timing each task in the production of goods to eliminate wasted time and increase efficiency. Significant inventions that advanced the textiles industry during the second industrial revolution are outlined in Table 1.2. The development of many synthetic fibers such as acetate, acrylic, modacrylic, lyocell, polyester, and spandex ensued during the twentieth century.

Ladies coat factory

■ Third Industrial Revolution

The **third industrial revolution** is an era focused on economic sustainability and climatic change. Some economists date it as early as 1974 with the major advances in information technology, whereas others claim it began in the early 2000s with the emphasis on green energy and global warming. Hans Sennholz, author of *The Underground Economy*, wrote, "The third industrial revolution is now making its appearance in the United States and other industrial countries . . . It is an 'information revolution' that greatly expands the scope of tradable services and tends to move many service jobs offshore to India, China, and other industrial newcomers where labor is much cheaper" (2006). Jeremy Rifkin, adviser to the European Union and author of bestsellers on economic issues, has defined the three critical challenges of the latest industrial revolution as the global economic crisis, energy security, and climate change. As with the first and second industrial revolutions, it will take time and resources to find solutions for the challenges faced by industry today.

Textile advances in the development of fibers have continued into the twenty-first century with technologically complex fibers including nano (diameters less than 0.5 micron), biomedical (with electronic sensors that communicate information about the biological conditions of the wearer's body), high-performance hybrid/multifunction fibers (which absorb and evaporate moisture and

Fabric made from organic cotton

Apparel manufacturing plant

perspiration away from the body while offering antimicrobial properties), as well as renewable, sustainable, and biodegradable fibers such as bamboo and organic cotton. These smart textiles bring added value to the customer through performance improvements such as regulating body temperature, administering medication, and providing aesthetic changes such as changing color or lighting up. The technology of 3D printed textiles and garments is improving and will continue to grow in importance in the twenty-first century.

GLOBAL PRODUCTION TODAY

Despite great technological advances to streamline production over the past few centuries, the manufacturing of fashion goods still remains labor-intensive, driving companies to seek low wages in order for their products to remain profitable and competitive in today's marketplace. An increased awareness of global climatic changes has inspired some companies, as well as governments, to explore eco-friendly and socially responsible options for manufacturing goods.

According to Anastasia Charbin, Lectra's worldwide marketing director for fashion and apparel, the most significant challenges the apparel industry faces are "reorganizing the supply chain to be more responsive to consumer demand, bringing quality products with unique styling to market ever faster and linking point-of-sale systems to production. Fast fashion has created the need to turn product replenishment from a push (pushing things to the market that the industry thinks consumers will want) to a pull, that is, responding quickly to market demand and using these market 'wants' to pull product from production . . .

Protecting profit margins is also a very big challenge today . . . To remain profitable, the supply chain needs to find innovative ways to reduce end-to-end costs, particularly in the main apparel production regions. Saving material, improving process and eliminating waste have become necessary; as well as ways to drive innovation via the product itself" (Barrie, 2015). Social media has also added pressure to the apparel supply chain by increasing awareness of products and driving demand.

Advances in information technology such as **electronic data interchange (EDI)**, **product data management (PDM)**, and **product life-cycle management (PLM)** have significantly reduced the time it takes to communicate changes across the global supply chain by making information immediately available via the internet or any digital means. Electronic data interchange allows trading partners, logistics services, and vendors to automatically exchange data and collaborate to build and manage their supply chain. Use of this software allows for faster communication of information while reducing processing times and increasing accuracy of data. Product life-cycle management involves the digital representation and management of information for a product with respect to supply chain processes and product data management throughout the product's life cycle from initial concept development to the end consumer. Product data management, a component of product life-cycle management, utilizes software to monitor and track information about product specifications with regard to materials, design, development, and manufacturing. This technology provides a means for companies to track the costs associated with producing a product. These advances in communication have allowed companies to shorten the supply chain cycle, thereby bringing goods to the consumer faster. Fast-fashion and speed-to-market programs have become increasingly important as companies seek ways to meet customer demand and reduce product development cycle time.

References

Barrie, L. (2015, April 1). *Apparel software trends 2015: Supply chain challenges.* Retrieved October 17, 2015, from http://www.just-style.com/management-briefing/supply-chain-challenges_id124803.aspx

Bellis, M. (2009a). *Industrial revolution: Timeline of textile machinery.* Retrieved December 21, 2009, from http://inventors.about.com/library/inventors/blindustrialrevolutiontextiles.htm

Bellis, M. (2009b). *Pictures from the industrial revolution.* Retrieved December 21, 2009, from http://inventors.about.com/od/indrevolution/ss/Industrial_Revo.htm

Bellis, M. (2009c). *19th century timeline.* Retrieved December 21, 2009, from http://inventors.about.com/od/timelines/a/Nineteenth.htm

FabricLink, 2006. *Fabric trademark and brand name index.* Retrieved February 11, 2010, from http://www.fabriclink.com/search/fabric-search.cfm

Fashionproducts.com. (n.d.). *Fashion apparel industry overview.* Retrieved December 21, 2009, from http://www.fashionproducts.com/fashion-apparel-overview.html

Gaddis, R. (2014, May 7). *What is the future of fabric? These smart textiles will blow your mind. Forbes* Lifestyle. Retrieved October 27, 2015, from http://www.forbes.com/sites/forbesstylefile/2014/05/07/what-is-the-future-of-fabric-these-smart-textiles-will-blow-your-mind/

Greenwood, J. (1997). *The third industrial revolution: Technology, productivity, and income inequality.* Washington, DC: AEI Press.

Hills, Inc. (n.d.). Polymetric nanofibers: Fantasy or future. Retrieved February 11, 2010, from http://www.hillsinc.net/Polymeric.shtml

Hoshi, T. (2009). *Second industrial revolution.* Retrieved December 21, 2009, from http://www.viswiki.com/en/Second_Industrial_Revolution

IPA. (2009). *IPA provides useful information about the apparel manufacturing industry.* Retrieved December 21, 2009, from http://www.internationalprofitassociates.net/stats/apparel.asp

Johnson, I., Cohen, A. C., & Sarkar, A. K. (2015). *J. J. Pizzuto's fabric science* (11th ed.). New York: Fairchild Books.

Lebby, M. S., Jachimowicz, K. E., & Ramdani, J. (2000). *U.S. Patent 6080690—Textile fabric with integrated sensing device and clothing fabricated thereof.* Retrieved February 11, 2010, from http://www.patentstorm.us/patents/6080690/fulltext.html

Netter, T. (2005, August). The new era of textile trade: Taking stock in the post MFA environment. *World of Work, 54,* 28–30.

Rifkin, J. (2009). *About Jeremy Rifkin.* Retrieved December 22, 2009, from http://www.foet.org/JeremyRifkin.htm.

Saheed, A. H. H. (2006, May 1). *New trends in the global apparel marketplace after first year of quota expiry.* Retrieved December 21, 2009, from http://www.allbusiness.com/asia/4089757-1html

Sennholz, H. F. (2006, April 3). *The third industrial revolution.* Retrieved December 21, 2009, from http://mises.org/story/2105

Swicofil A. G Textile Services. (n.d.). *Rayon Viscose.* Retrieved December 22, 2009, from http://www.swicofil.com/products/200viscose.html

Tortora, P. G., & Marcketti, S. B. (2015). *Survey of historic costume* (6th ed.). New York: Fairchild Books.

U.S. Department of Labor. (2009, December 17). Career guide to industries, 2010–2011 edition: Textile, textile product, and apparel manufacturing. Retrieved December 21, 2009, from http://www.bls.gov/oco/cg/cgs015.htm

CHAPTER 2

Apparel Supply Chain

The apparel industry's **global supply chain** includes all processes from fibers and fabric development to garment production, finishing, packaging, and distribution to retail venues.

Ellen Martin, vice president of Information and Supply Chain Systems at VF Corporation, stated, "Apparel has the hardest supply chain of any business." Aspects of the apparel business that add to the difficulty in manufacturing and distribution are manual *bundling*, sewing, and trimming operations; incessant demand for styling changes based on fashion and seasonal trends; and companies striving to cut costs by sourcing fabrics, trims, and labor from areas around the globe, which ultimately affects timing and distribution. High technology has helped speed up fiber and fabric production, product design, pattern development and fit, color communication, fabric spreading, cutting and preassembly or preproduction processes, ticketing, and tracking distribution and reorders in order to shorten the product development cycle.

Garment worker

NORTH AMERICAN INDUSTRY CLASSIFICATION SYSTEM (NAICS)

The U.S. Economic Classification Policy Committee (ECPC), in collaboration with Mexico's Instituto Nacional de Estadística, Geografía e Informática (INEGI) and Statistics Canada, developed a classification system for grouping similar industry procedures into economic activities. These three countries created the **North American Industry Classification System (NAICS)**. The United States, Canada, and Mexico, trading partners of the North American Free Trade Agreement (NAFTA), utilize the NAICS for organizing industries according to likenesses in production processes to provide means for statistical comparison and analysis among products manufactured in these countries. NAFTA carefully reviews and updates this classification system every five years, in order to correspond to economic changes representative of these three countries. NAICS uses a six-digit numeric system.

- First two numbers correspond to the sector.
- Third number identifies the subsector.
- Fourth number identifies the industry group.
- Fifth number identifies NAICS industry.
- Sixth number designates the national industry (Mexico, Canada, or 0 if others are the same as the United States).

NAICS divides the apparel supply chain into three major categories or sectors that include manufacturing, wholesale trade, and retail trade.

■ Manufacturing (Sector 31–33)

Within the manufacturing sector, two specific subsectors apply to apparel products: textile mills (subsector 313) and apparel manufacturing (subsector 315).

Textile Mills Businesses that develop, prepare, and convert natural or manufactured fibers into nonwoven fabrics or spin them into yarns that are woven or knitted into fabric yardage. As stated in the *NAICS*, this sector also includes finishing processes such as "bleaching, dyeing, *printing* (e.g. *roller*, *screen*, *flock*, *plisse*), stonewashing, and other mechanical finishing, such as preshrinking, shrinking, sponging, calendaring, mercerizing and napping; as well as cleaning, scouring, and the preparation of natural fibers and raw stock."

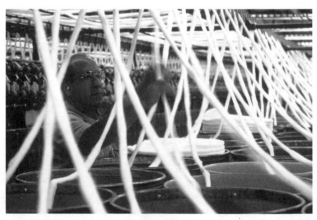

Fiber mill

Fiber, Yarn, and Thread Mills 3131 include

- 313110 Yarn Spinning Mills, Yarn Texturizing, Throwing, Twisting and Winding, Thread Mills, Hemp Yarn Producers

Fabric mill

Fabric finishing/coating mill

Fabric Mills 3132 include

- 313210 Broadwoven Fabric Mills
- 313220 Narrow Fabric Mills and Schiffli Machine Embroidery
- 313230 Nonwoven Fabric Mills
- 313240 Knit Fabric Mills for Warp (flat) and Weft (circular) Knits, Knitting and Finishing, Manufacturing, Dyeing, and Finishing of Lace

Textile and Fabric Finishing and Fabric Coating Mills 3133 include

- 313310 Textile and Fabric Finishing Mills, Converters
- 313320 Fabric Coating Mills

NAICS: Apparel Manufacturing

Apparel Manufacturing Subsector 315

Apparel Manufacturers Businesses that cut and sew garments from purchased fabrics, those that knit fabrics that are then cut and sewn into garments, or those that knit apparel products; combining mill and apparel manufacturing functions. This sector includes traditional manufacturers as well as contractors who manufacture all or part of a garment.

Traditional Manufacturers Apparel and textile production facilities or factories owned and operated by one company. All aspects of apparel design and assembly take place in-house.

Contractors Independent businesses hired by firms to provide production services to manufacture entire garments, product lines, or partially complete component parts. All or part of the apparel manufacturing process is outsourced. Examples of contractors include

- *Jobbers*
- *Cut, Make, and Trim (CMT)*
- *General Contractors*
- *Specialty Contractors*

Apparel Knitting Mills 3151 include

- 315110 Hosiery and Sock Mills
- 315190 Other Apparel Knitting Mills (underwear, outerwear, nightwear)

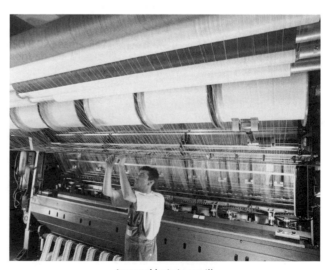

Apparel knitting mill

Apparel cutting contractor

Apparel sewing contractor

Cut and Sew Apparel Manufacturing 3152 include

- 315210 Cut and Sew Apparel Contractors
- 315220 Men's and Boy's Cut and Sew Apparel Manufacturing
- 315240 Women's, Girl's, and Infants' Cut and Sew Apparel Manufacturing
- 315280 Other Cut and Sew Apparel Manufacturing. "Examples of products made by these establishments are fur or leather apparel, sheep-lined clothing, team athletic uniforms, band uniforms, academic caps and gowns, clerical vestments, and costumes."

Apparel Accessories and Other Apparel Manufacturing 3159 include

- 315990 Apparel Accessories and Other Apparel Manufacturing. "Examples of products made by these establishments are belts, caps, gloves (except medical, sporting, and safety), hats, and neckties."

Sources: Cut and Sew Apparel Manufacturing 315280—p. 276 and Apparel Accessories and Other Apparel Manufacturing 315990—pp. 275–276, Executive Office of the President, Office of Management and Budget. (2012). North American industry classification system: United States.Baton Rouge, LA: Claitor's Publishing Division.

NAICS: Wholesale Trade

■ Wholesale Trade

Sector 42 is designated as wholesale trade. Within this sector only one subsector applies to apparel products:

- Merchant Wholesalers of Nondurable Goods are in subsector 424.

Merchant Wholesalers, Nondurable Goods Subsector 424

Wholesalers Businesses that sell textiles, textile products, and apparel goods to retail companies for the purpose of reselling the products to consumers.

Nondurable Goods Apparel, textiles, and textile products with a natural life span of three years or less.

Apparel, Piece Goods, and Notions Merchant Wholesalers 4243 include

- 424310 Piece Goods, Notions, and Other Dry Goods Merchant Wholesalers
- 424320 Men's and Boy's Clothing and Furnishings Wholesalers
- 424330 Women's, Children's, and Infants' Clothing and Accessories Merchant Wholesalers

Apparel wholesale distributor

■ Retail Trade

Sector 44–45 is designated as retail trade. Within this sector are two specific subsectors that apply to new apparel products:

- Clothing and Clothing Accessories Stores Subsector 448
- Nonstore Retailers Subsector 454

Retailers Businesses that purchase textiles, textile products, and apparel goods from wholesale companies for the purpose of reselling products to end consumers.

Store Retailers (Brick-and-Mortar Stores) Businesses that merchandise and sell products in locations that attract foot traffic.

Nonstore Retailers Businesses that serve the same purpose as store retailers except they provide greater purchasing convenience to customers through online stores, printed catalogues, and television shopping networks.

Clothing and Clothing Accessories Stores Subsector 448

Store retailers sell apparel and accessory items. As outlined in the *NAICS*, "Establishments in this subsector have similar display equipment and staff that is knowledgeable regarding fashion trends and the proper match of styles, colors, and combinations of clothing and accessories to the characteristics and tastes of the customer."

Clothing Stores 4481 include

- 448110 Men's Clothing Stores
- 448120 Women's Clothing Stores
- 448130 Children's and Infants' Clothing Stores
- 448140 Family Clothing Stores
- 448150 Clothing Accessories Stores
- 448190 Other Clothing Stores. Examples of these types of establishments include "Bridal gown (except custom) shops, Leather coat stores, Costume shops, Lingerie stores, Fur apparel stores, Swimwear stores, Hosiery stores, Uniform (except athletic) stores."

Nonstore Retailers Subsector 454

Merchandising methods used by nonstore retailers include infomercials, direct mailers, printed catalogues, and the internet.

Electronic Shopping and Mail-order Houses 4541 includes

- 454111 Electronic Shopping
- 454113 Mail-Order Houses

Store retail

Nonstore retail

Source: Clothing Stores 448190—p. 586, Executive Office of the President, Office of Management and Budget. (2012). North American industry classification system: United States. Baton Rouge, LA: Claitor's Publishing Division.

References

Garbato, D. (2004, May 1). Apparel vendors link a global chain. *Apparel Magazine*. Retrieved February 10, 2008, from http://www.apparelmag.com/ME2/dirmod.asp?sid=50FC6DCEA75B4FCB95F591F342D4F3B1&nm=Thought+Leadership&type=Publishing&mod=Publications%3A%3AArticle&mid=8F3A7027421841978F18BE895F87F791&tier=4&id=5F48FD3CE1B0434CB767D77740F9D144

Executive Office of the President, Office of Management and Budget. (2012). *North American industry classification system: United States*. Baton Rouge, LA: Claitor's Publishing Division.

CHAPTER 3

Brand Categories and Price Point Classifications for Mass-Produced Apparel

Apparel products are accessible in the marketplace at different prices and under a variety of brand names. A **brand** represents the reputation of a product, product line, or company that is conveyed through brand image, word mark, logo, product design and quality, marketing, promotion, distribution of goods, and customer service.

BRAND CATEGORIES

The three primary brand categories for mass-produced apparel products are branded, private brands, and licensed brands. Within the categories of private and licensed brands, there are fine distinctions.

■ Branded

Branded or National Brand or Wholesale Brand Products sold under a trademarked name to retailers that sell other branded products. Examples include Coach®, Jockey®, Levi's®, Polo Ralph Lauren®, and Seven for All Mankind®. Retailers who sell branded products include such stores as Target®, JCPenney®, Macy's®, and Nordstrom®.

Branded/National brand

■ Private Brand

Private Brand Products developed under a trademarked name owned by a retailer for the purpose of increasing margin and competing with branded products. Distribution and sale of private-brand goods are restricted to the retailer or company developing them. Private brands are composed of private-label products and store-brand products. Examples of these private-brand distinctions include

- *Private Label*—Merchandise developed by a retailer to sell in its stores alongside branded products. Examples include St. John's Bay® at JCPenney®, BP® at Nordstrom®, INC® at Federated Department Stores®, and George® at Walmart®.

- *Store Brand*—Merchandise developed by a retailer under the same trademarked name as the store, which sells only private-brand merchandise. Examples include Abercrombie & Fitch®, Ann Taylor®, Eddie Bauer®, Gap®, J.Crew®, and Victoria's Secret®.

Private brands

■ Licensed Brand

Licensing or Licensed Brand Products developed as the result of a contractual agreement between two companies granting exclusive permission to a manufacturer or retailer to develop, produce, and sell products using another firm's trademarked name, logo, image, character, or exclusive brand name. Licensing agreements can include the development of branded products, private brand products, or a combination of the two. The intellectual property of the brand is licensed for use or can be owned or controlled through a long-term licensing agreement. Examples of licensed brands include

- Paul Frank®
- Under Armour®
- Rachel Zoe®
- Martha Stewart Collection® for Macy's®
- Simply Vera® Vera Wang for Kohl's®

Licensed brand

The apparel industry has six general price classifications for mass-produced apparel products. **Price** is the amount designated by the seller to be paid by the customer in exchange for a product or service.

Price point refers to the range of prices, lowest to highest, upon which competitive products are offered in the marketplace. These price points fit into **price classifications** (budget, moderate, better, contemporary, bridge, and designer) for mass-produced apparel goods. Products should be distinctive enough in quality level of fabrics, findings, construction techniques, and details for the consumer to discern obvious distinctions between the price classifications.

Branded, private-label, and licensed products can be found within all price point classifications. Apparel product styling and design ranges from basic to fashion forward (contemporary) apparel items that are offered at all price points.

■ Budget Price Point or Budget

The lowest price category for mass-produced apparel products, geared toward a wide range of market segments. Mass market appeal, value-driven products, and low prices distinguish apparel brands and retailers within this price classification. Retailers include H&M®, Old Navy®, Target®, Uniqlo®, and Wal-Mart®, to name a few. Brand examples include

Cherokee®	Liz Lange Maternity for Target®
George®	Mossimo Supply Co®
Joe Boxer®	Xhilaration®

■ Moderate Price Point or Moderate

Average prices for mass-produced apparel products geared toward meeting the needs of middle-income families and individuals. Broad appeal, value, and quality in relation to price are important factors for selection at this price classification. Retailers include Charlotte Russe®, Gap®, JCPenney®, Kohl's®, and Limited®, to name a few. Brand examples include

a.n.a. ®	Lands End®
Arizona®	Lee®
Arrow®	Nicole by Nicole Miller®
Chaps®	Style&co®

Budget price point

Moderate price point

PRICE POINT CLASSIFICATIONS (continued)

■ Better Price Point or Better

Above-average prices for mass-produced apparel products with the consumer perception and expectation of better-quality fabrics and more advanced construction details. Retailers include Anthropologie®, Banana Republic®, Dillard's®, J.Crew®, and Macy's®, to name a few. Brand examples include

A.B.S.®	Jones of New York®
AK Ann Klein®	Lauren by Ralph Lauren®
CK Calvin Klein®	Nine West®
INC International®	Polo Ralph Lauren®

■ Contemporary Price Point or Contemporary

A price classification between better and designer that is similar to bridge but offers customers in the junior and misses markets very trendy fashion-forward apparel at a lower price than designer brands. Retailers include Bloomingdale's®, Nordstrom®, Saks Fifth Avenue®, and Theory®, to name a few. Brand examples include

Alice + Olivia®	Elizabeth and James®
Phillip Lim®	Kate Spade®
Michael Kors®	Rag & Bone®
Rebecca Minkoff®	Tory Burch®

Better price point

Contemporary price point

■ Bridge Price Point or Bridge

Mass-produced apparel products priced between the better and designer price classifications with the customer perception and expectation of high-quality fabrics and elements of designer apparel at a price point lower than designer apparel products. The target market is smaller than the better price classification. Retailers include Bloomingdale's®, DKNY®, Armani Collezioni®, Nordstrom®, and Saks Fifth Avenue®, to name a few. Brand examples include

Ann Klein New York®	Ellen Tracy®
Dana Buchman®	M Missoni®
D&G Dolce&Gabana®	Marc by Marc Jacobs®
Elie Tahari®	Rebecca Taylor®

Bridge price point

■ Designer Price Point or Designer

The highest price classification for mass-produced apparel products with exclusive design, high-quality fabrics, and construction details for a narrowly defined niche target market. Retailers include Barneys New York®, Bergdorf Goodman®, Fred Segal®, and Neiman Marcus®, to name a few. Brand examples include

Giorgio Armani®	Gucci®
Chanel®	Louis Vuitton®
Dior®	Prada®
Escada®	Zac Posen®

Designer price point

CHAPTER 4

Apparel Product Categories

Apparel product or merchandise categories are used to classify products of similar function, use, and style. Some products cross men's, women's, and children's categories, whereas others are specific to one gender, such as men's furnishings, or age group in conjunction with height and weight, such as infant apparel.

APPAREL MERCHANDISE

Merchandise within apparel product categories can be sold as separates or multipiece styles. **Separates** are apparel items that are priced and sold individually. These garments are not designed to coordinate with other pieces in the line, although in some cases they might. **Coordinated separates** are apparel items designed to coordinate with each other to provide the customer with opportunities for mixing and matching items in the line. Coordinated separates are also priced individually. **Multipiece styles** are ensembles made up of two or more pieces priced as one unit.

■ Infant Apparel (Infant Wear or Infants)

Apparel created and specifically designed to meet the needs of infants in sizes preemie, newborn, 0 to 3 months, 6 months, 9 months, 12 months, and sometimes 18 and 24 months. Apparel items include the following:

- Booties and mittens
- Caps and hats
- Coats and jackets
- Diaper covers
- Footed and footless coveralls
- Formal wear, suits, tuxedos, christening, or baptism attire
- Gowns
- Layettes (caps, gowns, onesies, shirts, pants, sweaters)
- Onesies, bodysuits, and creepers
- Pants and shorts
- Rompers and overalls

- Skirts and skorts
- Sleepers
- Snowsuits and outerwear
- Socks and tights
- Sweaters
- Swimwear
- Tops and shirts
- Undershirts
- Vests

Infant apparel is typically sold as multipiece styles, although some pieces are sold as separates.

Infant apparel

Toddler apparel

■ Toddler Apparel (Toddler Wear or Toddlers)

Apparel created and specifically designed to meet the needs of children who are walking but still wearing diapers. Toddler sizes 2T, 3T, and 4T, like infant apparel, correspond to a child's age, height, and weight. Apparel items include

- Bodysuits
- Coats and jackets
- Diaper covers
- Formal wear, suits, tuxedos, christening or baptism attire
- Hats and mittens
- Jumpers
- Leggings
- Pajamas and loungewear
- Pants and shorts
- Robes and cover-ups
- Rompers and overalls
- Skirts, scooters, and skorts
- Sleepwear
- Snowsuits and outerwear
- Socks and tights
- Sweaters
- Swimwear
- Tops and shirts
- Undershirts and underpants
- Vests

Toddler apparel is sold as multipiece styles and as separates.

■ Children's Sleepwear and Underwear

Boys' and girls' undergarments, sleepwear, and loungewear items include

- Bathrobes
- Briefs and boxer shorts
- Pajamas, night shirts, nightgowns
- Panties
- Thermal underwear
- T-shirts (long sleeve and short sleeve) and tank tops

Children's sleepwear and underwear use numeric sizing or unisex sizing such as XS, S, M, L, and XL.

Children's sleepwear and underwear

■ Apparel Accessories

Women's and children's items worn to accessorize an apparel ensemble for aesthetic appeal or function include

- Belts and suspenders
- Caps, hats, and millinery
- Gloves and mittens
- Hosiery (stockings, tights, thigh highs, pantyhose) and socks
- Neckwear ties and scarves

Numeric sizing, unisex sizing, and one-size-fits-all may be used. Some items—such as belts, gloves, and hats—have numeric sizing based on body circumference. These items are primarily sold as separates. Gloves, mittens, and hosiery items are sold as individual pairs or, in the case of hosiery, multiple-pair packages.

Apparel accessories

■ Activewear (Active Sportswear or Athletic Apparel or Athleisure)

Apparel items created and specifically designed to meet the needs of men, women, and children while exercising, although some individuals choose to wear activewear items as casual sportswear with no intention of exercising. Unisex sizing such as XXS, XS, S, M, L, XL, and XXL is used. Activewear garments include

- Bathing suits
- Bodysuits
- Caps and hats
- Jackets and hoodies (hooded jackets)
- Jogging suits
- Leggings and skirts for girls and women
- Pants and shorts
- Socks
- Sports bras and camisoles for girls and women
- Swimwear
- T-shirts (long and short sleeve) and tank tops
- Warm-ups and sweat suits

Activewear garments are primarily sold as separates.

Activewear

Career apparel

Dresses

■ Career Apparel (Tailored Clothing)

Men's and women's tailored business attire. Tailored apparel includes

- Suits (jackets, trousers, skirts)
- Fitted and tailored shirts
- Vests
- Women's blouses and dresses

Career apparel is sold as multipiece styles and as separates. Tailored garments sold as separates can also cross over into sportswear. Career apparel is dressier and more formal for day than sportswear. Numeric sizes are used for career apparel and tailored clothing.

■ Dresses

One-piece-style garments with a skirted lower portion designed for women and girls. Styles range from casual to formal. Numeric and unisex sizing XXS, XS, S, M, L, and XL are used.

■ Formalwear (Eveningwear or Special Occasion)

Apparel designed for special and ceremonial occasions. Formalwear includes

- Bridal wear
- Cocktail dresses
- Evening gowns
- Evening suits
- Holiday apparel
- Prom gowns
- Tuxedos

Special occasion attire for women and girls is typically made from dressier specialty fabrics such as brocade; velvet; lace; taffeta; chiffon; organza; faille; satin; and sequined, beaded, and embroidered fabrics. Men's and boy's formalwear is often made from worsted wool or blended suiting fabrics and can be accented with satin or braided trim details. Velvet and brocade fabrics are also used. Numeric sizing is used for formal attire because precise fit is often critical to the aesthetic appeal.

Formalwear

Men's furnishings

Men's suiting

Men's Furnishings

Apparel and accessory items designed for men. Furnishings include

- Bathrobes and wraps
- Belts
- Briefs, boxer shorts, boxer briefs, bikini briefs, trunks, and thongs
- Caps and hats
- Cufflinks
- Gloves
- Pajamas and nightshirts
- Scarves
- Socks
- Tailored dress shirts (sized—neck and sleeve length)
- Ties, pocket squares, handkerchiefs
- Thermal undershirts and pants
- T-shirts (long sleeve and short sleeve) and tank tops

Numeric sizing or unisex sizing such as S, M, L, XL, XXL, XXXL, and one-size-fits-all may be used. Some items—such as belts, gloves, and hats—have numeric sizing based on body circumference. Tailored dress shirts have numeric sizing indicating the neck circumference and sleeve length. Furnishings are primarily sold as separates or in pairs.

Lingerie (Loungewear, Sleepwear, or Intimate Apparel)

Women's undergarments, shapewear, foundation garments, and nightwear including

- Babydoll, chemise, camisole, and tap pant
- Bathrobe and bath wrap
- Bra and bustier
- Body shapers, foundation garments, waist cinchers, girdles
- Camisoles, tank tops, T-shirts (long sleeve and short sleeve)
- Pajamas, nightshirts, nightgowns, boxer shorts
- Panties—bikini briefs, boy shorts, high-cut and low-rise briefs, hipsters, thongs
- Slips and liners
- Thermal undershirts and pants

Numeric sizing is used for bras, foundation garments, and items with built-in bras; the band size (rib cage measurement plus 5 inches, or if the rib cage circumference is greater than 33 inches, 2 inches are added) accompanied by cup size (examples 29A, 34B, 39DDD). For most other sleepwear and loungewear items, unisex sizing such as XXS, XS, S, M, L, and XL is used.

Sleepwear

Outerwear

■ Outerwear

Men's, women's, and children's garments designed to be worn over an apparel ensemble to provide coverage or warmth. Outerwear items include

- Barn coats
- Down jackets
- Dress coats
- Fur and leather coats
- Parkas, stadium jackets, and anoraks
- Ponchos and shrugs

- Pullover jackets
- Rain coats and slickers
- Shawls and wraps
- Ski apparel and down jackets
- Trench coats and over coats
- Windbreakers

Sportswear

Uniforms

■ Sportswear

Apparel ranging from casual to dressy and from basic to trendy garments designed to meet the needs of men, women, and children. Sportswear items include the following:

- Jackets, blazers, sport coats
- Pants, trousers, slacks, and jeans
- Pullovers
- Woven and knitted shirts
- Skirts and skorts
- Sweaters
- Tailored or casual shorts

Sportswear items are sized numerically or with unisex sizing.

Separates sportswear—Apparel designed as individual pieces that may or may not coordinate with other items in a line. Garments are priced separately.

Coordinated sportswear—Apparel designed to be mixed and matched to create several looks. Garments are priced separately.

■ Uniforms (Work Wear)

Men's, women's, and children's apparel designed to provide a standardized appearance. Uniforms are worn for a variety of professions, recreational activities, sports, and school attire, where uniformity in appearance is required. Apparel uniforms include

- Knit shirts and tops
- Dress shirts
- Jackets and coats
- Pants and shorts
- Outerwear
- Skirts
- Sweaters
- Ties

Uniforms and work wear use numeric sizing as well as unisex sizing such as XXS, XS, S, M, L, XL, and XXL.

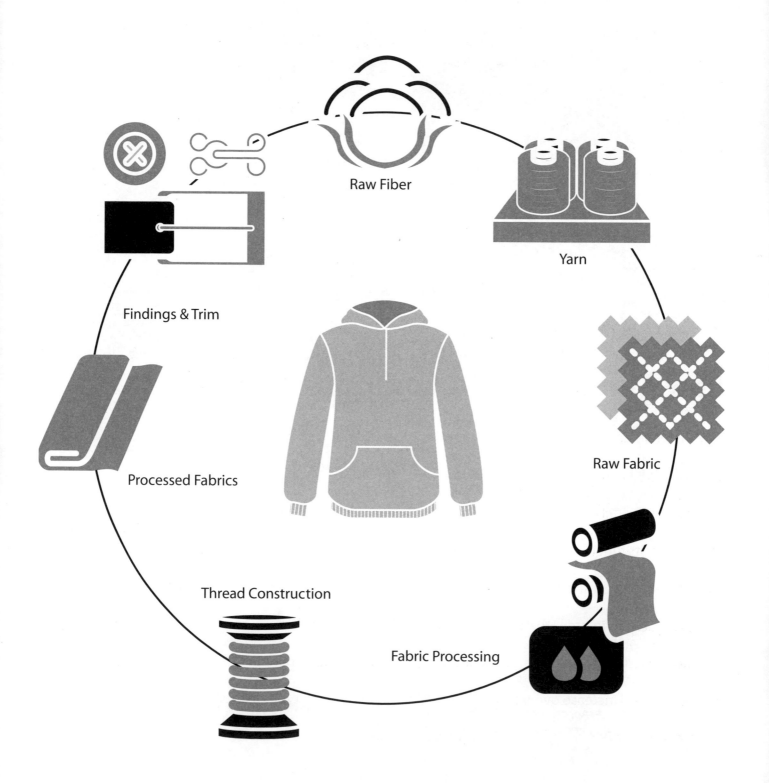

Raw Fiber

Yarn

Raw Fabric

Fabric Processing

Thread Construction

Processed Fabrics

Findings & Trim

Raw Materials and Component Parts

Raw materials and components are integral parts of apparel products. They contribute to a garment's overall aesthetic appeal and more importantly its function and performance. It is critical to have a strong understanding of these materials in order to make informed selection decisions to enhance the quality of products and increase overall customer satisfaction. Part Two of this book will provide an overview of raw materials; fabric and thread specifications; and component parts that add closure, structure, and support as well as those that provide aesthetic appeal used in garment production. The importance of color in regard to selection, communication, and management are highlighted. In additional, garment label types as well as content and compliance will be discussed.

CHAPTER 5

Raw Materials

Fibers, yarns, and unfinished fabrics used by mills and manufacturers to create apparel products and accessories are **raw materials**. Fabric is produced from natural fibers or manufactured filaments that are spun, twisted, cured, shrunk, bulked, or manipulated in other ways to create yarn for weaving or knitting. Yarns are woven, knitted, knotted and twisted, or felted in different formations to produce a variety of fabrics.

FIBERS

The smallest unit of a fabric's structure is a **fiber**. The minimum length-to-width/diameter ratio for a fiber is 100 to 1. Fibers used in apparel products are cellulose derived from plants, protein from animals, or synthetic chemicals. Fibers are available in filament or staple forms.

Filament Comparatively long fibers that are measured in meters or yards that are used as *filament yarn*, or cut into *staple (tow)* to be spun into yarns or woven, knitted, or processed into nonwoven fabrics. The only natural filament fiber is silk, typically 1,463 meters (1,600 yards) in length. All others are synthetic.

Filament

Staple Short fibers measured in millimeters or inches ranging from 5 millimeters (⅜ inch) to 500 millimeters (19.5 inches) in length. Staple-length fibers appear naturally in cellulosic fibers such as cotton or flax. They may also be cut from filament fibers. Staple fibers are spun into yarns or made into fabrics.

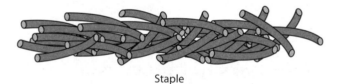

Staple

Tow Synthetic filament fiber strands that are cut down into staple lengths, ranging from 2.5 millimeters (1 inch) to 203 millimeters (8 inches), to be spun into yarns or made into fabrics.

Cellulosic Fibers (Cellulose Fibers) Fibers made from the cell walls of seeds, leaves, stems, or bast, which is the woody portion of specific types of vegetation. Examples of cellulosic fibers include

- Cotton
- Flax (linen)
- Hemp
- Jute
- Ramie
- Sisal

Protein Fibers Fibers that are naturally found in animal hair, feathers, and silk. Protein fibers include

- Alpaca
- Angora
- Camel hair
- Cashgora
- Cashmere
- Down
- Horsehair
- Llama
- Mohair
- Silk
- Vicuna
- Wool

Synthetic Fibers Fibers composed of **monomers** (molecules that can be chemically bound) linked together to form chain-type structures called **polymers**. Fibers composed of chemical polymers are extruded into filaments. Synthetic fibers include

- Acrylic
- Aramid
- Elasterell-p
- Lastol
- Modacrylic
- Nylon (polyamide)
- Olefin
- Polybenzimidazole (PBI)
- Polybutylene terephthalate (PBT)
- Polyester
- Polyethylene
- Polyethylene terephthalate (PET)
- Polylactic acid or Polylactate (PLA)
- Polypropylene
- Polytrimethylene terephthalate (PTT)
- Polyurethane
- Saran
- Spandex (elastane)
- Vinal or polyvinyl alcohol (PVA)
- Vinyon

Natural Fibers Fibers produced from plants (**cellulose based**) or animals (**protein based**).

Manufactured Fibers Fibers produced by synthesizing polymers derived from chemical compounds or polymers derived from modified naturally occurring compounds; formed from substances other than fibers. These polymers are converted into fiber form by extrusion through a spinneret. Manufactured fibers derived from chemical compounds include

- Acrylic
- Anidex
- Aramid
- Elasterell-p
- Fluoropolymer
- Lastol
- Lastrile
- Melamine
- Modacrylic
- Novoloid
- Nylon
- Nytril
- Olefin
- Polyamides
- Polybenzimidazole (PBI)
- Polybutylene terephthalate (PBT)
- Polyester
- Polyethylene
- Polyethylene terephthalate (PET)
- Polylactic acid or polylactate (PLA)
- Polypropylene
- Polytrimethylene terephthalate (PTT)
- Polyurethane
- Polyvinyl
- Rubber
- Saran
- Spandex
- Sulfar
- Vinal
- Vinyon

Some fibers derived from cellulosic fibers become manufactured fibers during processing. Manufactured fibers derived from modified natural compounds include

- Acetate and triacetate
- Azlon
- Bamboo
- Lyocell
- Rayon
- Viscose

A **yarn** is composed of staple or filament fibers conducive to the formation of textiles by weaving, knitting, or knotting, or chemical, mechanical, or thermal bonding. The composition of a yarn consists of fiber content, fiber length, ply, and twist.

Singles Yarn

Singles Yarn A yarn formed by twisting fibers or multiple filaments together. When the yarn is twisted in the reverse direction, the fibers can be pulled from it. A singles yarn can also consist of one continuous filament fiber.

Ply Yarn

Ply A twisted strand of two or more singles yarns. The number of ply depends on the qualities desired in the yarn:

- Strength
- Smoothness
- Diameter
- Construction
- Use

Twist The number of turns applied to a yarn to hold the fibers together.

Z-twist

Z-twist The direction in which the twist of a yarn is applied. Z-twist yarns, when held vertically, create spiral diagonal lines that extend from left to the upper right, forming the same type of line as indicated by the middle portion of the letter *Z* (/). These yarns become tighter when twisted on their axis in the right direction.

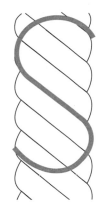

S-twist

S-twist The direction in which the twist of a yarn is applied. S-twist yarns, when held vertically, create spiral diagonal lines that extend from right to the upper left, forming the same type of line as indicated by the middle portion of the letter *S* (\ ). These yarns become tighter when twisted on their axis in the left direction.

Turns per Inch (TPI), Turns per Meter (TPM), or Turns per Centimeter (TPCM) The amount of twist added to a length of yarn when one end is rotated while the other is held stationary. The amount of twist added to a yarn affects

- *Abrasion resistance*—The greater the twist, the more resistant to abrasion, because fewer loose fibers are on the surface of the yarn.
- *Appearance*—The greater the twist, the smoother and more lustrous the appearance.
- *Cost*—The greater the twist, the more expensive the yarn.
- *Performance*—Greater twist can increase the overall durability and performance of the yarn.
- *Strength*—Greater twist can provide greater resistance to breakage.

Filament Yarn Manufactured or silk fibers drawn and twisted together to form a yarn. Filament yarns can be smooth or textured.

Monofilament Yarn A yarn composed of a single continuous filament.

Spun Yarn Staple fibers twisted together to form a yarn. Fibers must have a minimum length of 5 millimeters (⅜ inch) in order to be spun into yarn.

Textured Yarns Filament or spun yarns mechanically processed with heat or chemicals to create bulk or stretch. Textured filament yarns create the appearance of a spun yarn.

Yarn Number (Yarn Size) Method for measuring the fineness of a yarn. Yarn number systems include *direct* and *indirect*.

YARNS (continued)

Direct Yarn Number Yarn number system for measuring the mass/weight per unit length of filament yarn: the larger the yarn, the higher the number. This system is used for measuring silk and manufactured filament yarns. The direct yarn number system is further delineated into the following categories:

Denier—Used to describe the mass per unit length of filament yarns (silk or manufactured; grams per 9,000 meters).

Tex—Used to describe the mass per unit length of spun yarns made from silk or manufactured fibers (grams per 1,000 meters).

Kilotex—Used to describe the mass per unit length of thick spun yarns made from silk or manufactured fibers (kilograms per 1,000 meters).

Decitex—Used to describe the mass per unit length of fine filament yarns (silk or manufactured; grams per 10,000 meters).

Indirect Yarn Number Yarn number system for measuring the length per unit of mass/weight of spun yarn made from staple fibers: the finer the yarn, the higher the number. This system is used for measuring cotton, linen, and wool yarns. The indirect yarn number system is further delineated into the following categories:

Cotton Count—Used to describe the length per unit of mass/weight of cotton and cotton blend yarns (840 yards per pound).

Lea—Used to describe the length per unit of mass/weight of linen and linen-like fiber yarns (300 yards per pound).

Metric—Used to describe the length per unit mass/weight of all spun yarns (1,000 meters per pound).

Run—Used to describe the length per unit of mass/weight of coarse woolen and woolen blend yarns (1,600 yards per pound).

Worsted—Used to describe the length per unit of mass/weight of fine worsted wool, worsted wool blends, and acrylic yarns (560 yards per pound).

YARN SPECIFICATIONS

A **specification** is a detailed list or description of the standards to be met as well as the means for determining whether or not requirements for the material or product are satisfactory. The contents of specifications will vary depending on the product (e.g., yarn, trim, finding, fabric, or garment). Detailed specifications for yarns are important, as they relate to the manufacturing of woven, knitted, or braided/knotted materials for apparel production. **Yarn specifications** include detailed statements describing yarn composition, characteristics and performance requirements, and color standards for manufacturing. Yarn specifications include

- Dye specifications and color standards
- Fiber content
- Yarn type
- Yarn structure
- Yarn twist
- Number of turns per inch
- Single or number of plied yarns
- Yarn number and yarn number system
- Strength and elongation requirements and tolerances
- Tolerance for yarn defects and threshold levels for acceptable degrees of irregularity

Fabric structure is the result of the process by which fiber or yarn becomes cloth. The terms *cloth*, *material*, and *textile* are interchangeable with *fabric*. Fabric structures range from woven, knit, nonwoven, and braided or knotted materials. Any combination of finishes or treatments may be applied to the fiber, yarn, or goods at one or more stages of production, whether for functional, decorative, or permanent purposes. Finishes and treatments affect the hand, weight, and texture of finished materials. Variations and combinations of fiber, yarn, construction (structure), and finish determine the design potential of the finished fabric, including how it may be draped. Fabric selection for a garment depends on

- Design and style of the garment
- Type of garment
- Purpose, function, and use of the garment
- Care of the garment
- Additions of findings and trimmings
- Method of construction

■ Wovens

All woven fabrics possess a **weave structure**. This is the manner in which *warp* and *filling* yarns are interlaced at 90-degree angles to each other to form a woven fabric. The method used to interlace the yarns determines the weave structure. Basic weave structures include

- Plain weave
- Twill weave
- Satin weave

Fabric width depends on the size of the loom or the manufacturer's specifications. The number of harnesses determines the construction of woven goods. A **harness** is the mechanism on a loom that looks like a rectangular frame that holds the **heddles**, needle-like wires threaded with yarns. The harnesses are raised and lowered to create a path for the shuttle to pass through during the creation of woven material. Two harnesses for plain weave; three or more for twill weave; five to twelve for satin weave; as many as forty for jacquard.

More complex weaves such as the leno weave, pile weave, and double cloth structures create a different type of surface interest than the basic weaves. Woven designs created by dobby, jacquard, clip-spot, or color-and-weave effect patterns also create interest.

Warp (Ends) Yarns that run parallel to the selvage of the fabric, also known as lengthwise grain (green).

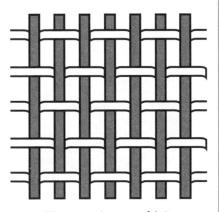

Warp yarns in woven fabric

Filling (Weft) Yarns that run perpendicular to the selvage of the fabric, also known as crosswise grain (white).

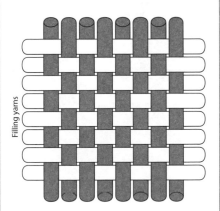

Filling yarns in woven fabric

Selvage The narrow, tightly woven finished edges of the fabric that run parallel to the warp yarns.

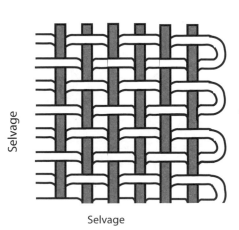

Selvage

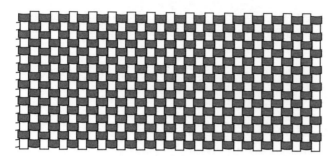

Plain weave construction

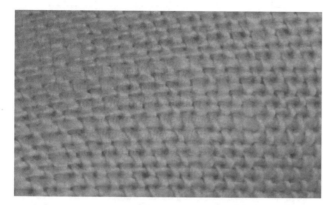

Plain weave (balanced)

Plain weave (unbalanced)

Plain Weave A basic weave structure in which filling yarns are passed over and under each warp yarn, alternating each row. Plain weaves can be balanced or unbalanced.

Balanced—The number of warp and filling yarns are identical in numbers, size, and type.

Unbalanced—The number of warp yarns is different in size, type, or number from the filling yarns (thicker), giving the fabric a ribbed texture.

Fabrics that utilize a plain weave structure include

- Batiste
- Bengaline
- Broadcloth
- Burlap
- Butcher cloth
- Calico
- Canvas
- Challis
- Chambray
- Cheesecloth
- Chiffon
- Chintz
- Crepe
- Crepe de chine
- Crinoline
- Damask
- Dotted Swiss
- Duck
- Faille
- Flannel (can be constructed with a plain or twill weave)
- Gauze
- Georgette
- Gingham
- Madras
- Moiré
- Muslin
- Organdy
- Organza
- Ottoman
- Percale
- Plissé
- Pongee
- Poplin
- Ripstop
- Sailcloth
- Shantung
- Sheeting
- Taffeta
- Tweed
- Toile
- Voile

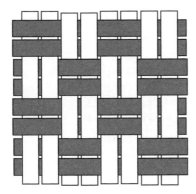

Basket weave construction

Basket weave

Basket Weave An unbalanced variation of a plain weave in which two or more yarns in the warp direction are passed over and under with two or more filling yarns, alternating each row.

Basket-weave structures include

- Hopsack
- Monks cloth
- Oxford cloth

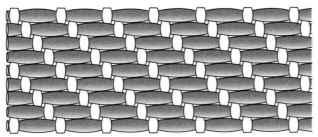

Twill weave construction

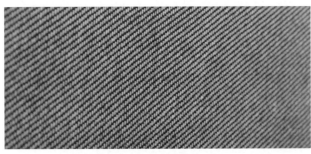

Twill fabric (right-hand twill)

Twill fabric (left-hand twill)

Twill Weave A basic weave structure in which the filling yarn is carried over two or more warp yarns and then under one or more yarns to the left or right in subsequent rows. Right-hand twill weaves create a diagonal line that extends from the lower left to the upper right. Left-hand twill weaves create a diagonal line that extends from the lower right to the upper left.

Even twill—The number of filling yarns passing over and under warp yarns is the same (for example, 3/3).
Uneven twill—The number of yarns on the face of the fabric is different from those on the back. Uneven twill fabrics can be warp-faced or weft-faced.
Warp-face twill—The warp yarns create the diagonal effect because more of these yarns are on the surface of the fabric (for example, 3/2).
Weft-face twill—The filling, or weft, yarns create the diagonal effect because more of these yarns are on the surface of the fabric (for example, 2/3).

Fabrics with a twill-weave structure include

- Cavalry twill
- Chino
- Denim
- Drill
- Flannel (can be constructed with a plain or twill weave)
- Gabardine
- Herringbone
- Houndstooth
- Serge
- Sharkskin
- Surah
- Whipcord

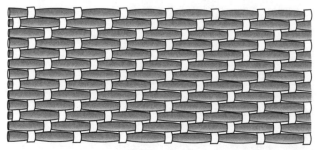

Satin weave construction

Satin weave

Satin Weave A variation of an extremely unbalanced twill weave having four or more yarns float on the surface before passing under one yarn.

Warp-face satin weave—The warp yarns float on the surface of the fabric (for example, 4/1 or 5/1).
Weft-face satin weave—The filling or weft yarns float on the surface of the fabric (for example, 1/4 or 1/5).

Satin weave structures include

- Antique satin
- Brushed-back satin
- Charmeuse
- Crepe-back satin
- Duchess satin
- Peau de soie
- Sateen
- Satin
- Slipper satin

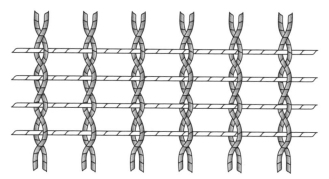

Leno weave construction

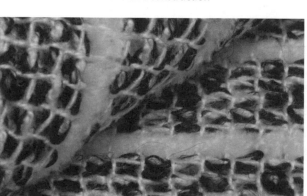

Leno weave

Leno Weave An advanced weave structure in which a pair of warp yarns is twisted back and forth, creating a loop in which the filling yarn is caught and held in place. Leno weave structures include

- Grenadine
- Marquisette

This weave structure is not as widely used in apparel fabrics as it is in home textiles for curtains and agritextiles. The leno weave is used to create chenille yarns that can be woven or knitted into fabric.

Corduroy

Pile Weave An advanced weave structure created by weaving an additional set of warp or filling yarns into the base (ground) yarns that appear as loops on the surface of the fabric. These loops can remain or be cut. Fabrics that utilize the pile weave structure include

- Corduroy
- Terrycloth
- Velveteen

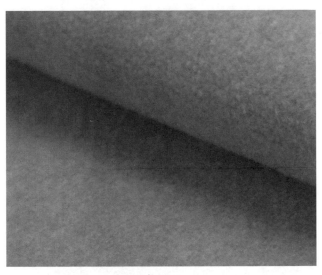

Velveteen

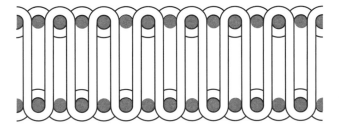

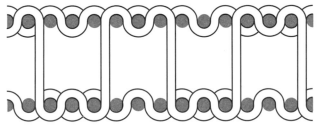

Double cloth weave construction

Matelassé

Double Cloth Weaves An advanced weave structure created by weaving two fabrics on the same loom, above and below each other, having the two layers interlock by another set of yarns that interlaces both fabrics to attach them together or as one cloth. Double weave structures include

- Double cloth
- Kersey
- Matelassé
- Melton
- Velvet

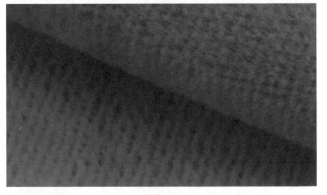

Velvet

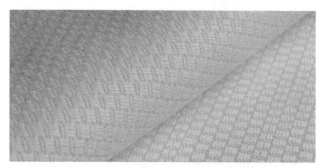

Dobby weave

Dobby weave

Dobby Weave An advanced weave structure that creates a geometric pattern in the fabric. Dobby weave fabrics include

- Birdseye
- Huckaback
- Piqué (can be constructed using a dobby or jacquard weave)
- Shirting madras
- Waffle cloth

Brocade

Jacquard Weave An advanced weave structure that creates a motif or figured pattern in the fabric. Jacquard weaves include

- Brocade
- Brocatelle
- Damask
- Piqué (can be constructed using a dobby or jacquard weave)
- Tapestry

Damask

Tapestry

■ Knits

A fabric structure constructed through the process of interlocking loops. **Knit** fabrics consist of a series of **stitches** that are formed by needles. These stitches are produced by one or more interlocking loops of yarn ends or equivalent material. The direction in which the loops are formed determines the knit structure. The two general classifications of knitted structures are *weft knits* and *warp knits*.

In knit fabrics, wales and courses are comparable to the warp and filling in woven fabrics. **Wales** are the vertical columns of stitches or loops in the lengthwise direction of the fabric. **Courses** are the horizontal rows of stitches or loops in the crosswise direction of the fabric. **Gauge**, also spelled *gage*, indicates the number of wales per inch in a knitted fabric, fineness of the knit, the number of needles per inch used in a machine to create a knit fabric, and size of the stitch.

Variations in the pattern of knits are achieved by changing the arrangement of the basic stitch or loop. The basic nature of the structure of knits offers stretchability not found in woven goods. The ability of a knit to stretch varies according to the direction and complexity of the formation of the loops, the size of the stitch (gauge), and the weight of the yarn (denier). Knits can be manufactured to stretch in either the course or wale direction, or both, depending on the elasticity desired.

Knitting machines produce either tubular or flat goods in a variety of widths depending on the type of machine and the specifications of manufacturers. Tubular and flat goods are used for cut and sew production of knit garments. Flatbed knitting machines can produce full-fashioned or knit-and-wear garments knitted to fit the shape of the body through the addition or subtraction of stitches during the knitting process. Preshaped, two-dimensional knitted pieces of a garment are produced by the knitting machine and emerge ready to be stitched together. Linking or looping is the process of joining knit trims to the garment by means of an elastic chain stitch seam. The machine operator must match each stitch along the garment panel with each stitch along the edge of the trim piece before they can be joined together.

Knit and wear garments can also be produced on some flatbed knitting machines. Similar to full-fashioned, knit and wear produces preshaped three-dimensional knitted garments to fit the shape of the body but do not require additional stitching for assembly, therefore eliminating preproduction and assembly operations such as cutting, sewing, and linking. These garments emerge ready to wear.

Four stitches can be used in all knitted fabrics:

- Knit or plain stitch
- Purl or reverse knit stitch
- Missed stitch
- Tuck stitch

Knit and wear garment

Weft Knit Identified by one continuous yarn forming courses across the fabric. A single yarn passes horizontally to all needles to construct loops in a course or row. Each new course is added to the last row of stitches. These knits are characterized by their moderate to high amount of stretch in the course (crosswise) direction. The amount of stretch provided in the wale (lengthwise) direction varies. These knits are prone to run but only from the last knitted yarn end or if the yarn is cut.

Weft knit structures include

- Balbriggan
- Bourrelet
- Cable knit
- Double knit
- Faux fur
- Fleece
  (weft insertion jersey)
- French terry
  (weft insertion jersey)
- Interlock
- Jacquard jersey
- Jersey knit
- Knit terry
- Lacoste
- Lisle
- Matte jersey
- Pile jersey
- Piqué
- Pont di Rome
- Purl knit
- Rib knit
- Stockinet or stockinette
- Velour

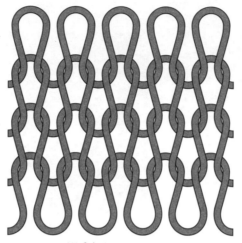

Weft knit construction

Rib knit

Weft Insertion Jersey A fabric in which a crosswise yarn is inserted into the loops of the courses as they are knitted. The inserted yarn provides stabilization in the crosswise direction and may also give strength, decoration, and nap to the finished fabric. Weft insertion knits include

- Fleece
- French terry

French terry

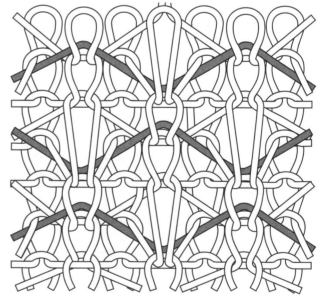

Weft insertion construction

Warp Knit Identified by a series of yarns forming wales in the lengthwise direction of the fabric. Each course stitch is formed by a different yarn. Courses are joined together by the adjacent course or row. These knits are characterized by their lack of stretch in the lengthwise direction. The amount of stretch provided in the crosswise direction varies. Warp knits will not ravel or run.

Warp knit structures include

- Bobbinet
- Crochet
- Filet
- Gossamer
- Illusion
- Intarsia
- Lace
- Mesh (knitted)
- Milanese
- Point d'esprit
- Pointelle
- Polar fleece
- Power net
- Raschel knit
- Simplex
- Thermal knit
- Tricot knit
- Tulle

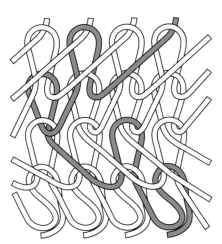

Warp knit construction

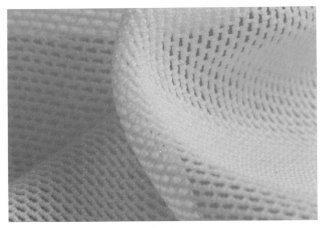

Mesh

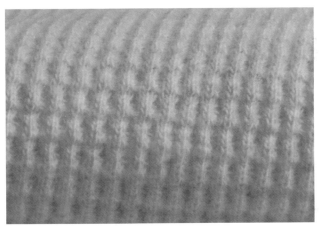

Thermal knit

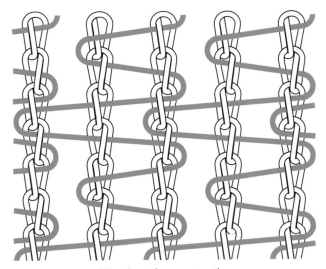

Warp insertion construction

Warp Insertion A yarn is inserted vertically, and the loops of the wales are formed around the insertion as they are knitted. The inserted yarn provides stabilization in the lengthwise direction and may provide strength and decoration to the finished fabric.

Warp insertion knits include

- Mali
- Malimo

■ Twisted Fabric Structures

Openwork fabric structures such as lace and net are made by twisting and knotting, looping, knitting, or stitching a network of thread or yarn together.

Lace An openwork fabric structure created through twisting and knotting is produced in a wide range of widths, weights, textures, and motifs, with or without decoratively finished edges. The intricacy and density of the design, fiber content, yarn size and type, and the number of yarns per square inch/meter determines the quality.

Lace fabrics include

- Alençon
- All-over
- Antique
- Battenberg
- Belgian
- Bobbin lace
- Bobbinet
- Brussels
- Chantilly
- Cluny
- Cordonnet
- Leavers
- Macramé
- Nottingham
- Torchon
- Valenciennes

Most machine-made lace is manufactured as raschel warp knits, which are quickly produced at a low cost.

Chantilly lace

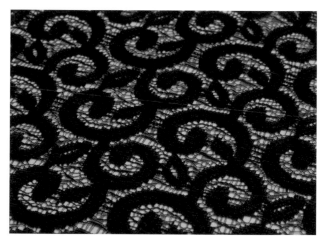

Cluny lace

Net An openwork fabric structure created through twisting in a variety of widths. Net fabric structures include

- Bobbinet
- Tulle

Most machine-made net is raschel or tricot warp knits, due to the speed and low manufacturing cost.

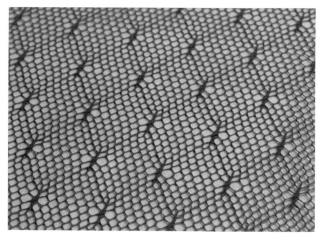

Bobbinet

■ Nonwovens

A **nonwoven fabric** is made from a fiber web structure rather than from yarns. A **fiber web structure** can be produced chemically with bonding agents, mechanically through fiber entanglement, or thermally by fusing the fibers together with heat. The method for manufacturing nonwoven fabrics varies with the nature of the fiber, web formation, and bonding agents used. Depending on the technique, the fibers may be laid in a parallel, cross, or random web formation. Nonwoven fiber web structures and their processes for fabric formation include

Nonwoven fabric

- *Dry-laid* and *wet-laid* web formations, in which either needle punching mechanically locks fibers together or chemical adhesives bond the fibers together.
- *Hydroentangled* or *spun-laced* web formations, in which high-pressure water jets mechanically lock the fibers together.
- *Melt-blown* and *spun-bonded*, *spun-laid*, or *flash-spun* web formations, in which heat and pressure bond the fibers together.

Some manufacturers use a combination of the preceding processes for fiber web and fabric formation.

Nonwoven fabrics can be manufactured with a fusible coating that allows them to be thermally bonded to other fabrics. Fusible nonwoven fabrics add shape or support as interlining materials in apparel products. These fusible fabrics are available in a variety of widths depending on roller beds and the specifications of manufacturers.

Composite (Compound Fabric Structures) A fabric formed by a process in which an outer or face fabric is joined to a backing or lining ply by an adhesive, bonding, foam fusing, or thermoplastic agent. Bonding or laminating changes the hand of the outer layer, stabilizes open weaves, reinforces a stretch or pliable surface, acts as a backing, and provides stability to the face fabric. Laminated fabrics include foam between the face and the underply, whereas bonded fabrics are fused directly to the underply. Composite fabrics can also provide a protective membrane.

Composite fabric

Bonded composite

Felt

Felt A nonwoven fabric structure produced by the application of moisture, heat, agitation, and pressure to a web of fibers, forming an interlocking, uniform matted material. Unlike warp, weft, or selvage, felt does not have a system of threads. It will not fray or ravel. Felt is produced in a variety of widths, from 60 to 90 inches (1.5 to 2.3 m), depending on the steam box and rollers or specifications of the manufacturers. Apparel felts are 1/16 to 1/8 inch (1.6 to 3.2 mm). Fibers used in producing felt are wool, fur, or mohair, which may be blended with cotton and/or rayon.

Metallic film

Laminated supported film

Film A sheet of clear or opaque material formed from thermoplastic polymer. Film is produced in a variety of textures ranging from smooth to rough and in finishes ranging from shiny to matte. It can provide a protective membrane. Available in a variety of widths, and in a single ply or as a **supported film** when fused or laminated to a woven or knitted backing to simulate leather or suede.

Examples of film include

- Polyethylene
- Polyurethane
- Polypropylene
- Saran
- Vinyl/vinyon

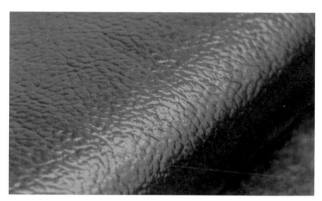

Fused supported film

Fur pelts

■ Animal Skins

Some materials used for apparel and accessories are not made from woven, knitted, or nonwoven manmade textiles but rather from animal skins, hides, or pelts. **Animal skins** come from small animals and **hides** from larger animals.

Fur

Fur is a dressed (preserved) animal pelt containing both skin and hair of the animal. Furs include

- Beaver
- Broadtail sheep, Borrego
- Calf
- Chinchilla
- Ermine
- Fox
- Kangaroo
- Kid
- Lynx
- Mink
- Muskrat
- Mongolian sheep and lamb
- Nutria
- Persian lamb
- Pony
- Rabbit
- Raccoon
- Sable
- Seal
- Sheep
- Squirrel
- Wolf

Dressing Chemical process to preserve fur to maintain suppleness and prevent rotting.

Pelt Fur that has not been chemically processed.

Leather

Leather is the skin or hide of an animal that is chemically processed into one of a variety of surfaces, thicknesses, and colors. Referred to as smooth leather, suede, or split leather, each skin differs in size, color, and surface markings. The irregular shape of a finished skin is determined by the animal. Skins and hides are sold by the square foot. Each skin is marked at the tail end on the wrong side, indicating its total length. The thickness of the skin determines the number of ounces (grams) that 1 square foot equals. Chemical processing maintains the suppleness and prevents rotting.

Animal skins and hides used for leather apparel and accessories products include

- Alligator (endangered)
- Buckskin
- Crocodile
- Eel skin
- Calfskin, cowhide
- Deerskin, doeskin
- Elephant (endangered)
- Elk
- Goatskin, kidskin
- Horse, pony
- Kangaroo
- Lizard
- Ostrich
- Pigskin
- Snakeskin
- Sheepskin, lambskin

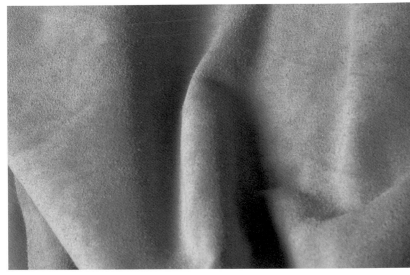

Suede

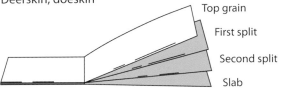

Top grain
First split
Second split
Slab

Split leather illustration

Split Leather From a thick hide that is processed into thinner sheets to obtain a rough surface on both sides.

Suede The flesh side of the hide or skin that is processed to obtain a soft nap on the surface.

Tanning Chemical process to preserve leather to maintain suppleness and prevent rotting.

Top-Grain Leather Outer surface of the hide or skin with the hair removed.

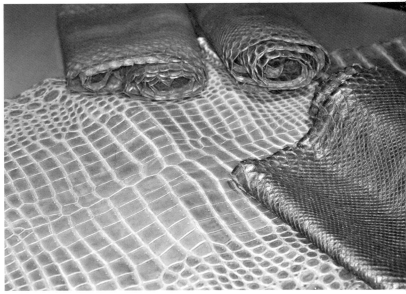

Crocodile leather

■ 3D Printed Textiles

Designers have been experimenting with **3D printing** of apparel and accessories for several years, and garments have been featured on runways since 2010. Traditional 3D printers shape layers of synthetic materials to form a seamless finished product. Garments that are 3D printed are commonly constructed of intricately designed connections, like mesh or chainmail, that offer flexibility and permit the garment to move in a similar way to traditionally made fabrics. Research and development teams are working on 3D printed fabrics that are lightweight, flexible, and supple, which allows them to behave like woven fabrics. According to articles published by 3D Printing Industry and 3DPrint.com, the Electroloom is the world's first 3D fabric printer, which is very different from other traditional 3D printers. It can be compared to the process of electroplating metals but is used to create a **Field Guided Fabrication (FGF)**. "FGF is essentially an electro spinning process that takes a liquid solution, converts it into solid fibers that are then deposited and bonded onto a 3D mold. The 3D mold is placed inside a chamber with an internal electric field that guides and bonds the fiber onto a mold" (Tampi, 2015). The 3D printed cloth is made from a solution of micro or nano-fibers composed of polyester and cotton. A silk and acrylic blend is in development. The Electroloom allows for natural fibers to be blended with synthetic fibers to 3D print textiles and apparel products.

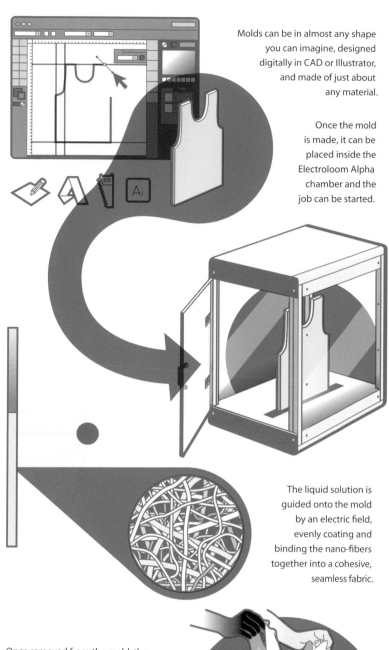

Molds can be in almost any shape you can imagine, designed digitally in CAD or Illustrator, and made of just about any material.

Once the mold is made, it can be placed inside the Electroloom Alpha chamber and the job can be started.

The liquid solution is guided onto the mold by an electric field, evenly coating and binding the nano-fibers together into a cohesive, seamless fabric.

Once removed from the mold, the unique material can flex, drape, and fold just like the fabrics you know and love.

Congratulations! You've now created your own custom designed future fabric. You can now reuse, reshape, or create an entirely new mold for future projects.

3D printed textile

References

ASTM International. (2016). *2016 ASTM International standards*: (Vol. 7.01) Textiles (1). West Conshohocken, PA: Author.

Bubonia, J. E. (2014). *Apparel quality: A guide to evaluating sewn products*. New York: Fairchild Books.

Celanese Acetate LLC. (2001). *Complete textile glossary*. Charlotte, NC: Author.

Hipolite, W. (2015, May 16). *The Electroloom becomes the world's first 3D printer of fabric – launches Kickstarter*. Retrieved November 1, 2015, from http://3dprint.com/65959/electroloom-3d-fabric-printer/

Humphries, M. (2009). *Fabric reference* (4th ed.). Upper Saddle River, NJ: Pearson Prentice Hall.

Johnson, I., Cohen, A. C., & Sarkar, A. K. (2015). *J. J. Pizzuto's fabric science* (11th ed.). New York: Fairchild Books.

Kaldolf, S. J. (2007). *Quality assurance for textiles and apparel* (2nd ed.). New York: Fairchild Books.

Kaldolf, S. J. (2010). *Textiles* (11th ed.). Upper Saddle River, NJ: Pearson.

Raviv, N. (2015, January 15). *3D printing: Future of eco friendly fashion?* Retrieved November 1, 2015, from http://blog.sproutwatches.com/index.php/2015/01/3d-printing-future-of-eco-friendly-fashion/

Shephard, R. (2003). *Lace classification system*. Retrieved November 1, 2015, from http://www.powerhousemuseum.com/pdf/research/classification.pdf

Tampi, T. (2015, May 16). *Electroloom, 3D printing, & the dawn of a new age of clothing*. Retrieved November 1, 2015, from http://3dprintingindustry.com/2015/05/16/electroloom-3d-printing-the-dawn-of-a-new-age-of-clothing/

Color

Color is created by the absorption and reflectance of light. The human brain interprets light waves in the electromagnetic spectrum as color. The viewer's eye contains light receptors that communicate messages to the brain. The brain then translates the visual perception of light into color. Color does not exist in the absence of light.

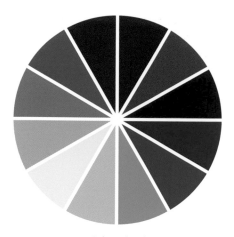

Color wheel

Analogous

Complementary

The visual spectrum is composed of seven color classes: red, orange, yellow, green, blue, indigo, and violet. Each color classification consists of a visual wavelength that can be further broken down into hue, value, and saturation. **Hue**, the purest form of a color, is directly associated with the color's wavelength. **Value**, or **luminance**, is the lightness or darkness of a color communicated through *tints* (lightened hues), shades (darkened hues), and midtones. Brightness can be used interchangeably with the terms luminance and value. **Saturation**, also known as *chroma* or *intensity*, measures the purity of a color expressed by its sharpness or dullness. When colors are used in combination with each other, they form a **color scheme**.

Examples of color schemes include the following:

- Achromatic
- Analogous
- Complementary
- Double complementary or tetradic
- Monochromatic
- Neutral or monotone
- Split complementary
- Triadic

Double complementary/tetradic

Split complementary

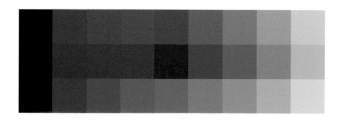

Value (shades and tints)

Triadic

Achromatic

Achromatic (or Colorless) The color prism does not contain achromatic colors. Achromatic colors include

- White
- Black
- Shades of gray; gray scale

Neutral or Monotone Variations in value for a single neutral hue. Colors absent from the color wheel such as beige, taupe, and brown, as well as achromatic colors such as black, gray, and white. An example of monochromatic color scheme could include

- Ecru
- Ivory cream
- Toffee
- Brown sugar
- Bitter chocolate

COLOR TRENDS

The fashion industry is known for constant change and innovation in color and design trends. **Color trends** are a selection of important hues for a particular season forecasted by **trend forecasting services**, which conduct market research on color to ascertain trends that will provide direction for future seasonal color palettes. According to Augustine Hope and Margaret Walch, authors of *The Color Compendium*, "Although change and variation make color more appealing to human beings, there is always a certain consistency of preference for a few rather than many hues. Therefore, color forecasters need to calculate the exact shade in which to render perennially popular volume sellers." In their market research, trend forecasting services gather and analyze data on consumer preferences and lifestyle changes; observe events in world capitals; consider cultural, economic, political, and social influences; and evaluate media persuasions. Industry leaders in color forecasting include

- **Color Association of the United States (CAUS)** Founded in 1915, CAUS relies on the expertise of a committee of eight to ten industry professionals for color direction. The spring/summer and fall/winter color forecasts are published each March and September, and are available for interiors and men's, women's, and youth apparel. CAUS is the oldest color forecasting service in the United States. Its color and vintage pattern archives date back to 1915 and are available for use by members. CAUS also provides continuing education programs to strengthen industry professionals' knowledge of color and application. This association publishes its forecasts twenty months in advance of a season.
- **Color Marketing Group (CMG)** Founded in 1962, CMG has approximately 400 international members who attend semiannual conferences to collaboratively provide color direction. During these conferences, color designers meet in more than twenty-four concurrent workshops to develop forecasts for the season. CMG publishes Color Directions® forecasts twice yearly. This nonprofit organization provides color forecasts for a multitude of industries. Forecasts are published nineteen months or more in advance of a season.
- **Global Color Research** Founded in 1999, Global Color Research relies on a team of experts to create forecasts. Their trend forecast, *Mix Magazine®*, is published four times a year for the fashion and design industries. Forecasts are published twenty-four months in advance of the season.
- **Pantone Color Institute®** Founded in 1963, Pantone's research and information center is focused on understanding color and how it affects human emotions, perceptions, and physical states. *PANTONE VIEW Colour Planner* is published twice annually, providing fall/winter and spring/summer color forecasts for activewear, cosmetics, industrial design, menswear, and women's wear. Forecasts are published twenty-four months in advance of a season.

COLOR TRENDS (continued)

Forecasting services develop season **color palettes** of five to seven coordinating colors based on a theme. Designers and product developers evaluate forecasted palettes from multiple sources and evaluate what colors are most appropriate for their brand and target customer.

Accent Color A color used sparingly to provide emphasis in a color palette or color story.

Core Color A brand's signature hue that is incorporated into the color palette for every season or during particular seasons such as fall, spring, holiday, or resort.

Color Discord Colors that clash; visually conflicting or disturbing colors; unharmonious colors that appear widely separated on the color wheel with the exception of complementary or triadic colors.

Accent color

Core color

Color discord

Color Story Color theme for a line within a collection. The color palette provides the theme.

13-0535 TC   16-0230 TC   17-1644 TC   12-2905 TC   13-2005 TC

Color Story

Colorway The colors a garment is offered in; or an arrangement of palette colors in a print, weave, or knit design.

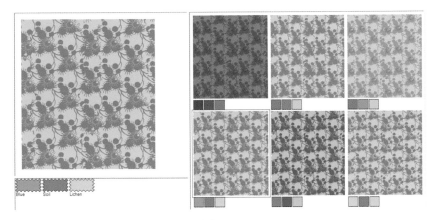

Colorway

Dominance (Tonality) The dominant color within a collection, which elevates the importance of one hue or color family to set a main theme. When two colors are used together, one will be dominant and the other will become secondary. When more than two colors are used, there is one dominant color and all other colors become subordinate.

Dominance (tonality)

COLOR MANAGEMENT

Color is a critical design factor to consider when developing apparel and textile products. It is a primary element that attracts a customer to a particular item. People respond emotionally to color based on their psychological experiences, cultural surroundings, and personal aesthetic. Accurate color communication is crucial in the apparel industry and is the basis for comparing, matching, measuring, and specifying color information. **Color management** is the process of accurately communicating color standards by comparing digital spectral data to physical or digital samples to make sure good-quality color matches occur between color specifications and dyed or printed materials and findings from the initial design concept through production. Color must be managed and controlled throughout the manufacturing process to ensure customer satisfaction.

■ Color Spaces

There are a variety of ways to define color. **Color spaces**, also known as color models, provide precise numeric formulations for defining, naming, and reproducing exact color matches for electronic input and output devices such as scanners, computer monitors, and printers. Color spaces are how colors are mixed in a digital environment. In fashion production, they are used to create and manipulate electronic files that contain color. Color spaces include

RGB	CMYK (CMY)	XYZ
HSV (HSL)	L*a*b*	

RGB Red, green, and blue are the primary colors in this model. Thomas Young and Hermann von Helmholtz developed the theory of trichromatic color vision during the nineteenth century. These physicians determined that the human eye has three types of photoreceptor cones for seeing color. Each cone responds to a different wavelength of light when it makes contact with the retina. Young and Helmholtz classified these cones as red, green, and blue (Young-Helmoltz three-colour, 2009). RGB utilizes additive color principles, meaning that primary colors are mixed in various combinations to create different colors. Equal proportions of two primary colors create secondary colors. Unequal proportions of two or three primary colors create additional hues. When equal amounts of all primary colors are added, white is created. The absence of all primary colors creates black. Input devices such as computer monitors and scanners utilize RGB color space.

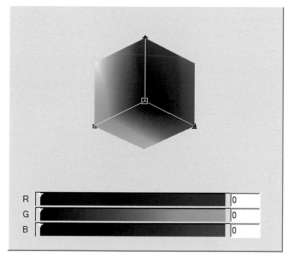

RGB

HSV (HSL) Hue, saturation, and value (luminance) models work with the same additive color principles for color mixing as RGB. Hermann von Helmholtz introduced these three variables to characterize color in his *Manual of Psychological Optics* in 1860. Hue identifies the color; saturation measures the variation of purity of a color expressed by its sharpness or dullness; and value (luminance) refers to the lightness or darkness of a color that is communicated through tints, shades, and midtones. HSV (HSL) more accurately defines perceptual color relationships than other color spaces.

HSV (HSL)

CMYK (CMY) Cyan, magenta, and yellow are the primary colors in this model. CMYK utilizes *subtractive color* principles. Subtractive colors become darker when mixed together. The absence of all primary colors creates white. CMYK uses a fourth color, "key," which represents black and allows for true black to be printed. Output devices such as printers for fabric and paper utilize CMYK color space.

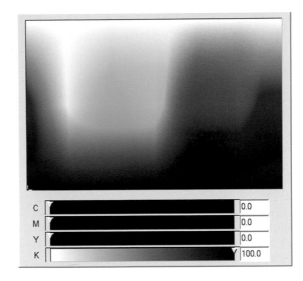

CMYK

L*a*b* Three coordinates of this color space are L*, which represents lightness of a color; a*, which indicates the position between red and green (positive values designate red; negative values, green); and b*, which designates the position between yellow and blue (positive values designate yellow; negative values, blue). Unlike color spaces based on additive or subtractive principles, color space based on chromatic value depicts all of the colors visible to the human eye, which more closely resembles how the eye perceives light than other color spaces. Developed in 1976 by the Commission Internationale d'Eclairage (CIE), this color space is derived from the 1931 CIE Standard Colour Table or Standard Valency System. Color formulas are calculated with simple formulas derived from XYZ color space. Spectrophotometers communicate digital color readings using L*a*b*.

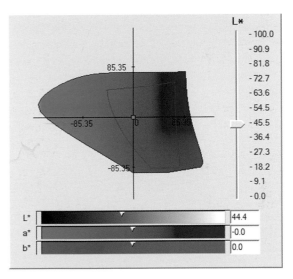

L*a*b*

XYZ X, y, and z coordinates are used to mathematically determine how a color is perceived by the human eye. Colors are produced using three linear light components to represent direct measurements of visual perception. In the RGB system, some colors may be represented with negative values in order to achieve the specified color. When RGB is converted to XYZ, all colors are represented as a set of positive values. The Commission Internationale d'Eclairage developed the XYZ color space, originally called the CIE Standard Colour Table or Standard Valency System, in 1931.

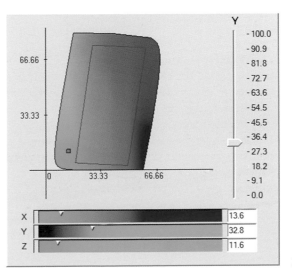

XYZ

COLOR STANDARD

A **color standard** identifies the specific hue for matching fibers, yarns, fabrics, threads, trims, and findings. Standard systems for color notation have been developed by *Munsell*, *Pantone*, and *SCOTDIC* to aid in the communication of color.

■ Munsell®

The first **Munsell®** color system for communicating color was published in 1915. The five major hue families used in this system are purple, blue, green, yellow, and red, which are represented in a three-dimensional model. Minor hue families include yellow-red, green-yellow, blue-green, purple-blue, and red-purple. The color space used for color communication is hue, value, and chroma (saturation). Hue is represented as a circle. Value is located along the central axis, and chroma is indicated by distance from the central axis. One hundred hues (color families) are represented in this system.

The Munsell color system is owned by X-Rite, a global leader in color measurement and analysis. A variety of industries use this system to provide precise color communication. Munsell accurately communicates color requirements to mills, dye houses, and fabric converters in order to precisely match the desired hues for production of textile products.

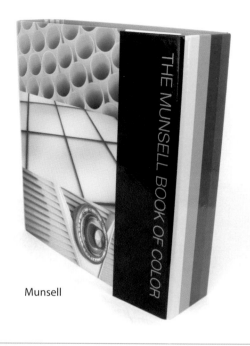

Munsell

■ Pantone®

In 1963, the founder of Pantone, Inc.® pioneered a system for specifying color, and today the company is recognized around the world as the authority on color. **Pantone** is a standardized color-matching system widely used by the fashion and textiles industry, among a wide range of other industries, to specify and control color throughout the product development and manufacturing processes. This standardized classification system for communicating color is known as the PANTONE FASHION + HOME color system, which contains 1,925 colors printed on either paper or cotton. *HSL* color space is used for color communication.

Using a handheld instrument called a spectrocolorimeter, a designer takes the digital color measurement of a flat object and immediately finds the closest Pantone color match using specialized software. The instrument reduces time spent matching found colors against color standards.

Pantone, Inc., has partnered with Clariant International, Ltd., one of the largest global textile colorant producers, to specify dye formulations and pigment mixing for precise color matching for production. This color management specification system provides designers and product developers with accurate color matching while significantly reducing the time and cost of the color development process.

Pantone

■ SCOTDIC®

SCOTDIC® is a standardized color-matching system used by the fashion and textiles industry to specify and control color throughout product development and manufacturing processes. SCOTDIC uses the *Munsell®* color system as the basis for color identification and communication.

Three color systems are available, each dyed on a specific type of fiber. The cotton system includes 2,300 color choices, the polyester system has 2,468 color choices, and the wool system consists of 1,100 color choices. SCOTDIC is owned by Kensaikan International, Ltd., a Japanese company that specializes in dyeing. Designers have used the textile color system for color matching on fabric since its introduction in 1982.

SCOTDIC

Colorant A substance applied to a fiber, yarn, fabric, or garment that alters the transmittance or reflectance of visible light by adding color. Examples of colorants include

Brighteners	Pigments
Dyes	Tints

Coloration The hue of a material or arrangement of colors in a fabric design; adding color to a *substrate*.

Colorant

Colorimetry The science of digitally measuring color with an instrument.

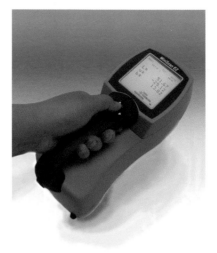

Colorimetry bench spectrophotometer

Handheld spectrophotometer

Color Fidelity The ability of colors to match when created using different color spaces or color systems.

Colour Index™ The international reference guide to colorants. The index is published by the American Association of Textile Chemists and Colorists (AATCC) and the Society of Dyers and Colourists (SDC). Contents of the index include

- Generic colorant names and chemical formulations
- Constitution numbers (chemical classification numbers) assigned to identify colorants

- Listing of commercial products available in the marketplace
- Product names listed by manufacturer
- Physical forms of colorants (i.e., powder, liquid dispersion)
- Uses

Gamut The defined capacity of colors within a color space. When a color is out of gamut, it cannot be reproduced within that color space.

COLOR EVALUATION

The process of assessing color at many different stages of design development and production is known as **color evaluation**. Color must be continually monitored and controlled to ensure consistent color matching and precise color reproduction. **Colorimeters** or **spectrophotometers** are instruments used to digitally measure the percentage of light reflected at each wavelength along the visible spectrum, providing a numeric representation of a color. This numeric depiction of a hue is known as **spectral data**. Colors found in a naturally occurring spectrum can be identified by their **spectral color curves**. Color standards are sent to *converters*, and the color-matching process begins. Fabric samples are dyed or printed to match color standards. These colored samples, called **lab dips**, are then evaluated against the standard to determine if they match. When a material registers the same or near-identical spectral data as the color standard, it is considered a **color match**. Today lab dips can be digital representations of the color and fabric that are evaluated visually on a computer screen or physical samples evaluated in person under various lighting conditions to ensure consistent color.

Color Approval When a lab dip meets the specified requirements for a color match. Once colors are approved, production of materials begins.

Color Calibration Process of matching digital color standards displayed on a computer screen with the output of a printer to ensure accurate and consistent color communication.

Color Measurement Spectral data of a material obtained through the use of a colorimeter or spectrophotometer that provides a numeric representation of the color.

Color Production Standard A color standard that is reproducible for manufacturing that identifies the specific hue to be matched for fibers, yarns, fabrics, threads, trims,

and findings to ensure color consistency throughout production. It is a challenge to match the colors of materials and garment components when each medium may require different chemical formulations to arrive at the same color to ensure they match.

Color Specifications Defined set of requirements for matching color standards and the dye or pigment formulations for reproduction on specified materials, to obtain the desired color standards.

Metamerism When colors match under certain lighting conditions and not in others. For example, if a customer purchases a navy turtleneck and brings it home to find the collar and cuffs do not match in incandescent light but did match under the fluorescent lighting used in the retail store.

References

AATCC. (2016). *Technical manual of the American Association of Textile Chemists and Colorists*. (Vol. 91). Research Triangle Park, NC: Author.

ASTM International. (2016). *2016 International standards*. (Vol. 07.01). West Conshohocken, PA: Author.

Clariant International Ltd. (2007). *Color competence in cooperation with Pantone: A SMART partnership for the textile market* [Brochure]. Muttenz, Switzerland: Author.

Color Association of the United States. (2015a). *About the Color Association*. Retrieved October 31, 2015, from http://www.colorassociation.com/pages/2-about

Color Association of the United States. (2015b). *Color Standards*. Retrieved November 1, 2015, from http://www.colorassociation.com/pages/21-color-standards

Color Marketing Group. (2015). *About CMG*. Retrieved November 1, 2015, from http://www.colormarketing.org/about-cmg

Gilbert, D. (2005, November 15). Made in the shade. *WWD*, 6–7.

Global Color Research. (2015) *About Global Color Research*. Retrieved November 1, 2015, from http://www.globalcolor.co.uk/about/

Hermann von Helmholtz. (n.d.). Retrieved November 1, 2015, from http://www.wwd.com

Hope, A., and Walch, M. (1990). *The color compendium*. New York: Van Norstrand Reinhold.

Lilien, O. M. (1985). *Jacob Christoph Le Blon, 1667–1741: Inventor of three-and four-colour printing*. London: Hiersemann.

McLaren, K. (1976). The development of the CIE 1976 (L*a*b*) uniform colour-space and colour-difference formula, *Journal of the Society of Dyers and Colourists*, *92*, 338–341.

Pantone Inc. (2015). *About us: Who we are*. Retrieved November 1, 2015, from http://www.pantone.com/about-us?from=topNav

Society of Dyers and Colorists, and American Association of Textile Chemists and Colorists. (2015). *Introduction to the Colour Index*[TM]: *Classification system and terminology*. Retrieved November 1, 2015. http://colour-index.com/introduction-to-the-colour-index

SCOTDIC (2015). *SCOTDIC: The world textile color system*. Retrieved November 1, 2015, from http://www/scotdic.com

X-Rite. (2015). *Munsell color*. Retrieved November 1, 2015, from http://www.xrite.com/top_munsell.aspx

Young-Helmholtz three-colour theory. (2015). In *Encyclopedia Britannica*. Retrieved November 1, 2015, from Encyclopedia Britannica Online: http://www.britannica.com/science/Young-Helmholtz-three-color-theory.

Color plate 1 Dyeing

Color plate 2 Dyeing

Color plate 3 Flat print

Color plate 4 Tonal print

Color plate 5 Coordinated prints

Color plate 6 Rotation cast buttons

Color plate 7 Assembled/combination buttons

Color plate 8 Embroidery

Color plate 9 Embroidery

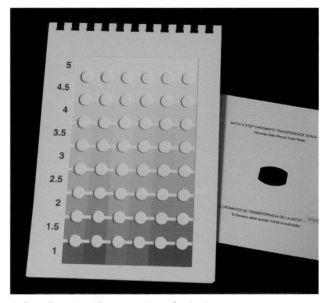

Color plate 10 Chromatic Transfer Scale

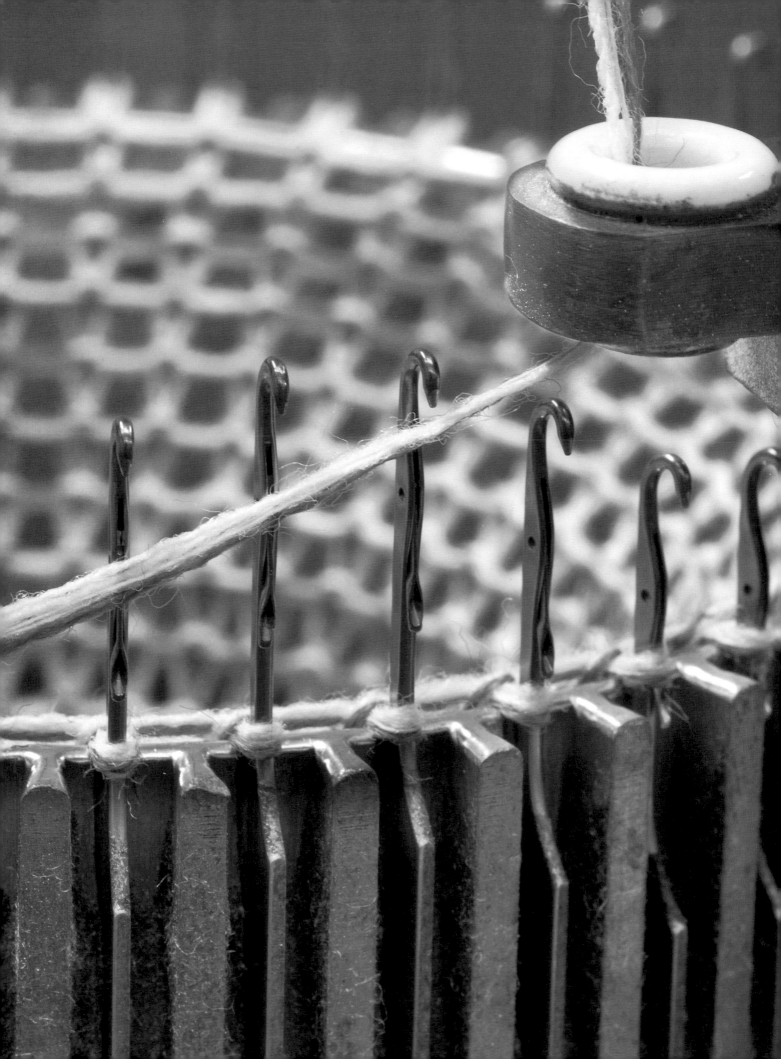

CHAPTER 7

Fabric Specifications

Designers consider many factors when selecting textiles for wearing apparel. Fabric classifications and characteristics regarding aesthetic desirability and performance are specified in relation to the garment's design and intended use.

FABRIC CATEGORIES

Fabrics are classified into two general categories: basic and novelty. **Basic fabrics** are core materials designers rely on from season to season or year to year. Basic goods are updated from one season to the next through changes in color, fiber content, finish, pattern, or print design. Basic goods are typically less expensive because they are produced and ordered in larger quantities. These goods are typically stocked materials. Examples of basic fabrics include

Broadcloth	Jersey
Chino	Knit pique
Corduroy	Oxford cloth
Denim	Polar fleece
Fleece	Poplin
Gabardine	Rib knit
Interlock	Thermal cloth

Basic fabric

Novelty fabrics are distinctive materials produced in limited production runs and are more expensive than basic goods. Novelty fabrics may contain specialty fibers or yarns, unusual knit or weave structures, or unique prints or pattern designs.

Novelty fabric

Designers and product developers need to know the weight of the fabrics they are designing garments with because weight affects how a garment will hang and drape on the body. The two systems used to measure fabric weight are the **International System of Units (Système International d'Unites)**, known as **SI units** and **U.S. customary units (English System)**. SI is the designation for metric units of measurement used internationally. U.S. customary units is the designation for the English units of measurement used in the United States.

Fabric weight is the mass per unit area of a material. **Mass per unit area** can be conveyed as ounces per square yard (grams per square meter) or ounces per linear yard (grams per linear meter). Additionally, fabric weight can be communicated inversely as linear yards per pound (linear meters per kilogram). Factors influencing fabric weight include fiber content, yarn size, number of yarns per inch (per 25 mm) in the warp and filling directions of woven materials, or the number of loops in the wale and course directions of knitted fabrics.

Designers, manufacturers, and suppliers typically refer to fabrics as top weight or bottom weight. **Top-weight** fabrics are those weighing 6 oz/sq yd (203.43 g/m^2) or less. **Bottom-weight** fabrics weigh 8 oz/sq yd (271.25 g/m^2) or more. Common fabric weight ranges and uses are as follows:

- *Extra-light top-weight fabrics*—1 to 3 oz/sq yd (33.91 to 101.72/m^2); used for sheer blouses, lingerie, tissue-weight knitted tops, and T-shirts.
- *Light top-weight fabrics*—4 to 6 oz/sq yd (135.62 to 203.43 g/m^2); used for blouses, casual shirts, dresses, dress shirts, knitted tops, pajamas, sweaters, T-shirts, undergarments.
- *Tropical-weight fabrics*—4.5 to 8.5 oz/sq yd (152.58 to 288.20 g/m^2); used for dresses, jackets, knitted tops, suits intended for wear in the summer or hotter climates, trousers.

- *Bottom or medium-weight fabrics*—7 to 9 oz/sq yd (237.34 to 305.15 g/m^2); used for coats, pants, dresses, jackets, jeans, knitted tops, pants, shorts, skirts, suits for all-season wear, sweaters, sweatshirts, trousers.
- *Heavy bottom-weight fabrics*—10 to 12 oz/sq yd (339.06 to 406.87 g/m^2); used for coats, parkas, denim garments, jackets, jeans, pants, cold-weather suits, sweaters, sweatshirts, sweatpants, trousers.
- *Extra-heavy bottom-weight fabrics*—14 to 16 oz/sq yd (474.68 to 542.49 g/m^2); used for denim garments, jackets, jeans, pants, sweaters, sweatshirts, sweatpants, winter coats, and parkas.

Ounces per Square Yard Fabric weight reported as the mass per unit area of a piece of fabric that measures 36 inches by 36 inches.

Grams per Square Meter Fabric weight reported as the mass per unit area of a piece of fabric that measures 100 centimeters by 100 centimeters.

Ounces per Linear Yard Fabric weight reported as the mass per unit area of a piece of fabric that measures 36 inches by the total width of the material in inches.

Grams per Linear Meter Fabric weight reported as the mass per unit area of a piece of fabric that measures 100 centimeters by the total width of the material in centimeters.

Linear Yards per Pound Fabric weight reported as the number of yards of fabric equal to 1 pound of material in a particular width in inches.

Linear Meters per Kilogram Fabric weight reported as the number of meters of fabric equal to 1 kilogram of material in a particular width in centimeters.

Yield for Knitted Fabrics The number of square yards per pound of fabric.

Momme The Japanese unit used for measuring the weight of silk fabrics. The weight of silk fabric may also be reported in grams. 28 grams = 1 ounce; 1 ounce = 8 momme (mm).

FABRIC WIDTH

The distance measured, without tension, across a flat material from one *selvage* to the other is known as **fabric width**. Fabric width is measured in inches or centimeters and reported in whole numbers such as 58" (147 cm) or as a range 58/60" (147/152 cm). Measurements are taken at various intervals along the length of the fabric to provide the most accurate width information. The width of fabrics can vary depending on the size of the loom or knitting machine used to make the material and the amount of shrinkage that can occur during finishing. When a width range is provided, it is typically due to variations in shrinkage of the fabric that occurs during finishing; so, for example, some portions of the fabric measure 44 inches (112 cm) in width, whereas others measure 45 inches (114 cm).

Fabric width of circular knits is determined by measuring the diameter of the flattened tubular goods. Knowing the width of the fabric is important for determining the amount needed for a garment, laying out garment parts for cutting to provide the best utilization of fabric to avoid unnecessary waste, and calculating the cost of fabric consumption or yield for a garment.

Wider fabrics typically provide better utilization than narrow goods because less yardage is needed. The width of woven fabrics typically ranges from 12 inches (30 cm) to 120 inches (305 cm). Most woven fabrics used for apparel are 45-inch (114 cm) and 60-inch (152 cm) widths. The width of knitted fabrics usually ranges from 36 inches (91 cm) to more than 200 inches (508 cm). Materials having a width of 36 inches (91 cm) or less are considered narrow fabrics. Some specialty fabrics may be as narrow as 12 inches (30 cm). Materials having widths of 72 inches (183 cm) or more are considered wide fabrics and are used for soft home products and home furnishings.

FABRIC PUT-UP

The manner in which textile material is packaged is called **put-up**. Apparel manufacturers purchase fabrics from mills or **converters** in a rolled put-up. Converters purchase **greige goods** (unfinished fabrics) and apply *finishes* specified by designers or product developers. Typically, fabric is rolled onto a cardboard tube that holds 60 to 100 yards (55 to 90 meters). Open-width or tubular knitted fabrics are packaged in a rolled put-up weighing 35 to 50 pounds (560 to 800 ounces). Some fabrics are put-up in 1,000-yard lengths for greater efficiency in high-volume apparel manufacturing.

Put-up of greige goods

Colorants are used to apply color to fibers, yarns, fabrics, and garments. Colorants include dyes, pigments, and optical brighteners to enhance the appearance of fabrics (see Color plates 1 and 2).

■ Dyes

Dyes are complex organic molecules that appear to the eye as color and can be dissolved in water. The two component parts of a dye molecule are the color segment known as the **chromophore** and the **auxochrome**, which provides solubility and bonding capabilities. Most dyes are **substantive**, meaning they are absorbed by the fibers without the need for a binder or **mordant**. Mordants help the material hold the dye. Not all dyes are accepted by all fibers. Major dye classes follow.

Dyeing

Dyeing of fabrics

Machine for drying fabrics after dyeing

Acid (Anionic) Dyes Dye class used to add color to protein-based fibers (i.e., cashmere, silk, and wool), as well as synthetics (i.e., acrylic and nylon). These dyes offer a wide range of colors, including bright hues. Performance ratings of acid/anionic dyes on colorfastness tests are shown in Table 7.1.

TABLE 7.1

Colorfastness Performance for Acid or Anionic Dyes

Test	Performance Rating
Crocking (color ruboff)	Good
Drycleaning	Excellent
Laundering	Poor
Light (sun or artificial light source)	Good
Perspiration	Poor to good

(Celanese Acetate LLC, 2001; Humphries, 2009; Leonard, 2007)

Azoic (Developed or Naphthol) Dyes Dye class used to color or print on cellulose-based fibers (i.e., cotton, hemp, linen, and ramie). These dyes offer a good assortment of bright shades in deep, rich colors. Performance ratings of azoic/developed/naphthol dyes on colorfastness tests are shown in Table 7.2.

TABLE 7.2

Colorfastness Performance for Azoic, Developed, or Naphthol Dyes

Test	Performance Rating
Crocking (color ruboff)	Poor for dark shades
Laundering	Good to excellent
Light (sun or artificial light source)	Excellent

(Celanese Acetate LLC, 2001; Humphries, 2009; Leonard, 2007)

Basic (Cationic) Dyes Originally created for dyeing silk and wool fiber, is now used to color acrylic, modacrylic, nylon, and polyester fibers. These dyes offer a complete range of intense and brilliant hues, some fluorescent. Performance ratings of basic/cationic dyes on colorfastness tests are shown in Table 7.3.

Today, silk and wool fibers are dyed using other dye classes such as *acid* and *reactive* that provide better colorfastness performance.

TABLE 7.3

Colorfastness Performance for Basic or Cationic Dyes

Test	Performance Rating
Crocking (color ruboff)	Excellent
Laundering	Excellent
Light (sun or artificial light source)	Good
Perspiration	Excellent

(Celanese Acetate LLC, 2001; Humphries, 2009; Leonard, 2007)

Direct Dyes Dye class used to color cellulose-based fibers (i.e., cotton, hemp, jute, linen, ramie, and rayon). These dyes offer a wide range of colors in light, medium, and dull shades. Direct dyes require a mordant to keep the dye affixed to the fibers. Performance ratings of direct dyes on colorfastness tests are shown in Table 7.4.

TABLE 7.4

Colorfastness Performance for Direct Dyes

Test	Performance Rating
Crocking (color ruboff)	Good on dry but poor on wet fabric
Laundering	Poor to good
Light (sun or artificial light source)	Fair

(Celanese Acetate LLC, 2001; Humphries, 2009; Leonard, 2007)

Disperse Dyes Originally created for dyeing acetate and triacetate, this dye class is also widely used for coloring most manufactured fibers such as acrylic, modacrylic, nylon, and polyester fibers. These dyes offer a good color assortment with the exception of black and dark hues. Performance ratings of disperse dyes on colorfastness tests are shown in Table 7.5.

TABLE 7.5

Colorfastness Performance for Disperse Dyes

Test	Performance Rating
Crocking (color ruboff)	Good on dry but poor on wet fabric
Drycleaning	Good to excellent
Laundering	Good on acrylic, modacrylic, and nylon; poor on acetate; excellent on polyester
Light (sun or artificial light source)	Fair to good
Perspiration	Good

(Celanese Acetate LLC, 2001; Humphries, 2009; Leonard, 2007)

Reactive Dyes Dye class used to color cellulose-based fibers such as cotton, cotton blends, and linen is also used to dye nylon, silk, and wool fibers. These dyes offer a wide assortment of bright colors. Reactive dyes are a type of anionic dye. During the dyeing process, the introduction of alkali causes a reaction with the fiber's hydroxyl groups creating a link between the fiber and the dye. Performance ratings of reactive dyes on colorfastness tests are shown in Table 7.6.

TABLE 7.6

Colorfastness Performance for Reactive Dyes

Test	Performance Rating
Crocking (color ruboff)	Poor to good
Laundering	Excellent
Light (sun or artificial light source)	Excellent

(Celanese Acetate LLC, 2001; Humphries, 2009; Leonard, 2007)

Sulfur Dyes Dye class used mainly to color cotton, a cellulose-based fiber. These dyes offer a good range of muted colors and are the most widely used as black dye. Performance ratings of sulfur dyes on colorfastness tests are shown in Table 7.7.

TABLE 7.7

Colorfastness Performance for Sulfur Dyes

Test	Performance Rating
Crocking (color ruboff)	Poor to good
Laundering	Excellent
Light (sun or artificial light source)	Good to excellent

(Celanese Acetate LLC, 2001; Humphries, 2009; Leonard, 2007)

Vat Dyes Dye class used to color cellulose-based fibers (i.e., cotton, linen, and rayon). These dyes offer a limited color assortment having dull shades. Performance ratings of vat dyes on colorfastness tests are shown in Table 7.8.

TABLE 7.8

Colorfastness Performance for Vat Dyes

Test	Performance Rating
Crocking (color ruboff)	Good
Laundering	Excellent
Light (sun or artificial light source)	Excellent
Perspiration	Excellent

(Celanese Acetate LLC, 2001; Humphries, 2009; Leonard, 2007)

Pigments

Pigments are not dyes. They do not penetrate fibers and are not water soluble like dyes. Pigments require binding agents to adhere to the surface of the fiber, yarn, or fabric. They offer a limited range of dull shades and fluorescent colors. Dark pigments have a tendency to stiffen fabrics. Achieving a distressed appearance is very economical with pigments because the colorant stays on the fabric surface rather than penetrating the fibers. Performance ratings of pigments on colorfastness tests are shown in Table 7.9.

TABLE 7.9
Colorfastness Performance for Pigments

Test	Performance Rating
Crocking (color ruboff)	Poor to fair
Laundering	Fair to good on light to medium shades; poor to fair on dark shades
Light (sun or artificial light source)	Excellent

(Celanese Acetate LLC, 2001; Humphries, 2009)

Optical Brighteners

Optical brighteners, also known as **fluorescent dyes** or **whiteners**, are colorless compounds with luminous qualities that absorb the ultraviolet radiation in light and reflect the radiation in the visible spectrum at longer wavelengths, giving the appearance of an intensely bright white. When fabrics treated with optical brighteners are exposed to ultraviolet florescent lighting (black light), they glow. There are three types of optical brighteners: anionic, cationic, and nonionic. Anionic optical brighteners are used on cotton, nylon, silk, and wool fibers. Cationic optical brighteners are used on acrylic and polyester fibers. Nonionic optical brighteners are used on all synthetic fibers. Performance ratings of optical brighteners, fluorescent dyes, or whiteners on colorfastness tests are shown in Table 7.10.

TABLE 7.10
Colorfastness Performance for Optical Brighteners

Test	Performance Rating
Crocking (color ruboff)	Excellent
Laundering	Good
Light (sun or artificial light source)	Good to excellent

(Celanese Acetate LLC, 2001; Esteves, 2004)

Price Classifications for Colorants

The price of colorants depends on the type of dye, pigment, or optical brightener applied to the fiber, yarn, or fabric. Price classifications for the different types of dyes, pigments, and brighteners are shown in Table 7.11.

TABLE 7.11
Price Classifications for Colorant Types

Price Classification	Colorant Type
Economical/Low Cost	Direct dyes Optical brighter Sulfur dyes
Low to Average Cost	Acid/Anionic dyes Pigments
Average Cost	Azoic/Developed/Napthol dyes Disperse dyes
Above Average Cost	Basic/Cationic dyes Vat dyes
Expensive/High Cost	Reactive dyes

A **textile print** is a design with a pattern repeat and **colorway** that is applied to a fabric. A colorway is the selection of palette colors used in a print for a particular season. Textile prints can be classified into flat and tonal prints. **Flat prints** (see Color plate 3) contain one or more designs or **motifs** that possess distinct divisions of color that are clearly defined from the background or **ground**. The repetition of motif creates the print design. **Tonal prints** contain motifs that can be hard to distinguish from the background (see Color plate 4). One motif may blend in with another due to subtle color variations. Examples of tonal prints include batik, tie-dyed, and watercolor designs. An assortment of pattern designs that share a common theme is known as a **print collection**. Print designs within the collection are independent of each other and are not intended for use together; however, they build a unifying relationship among all of the designs within the line.

Coordinated prints are specifically designed to be used together within an ensemble or garment. Color and motif are significant unifying factors when developing print coordinates. The designer creates a **master print** first and subsequently develops **derivative print** designs to coordinate with and complement the original design. Derivative designs can contain as little as one motif and as few as two colors from the master print (see Color plate 5). Additional motifs can be introduced into derivatives as long as all of the print designs are harmonious and coordinate with each other.

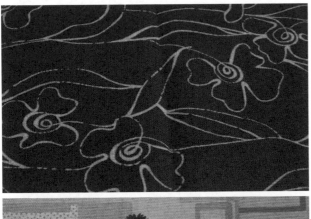

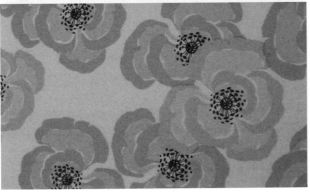

Flat prints

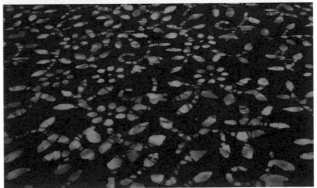

Tonal prints

PRINT DESIGN AND DEVELOPMENT (continued)

■ Print Repeat Styles

The **motif arrangement** or **layout** is the way in which one motif is positioned next to another. A **repeat** or **repeatable tile** is the specific arrangement of one or more motifs within an area where no two designs appear in the same way. The repeatable tile is repeated to create a pattern on fabric. Motifs in a repeat arranged in close proximity to each other create a **packed** or **tight layout**. The terms **open** or **spaced layout** describe the arrangement of a repeat that contains a significant amount of ground between motifs. **Open-and-closed layouts** contain clusters of motifs in an unbalanced or uneven distribution within the repeat. **Coverage** defines the area within a repeat that is occupied by motifs. For example, 50 percent coverage would indicate the equal distribution of space between the motifs and the background.

Repeatable tile

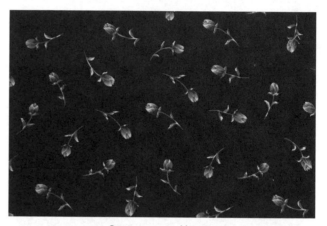

Open or spaced layout

Open-and-closed layout

Packed or tight layout

The directional arrangement of motifs within a repeat can affect the design of the fabric and its use. **One-way designs** contain motifs that are right-side-up and arranged in the same direction (e.g., arrows pointing in the same direction). **Two-way designs** contain motifs that are arranged in two directions (e.g., arrows pointing down and arrows pointing up). **Four-way designs** contain motifs arranged in four directions (e.g., arrows pointing up and down and arrows pointing to the left and to the right).

Tossed designs contain motifs arranged in all directions. Tossed designs appear to have a random layout and are not restricted by a specific direction.

A **pattern repeat** is the repetition of the repeatable tile in a specific repeat style. Print repeat styles include straight, drop, slide, and toss arrangements. Print layout styles include border prints, engineered prints, and direct-to-garment prints.

One-way design

Four-way design

Two-way design

Tossed design

Straight Repeat Pattern repeat displayed symmetrically in columns and rows.

Straight repeat

Drop Repeat Pattern repeat displayed in a diagonal layout where the repeat appears above or below the previous adjacent repeat. A repeat that is dropped ½ inch is known as a half-drop.

Drop repeat

Slide Repeat Pattern repeat displayed in a diagonal layout where the repeat is shifted to the left or right of the adjacent repeat. A repeat that is shifted ½ inch to the right or left is known as a half-slide.

Slide repeat

Allover Repeat Multidirectional configuration that appears random.

Allover repeat

Border Print Incorporates a stripe or border repeat of motifs displayed along one or more edges of the fabric. Border prints can contain solid blocks of color or an arrangement of motifs in addition to the border.

Border print

Engineered Print or Placement Print A print design that does not repeat within a garment panel and is created to fit specific dimensions; a single motif arrangement. Designers create engineered prints for a specific part of a garment (i.e., the front or back panel of a skirt, the front panel of a blouse, a scarf). Each engineered print is repeated along the yardage of the fabric independent of the others.

Engineered print

Direct-to-Garment Print The fabric design is engineered and printed as individual garment pattern pieces. After print processing, the fabric can go straight to cutting.

Direct-to-garment print

PRINT DESIGN AND DEVELOPMENT (continued)

■ Categories of Prints

The motifs used in print repeat designs determine the way a textile print is classified. **Realistic prints** contain motifs that appear close to or true to life, whereas **stylized prints** include simplistic, one-dimensional motifs that appear more abstract. Common print categories include conversational, floral, documentary, traditional, textures and weaves, and abstract and geometric designs.

Realistic prints

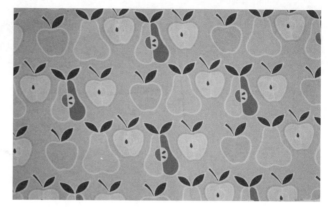

Stylized prints

Abstract Prints Fabric designs containing motifs of shapes and forms so stylized they are not identifiable objects.

Abstract prints

Conversational Prints Fabric designs containing motifs of identifiable objects. These prints may contain one motif or a series of related motifs tied to a central theme that tells a story. *Hidden conversational prints* reduce the overall importance of the individual motifs through their closely arranged allover print layout. Conversational prints can be subcategorized into the following classifications and themes:

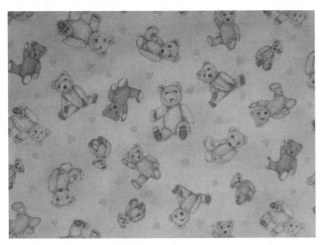

Juvenile design

Juvenile designs Contain motifs relating to themes that appeal to children, such as

Animals	Holidays or seasonal objects
Candy	School
Children's activities	Toys
Fairy tales	Vehicles

Adult prints

Adult designs Contain motifs relating to themes that appeal to adults, such as

Animal prints
Current events
Fashion accessories
Home (e.g., kitchen gadgets, food items, furniture)
Nautical
Nostalgic items
Sports

Floral Prints Fabric designs containing motifs of plant life such as flowers, leaves, plants, or trees.

Floral print

Geometric Prints Fabric designs containing lines and curves that create shapes such as circles, cubes, rectangles, spheres, squares, and triangles. Designers may use motifs singly or in groups that overlap or mesh together. Geometric prints can also simulate stripe, plaid, and check woven fabrics.

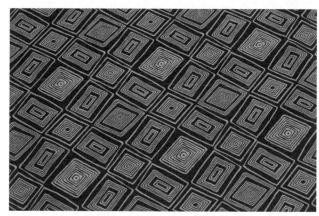

Geometric print

Texture Prints Fabric designs containing ground textural effects to create subtle surface interest. Texture prints can be subcategorized into the following classifications:

Organic texture prints Contain motifs based on forms found in nature. Examples of textural motifs include

Animal and reptile skins and fur	Pebbles or rock
Bark	Sand
Clouds	Seashells
Coral	Waves
Feathers	Wood
Grasses	

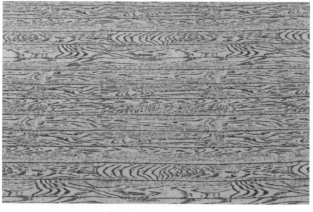

Organic texture print

Artificial effects Contain irregular motifs that provide texture to the fabric background. These special effects mimic artistic tools. Examples of artificial print effects include

Air brush	Spatter brush
Mosaic	Water droplets
Sponge	

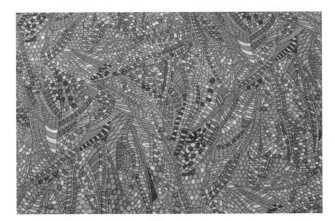

Mosaic

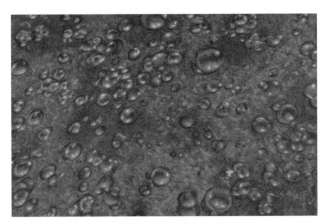

Water droplets

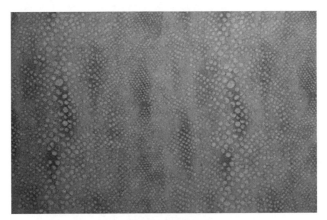

Graphic texture

Graphic textures Contain simple, stylized geometric shapes that create an overall ground effect.

PRINT DESIGN AND DEVELOPMENT (continued)

Traditional Prints Fabric designs containing classic motifs that have not changed much over time. Traditional prints can be subcategorized into the following classifications:

Calico prints Contain closely packed floral or geometric motifs that have close coverage.

Documentary prints Contain motifs and colors specific to a culture, ethnic group, historical period, geographic region, or country. These prints may be either reproductions or close interpretations.

Foulard prints Contain small classic motifs, often geometric in shape, in a specific repeat arrangement (such as a straight, drop, or slide) that conveys an elegant conservative style.

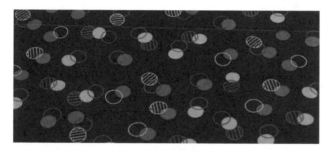

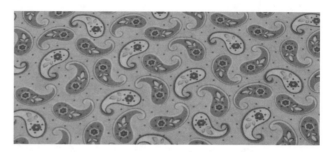

Little nothing prints Contain small, simplistic-shaped motifs such as circles, crescents, lines, squares, squiggles, and triangles arranged in an open-spaced tossed-repeat style. Colors of shapes are simplified to one to three colors.

Paisley prints Contain vegetal motifs shaped like droplets inspired by the Indian bodhi tree leaf. These designs are typically very detailed and offered in rich colors.

Weave Prints Fabric designs with motifs that simulate weave or knitted structures. Examples of weave prints include simulated

- Basket weave
- Crochet knit
- Lace
- Twill weave
- Woven straw

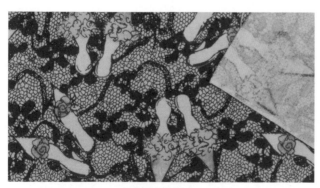

Simulated lace

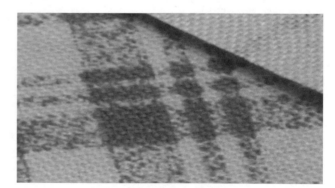

Simulated twill weave plaid

■ Textile Printing Methods

Designers create print designs and manufacturers produce sample yardage. Setup of some printing methods can be labor-intensive and require screens to be created for transferring the design to the material. After setup, the manufacturer does a test run, or **strike-off**, to check for accuracy and alignment of colors within the print design. **Registration** refers to the alignment of each color within a pattern design.

Fabric minimums designate the smallest amount of fabric yardage that can be ordered. Fabric is printed in different **run lengths**, depending on the purpose and yardage required. **Sampling** is a very small run length of 3.3 yards (3 meters) of fabric that is printed and submitted for evaluation and approval. Sampling may be submitted several times before it is approved and production begins. When sample yardage is evaluated, color match and registration are key factors. Color must be accurate and be precisely aligned for aesthetic and quality purposes. **Coupon printing** is a small run length of 33 yards (30 meters) of fabric. **Collection** or **catalogue printing** is a run length of 109 yards (100 meters) of material. Typically, a minimum run length of 109 yards (100 meters) is used for production yardage by small to midsize brands and apparel manufacturers. **Production printing** is a minimum run length of 328 yards (300 meters).

The most common methods for printing textile production yardage include flatbed screens, rotary screens, and digital printing. Approximately 99 percent of production fabric yardage is printed using flatbed or rotary screen systems, although digital printing is becoming increasingly more important.

Flatbed Screen Printing (Automatic Screen Printing)

An intermittent printing method that utilizes screens made of nylon mesh. Screens are coated with a photosensitive film and processed to remove the film only in portions containing the pattern design. The screen is stretched onto a metal frame and loaded onto a continuous rubber belt known as a *printing blanket*. Whole rolls of fabric are loaded and printed at one time. Fabric moves along a belt and stops at each screen, where a squeegee passes over the screen, transferring colorant paste to the fabric. Each color requires its own screen. The maximum range of colors in prints using this method is 12 to 16. Flatbed screen printing output is approximately 500 yards per hour (450 meters per hour) and is used for small-scale production or more complex work.

Flatbed screen printing

Rotary screen printing

Rotary Screen Printing A continuous printing method where the cylinder-shaped screens are made of metal mesh. Screens are engraved with the design. Whole rolls of fabric are loaded and printed at one time. The fabric moves along a continuous rubber belt known as a *printing blanket*, and the cylinder rolls over the fabric, transferring the print design to the material.

Each color requires its own screen. The maximum range of colors in prints using this method is 12 to 16. Although the rotary screen printing process can accommodate maximum color ranges of 24 to 32, these designs are very expensive to prepare, therefore increasing the fabric cost significantly. Dyes or pigment pastes can be used. The maximum output for rotary screen printing using pigment pastes is approximately 120 yards per minute (100 meters per minute). When dyes are used, the maximum speed must be reduced to 45 to 90 yards per minute (40 to 80 meters per minute). Rotary screen printing is used for large-scale production runs. The repeat design is limited to the diameter of the cylinder. Common cylinder sizes include 25 inches, 27 inches, 32 inches, and 36 inches.

Digital printing

Digital Printing A continuous printing method using an inkjet printer that directly applies dye from the printhead to pretreated fabric. The CMYK (cyan, magenta, yellow, and black) color space for mixing and printing colors is used. The printhead applies tiny droplets of ink to mix the colors that appear on the fabric's surface. Development of digital printing ink technology continues as chemists research formulations to eliminate additional postprocessing needed to fix the color to the surface of fabric such as pigment-based and nano colorants (dye or pigment particles having dimensions smaller than 100 nanometers). With this method, fabric designs can be printed with virtually unlimited colors and without repeats. Photorealism can be achieved as well. The maximum output for the quickest digital printers is less than 120 yards per hour (100 meters per hour). Digital printing also allows for direct-to-garment printing.

■ Colorant Application

In textile printing, dyes and pigments are applied to the face of the **substrate** (base material). The same dye classifications defined in the colorants section are used for printing, except the chemical colorants are not dissolved in a dye bath. Printed fabrics are typically referred to as dry, wet, or digital prints.

Dry Prints (*Pigment Prints*) Powdered pigments are adhered to the material with resin binders that require curing with dry heat to complete the printing process. The print is applied to the substrate by flatbed or rotary screen printing methods. Performance ratings of dry or pigment prints to colorfastness tests are shown in Table 7.12.

TABLE 7.12
Colorfastness Performance for Dry/Pigment Prints

Test	Performance Rating
Abrasion	Poor
Crocking (color ruboff)	Poor
Laundering	Good
Light (sun or artificial light source)	Good

(EPA 1995; Humphries, 2009; Maguire, Garland, Pagan, & Nienke, 2009; Stefanini, 1996; Thiry, 2007)

Wet Prints Liquid dyes are thickened to form a paste used for printing. Wet prints require more labor-intensive processing after printing—such as *aging*, where steam is applied to the fabric—followed by washing and rinsing processes to remove agents used to thicken the pigments. Printers utilize flatbed or rotary screen printing methods to apply prints to substrates. Performance ratings of wet prints to colorfastness tests are shown in Table 7.13.

TABLE 7.13
Colorfastness Performance for Wet Prints

Test	Performance Rating
Abrasion	Good
Crocking (color ruboff)	Good
Laundering	Good
Light (sun or artificial light source)	Good

(EPA 1995; Humphries, 2009; Maguire, Garland, Pagan, & Nienke, 2009; Stefanini, 1996; Thiry, 2007)

Digital Prints Printers use disperse dyes or pigment inkjet inks. Digital prints require labor-intensive processing after printing such as aging. Viscosity of the dye or ink determines the level of processing required after printing to achieve acceptable colorfastness levels. High-viscosity pigment inks contain binders, whereas low viscosity inks do not contain any binding agent, therefore requiring a separate application after printing. Digital inkjet printers apply the print to the substrate. Performance ratings of digital prints to colorfastness tests are shown in Table 7.14.

TABLE 7.14
Colorfastness Performance for Digital Prints

Test	Performance Rating
Crocking (color ruboff)	Good
Laundering	Good
Light (sun or artificial light source)	Good

(EPA 1995; Humphries, 2009; Maguire, Garland, Pagan, & Nienke, 2009; Stefanini, 1996; Thiry, 2007)

■ Price Classifications for Printing

The price of printing on textiles varies depending on the type of dye or pigment and the method used to apply it to the fabric. Following are price classifications for the different types of prints.

Economical/Low Cost
- Sampling using digital printing
- Low-volume yardage using digital printing
- High-volume production yardage using rotary screen (screen setup and sampling are expensive)

Average Cost
- Sampling and setup using flatbed screen printing
- Moderate- to low-volume yardage using digital printing
- Moderate- to high-volume flatbed screen printing

Expensive/High Cost
- Sampling and setup using rotary screen printing
- Low-volume yardage using rotary screen printing
- High-volume production yardage using digital printing

PRINT DESIGN AND DEVELOPMENT (continued)

■ Exclusive Fabrics

When selecting and ordering fabrics for an apparel line, a designer has many factors to consider. Some purchase **stock materials** produced in large quantities and ready to ship; others work with mills or textile converters to develop custom or exclusive fabrics. **Developed fabrics** are custom materials made to specifications to provide an exclusive fabrication for a brand. Developed fabrics include custom prints and yarn-dyed patterns.

Confined Prints Custom print designs owned by a company for their exclusive use.

Open Prints Stock print designs owned by a fabric manufacturer and available for sale.

Structural Fabric Design Custom fabric designs or patterns woven or knitted into the structure of the material created for exclusive use by an apparel manufacturer or brand.

Intarsia Knit Structural designs knitted into the fabric to create a picture or image by utilizing multiple colored yarns and can also incorporate different yarn styles.

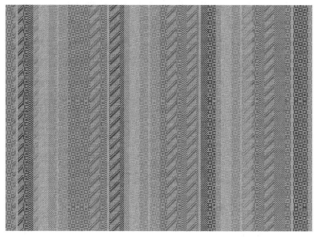

Structural fabric design with multiple weave structures

Intarsia knit fabric

Fair Isle Knit Bands or rows of geometric designs knitted into the structure of the fabric that can appear as an all-over design, a border, or panel on a garment. Traditional Fair Isle knits are typically limited to five colors with two colors used per row.

Yarn-Dyed Fabrics Design or pattern of the material is woven or knitted into the structure as it is created. Yarn-dyed fabric can be stock or structural designs.

Fair Isle knit fabric

Yarn-dyed woven fabric   Yarn-dyed knit fabric

Finishing is a chemical or mechanical process performed on textiles, in order to change the properties of a material, to produce desired effects for the intended end use of the product. Mechanical processes that physically change the appearance of the fabric are referred to as **dry finishes**. When liquid or foam chemicals are applied to fabrics, then dried or cured in order to physically change performance characteristics, they are referred to as **wet finishes**. **Aesthetic finishes** change the appearance, hand, or drape of fabrics. Examples of aesthetic finishes include calendaring, flocking, fulling, mercerizing, napping and sueding, plissé, shearing, softening, stiffening, and washing.

Calendaring Mechanical process of ironing or pressing textiles under high-pressure cylinders at high speeds. The surface of the cylinders and rate of speed the fabric is passed through determine the type of surface finish applied. Some fabrics are treated with resins or waxes as part of the process to achieve the desired finish. Calendaring fabric can give it

- Embossed surface
- Glazed appearance
- Slight sheen to high luster
- Moiré effect

Flocking Mechanical process utilizing adhesive to attach tiny fiber particles to the surface of fabric. If fiber particles are given an electrostatic charge, they attach to fabric in an upright position; otherwise, they are adhered in random positions. Flocking fabric gives it

- Surface interest to create a pattern or overall raised uniform surface
- Surface texture similar to suede or velvet

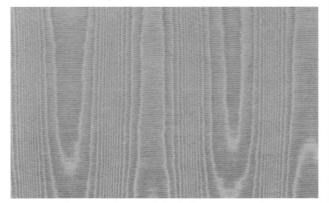

Moiré effect

Flocking

Pressing textiles under high-pressure cylinders

Spray binding flocking machine

Fulling Mechanical process of felting wool in a controlled environment of moisture, heat, and friction. The amount of friction applied determines the level of felting that occurs. Fulling fabric gives it

- Improved fabric hand
- Increased fabric density and thickness
- Smooth surface texture
- Improved softness

Fulling

Mercerizing Chemical bath of caustic solution applied to tension-controlled fabric. Mercerizing provides aesthetic and functional finish qualities. Mercerizing fabric results in

- Enhanced luster
- Increased strength
- Increased affinity for dye penetration
- Improved fabric drape and hand

Mercerized jacket

Napping and Sueding Mechanical processes used to raise fibers on the surface of fabrics by means of brushing or sanding. In napping, the fabric surface is passed between rotating cylinders with a bristled surface made of fine bent wires. In sueding, the fabric surface is passed over rotating cylinders with an emery surface similar to sandpaper. Some fabrics are sheared after these processes to provide consistency and uniformity to the fabric surface. Napping and sueding a fabric gives it

- Brushed surface
- Improved fabric hand
- Improved softness
- Increased insulation properties

Napping and sueding

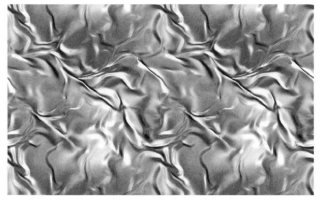

Plissé

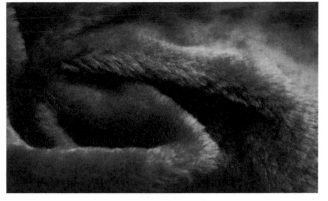

Shearing

Plissé Process of applying a chemical paste of sodium hydroxide to fabric, causing it to shrink in the areas where paste is present. Plissé processed fabrics have a puckered effect.

Shearing Mechanical process of passing fabric over cutting blades to trim surface fibers of napped or pile fabrics. Shearing gives consistency and uniformity to fiber lengths on the fabric's surface.

Softening machine

Softening Chemical and mechanical processes used to soften fabric and improve drape and hand. Common methods include application of silicone, emulsified oils and waxes, or cationic detergents.

TEXTILE FINISHES (continued)

Stiffening Process of applying a chemical solution of starch or acid to fabric that is then dried or cured. Stiffening a fabric makes it crisper and more rigid.

Stiffening applied to shirt fabric

Washing Process of mass production laundering with enzymes, stones, or bleach to distress a fabric's surface. In *enzyme washing*, cellulase is used to attack the cellulose fibers to weaken them and remove surface fuzz. In *stone washing*, pumice stones abrade the fabric. In *acid washing*, pumice stones are wet with an oxidizing chemical of sodium hypochlorite and used in the laundering process to abrade and bleach the fabric. Washing is most widely used on denim products. Washing a fabric gives it

- Distressed, faded, or worn appearance
- Improved softness
- Lightened color

Stone washing

Acid washing

Functional finishes change performance characteristics of fabrics. Examples of functional finishes include antimicrobial, antistatic, crease-resistant, durable press, flame-resistant, insect control, shrinkage control, soil release, water- and stain-repellant, and waterproof.

Antimicrobial, Antiseptic, or Antibacterial Chemical solutions applied to fabrics or incorporated into fibers as they are produced in order to

- Control spread of germs, disease, and reduce risk of infection
- Inhibit growth of bacteria, fungus, mold, and mildew
- Protect against damage and decay
- Protect against dust mites and insects
- Protect against odor

Antistatic Chemical solutions applied to fabrics or incorporated into fibers as they are produced in order to

- Attract moisture
- Eliminate or reduce static buildup

Crease-Resistant Chemical resin solutions applied to fabrics in order to reduce wrinkling during wear. Ironing is still required for garments treated with this finish.

Durable Press (Permanent Press or Wrinkle-free) Chemical treatment of ammonia or resin followed by curing or heat-setting in order for fabrics to resist, remove, or shed wrinkles.

Flame-Resistant Chemical solutions applied to fabrics followed by curing or drying in order for fabrics to slow the ignition rate of fabric when a flame is introduced and to slow the rate of burning once the material is ignited.

Insect Control (Insect Repellant or Insecticide) Chemical solutions applied to fabrics typically during the dyeing process to make the fibers unpalatable to insects or larva such as carpet beetles, crickets, cockroaches, moths, silverfish, spiders, and other types of insects.

Shrinkage Control Mechanical or chemical processes used for controlling fabric shrinkage. Compressive shrinkage is the mechanical process used to finish cellulose-based woven and knitted fabrics. Chemical resins or solutions are applied to fabrics made from hair fiber or some cellulose-based fibers. Manufacturers use heat-setting to control shrinkage in nylon, polyester, and acrylic fabrics.

Soil Release Chemical resins applied to fabric to increase *wetting* (absorbency) to facilitate soil release during laundering.

Water and Stain Repellant Chemical emulsions, solutions, or waxes applied to fabrics to make them resistant to stains or water.

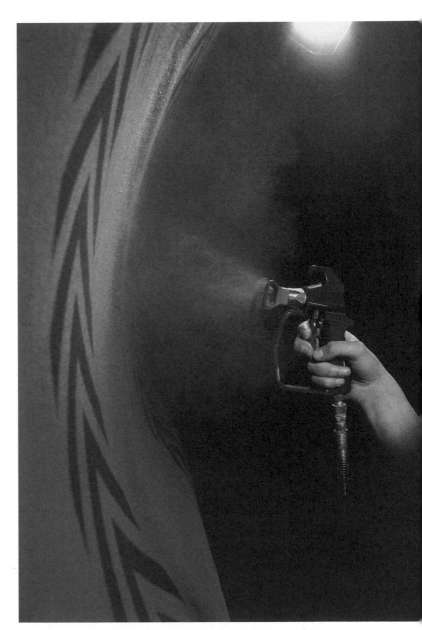

Flame-retardant finish being applied to fabric.

Waterproof Laminate film coating applied to prevent water from passing through the fabric.

Not all finishing processes produce permanent results. Finishes are categorized as permanent, durable, semi-durable, and temporary.

TEXTILE FINISHES (continued)

Permanent Finish Fabric is subjected to chemical or mechanical treatment in order to retain specified characteristics for the useful life of the garment. Finishing processes producing permanent finishes include

- Calendaring
- Fulling
- Mercerizing
- Napping and sueding
- Plissé
- Shearing
- Stiffening (Acid)
- Washing
- Waterproof

Durable Finish Fabric is subjected to chemical or mechanical treatment in order to retain specified properties or characteristics. The finish is weakened with each cleaning. Toward the end of the useful life of the garment, the finish may be virtually removed. Finishing processes producing durable finishes include

- Antimicrobial/antiseptic/antibacterial
- Calendaring
- Durable press/permanent press/wrinkle-free
- Flame-resistant
- Insect control/insect repellant/insecticide
- Soil release
- Water and stain repellant

Semi-Durable Finish Fabric is subjected to chemical or mechanical treatment in order to retain specified properties or characteristics. The finish is virtually removed after several cleanings. Some semi-durable finishes are renewed when drycleaned or laundered. Finishing processes producing semi-durable finishes include

- Antistatic (Fiber)
- Crease-resistant
- Flame-resistant
- Softening

Temporary Finish Fabric is subjected to chemical or mechanical treatment in order to maintain specified properties or characteristics. The finish is removed after one cleaning. Finishing processes producing temporary finishes include

- Antistatic (Fabric)
- Calendaring
- Softening
- Stiffening (Starch)

FABRIC SPECIFICATIONS

Aesthetic and physical performance of sewn products depends in no small part on detailed specifications for textile fabrics. **Fabric specifications** include detailed statements describing fiber content, yarn composition, fabric structure and construction, weight, characteristics and performance requirements, finishes, and color standards for manufacturing. Fabric specifications include

- Fiber content, size, and length
- Yarn type
- Yarn structure
- Yarn twist and number of turns per inch
- Single or number of ply yarns
- Yarn number
- Knit or weave type
- Yarn count
- Fabric weight
- Fabric width
- Fabric density
- Defect tolerances
- Color standards
- Color identification information from vender's color card or dye or pigment specifications
- Finishes
- Appearance requirements and tolerance
- Abrasion requirements and tolerances

- Chemical resistance requirements and tolerances
  - Acids
  - Alkalis
  - Bleaching
  - Drycleaning
  - Insects/microorganisms
  - Laundering
  - Mineral acids
  - Moisture regain
  - Organic solvents
- Colorfastness requirements and tolerances
  - Atmospheric contaminants
  - Bleach
  - Crocking (rubbing)
  - Drycleaning
  - Laundering (home and commercial)
  - Light
  - Perspiration
- Dimensional stability requirements and tolerances
- Flammability requirements and tolerances
- Strength and elongation requirements and tolerances
- Thermal property requirements and tolerances

References

ASTM International. (2016a). *2016 ASTM International standards*. (Vol. 07.01). West Conshohocken, PA: Author.

ASTM International. (2016b). *2016 ASTM International standards*. (Vol. 07.02). West Conshohocken, PA: Author.

Celanese Acetate LLC. (2001). *Complete textile glossary*. Charlotte, NC: Author.

BASF. (2015). *Optical brighteners*. Retrieved November 1, 2015, from https://www.dispersions-pigments.basf.com/portal/basf/ien/dt.jsp?setCursor=1_556358

EPA. (1995). 4.11 Textile fabric printing. In *AP 42: Chapter 4, Evaporation loss sources* (Vol. 1, Ed. 5). Retrieved November 1, 2015, from http://www.epa.gov/ttnchie1/ap42/ch04/final/c4s11.pdf

Esteves, F. (2004, June 22–24). *Optical brighteners effect on white and colored textiles*. World textile conference: 4th AUTEX conference. Retrieved November 1, 2015, from http://repositorium.sdum.uminho.pt/bitstream/1822/2021/1/Optical.pdf

Fisher, R., & Wolfhal, D. (1993). *Textile print design*. New York: Fairchild.

Glock, R. E., & Kunz, G. I. (2005). *Apparel manufacturing sewn product analysis* (4th ed.). Upper Saddle River, NJ: Pearson Prentice Hall.

Humphries, M. (2009). *Fabric reference* (4th ed.). Upper Saddle River, NJ: Pearson Prentice Hall.

Johnson, I., Cohen, A. C., & Sarkar, A. K. (2015). *J. J. Pizzuto's fabric science* (11th ed.). New York: Fairchild.

Kadolph, S. J. (2010). *Textiles* (11th ed.). Upper Saddle River, NJ: Pearson.

Leonard, C. (2007, September). Dye classes: The basics. *AATCC Review, Magazine for Textile Professionals, 7*(9), 28.

Maguire King, K., Garland, G., Pagan, L., & Nienke, J. (2009, February). Moving digital printing forward for the production of sewn products. *AATCC Review: Journal for Textile Professionals, 9*(2), 33–36.

Provost, J. (2009). *Textile ink jet printing with pigment inks*. Retrieved November 1, 2015, from http://provost-inkjet.com/resources/Textile+Ink+Jet+Printing+with+Pigment+Inks.pdf

Regan, C. L. (2008). *Apparel product design and merchandising strategies*. Upper Saddle River, NJ: Pearson Prentice Hall.

Stefanini, J. P. (1996, September). Jet printing for the textile industry. *AATCC Textile Chemist and Colorist, 28*(9), 19–23.

Thiry, M. C. (2007, September). Pretty as a picture: Traditional screens and newcomer digital vie to print beautiful fabrics. *AATCC Review, Magazine for Textile Professionals, 7*(9), 22–27.

CHAPTER 8

Thread Specifications

Sewing thread is a strong, slender strand or ply composed of flexible yarns made from fibers or filaments, bonded cords, or monofilaments that pass through an industrial sewing machine needle at high speeds, form uniform stitches, and suit the intended use of sewn products.

Thread is an essential component to assemble garment parts, finish edges, and add decorative details. Proper thread selection is important and should be based on fabric type and fiber content to be sewn, type of seam construction and desired seam strength, type of sewing machine and equipment, product end use, desired performance, and life span. These factors affect appearance, cost, and performance, and during production, ease and efficiency of sewing.

TYPES OF THREAD FIBERS

Natural fibers, manufactured fibers, and synthetic fibers are used in making industrial sewing thread for garment production. The most common natural fiber used for industrial sewing thread is cotton. Other natural fibers used in specialty thread manufacturing include hemp, jute, linen, ramie, silk, and wool. Natural fibers are available only in staple lengths and do not provide uniformity or strength that synthetic fibers offer. Although natural fibers are affected by changes in climate, they do offer good heat resistance and are used for **overdye** (process of adding supplementary dye color to yarn-dyed fabrics or piece-dyed garments for the purpose of creating unique colors) or garment dye applications. Natural fibers are fairly colorfast and resistant to abrasion and chemicals.

In addition to natural fibers, manufactured and synthetic fibers are used in thread construction. The manufactured fiber used in industrial sewing thread is rayon. This regenerated cellulose compound is extruded into filaments and used in this form or cut into staple lengths.

Rayon thread provides moderate strength but low **elongation** (an increase in length when force is applied). Like thread made from natural cellulose fibers, rayon thread is also affected by climatic changes, offers good heat resistance, is colorfast, and resists abrasion and chemicals. Rayon thread provides high sheen that is desirable for embroidery applications.

Synthetic fibers, made from chemical polymers, are extruded into filaments that can be used as is or cut into staple lengths. The most common synthetic fibers used for industrial threads are nylon and polyester. Threads composed of aramid and spandex fibers are used for garments that require particular performance characteristics such as flame or heat resistance or for stretch. Synthetic fibers are strong, colorfast, and resistant to abrasion and chemicals, and provide high elongation. Polyester threads are used in most apparel applications, whereas nylon is more widely used for accessory items such as footwear, handbags, and luggage.

THREAD CONSTRUCTION METHODS

Staple fibers or filaments are spun or extruded, bonded, and twisted to form a unit or cord called a **strand**. An extrusion process with no twist creates monofilament threads. Thread construction methods used for apparel include air-entangled (locked), core spun, monofilament, spun, and textured. Thread construction methods for other uses include monocord and twisted multifilament.

Air-Entangled (Air Jet or Locked) Thread Continuous polyester filaments are passed through high-pressure air jets, which entangle the filament fibers. Then the yarn is twisted to form an air-entangled thread.

Air-entangled thread

Core Spun Thread A continuous filament of polyester fiber wrapped with a spun yarn of cotton (or other natural fiber) or polyester staple. The thread is then formed by twisting two or more single yarns together. This type of thread wrapped in cotton provides washdown (fading). Core spun thread is commonly used for seam construction, covering raw edges, topstitching buttonholes, and attaching buttons. For embroidery thread, the polyester core is wrapped with metallic-coated polyester.

Core spun thread

Monocord Thread Continuous filaments of nylon fibers minimally twisted together to form a single flat cord of yarn that is bonded during finishing. Monocord thread is typically not used in apparel products but reserved for heavy-duty sewing applications such as construction of footwear, handbags, and luggage.

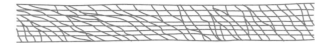

Monocord thread

Monofilament Thread Single continuous nylon filament fiber commonly used to *blind stitch* the hems of garments.

Monofilament thread

Spun Thread Staple fibers of cotton or polyester twisted together to form a yarn. Two or more singles yarns are twisted together to form a plied yarn known as spun thread. Manufacturers commonly use this type of thread for seam construction and covering raw edges, topstitching buttonholes, and attaching buttons.

Spun thread

Textured Thread Continuous filaments of polyester or nylon fibers are textured and heat-set to maintain bulk. This type of thread is commonly used for seam construction, covering raw edges, topstitching buttonholes, and attaching buttons. Textured thread is popular for knit fabrics due to its elongation and stretch.

Textured thread

Twisted Multifilament Thread A ply yarn formed by twisting together two or more *singles yarns* (twisted continuous nylon or polyester filaments). Heavy-duty sewing applications such as construction of footwear, handbags, luggage, and furniture use this type of thread. For embroidery applications, continuous polyester or rayon filament singles yarns twisted to form a ply thread are finished to provide a matte or shiny appearance.

Twisted multifilament thread

The number of strands twisted or bonded identifies the finished thread as monocord, two-, three-, four-, or six-ply. Thread strength is determined by the size, twist, balance, yarn finish, and number of plies, as well as the inherent fiber characteristics. Single-strand yarns typically have an S-twist, whereas ply yarns have a Z-twist. Most ply sewing threads are created with Z-twist, because S-twisted yarns tend to unwind during stitching.

Balanced Twist Singles yarns of a ply thread have S-twist, and the ply yarns have Z-twist. Each twist direction contains a specific number of turns per inch to balance the thread. Balancing the twist of thread prevents kinking or twisting back on itself during sewing. Embroidery threads are different in that singles and ply yarns both possess Z-twist to prevent missed stitches and loops from forming on the surface of the embroidery during production due to multidirectional stitches.

Ply Security (Ply Adhesion) The integrity of thread, that is, its ability to maintain its structure and not unravel during sewing.

THREAD SIZE

Thread size is the diameter of the thread. Thread size is typically indicated by **ticket number**, which is the numeral assigned to designate the **linear density** or mass per unit length of the thread. That numeral is given in *tex*, which indicates the number of grams per 1,000 meters of undyed or finished thread. Tex, a *direct yarn number system*, is used to approximate the minimum amount of fiber present in the thread. Larger numbers, such as T-90 or T-105, indicate coarser threads, containing more raw fiber. Smaller numbers, such as T-18 or T-24, indicate finer threads containing less raw fiber. Thread manufacturers use a ticket number to designate thread size and indicate how much fiber is in the thread. ASTM D 3823 Standard Practice for Determining Ticket Numbers for Sewing Threads can be used to convert yarn number to ticket number. Thread is typically sold by length rather than weight.

Common thread tex sizes, referred to as ticket numbers for industrial sewing thread, are paired with the appropriate fabric weights in Table 8.1.

TABLE 8.1
Thread Ticket Numbers for Industrial Sewing Threads Used for Various Fabric Weights

Thread Ticket Numbers	Fabric Weights
T-18, T-21, or T-24	2-4oz/sq yd (67.81–135.62g/m²)
T-24, T-27, or T-30	4-6oz/sq yd (135.62–203.43 g/m²)
T-30, T-35, T-40, or T-50	6-8oz/sq yd (203.43–271.25g/m²)
T-50, T-60, or T-70	8-10oz/sq yd (271.25–339.06g/m²)
T-80, T-90, T-105, T-120, or T-135	10-14oz/sq yd (339.06–474.68g/m²)

(American & Efird, Inc., 2009a)

Sewing Thread Needle Size The metric diameter of a needle measured in hundredths of a millimeter. For example, a 65 needle is 0.65 mm in diameter, and a 120 needle is 1.20 mm in diameter. The size of the needle's eye is proportional to the thickness of the thread. To form stitches properly, the thread must pass through the needle's eye with a specific amount of drag and tension. Needle size must be appropriately selected for the type and weight of fabric as well the size and type of thread. Minimum metric needle sizes are paired with thread ticket numbers and organized by types of thread used for apparel production in Table 8.2.

TABLE 8.2
Minimum Metric Needle Sizes for Thread Types, along with Thread Ticket Numbers

Type of Thread	Thread Ticket Numbers	Metric Needle Sizes (Thread Size)
Air Entangled (Locked Threads)	T-21	70
	T-27	75
	T-40	90
	T-45	100
	T-60	110
	T-90	120
	T-135	150
Core Spun Threads	T-16	65
	T-18	70
	T-24	70
	T-30, T-35	80
	T-40	90
	T-50, T 60	110
	T-80	120
	T-105	125
	T-120	130
	T-135	140
Spun Threads	T-16	65
	T-18 to T-21	65 to 75
	T-27	75
	T-30	80
	T-40 to T-45	90
	T-60 to T-70	110
	T-80 to T-90	120
	T-105	125
	T-120	130
	T-135	140
Textured Thread	T-18	60
	T-24	65
	T-35	75
	T-50	90
	T-70	110
	T-105	140

(American & Efird, Inc. 2009b, c; Coats, 2015)

Ready-wound bobbins

Cheese package

Cone package

Cop package

Ready-Wound Bobbins Sewing machine bobbins sold prewound with the same type of thread as the *lockstitch machine*'s upper needle or with twisted multifilament or monochord thread.

Thread Package Paper or plastic container or holder on which thread is wound. Types of thread packages include

- *Cheese*—Flangeless cylinder
- *Cone*—Conical shape
- *Cop*—Tube with tapered ends

DYEING

Color is added to thread through **package dyeing**. During this dyeing process, wound thread packages are placed on perforated spindles and lowered into a pressurized chamber where the dye is forced through the thread package to penetrate the yarns from the inside out. Threads made from cotton or rayon are dyed using one of the following dye classes (listed in order of colorfastness, starting with the best):

- Vat
- Fiber reactive
- Azoic or naphthol
- Developed
- Direct

Thread hues available from thread manufacturers' color cards are evaluated against color standards from approved lab dips to ensure good matches between the thread, fabric, trims, and findings. Selection from existing stock colors reduces cost and time to market. **Dyed to match** (DTM) thread is often specified when existing stock does not provide the color needed to match the color specification. Dye formulations are created specifically for clients to match their color standards. Due to the variety of fabric textures used for apparel, manufacturers cannot solely rely on spectrophotometer readings to match thread color. When stitches are applied to fabric, the way in which the light is absorbed or reflected off the surface of the fabric affects how the thread color appears.

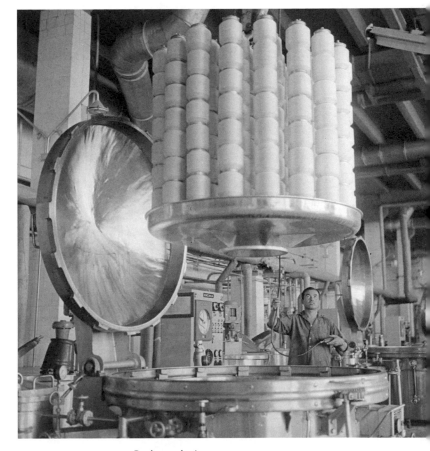

Package dyeing

DYEING (continued)

Prepared for Dyeing (PFD) A type of cotton thread used for constructing apparel to be garment dyed. PFD threads are used with greige goods, so the thread and garment fabric are dyed simultaneously in order to match the color. These threads do not contain *finishes*, *optical brighteners*, or sizing (starch) that can interfere with dyeing.

Ready for Dyeing (RFD) A type of polyester or nylon thread used for constructing apparel to be garment dyed. RFD threads are used with greige goods, so the thread and garment fabric are dyed simultaneously in order to match the color. These threads do not contain *finishes*, *optical brighteners*, or sizing (starch) that can interfere with dyeing.

FINISHING PROCESSES

Bonded thread

A **thread finish** is applied to enhance the desired qualities for end use. Thread finishes include bonding, gassing, glazing, and mercerization.

Bonded Resin applied to a multifilament nylon or polyester yarn to encase the filaments to form a smooth, strong coating on the threads' surface. Bonding is applied to the following thread constructions:

- Twisted multifilament
- Monocord

   Bonded yarns are used for sewing coated fabrics and heavyweight fabrics for apparel, but are mainly used for handbags, luggage, and shoes.

Gassed Cotton threads move through a flame at a high rate of speed to reduce the protrusion of fiber ends or fuzz on the threads' surface and enhance sheen. Cotton threads are gassed prior to mercerization. Gassing is used on spun thread.

Gassed thread

Glacé thread

Mercerized thread

Glacé (Glazed) Starch, wax, or special chemicals applied to cotton threads through brushing or polishing under heat-controlled conditions to produce a durable, glossy finish. Glazing reduces the possibility of thread untwisting during sewing. Glacé is applied to spun thread.

This finish produces a very strong cotton thread not typically used in apparel but for stitching footwear, handbags, and luggage.

Mercerized Chemical bath of caustic solution applied to tension-controlled cotton thread to enhance luster and strength while increasing its dye penetrability.

Mercerized yarns are used in apparel production.

Soft finish

Lubricated thread

Soft Threads lubricated for ease of sewing but not otherwise finished or treated. Soft yarns are used in apparel production. These thread constructions use a soft finish:

- Air-entangled
- Core
- Monofilament
- Textured
- Twisted multifilament

Lubrication Silicone applied to thread to reduce friction during sewing. Such threads include

- Core spun wrapped in cotton or polyester staple fibers
- Spun made from cotton or polyester staple fibers

THREAD USE AND CONSUMPTION

Industrial sewing thread for apparel manufacturing is selected for those qualities most compatible with the fabric and type of garment. In a properly designed garment, seams are constructed so the thread will break before the fabric fails or tears. Thread type is selected with consideration for

- Compatibility with fabric fiber content
- Fabric type and weight
- Method of seam construction
- Machinery used
- Type of stitching, number of stitches per inch, location, and definition or distinction required (for topstitching)
- Garment type and intended use
- Care and life span of the garment
- Cost
- Quality level desired

TABLE 8.3
Thread Consumption for Men's, Women's, and Children's Apparel

Men's Garment Styles	Thread Consumption	Women's Garment Styles	Thread Consumption	Children's Garment Styles	Thread Consumption
Athletic pant	98 yds (90 m)	Athletic pant	98 yds (90 m)	Blouse and top for girls	56 yds (50 m)
Athletic short	67 yds (60 m)	Athletic short	67 yds (60 m)	Shirt for boys	82 yds (75 m)
Briefs and underwear	55–60 yds (50–55 m)	Blouse	92 yds (85 m)	Brief and underwear	44 yds (40 m)
Boxer short	120 yds (110 m)	Bra	63 yds (58 m)	Boxer short	87 yds (80 m)
Camp shirt	109 yds (100 m)	Brief and underwear	71 yds (65 m)	Dress shirt	101 yds (92 m)
Dress shirt, long sleeve	128 yds (117 m)	Camp shirt	109 yds (100 m)	Dress	98–118 yds (90–108 m)
Dress shirt, short sleeve	98 yds (90 m)	Camisole	60 yds (55 m)	Jean	142 yds (130 m)
Jacket, unlined	219 yds (200 m)	Dress, unlined	141–208 yds (129–190 m)	Knit polo shirt	98 yds (90 m)
Jacket, lined	384 yds (351 m)	Dress, lined	326 yds (298 m)	Nightgown	180 yds (165 m)
Jeans	197 yds (180 m)	Knit polo shirt	131 yds (120 m)	Pant	164 yds (150 m)
Jean jacket	230 yds (210 m)	Jacket, unlined	219 yds (200 m)	Pajama	109 yds (100 m)
Knit polo shirt	164 yds (150 m)	Jacket, lined	384 yds (351 m)	Parka	180 yds (165 m)
Overcoat	667 yds (610 m)	Jean	197 yds (180 m)	Skirt	77 yds (70 m)
Pajama	208 yds (190 m)	Jean jacket	230 yds (210 m)	Short	38 yds (35 m)
Parka	262 yds (240 m)	Overcoat	344 yds (315 m)	Swimwear	44 yds (40 m)
Raincoat	312 yds (285 m)	Nightgown	135 yds (123 m)	Tank top	27 yds (25 m)
Shirt	131 yds (120 m)	Pajama	208 yds (190 m)	T-shirt	27 yds (25 m)
Short, casual	77–93 yds (70–85 m)	Parka	262 yds (240 m)		
Short, tailored	151 yds (138 m)	Raincoat	295 yds (270 m)		
Suit, 2 piece	525 yds (480 m)	Short, casual	77–93 yds (70–85 m)		
Suit, 3 piece	580 yds (530 m)	Short, tailored	151 yds (138 m)		
Sweater	66 yds (60 m)	Skirt	198–399 yds (181–365 m)		
Sweatshirt	208 yds (190 m)	Suit	109 yds (100 m)		
Swimwear	55 yds (50 m)	Sweater	55 yds (50 m)		
Trouser and dress slack	295 yds (270 m)	Sweatshirt	208 yds (190 m)		
Tank top	38 yds (35 m)	Swimwear	82 yds (75 m)		
T-shirt, short sleeve	49 yds (45 m)	Trouser and dress slack	175 yds (160 m)		
T-shirt, long sleeve	131 yds (120 m)	Tank top	38 yds (35 m)		
Vest	60 yds (55 m)	T-shirt, short sleeve	44–49 yds (40–45 m)		
		T-shirt, long sleeve	131 yds (120 m)		
		Vest	60 yds (55 m)		

(American & Efird, 2012; Coats, 2015)

Thread consumption is the estimated amount of thread used during construction of sewn apparel products and includes waste as a factor. Some products utilize different types of thread and thread sizes depending on the sewing operation, seam construction and desired seam strength, stitch type, stitches per inch, edge finishing, cost, and stitch definition desired for different portions of the garment. The needle thread may also be different from the bobbin or under thread for the purpose of reducing overall thread cost for the garment. When different needle and bobbin threads are used, the needle thread is typically more expensive. Approximate thread consumption figures for common apparel products are shown in Table 8.3.

THREAD SPECIFICATIONS

Aesthetic and physical performance of sewn products depends largely on correct thread specifications. **Thread specifications** include detailed statements describing thread size and composition for each sewing operation of a garment, characteristics and performance requirements, and color standards for manufacturing. Thread specifications include

- Color standards
- Color identification information from vender's color cards or dye specifications for dye to match
- Fiber content
- Yarn type
- Yarn structure
- Twist
- Number of turns per inch
- Single or number of ply yarns
- Tex yarn number
- Thread size or ticket number
- Finish

- Thermal property requirements and tolerances
- Chemical resistance requirements and tolerances
  - Alkalis
  - Bleaching
  - Drycleaning
  - Insects or microorganisms
  - Laundering
  - Mineral acids
  - Moisture regain
  - Organic solvents
- Strength and elongation requirements and tolerances
- Abrasion requirements and tolerances
- Colorfastness requirements and tolerances
  - Bleach
  - Crocking (rubbing)
  - Drycleaning
  - Laundering (home and commercial)
  - Light (sunlight or artificial light source)
  - Perspiration

References

American & Efird Inc. (2009a). *Selection logic charts*. Retrieved November 1, 2015, from http://www.amefird.com/wp-content/uploads/2009/10/1ThreadSelection-Guide-for-Apparel-2-15-10.pdf

American & Efird Inc. (2009b). *Thread science*. Retrieved November 1 2015, from http://www.amefird.com/technical-tools/thread-education/thread-science/

American & Efird Inc. (2009c). *Thread selection guides*. [Brochure]. Mount Holly, NC: Author.

American & Efird Inc. (2012). *Estimating thread consumption*. Retrieved November 1, 2015, from http://www.amefird.com/wp-content/uploads/2012/09/Estimating-Thread-Consumption-.pdf

ASTM International. (2016). *2016 international standards* (Vol. 07.02). West Conshohocken, PA: Author.

Celanese Acetate LLC. (2001). *Complete textile glossary*. Charlotte, NC: Author.

Coats. (n.d.). *World of Coats astra product information*. [Brochure]. Charlotte, NC: Author.

Coats. (n.d.). *World of Coats dual duty product information*. [Brochure]. Charlotte, NC: Author.

Coats. (n.d.). *World of Coats epic product information*. [Brochure]. Charlotte, NC: Author.

Coats. (2015). *Apparel sewing: Product search*. Retrieved November 1, 2015, from http:// http://www.coatsindustrial.com/en/products-applications/apparel

Thiry, M.C. (2008, November). In stitches. *AATCC Review: International Magazine for Textile Professionals 8*, 24–26, 28–30.

CHAPTER 9

Support and Thermal Materials

Garment components are all materials and findings, including interior construction and finishing units, that influence the wear, appearance, and performance of a completed garment. **Support materials** are separate fabric plies applied as integral parts of the construction process. They support and reinforce garment sections and achieve a particular silhouette or other effect. They can also be separate components attached to the interior portion of garments to provide a clean finish. A designer selects support materials for compatibility with the garment type and end use, fabric weight, surface texture, fiber content, finish, and care method. Additionally, companion fabrics and support materials must be specified within tolerances for shrinkage and growth, appearance retention, resistance to abrasion, and colorfastness to a variety of sources.

INTERLININGS

An **interlining** is a separate ply of fabric between the facing or lining and the shell or outer fabric ply of a finished garment. An **underlining**, also known as a **backing**, is a ply of interlining fabric that provides both stability and thermal warmth to a garment. Underlining material is cut to duplicate a garment section and is applied to the back of the outer ply, where both outer and under plies are handled as one unit during garment production. When fusible interlinings are used, an entire roll or part of a roll of shell fabric is fused with the underlining (known as roll-to-roll fused), so when garment components are cut, they are ready to be sewn. An interlining is used to

- Maintain shape and prevent stretching and wrinkling of the area to which it is applied, such as necklines, lapped closures, yokes, waistbands, and pockets
- Provide support and crispness to collars, lapels, cuffs, pockets, tabs, and flaps
- Define shape and provide support to body sections of tailored suits, dresses, and coats

- Span the shoulder area of tailored jackets and coats
- Reinforce button and buttonhole areas
- Add body to hemlines and sleeve edges
- Add firmness to belts and waistbands
- Add warmth to the garment
- Provide stability for embroidering or structure for embossing

Various different types of interlinings are used for mass-produced apparel ranging in weight from 0.04 ounces per square yard (1.36 g/m²) to 4 ounces per square yard (135.62 g/m²). Interlinings are first categorized into fusible and sew-in materials and then by base *substrate*. **Fusible interlinings** are bonded to the back surface of shell fabrics through a precise combination of heat, time, and pressure. Bonding agents are resin coatings made from polyethylene or polyamide that are applied to woven, nonwoven, or knit substrates in the form of paste printing, dry-dot printing, or scatter or spray sintered coatings.

Paste Printing A cylindrical printing screen is used to apply the *resin paste* (mixture of adhesive powder, water, and other wetting agents) in the form of fine uniform dots onto the base fabric. After printing, heat is applied to evaporate the residual water to solidify the resin and bond it to the base cloth. Paste printed coatings create high-quality fusible interlinings used for top-collars of shirts and other garments made from lightweight and sheer fabrics.

Paste printing

Dry-Dot Printing A base fabric is passed between a heated roller and an engraved roller with small dots to hold the resin powder. As the fabric is passed through, the heat softens the resin, causing it to adhere to the base fabric. This type of fusible interlining works on a variety of fabric weights and garment applications. Typically, lightweight, smooth-surface fabrics need many small adhesive dots in order for the resin to properly penetrate the surface of the garment fabric to create satisfactory bond strength. On the other hand, heavyweight fabrics require larger but fewer dots. The number of dots per square centimeter can range from two to nine. Dry-dot printing creates a higher-quality fusible interlining than scatter or sinter coated substrates.

Dry-dot printing

Scatter (Spray Sintered) Coating A conveyer moves the base fabric while overhead sprayers apply resin to the fabric. The coated substrate is passed through an oven to soften the adhesive and press it into the base cloth. This type of resin coating works on a variety of fabric weights and garment applications. Scatter coatings are the most economical adhesives, but they do not offer the uniformity or quality of dot printed resins.

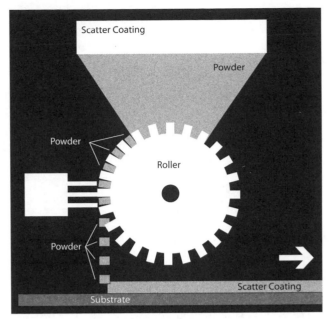

Scatter (spray sintered) coating

Each interlining manufacturer provides detailed specification sheets for each product with the formula for proper adhesion and performance for the useful life of the garment. According to Gerry Cooklin, author of *Fusing Technology*, "Each resin type has its own specific characteristics, and these have to be considered in relation to: (a) the style of the garment being produced, (b) the topcloth and the handle required, (c) the fusing equipment available in the factory, (d) the base cloth of the fusible, (e) the over-all cost, [and] (f) the durability to washing or drycleaning or both." **Sew-in interlinings** must be stitched to shell fabrics during production. Both fusible and sew-in interlinings can be woven, knitted, or nonwoven in their construction. Nonwoven fusible are the most commonly used interlinings, because they are quicker to apply than sew-in varieties and are more economical. Interlining fabrics are available starting with 50-yard or 50-meter rolled put-ups ranging in width from 20 inches (50.8 cm), 36 inches (91.4 cm), 45 inches (1.14 m), 60 inches (1.52 m), 66 inches (1.68 m), and custom widths, or can be precut to desired specifications.

Sew-in woven interlining

Knit Interlining Warp knit fabric made from fibers such as nylon, rayon, polyester, or a combination of fibers blended together to provide stability to designated portions of a garment. A variety of weights are available for compatibility with the shell fabric of a garment and work in both knit and woven garment applications. Common put-up for knit interlinings is 50- or 100-yard or 100-meter rolls. Roll size depends on the type of interlining selected. Typical applications include

- Waistbands to maintain shape and prevent stretching
- Tailored garments to maintain shape and prevent stretching of jacket fronts, shoulders, collars, lapels, cuffs, pockets, tabs, and flaps
- Button and buttonhole areas for reinforcement
- Hemlines and sleeve edges to add body

INTERLININGS _(continued)

Tricot Interlining Warp knit interlining of a close knit construction available in fusible and sew-in varieties. Tricot interlinings can be used in both knit and woven garment applications to provide drape and flexibility in garment applications and to provide elasticity.

Fusible interlining

Sew-in interlining

Weft Insertion Interlining Knit interlining with a crosswise yarn inserted in to the loops of the courses as they are knitted to provide strength and stability in the crosswise direction. *Moiré effect* is a common problem caused by applying weft insertion interlinings to twill weave fabrics. It occurs when the face of the garment fabric appears striped or water spotted due to the alignment of the adhesive pattern and the inserted yarns of the interlining. Typical applications include

- Waistbands to maintain shape and prevent stretching
- Tailored garments to maintain shape and prevent stretching of jacket fronts, shoulders, collars, lapels, cuffs, pockets, tabs, and flaps

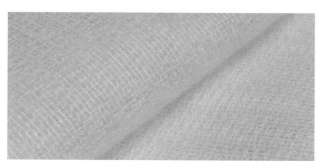

Weft insertion interlining

Woven Interlining Plain-weave-constructed sew-in or fusible material made from a variety of fibers such as cotton, rayon, polyester, mohair, wool, or a combination of fibers blended together to provide strength and stability to designated portions of a garment. A variety of weights are available for compatibility with the garment shell fabric. Woven interlinings must be cut *on-grain* or on the *bias* to avoid distortion of the woven garment and are available in fusible and sew-in varieties. Common put-up for woven interlinings is 50- or 100-yard or 100-meter rolls. Typical applications include

- Waistbands and belts to add firmness, maintain shape, and prevent stretching
- Tailored garments to provide shape and support to jacket fronts, shoulders, collars, lapels, cuffs, pockets, tabs, and flaps
- Button and buttonhole areas for reinforcement
- Hemlines and sleeve edges to add body

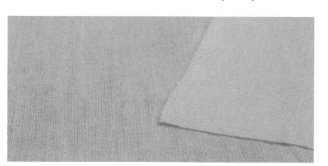

Woven interlining

Woven interlining

Ban-Roll Interlining Interlining made of woven stiff material that will not roll, crush, or curl when sewn into a waistband. Some varieties stretch. Ban-roll is premade and available in 1-inch (2.54 cm), 1¼-inch (3.18 cm), 1½-inch (3.8 cm), and 2-inch (5 cm) widths. Ban-roll is used on waistbands of skirts, shorts, pants, and trousers to provide structure and stability.

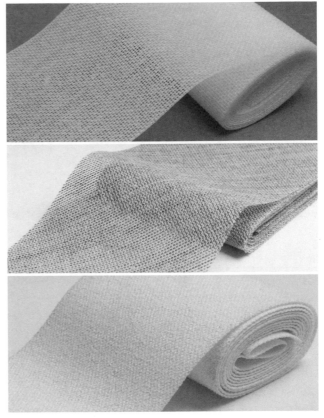

Ban-roll interlinings

Waistband Curtain Interlining made from a combination of woven materials that have been sewn together to form a premade waistband insert that, when cut to the appropriate length and sewn into the interior portion of the waistband of tailored trousers, pants, and skirts, provides structure and stability and conceals raw edges. Waistband curtain is manufactured as preassembled stock or can be customized in size, structure, and detailing such as the insertion of piping, a printed fabric, a woven tape with the brand name or logo, special stitching, and so on. Some waistband curtain is constructed with exposed elastic yarns or a rubberized textured surface in order to prevent men's shirttails from coming untucked during normal wear. Typical applications include waistbands of tailored skirts, shorts, pants, and trousers to provide structure, stability, and a clean finish.

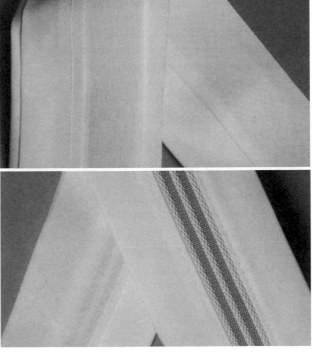

Waistband curtain

INTERLININGS (continued)

Wigan Woven or nonwoven fusible interlining made from cotton, rayon, polyester, or a combination of fibers. Wigan is available in a variety of widths ranging from 2-inch (5 cm), 2½-inch (6.35 cm), 3-inch (7.62 cm), or 4-inch (10.16 cm) precut 100-yard or 100-meter rolls and can be cut on straight grain or bias. Wigan is applied to provide structure and stability at sleeve and cuff hems.

Wigan interlining—Nonwoven fusible

Wigan interlining—Woven sew-in

Nonwoven Interlining Nonwoven constructed sew-in or fusible material made from a variety of fibers such as rayon, polyester, nylon, and acrylic, or a combination of fibers blended together. However, other fibers such as olefin, vinyon, cotton, and acetate can also be used to make nonwoven interlinings. A variety of weights and hand are available for compatibility with the shell fabric of a garment. Nonwoven interlinings work in both knit and woven garments. Unidirectional and multidirectional nonwoven interlinings are available when strength is needed in a particular direction of a garment or when material is a key cost factor. Fusible interlinings are more cost-effective than sew-in interlinings in mass production because they are less expensive to apply to fabrics. Common put-up for nonwoven interlinings is 50- or 100-yard or 100-meter rolls. Nonwoven interlinings can also be die cut for collars, plackets, waistbands, jacket fronts, and so on for ease during manufacturing. Typical applications include

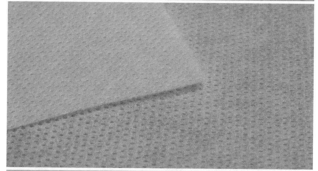

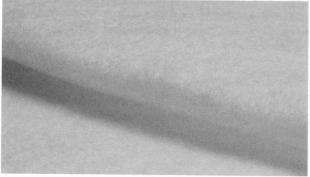

- Waistbands and belts to add firmness, maintain shape, and prevent stretching
- Tailored garments to provide shape and support to jacket fronts, shoulders, collars, lapels, cuffs, pockets, tabs, and flaps
- Button and buttonhole areas for reinforcement
- Hemlines and sleeve edges to add body
- Garments requiring thermal qualities

Nonwoven interlining

Stitch Reinforced Nonwoven Interlining (Stitched through Nonwoven Interlining) Nonwoven interlining containing rows of stitching to provide stabilization and added strength to tailored items. This product is a cost-effective alternative to sew-in woven interlinings. Typical applications include

- Waistbands and belts to add firmness, maintain shape, and prevent stretching
- Tailored garments to provide directional strength, shape, and support to jacket fronts, shoulders, collars, lapels, cuffs, pockets, tabs, and flaps
- Button and buttonhole areas for reinforcement
- Hemlines and sleeve edges to add body

Stitch reinforced nonwoven interlining

Stitch reinforced nonwoven interlining

Nonwoven Fusible Seam Tapes and Stays Strips of nonwoven fusible material of a predetermined length and width measured to accommodate seam lengths or garment areas that need stabilization. Nonwoven tapes and stays may or may not contain reinforcing stitches for added stabilization and strength. Typical applications include

- Seam reinforcement to prevent fabric tearing or breakage or seam construction at areas of strain
- Curved crotch and sleeve
- Armhole areas of lined sleeveless garments
- Unlined garments to cover seams where fabric may cause skin irritation
- Bias seams or edges to prevent stretching
- Corners of *slashes*, *plackets*, *gussets*, and *godets* for reinforcement

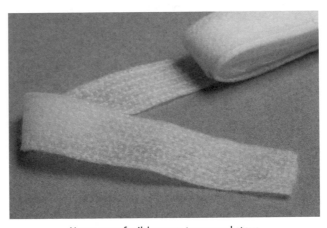

Nonwoven fusible seam tapes and stays

Cut-Away Nonwoven Interlining Nonwoven interlining that provides stabilization and support during embroidering that can be trimmed back with shears.

Cut-away nonwoven interlining

Backside of embroidering stabilized by
cut-away nonwoven interlining

Tear-Away Nonwoven Interlining Nonwoven interlining applied to the back of a garment to provide stabilization and support during embroidering that can be torn off afterward.

Tear-away nonwoven interlining

Backside of embroidering stabilized by
tear-away nonwoven interlining

Water-Soluble Stabilizer Clear, nonwoven fusible film applied to a garment area to stabilize fabric during application of embroidery, appliqué, and open-pattern decorative stitching. This stabilizer can be removed with water.

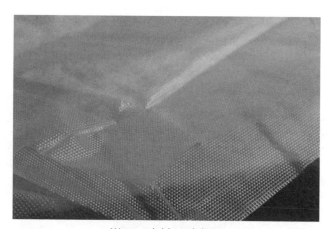

Water-soluble stabilizer

LININGS

A **lining** is a unit assembled in the same manner or similar silhouette as the garment unit. The type and quality of lining fabric selected is based on the type of shell fabric and weight, style of the garment, and price point. Lining materials can be manufactured from acetate, cotton, nylon, polyester, rayon, silk, and wool fibers. Linings can be designed and constructed to be free hanging or fully attached at the hem edge of the garment. Proper selection of lining material is important, and the lining should be compatible with the shell fabric, garment type, and end use.

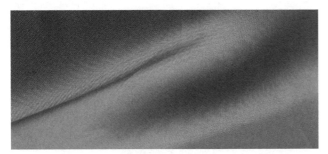

Bemberg rayon lining

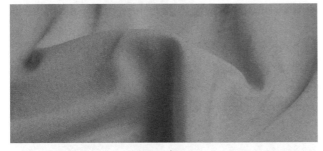

Polyester satin lining

Acetate lining

Cotton jersey knit

Apparel linings can be constructed from woven or knitted materials. **Woven linings** are the most commonly used materials for apparel items due to their stability and smooth surface. The majority of tailored and lined apparel items are made from woven fabrics. When shell fabrics contain spandex, it is important for a lining material to have the capability of stretching to the same extent as the outer fabric. When the shell fabric stretches more than the lining, the wearer's movement is restricted. **Knit linings** can provide stretch in the width direction or in both the width and lengthwise directions depending on the needs of the garment. These linings are sewn into knit garments and are used where stretch is an important factor for comfort and shape retention.

Linings can be sewn permanently into a garment or made to detach. The weight of the lining and method for refurbishment must be compatible with all garment components. Lining fabrics should be lighter in weight than the garment material to avoid distortion of the overall appearance and structure of the apparel item. The pattern for the lining is drafted separately. The garment lining is assembled separately and then attached to the rest of the garment during production. Linings

- Conceal raw edges and construction details inside the garment
- Facilitate the ease of donning and doffing
- Prevent the outer fabric from coming in direct contact with the body and causing skin irritation
- Provide warmth
- Prolong garment life

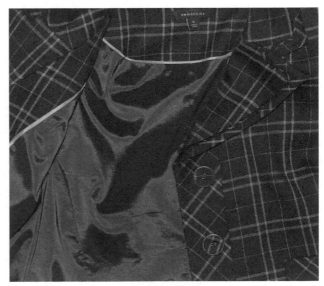

Fully lined jacket

Free-hanging lining

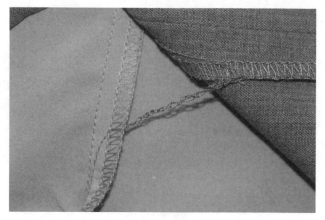

Swing tack

Free-Hanging Lining Unit assembled in the same manner or similar silhouette as the garment unit that is not sewn to the hem but rather attached to seam allowances by swing tacks. Free-hanging linings are attached to the shell fabric at the hem of dresses, skirts, trousers, jackets, coats, and furs.

Swing Tack Thread chain, typically 1½ inches (3.8 cm) in length, that attaches a free-hanging lining to seam allowances of a garment. Swing tacks are used to

- Prevent free-hanging linings from riding up
- Allow the lining to move while restricting it from hanging below the hem and showing on the outside of the garment

Partial Lining Unit assembled in a similar silhouette as a portion of the garment unit. Partial linings are used to

- Maintain shape of the garment area such as the seat of skirts, pants, or trousers or knees of pants and trousers
- Conceal construction details in the shoulder area of tailored jackets and coats

Partial lining

Detachable Lining Unit assembled in a similar silhouette as part of the garment unit that allows for the item to be worn year-round by simply removing the inner lining portion held in place by buttons, snaps, or a zipper. Detachable linings are used

- In trench coats, raincoats, and outerwear
- For all-weather garments

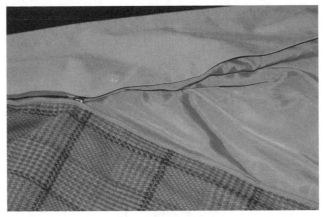

Detachable lining

References

Brown, P. & Rice, J. (2014). *Ready to wear apparel analysis.* (4th ed.). Upper Saddle River, NJ: Pearson.

Bubonia-Clarke, J. (1998). Bond strength, dimensional stability, and appearance of fused fabrics after professional cleaning [Doctoral dissertation, Texas Woman's University, 1998]. *Dissertation Abstracts International, 59,* no. 05B, 148.

Cooklin, G. (1990). *Fusing technology.* Manchester, United Kingdom: Trafford Press.

The Freudenberg Group. (n.d.; a). *Freudenberg nonwovens: Engineered for performance bonding technology* [Brochure]. Chelmsford, MA: Author.

The Freudenberg Group. (n.d.; b). *Fronts and facings* [Brochure]. Chelmsford, MA: Author.

The Freudenberg Group. (n.d.; c). *Tapes and stays* [Brochure]. Chelmsford, MA: Author.

The Freudenberg Group. (1992). *Fusing glossary* [Brochure]. Chelmsford, MA: Author.

Precision Custom Coatings Inc. (n.d.). *The fusible interlining handbook.* Totowa, NJ: Author.

WAWAK. (n.d). *Waistband curtain.* Retrieved November 1, 2015, from http:// store.atlantathread.com/wael.html

CHAPTER 10

Support and Shaping Devices

Support devices provide shape, structure, underpinning, and aid in the construction of garments. Support devices used for apparel construction and enhancement are selected with consideration for the overall aesthetic look and fit of a garment, type and style of the garment, and intended end use. Designers need to consider the type of support structure best suited for the garment application production, assembly methods, and garment refurbishment.

SHOULDER-SHAPING DEVICES

A **shoulder pad** is a shaping device in a triangular or rectangular arc configuration of padding that tapers to a diminishing thickness while maintaining maximum bulk along one edge. Cotton, polyester, and other synthetic fibers form the inner layer of the pad, which can be molded, needle punched, or stitched with outer layers of nonwoven or felt material to create shoulder pads. Exposed shoulder pads are covered with a lining material such as tricot or taffeta, whereas those that are completely contained within the garment and cannot be seen from the inside are typically left uncovered or raw. Shoulder pads can be stitched into the garment or have Velcro for attachment and removal. They are available in a variety of sizes, shapes, thicknesses, and weights depending on the desired shape and are sold in minimum quantities of 100 pairs. Shoulder pad varieties include

- Styles for raglan sleeves, set-in sleeves, and dropped sleeves
- Sleeve heads and sleeve puffs
- Uncovered (raw) or covered
- Sew-in or detachable
- Those manufactured to withstand repeated launderings or drycleanings

Shoulder pads are used to

- Emphasize or exaggerate the shoulder line of a silhouette
- Support shoulders of a garment for correct shaping
- Maintain and support the shoulder area of tailored coats and jackets

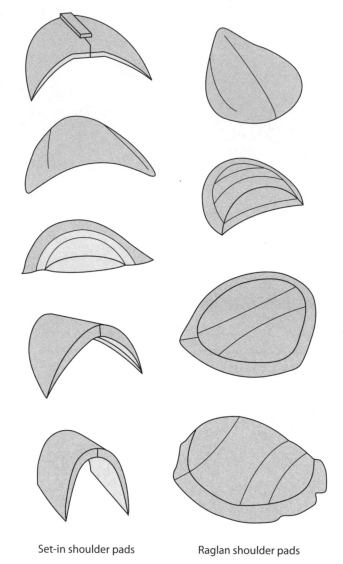

Set-in shoulder pads   Raglan shoulder pads

Sleeve Head Shoulder pad support made from a narrow strip of felted or nonwoven batting material that supports and shapes the top portion of the sleeve armhole at the shoulder.

Sleeve Puff Shoulder pad support made from a thin nonwoven material equal to or slightly firmer in handle than the shell fabric to support and shape a gathered or puffed sleeve design.

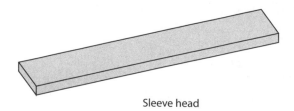

Sleeve head

Sleeve puff

TORSO SUPPORT AND SHAPING DEVICES

Garments manufactured with built-in shaping and support devices for the bust and torso are popular in today's marketplace.

Bra cups are molded from foam, latex, or synthetic batting or stitched into rounded conical shapes. They are available covered or uncovered and can be produced as separate cups or constructed as one unit. Bra cups are sized the same as brassieres and sold with order minimums starting at 100 pairs.

Bra cups are available in the following styles:

- Full cup
- Push-up full cup
- Demi cup or half pad
- Push-up demi cup or half pad push-up
- Rounded seamless
- Contour

- Filler pad
- Tear drop
- Seamless push-up
- Underwire bra
- Athletic wear and swimwear cups

Bra cups are used to

- Shape swimsuit tops and brassieres
- Support shape of strapless garments
- Support garments where separate bras would detract from the garment appearance

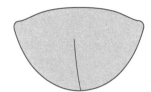
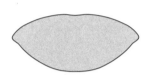
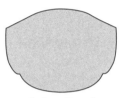

| Round seamless | Contour | Half pad | Swimsuit pad |

Lingerie Underwire Stainless steel wire or plastic boning shaped like a U and inserted into some brassieres and garments with built-in bras to provide firm support and shape to the bustline. Underwires are sold in pairs by the gross and by bra cup sizes.

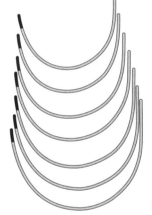

Lingerie underwire

Lingerie Separating Wire Stainless steel wire or plastic boning shaped like a U or V where the ends flare in, flare out, or are formed straight and inserted into the center front of some brassieres, swimwear, and eveningwear to provide firm support and separation of the bustline and shaping to the neckline of strapless garments. Separating wires are sold by the gross and sized by width and length.

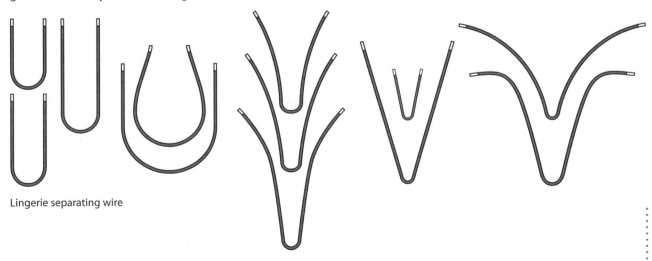

Lingerie separating wire

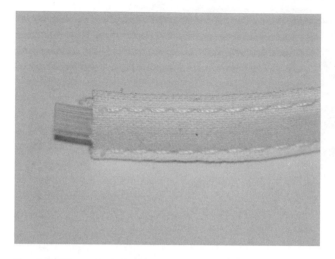

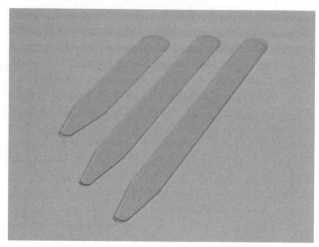

Boning (Stay Strip) Firm yet flexible nylon strip, ⅛ inch to 3.4 inches (3.2 to 19 mm) wide, concealed in a casing, or a flat, lightweight, flexible strip of stainless steel or plastic used to support the bust or torso. Boning can be applied to *princess line seams*, *darts*, center front or center back seams, collars, or other garment seams. Metal or plastic strips used for boning are available in premeasured lengths by the gross or put up on rolls of 150 yards (137 m). Boning is used to

- Support strapless bodices, *built-up waistlines* (*raised* or high-waist), or high-standing collars
- Prevent crushing of a cummerbund or rolling and crushing of wide-shaped belts
- Stiffen and maintain shape of corsets or bodices
- Maintain exaggerated silhouettes of dome skirts
- Produce hoop skirt silhouette in petticoats, evening and bridal gowns

Collar Stay Flat, narrow plastic or metal supporting strip rounded to a soft point at one end and slid into a stitched pocket or casing on the underside of a shirt collar. Collar stays can be printed with a brand name or logo and are sold by the gross. Collar stays are used to

- Maintain shape of collar points on tailored shirts
- Prevent end points of a collar from twisting, turning, or curling
- Support and maintain shape of stand-up collars
- Support pointed shirt cuffs

FABRIC TAPES AND STAYS

Seam tapes and stays are strips of material of predetermined lengths and widths measured to accommodate garment areas that need stabilization. Tapes and stays are available in fusible and sew-in varieties and are used to

- Reinforce seam construction of areas subjected to strain in order to prevent fabric tearing or breakage
- Reinforce curved crotch seams of pants, trousers, and shorts
- Stabilize curved seams of sleeves (i.e., dolman, batwing, and raglan styles)
- Cover seams to ensure comfort and wearability in unlined garments where fabric may cause skin irritation
- Prevent bias seams or edges from stretching

- Stabilize fold lines where facings and garments are cut in one
- Reinforce corners of slashes, *plackets*, *gussets*, and *godets*
- Prevent stretching and distortion of waistlines
- Stabilize waistlines of skirts to facilitate subsequent construction operations

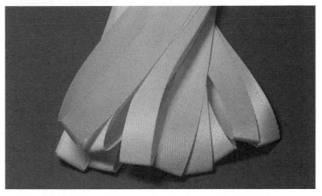

Bias Tape Bias-cut, *plain weave* strip of material, available in various widths with two prefolded ¼-inch (6.4 cm) edges, one of which is applied to the hem edge prior to hemming the garment. Bias tape is manufactured in cotton, rayon, silk, or synthetic fibers with prefolded edges in finished widths from ⅜ inch to 3 inches (9.5 to 38.1 mm) and available in single-fold or double-fold varieties and sold in 100-yard or 100-meter roll put-ups. Bias tape is used on

- Seams and hems to conceal raw edges of fabrics that unravel easily
- Hems that require stretch and flexibility
- Garments made of heavy fabrics where a self hem fold would create too much bulk

Twill Tape Firmly woven twill weave ribbon, ¼ to 1 inch (6.3 to 35.4 mm) in width, made from natural or synthetic fibers and sold in 100-yard or 100-meter roll put-ups. Twill tape is used as

- Reinforcing strip for stayed seams or taped seams
- Stabilization at fold lines of one-piece extended facings, extended pockets, slashed seams, or straight-edge closures

Lace Seam Binding Stretch or nonstretch lace ribbon produced in a variety patterns, available in 2-inch (5-cm) widths to be applied as hem facing. Lace seam binding is produced with natural or synthetic fibers to be compatible with the garment fabric and sold in 100-yard or 100-meter roll put-ups. Lace seam binding is used on

- Hems in place of seam tape or bias binding
- Facing edges
- Garment edge or as decorative detail insert

Ribbon Seam Binding Narrow, lightweight ribbon of natural or synthetic yarns, approximately ½ inch (1.3 cm) in width. Seam binding is produced in a variety of synthetic fibers for compatibility with the garment fabric. It is available in a bias cut to sew with ease around curved edges and is sold in 100-yard or 100-meter roll put-ups. Ribbon seam binding is used as

- Finish for hem edges, straight edge facings, and seams
- Reinforcing strip for taped seams
- Stay at seams and waistlines
- Stay for gathering and shirring
- Stay at fold lines of extended seams and facings

ELASTIC

Elastic is thread, cord, braided or woven ribbon, or fabric that has resilience and flexibility. Elastic is a product processed from spandex, latex, or rubber fiber that is cut, extruded, or rolled into cores, wrapped, and braided or woven; it also may be produced in flat, thin uncovered bands or strips. The stretchable core substance can be left raw or covered with cotton, nylon, polyester, polypropylene, or fiber-blended yarns. The amount of pliancy in elastic is determined by the fiber content, size, core, method of weaving or braiding, or intended use. Webbing or woven elastic retains its original width when stretched, whereas braided elastic becomes narrower as it is stretched. Both types of elastic may be applied to garments in a variety of methods. Elastic may be applied directly to a garment by *lock*, *zigzag*, or *overedge stitch* formations or may be enclosed in a casing. Elasticized shirring is made with multiple rows of elastic. Special-purpose elastics are required for pajamas, lingerie, loungewear, swimwear, and undergarments. The type of elastic selected depends on

- Garment construction
- Elastic width
- Fiber content of the garment
- Elastic gripping power
- Fabric weight and compatibility
- Garment type and style
- Garment use
- Garment care
- Figure or body type and size range

Decorative Elastic Band Woven or braided strip 1 to 3 inches (2.5 to 7.6 cm) in finished width, cut to a predetermined length and applied to draw in a garment edge. Available in solid colors, prints, and geometric designs and put up on 100-yard or 100-meter rolls. The degree of elasticity will vary by fiber, weave, braid, and manufacturing method. Decorative elastic band is used as

- Design detail, or fitting elements at the waistline, edge of sleeves, neckline, bottom of shorts or pant legs, or skirt hem
- Waistband insert
- Means for fitting garments spanning more than one size range

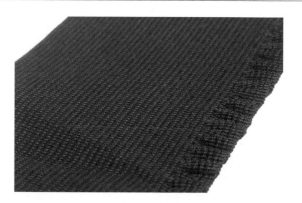

Elastic Braid Premeasured length of elastic, ribbon, or rib-type braid applied to draw up predetermined fullness to fit body measurements. Elastic varies from ¼ inch to 3 inches (.06 to 7.65 cm) in width and put up on 100-yard or 100-meter rolls. Type and size of elastic are selected based on the garment style and fabric. The degree of elasticity, type of yarn, and hand produced in braid construction determine the intended application. Elastic is available in soft or hard stretch. Elastic braid is used as

- Inside ply of waistbands, in self or applied casings or directly applied to garments
- Means for fitting garments without darts or plackets, or those spanning more than one size range
- Decorative design details at the edge of garments or spanning garment sections

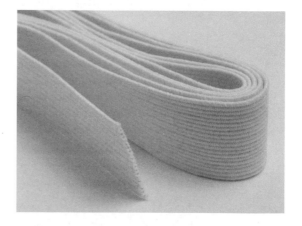

Nonroll Ribbed Elastic Rib patterned, noncurling core of rubber or spandex sheathed in natural or synthetic yarn, woven or braided ¾ inch to 2 inches (1.9 to 5.1 cm) in width and put up on 100-yard or 100-meter rolls. Elastic ribbon is used in

- Concealed waistbands or applied directly to garments
- *Self* or *applied casings*

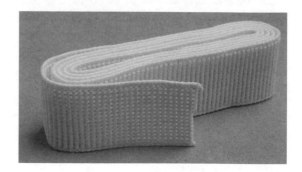

Elastic Cord Round or oval gimp-covered core of elastic sewn directly to the garment or enclosed in the bite of patterned machine stitches. Elastic cord is available in a variety of diameters and expandability and put up on 100-yard or 100-meter rolls. Elastic cord is used on

- Garment edges of sleeves, pant legs, or waistline
- Garments to produce a ruffle or flounce effect
- On garments in individual stands where delicate lines of gathering or multiple strands produce elasticized shirring
- Waistlines of one-piece garments
- Necklines, hem openings, and waistbands of infants' and children's wear
- Bodices for *smocking*

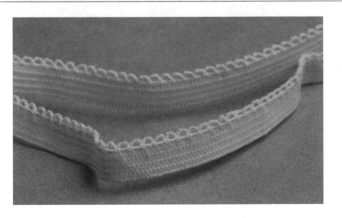

Decorative Elastic (Fancy Elastic) Thread-covered elastic core woven, knitted, or braided into a soft strip or band in a variety of widths and patterns. Decorative elastic may be woven with a picot finish along one or both edge lengths and can also be made in stretchable lace patterns. This type of elastic is softer than others and results in a less restrictive garment. Decorative elastic is used as

- Means of fitting waistlines and leg openings of infants' and children's wear and intimate apparel
- Edging on bras, bodysuits, and shape wear

Elastic Edging Yarn- or thread-covered elastic core woven, knitted, or braided into a ribbon with a scalloped, picot, or other decorative edge along one or both lengths. This decorative elastic can be applied on the outside or inside of a garment to extend beyond a garment edge. Elastic edging is made in widths up to ⅟₁₆ inch (1.6 cm) and put up on 100-yard or 100-meter rolls. Elastic edging is used where

- Other elastic may interfere with garment comfort
- Casings are inapplicable
- Decorative edges at the waist, neck, sleeve, or leg opening are desired

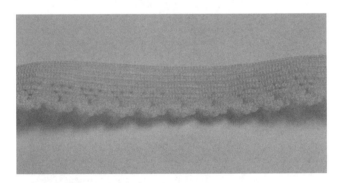

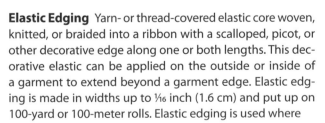

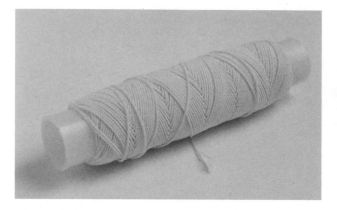

Elastic Thread Stretchable thread made of rubber or spandex wound and covered with cotton, synthetic, blended, or metallic yarn. The thread is firm and pliable with maximum stretch and recovery. It is put up on cones and designated by weight in grams rather than yards. Elastic thread is used in single or multiple rows to

- Produce elasticized shirring; waffle shirring, or an elasticized waistline; or shirred ribbon decorative waistband. The amount of control for elasticized shirring or gathering is determined by the length of the stitch, type and expandability of the elastic, and the number and spacing of parallel rows of stitching and their interrelationship with the fabric.
- Fit garments designed to accommodate more than one size range

Clear Elastic (Invisible Elastic) Transparent tape providing support and stability at seams or as a strap without detracting from the garment design. This type of elastic has low stretch. Clear elastic is made in finished widths of ¼ to ⅜ inch (6.4 to 9.5 mm) and put up on 100-yard or 100-meter rolls. Clear elastic is used as

- Tape in shoulders or neckline of garments made of lightweight knit fabric
- Hanger tapes to secure garments on hangers
- Invisible straps on a garment when fabric straps would detract from the garment design

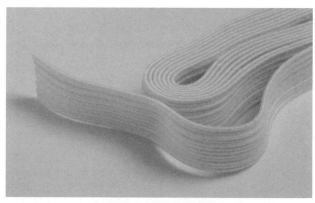

Elastic Webbing Soft, woven elastic band, ¾ inch to 1¼ inches (19 to 32 mm) in finished width, cut to a predetermined length and put up on 100-yard or 100-meter rolls. The woven construction allows the webbing to maintain its original width when stretched. Elastic webbing is used on

- Inside waistlines of boxer shorts, athletic shorts, and pajamas
- Garments spanning more than one size

Elastic for Swimwear Spandex core covered with nylon or polyester braided or woven into a band or ribbon with or without a decorative edge. Elastic is manufactured in widths and sizes for the leg, waist, bra, and neckline openings of garments. The width of elastic is chosen by location and application to the garment. Swimwear elastic is used as an edging at the top, waist, or leg openings of swimwear to retain resilience when wet.

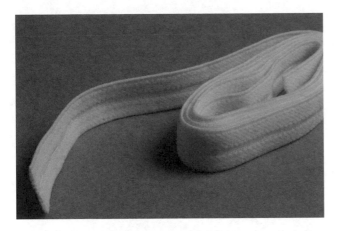

Buttonhole Elastic Tape Elastic tape with buttonholes positioned parallel with the finished edges of the tape at regular intervals. Whichever buttonhole offers the best fit is looped around a button that is sewn into the waistband. Buttonhole elastic tape is available in a variety of widths ranging from ½ to 1 inch (13 to 25 mm) wide and put up on 100-yard or 100-meter rolls. Buttonhole elastic tape is used to provide a means for adjusting stable waistband casings in children's or maternity garments.

Drawstring Elastic Elastic waistband webbing constructed with a drawstring inserted in the middle of the band and put up on 100-yard or 100-meter rolls. Drawstring elastic is used to allow some fit to the waistline prior to engaging the drawstring.

Non-Slip-Backed Elastic Elastic waistband webbing constructed with rows of rubber yarn on one surface or embossed or printed silicone adhered, woven, or knitted in to produce a nonslip surface on the waistband. Non-slip-backed elastic is used on trousers and skirt waistbands to hold tuck-in blouses and shirts in place.

References

CTS USA. (2015a). *Products: Elastic*. Retrieved November 2, 2015, from http://www.ctsusa.com/_e/dept/02/Elastics.htm

CTS USA. (2015b). *Products: Tapes*. Retrieved November 2, 2015, from http://www.ctsusa.com/_e/dept/04/Hanger_Tapes_Twill_Tape.htm

Richard the Thread. (2013). *Product catalog*. Retrieved November 2, 2015, from http://www.richardthethread.com/index.php?src=gendo cs&link=catalog&category=Main

Steinlauf and Stoller Inc. (2002). *Products*. Retrieved November 2, 2015, from http://www.steinlaufandstoller.com/products.htm

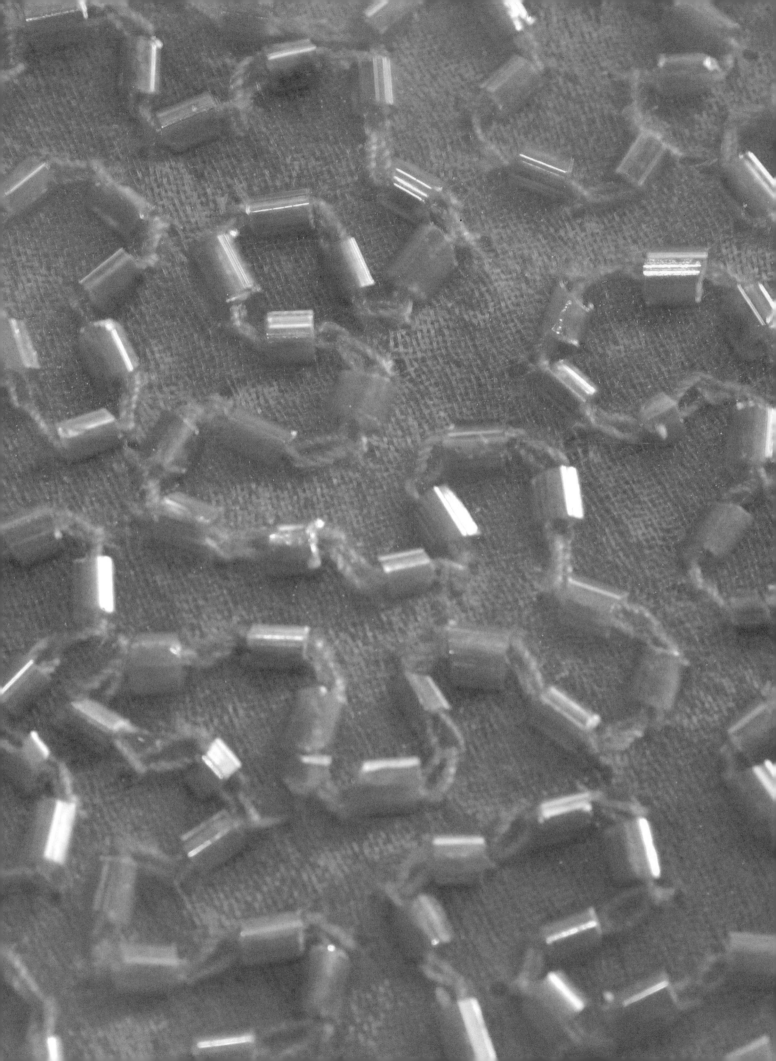

CHAPTER 11

Trim and Surface Embellishments

Designers and product developers use trim and other types of embellishments to add detail and interest to the surface of apparel products. Fashion trends often influence their use and application in garments.

TRIMS

Decorative linear materials that embellish garments are known as **trim**. Attached to the surface or inserted into a seam of an apparel item, they enhance the design and overall garment aesthetic. Trim can enhance the quality of a garment and is used to

- Add decorative effects on seams of collars, cuffs, plackets, pockets, princess lines, waistbands, and yokes
- Produce dimensional effects
- Emphasize a garment part or section
- Create a decorative pattern on the garment surface

Various forms of trim are used in apparel construction. The type, width, shape, and placement selected depends on

- Garment style and design
- Garment type
- Garment use
- Garment care
- Method of construction
- Compatibility with garment fabric
- Compatibility of shape, color, and size with the garment
- Cost

Braid Trim made from gimp yarns that interlace to create a decorative pattern. Braid is available in a variety of colors, patterns, and widths. Braid can be used to create a military inspired look.

Cording Soft cotton, cellulose, or synthetic yarn rope ⅛ to 1 inch (3.2 to 25.4 mm) in diameter, either twisted to form a cable or cylindrically shaped, that is sewn into a seam or attached to the face of the garment. Cording is available in a variety of fabrics, weaves, and filler sizes. Cording can be used to add body and stiffness for a standout effect at a hem edge and to outline and emphasize bands applied to a garment part or section.

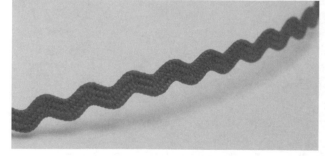

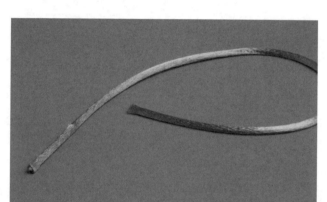

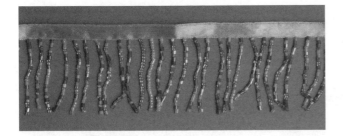

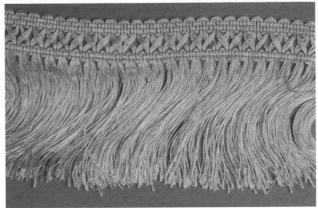

Fringe Tape or braid with threads or cords that hang free. The tape or braid is stitched onto the surface of the garment or inserted between seam plies. The free-hanging threads of fringe can be formed into tassels. Fringe is available in a variety of styles, colors, and widths. Fringe is used to

- Elongate a hemline
- Decorate horizontal seams
- Emphasize movement when a garment is worn

Lace Twisted and knotted yarns forming an openwork pattern fabric structure produced in a wide range of widths, weights, textures, and motifs. Floral motifs are the most common designs. Lace trim is available with or without decorative edge finishes such as scallops (a series of arcs that protrude out from the edges of the trim) and *picots* (tiny teardrop-shaped loops). The intricacy and density of the design, fiber content, yarn size and type, and the number of yarns per square inch or meter determine the quality. Lace helps create a pretty, feminine effect.

Passementerie Braid, cord, fringe, and tassel trims.

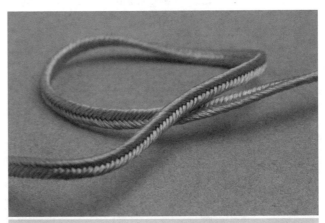

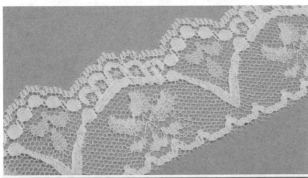

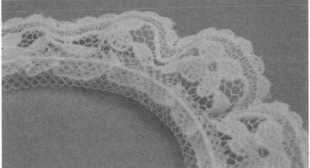

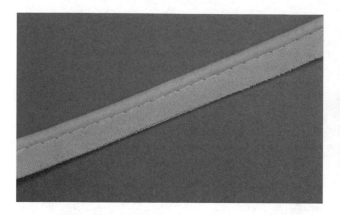 

Piping (Cordedge) Bias strip stitched with or without cord filler produced with a *seam allowance* that is inserted between plies of the seam, to show on the face of the garment. Piping is available in a variety of fabrics, weaves, and filler sizes. Piping is used to add body and stiffness for a standout effect at a hem edge or to outline and emphasize bands applied to a garment part or section.

Ribbon Narrow, firmly woven fabric produced with a plain, satin, or *picot* edge. Ribbon is available in a variety of woven constructions, widths, colors, and prints. Types of ribbon include

- Grosgrain
- Lace
- Jacquard
- Organdy or chiffon
- Satin (single or double faced)
- Velvet (single or double faced)

Ribbon can be used to

- Tape necklines or collars on the inside of knitted shirts to add decoration and stabilization
- Finish a hem or vent
- Add body and stiffness for a standout effect at a hem edge
- Create flowers, bows, and ties

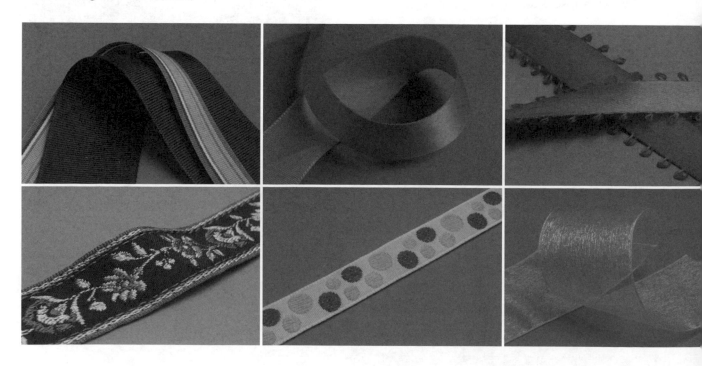

Surface embellishments are elements added to the face of a garment to change its aesthetic appearance. The use of surface embellishments to alter a garment's aesthetic appearance is limited only by the designer's imagination and knowledge of how to use them. Beads, embroidery, or screen printing will each create a different effect on a garment of the same shape.

Various forms of surface embellishments are used in apparel production for

- Embellishing a garment
- Design details
- Dimensional effects
- Decorative effects for collars, cuffs, pockets, and hems
- Emphasizing garment parts
- Creating a decorative focal point

The type, shape, and placement of surface embellishments selected depend on

- Garment style and design
- Garment type
- Garment use
- Garment care
- Method of attachment
- Compatibility of shape, color, and size with the garment
- Cost

Beads Very small ball, tube, or other shape with a hole in it. Beads can be strung and then affixed to the garment, sewn individually, or attached to a backing material and sewn as an appliqué. Beads are made from acrylic, glass, nut, shell, stone, or wood.

Appliqué Base fabric fused or stitched with thread, fabric, beading, sequins, or rhinestones.

Embossing Raised surface texture created with a special nonwoven or knit fusible backing, synthetic rubber mold design, and heat press. When heat and pressure are applied to the garment, the fusible interlining conforms to the mold.

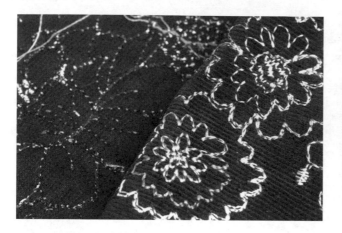

Embroidery Design created by stitching a pattern on the surface of a garment with thread (see Color plates 8 and 9). Embroidery is used to

- Add decorative patterns to hemlines or garment sections
- Add a logo, text, or object to a garment
- Personalize or customize a garment

Foiling Metallic surface design created by applying synthetic film with a heat press. When heat and pressure are applied to the film, it permanently bonds to the garment.

Rhinestones Faceted glass or plastic imitation gemstones produced in a variety of colors and sizes. Rhinestones on a garment produce a shimmering or sparkling effect.

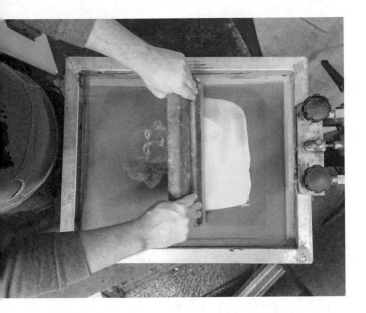

Screen Printing *Pigment* is applied to prepared screens, and pressure is used to transfer the graphic to the fabric. One screen is required for each color in the design. An economic alternative to screen printing is *heat transfer* (also known as *iron on*). Heat transfer designs are of lesser quality and are not as durable to wearing and washing.

Sequins Small thin discs or squares made from plastic, having a matte or shiny finish, with a center hole. Sequins can be attached as a string, sewn individually, or attached to a backing material and sewn as an appliqué. They are available in a variety of sizes and colors. Sequins are used to produce a shimmering effect.

Trapunto Embroidered pattern stitched on the surface of a garment area that is padded or corded to create a three-dimensional appearance.

Closures

Closures, or **fasteners**, are used to secure

garment sections together. They are designed

for a variety of specific functions. Fasteners

are used for decorative as well as functional

purposes. They may be used at the discretion

of the designer as a focal point of a garment to

add originality and to enhance its appearance.

Functional closures may be designed with concealed or surface-type fasteners. The type of fastener selected depends on

- Garment style and design
- Garment type
- Type of garment closure
- Garment use
- Garment care
- Fastener placement and position
- Method of application
- Fabric weight, type, and texture

BUTTONS

A **button** is a disk, knot, or other three-dimensional form that can be slipped through a buttonhole, loop, or narrow opening for the purpose of fastening a garment or part of an article of clothing.

Buttons are available in a wide range of sizes and are designated by **ligne (L)**, which is the unit of measurement indicating the diameter of a button. One ligne is equivalent to 0.025 inch (0.635 mm); therefore, a button with a 1-inch (25 mm) diameter would be referred to as 40 ligne (40L). Table 12.1 includes common button sizes.

Buttons are ordered by the **gross**, which is 144 units or 12 dozen. They can also be ordered by the **great gross**, 1,728 units or a dozen gross.

Buttons are made in many sizes, shapes, and contours. Dimensional variations of buttons include flat, dome, half-ball, and full-ball. Button surfaces may be smooth, raised, patterned, or adorned. Buttons may be used for decorative or functional purposes. Novelty buttons of irregular shapes, sizes, and designs can be used as trimming on apparel.

Flat button

Dome button

Half-ball button

Full-ball button

A wide variety of natural and man-made materials are used to make buttons for mass-produced apparel. Buttons can be manufactured from bone, glass, horn, leather, melamine, metal (stamped, cast, or plated), nylon, pearls or shells, plastic, polyester, rubber, tagua (a nut), urea formaldehyde, and wood. Button forms or molds may be covered with braid, cord, or fabric to complement the garment.

There are a variety of methods for producing buttons from man-made materials. These methods include compression molding, injection molding, rod casting, rotation or wheel casting, and sheet casting. These methods produce **blanks**, which are disks or forms that have not yet been fabricated into buttons. During the fabrication stage, blanks are shaped, holes are drilled, or *shanks* are inserted. Metal or metal alloy buttons are cast and finished. Buttons made from natural materials are typically die cut, sawed, or sliced, and then fabricated.

Compression Molded Application of pressure and heat to resins such as urea, melamine, or modified polyester to form buttons or blanks. Pearlescent pigments can be added during the molding process to produce imitation pearl buttons.

Compression molded

TABLE 12.1
Button Sizes

Ligne Number	Button Diameter
14L	5/16 inch (8 mm)
16L	3/8 inch (9.5 mm)
18L	7/16 inch (11.5 mm)
20L	1/2 inch (12 mm)
22L	9/16 inch (14 mm)
24L	5/8 inch (15 mm)
27L	10/16 inch (17 mm)
28L	11/16 inch (18 mm)
30L	3/4 inch (19 mm)
32L	13/16 inch (20 mm)
36L	7/8 inch (22 mm)
40L	1 inch (25 mm)
44L	1 1/8 inches (27 mm)
54L	1 3/8 inches (34 mm)
72L	1 3/4 inches (44 mm)

(M&J trimming, n.d)

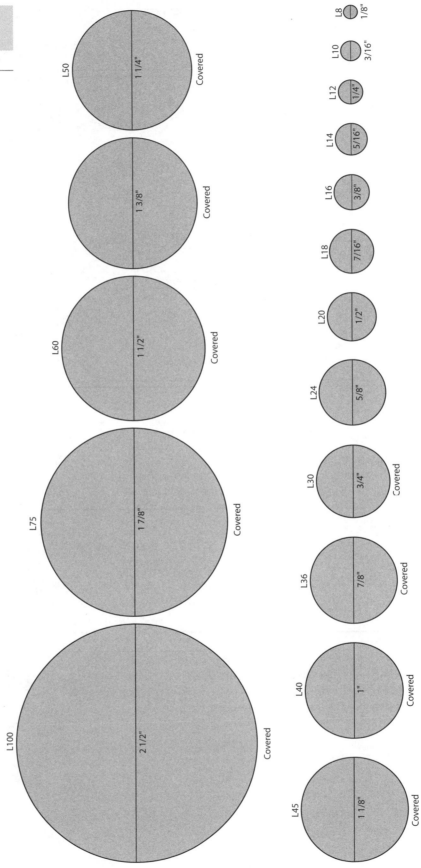

Ligne card

Injection Molded Liquid resin is injected under pressure into the hollow space of a closed mold. Method used to manufacture buttons made of rubber, plastic, polyester, and urea formaldehyde.

Metal Cast Molten metal and metal alloys are cast into individual mold chambers. Method used to manufacture metal buttons that can be used as is or plated to produce a variety of finishes.

Metal Stamped Metal or metal alloy sheets are stamped to form the shape and die cut and finished to fabricate the button. Method used for manufacturing metal buttons.

Rod Cast Modified polyester resin cast in tubing made of aluminum or glass. When set, the rods are sliced into blanks, cured, and made into buttons. Method used to manufacture multicolored and mottled or speckled buttons.

Rotation Cast (Wheel Cast) Modified polyester resin is cast in a rotating cylinder to form a sheet. The blanks are die cut, cured, and made into buttons. Method used to manufacture buttons with a specific orientation or special face such as a combination of multiple layers of colors, opaque white, mottles, and pearlescent (see Color plate 6).

Sheet Cast Polyester resin cast in gaskets placed between sheets of glass or open molds with gaskets. The blanks are die cut, cured, and made into buttons. Method used to manufacture buttons with a specific orientation or special face such as opaque white and pearlescent.

Buttons can be classified into three categories: sew-through, shank, and tack. The type of button selected depends on careful consideration of

- Garment style and design
- Garment construction
- Garment use
- Closure type and purpose

- Fabric type, weight, density, and texture
- Button size and shape
- Button design and type
- Number of buttons used
- Button placement and position
- Application method
- Garment wet processing (finishing)
- Garment care

Sew-through Button Disk having two, three, or four sewing holes, equidistant from the center, for attaching the button to the garment. A *flange* is the portion of the button where the holes or eyes are drilled or formed. Sew-through buttons can be sewn flat against the fabric or with a shank that is created with sewing thread that slightly elevates the button. Buttons can be attached to the fabric in a variety of different stitch designs. See Chapter 21 for the *ASTM D6193 Standard Practice for Stitches and Seams*, detailing the stitch attachment patterns for sew-through buttons. The face of sew-through buttons can be flat or domed. Some two-hole dome-shaped buttons have a recessed fisheye detail at the flange. Both two- and four-hole buttons can be produced with a *well*, or recessed portion, in the flange to add detail and mark the face side. Brand names, logos, and patterns can be cast, engraved, molded, or stamped into buttons. Sew-through buttons can be used on button fly closures, button-down collars, collar bands, cuffs, plackets, tab closures, pockets, suspender buttons, and waistband closures. Typical applications include

- Boxer briefs and boxer shorts
- Casual shirts, dress shirts, sport shirts, and sweaters
- Casual pants, shorts, and trousers
- Dresses and skirts
- Jackets, coats, and outerwear
- Lounge wear, sleepwear, and robes
- Suits and vests

Two-hole sew-through buttons

Two-hole fisheye sew-through buttons

Four-hole sew-through buttons

BUTTONS (continued)

Shank Button Three-dimensional form, in any shape, size, or surface pattern, with a protrusion on the underside containing a loop or hole made of metal or plastic for attachment to the garment. The *shank* contains an eye to sew through and conceals the point of attachment from the face of the garment. The stem and size of the shank vary with the type and use of the button. Shank styles include

Bell
Pin
Screw or stab
Tunnel
U

Shank buttons are used on items where the visible means of attaching the button would detract from the appearance of the garment and for closures on garments made of heavy and bulky fabrics. The button shank provides the space needed to accommodate the thickness of the garment ply and allows the button to rest on top of the buttonhole. It eliminates distortion and crowding of the buttonhole, permitting the closure to fasten smoothly. The shank does not show on the face of the garment. Shank buttons can be used on button placket closures and cuffs, pockets, tabs, and waistband closures. Typical applications include

- Blouses and sweaters
- Dresses and gowns
- Jackets, coats, and outerwear
- Loungewear, sleepwear, and robes
- Suit jackets (women's) and vests

See Chapter 21 for the *ASTM D6193 Standard Practice for Stitches and Seams*, detailing the attachment options for shank buttons.

Bell shank button

Pin shank button

Stab shank button

Tunnel shank buttons

U Shank buttons

Tack Button Brass, stainless steel, steel, or metal alloy cast button with a shank that is not sewn with thread but rather attached to the garment by a single or two-prong tack inserted through the back of the garment into the *collet*, or cap of the button. These buttons can be made with domed, flat (closed), open, or two-piece tops. Tack buttons can be fixed in place or have a swivel top and are available in all metal or with nylon inserted into the metal sheath cap, and threaded tack. Brand names, logos, and patterns can be cast into buttons. Tack buttons are used on garments made of denim or other sturdy fabrics on button placket closures, cuffs, pockets, tabs, and waistband closures. Typical applications include

- Jeans, skirts, shorts, and coveralls
- Casual jackets

Caper collet

Single prong tack

Assembled Button (Combination Button) Amalgamation of materials (such as plastic and metal or metal and metal) that have been affixed by gluing, swaging (shaping cold metal with a special tool to bend it into the desired shape), or stamping to provide contrast and detail. Assembled buttons can be used on button placket closures, cuffs, pockets, tabs, and waistband closures (see Color plate 7). Typical applications include

- Suit jackets (women's) and casual jackets
- Casual shirts and dresses
- Casual pants, jeans, and shorts
- Outerwear

Assembled button/combination button

Corded Button Twisting, looping, plaiting, or knotting of cord, *soutache braid*, or fabric tubing to create a button used with a loop or frog closure. When the button is formed as a sphere, it produces a Chinese ball button. Corded buttons can be used on button plackets, cuffs, and tab closures. Typical applications include

- Blouses and sweaters
- Coats and outerwear (women's)
- Suit jackets and vests

Corded buttons

Covered Button Two-piece form or mold; the top section is covered with a ply or plies of fabric or other material and clamped to the bottom shank base. The button may be fully covered, outlined by a metal rim, or decoratively stitched on the surface. Covered buttons can be used as a design detail when a button is to match, complement, or contrast the garment fabric, or to match corresponding trim. These buttons are used on button placket closures, cuffs, and pockets. Typical applications include

- Blouses and sweaters
- Coats and outerwear
- Dresses
- Loungewear, sleepwear, and robes
- Suit jackets and vests

Covered buttons

Toggle Oblong barrel-shaped or flat and long button, available as sew-through or with a shank; or a paired closure formed by two loops, one of which has a bar-shaped button affixed. Toggles are typically used where buttonholes would be difficult to construct, such as on garments made of heavy fabric or fur, as a design detail, or button placket or tab closure. Toggles are available in a variety of sizes, shapes, materials, and finishes. Typical applications include

- Coats and outwear
- Sweaters
- Vests

Toggle buttons

BUTTONHOLES AND OPENINGS

A **buttonhole** is an opening in a garment large enough to accommodate a button to pass through and remain secured. Buttonholes are constructed on the overlapping portion of a garment. Women's garments typically button right over left, and men's garments button left over right. **Horizontal buttonholes** are most commonly used for garment construction. **Vertical buttonholes** are used for garments that have hidden button closures or narrow *plackets*, and on some knit garments where a horizontal orientation would cause distortion to the garment during wear. There are three types of buttonholes: straight, bound, and slot. Each style has its variations. Loops can also be used in lieu of a buttonhole as part of a closure. The type and size of buttonhole or opening depends on

- Type of garment
- Garment design and style
- Fabric type and weight
- Purpose of the opening
- Method of application
- Button placement
- Button size and shape
- Number of buttons required

See Chapter 21 for the *ASTM D6193 Standard Practice for Stitches and Seams*, illustrating the buttonhole stitch formations.

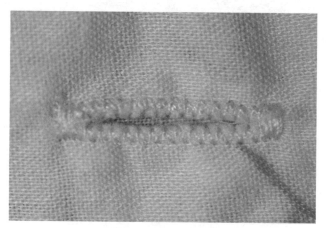

Straight buttonhole

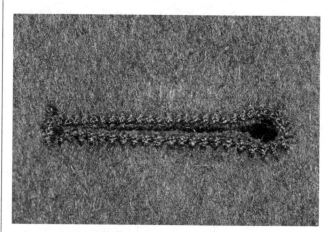

Keyhole (eyelet or eyelet-end) buttonhole

Straight Buttonhole Machine-stitched buttonhole created in a straight rectangular formation of zigzag stitches that can vary in density and secured with bar tacks (compact zigzag stitches used to reinforce points of stress) at the ends. Straight buttonholes can be used on button-down collars, button fly closures, collar bands, cuffs, plackets, pockets, tabs, and waistband closures. Garments that use straight buttonholes include

- Boxer briefs and boxer shorts
- Casual shirts, dress shirts, sport shirts, and sweaters
- Casual pants, shorts, and trousers
- Dresses and skirts
- Jackets, coats, and outerwear
- Lounge wear, sleepwear, and robes
- Suits and vests

Keyhole Buttonhole (Eyelet or Eyelet-end Buttonhole) Variation of a stitched buttonhole created with a straight rectangular formation of zigzag stitches that can vary in density and are secured at one end with a *bar tack*, while the other end is rounded into an eye formation. This eye provides more room to accommodate the button shank to avoid distortion when the garment is buttoned. Keyhole buttonholes can be constructed with filler cord and finished with a *bar tack*. Keyhole buttonholes can be used on button placket closures and cuffs, pocket and tab closures, and waistband closures. Typical applications include

- Blouses and sweaters
- Jackets, coats, and outerwear
- Dresses and gowns
- Loungewear, sleepwear, and robes
- Suits and vests

Bound Buttonhole (Welt Bound Buttonhole) Opening that is sewn with separate strips of fabric in matching or contrasting fabric that form the lips through which a button can be passed. Bound buttonholes are decorative and can add design detail to a garment when contrasting fabric is used on button plackets, cuffs, and pockets. Typical applications include

- Blouses and shirts
- Dresses and gowns
- Jackets, coats, and outerwear
- Loungewear and sleepwear
- Suits, tailored jackets, and vests
- Trousers

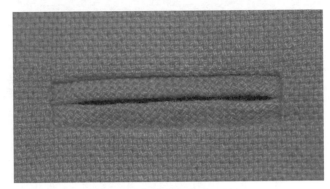

Bound buttonhole

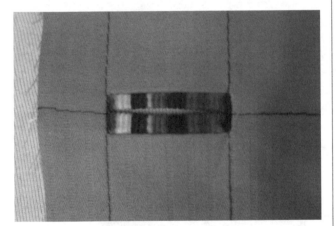

Corded bound buttonhole

Corded Bound Buttonhole A variation of a bound buttonhole sewn with corded piping in matching or contrasting fabric that forms more rounded lips in which a button can be passed through. Corded bound buttonholes are decorative and can add design detail to a garment when contrasting fabric is used on button plackets, cuffs, and pockets. Typical applications include

- Blouses and shirts
- Dresses
- Jackets, coats, and outerwear
- Suits and vests
- Trousers

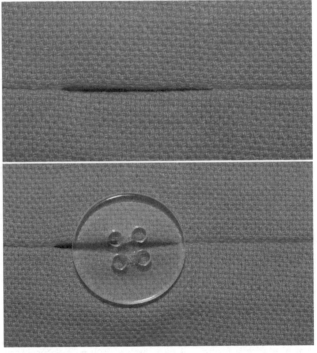

Slot buttonhole

Slot Buttonhole (In-Seam Buttonhole) Finished opening in a stitched seam where the placement of the button corresponds with a seam line. This style is typically planned as a decorative closure and selected for use when other types of buttonholes or openings would interfere with the garment design. For example, slot buttonholes work well in bands or inserts, pockets, tabs, waistlines, and yokes. Typical applications include

- Jackets, coats, and outerwear
- Dresses
- Suits and vest
- Trousers

Button Loops U-shaped or rounded formation of braid, cord, elastic, fabric, or thread chain sewn into a folded garment edge or seam. Loops are placed to extend beyond the edge of the garment. Button placement designed for a loop closure may be positioned as a center or lapped application. Loops can be made of matching or contrasting fabrics or materials, used individually or in a continuous row, or in place of a buttonhole as a decorative detail or closure. This style is typically used for garments made of lace or sheer fabrics where other buttonhole types would mar or detract from the fabric or garment design or on a single top closure at the neckline. For example, button loops work well in bands or inserts, plackets, and pockets of garments. Typical applications include

- Blouses
- Jackets, coats, and outerwear
- Dresses and gowns
- Suits (women's) and vests

Button loop

SNAP FASTENERS

A **snap** is a mechanism for attaching one garment part to another by means of a ball and socket that are joined together with the application of minimal compression and separated using perpendicular force. Snaps are available in a wide range of sizes that vary by snap type. The various types of snaps used for apparel production include sew-on, no-sew, covered, and snap tape. Snaps are purchased by the gross (144 units) or by the great gross (1,728 units). Snap sizes are designated by ligne just like buttons, with the exception of sew-on snaps.

Sew-on Snap Pair of opposing circular or square plates, molded with mating ball and socket; both designed with openings for attachment to a garment. See Chapter 21 for the *ASTM D6193 Standard Practice for Stitches and Seams*, illustrating the stitch attachment for sew-on snaps. Sew-on snaps are used

- On garments where there is little or no strain at the opening
- Where a smooth, flat closure is desired
- Behind decorative buttons when there is no buttonhole
- To fasten the top corner of an opening
- In a fly-front concealed closure
- In place of buttons and buttonholes on loosely fitted garments
- As part of a lingerie strap holder

Sew-on snap sizes 4/0 (0000) to 1/0 (0) are used on sheer and medium-weight fabrics. Sizes 1 to 4 are used on heavier fabrics. Snaps are manufactured in brass, black-enamel-coated metal, nickel, plastic, or clear nylon. Clear or transparent plastic snaps are used where metal snaps would detract from the garment appearance.

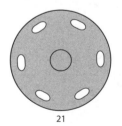

21   10   4   3   2   1   4/0   3/0   2/0   0

Sew-on snap sizes

No-Sew Snap Pair of metal plates molded with mating ball and socket designed with a pronged back plate that cleats through all garment plies, attaching the snap section to the garment. No-sew snap fasteners have four parts:

Snap Cap or Prong Cap— Visible part of the fastener when it is in the closed position. It has two functions: to anchor the socket in the material, and to be decorative or carry a brand logo or trademark.

Socket—Part of the fastener that the stud snaps into.

Stud or Post—Portion of the fastener that engages the socket and with it composes the actual closure. *Reversible stud* or *gypsy* is manufactured with an eyelet attached to facilitate back-to-back assembly with a socket or another stud, to make a double or reversible closure.

Post or Eyelet or Prong— The bottom part of the fastener when it is in a closed position, and serves only to anchor the stud in the material.

The surface of the snap may be decorative in finish, shape, and color. Logo designs or brand names can be stamped or molded into the surface. No-sew snaps are used on garments to facilitate ease of dressing and on industrial or professional garments where other fasteners are not applicable. Typical applications include

- Children's wear and sleepwear
- Casual shirts, work shirts, and western shirts
- Jeans, coveralls, and trousers
- Outerwear and leather jackets

Covered Snap Lightweight fabric-covered snap color-matched to the garment fabric; may be self-covered (with shell fabric of the garment) or ready-made. Covered snaps are used on garments where the shine of the metal would detract from the garment appearance Typical applications include

- Fur and outerwear
- Blouses and sweaters

Snap Tape Pair of woven tapes with opposing snaps attached at regular intervals. Tapes are available in a variety of widths, and snaps in a range of space intervals. Snap tape is designed for lapped applications to facilitate ease of dressing and on garments with detachable collars and cuffs. Typical applications include

- Children's wear and sleepwear
- Jackets and coats

Covered snap

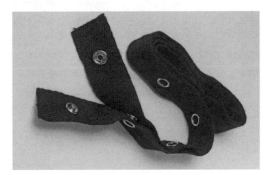

Snap tape

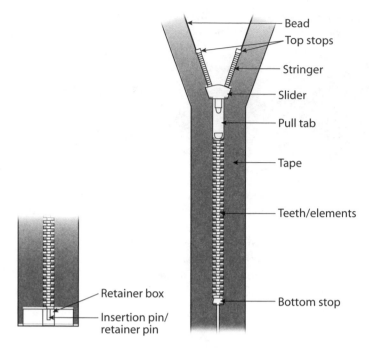

Bead
Top stops
Stringer
Slider
Pull tab
Tape
Teeth/elements
Bottom stop

Retainer box
Insertion pin/ retainer pin

Zipper component parts

A **zipper** is a fastening device that makes a complete closure by means of interlocking teeth or coils. Zippers have three main components: zipper tape, teeth, and slider. **Zipper tape** is a strip of material constructed of cotton, nylon, or polyester yarns that has a thicker cordlike inner edge called a **bead**. The **teeth**, also known as *elements*, are affixed to the bead of the tape and interlock together. When the teeth are locked together, they are called a **chain**. A **stringer** is one side of a chain that includes the assembly of the bead, elements, and tape. The **slider** is the component that moves along the chain and joins the teeth together to close the zipper or separates the elements to open it. The **stop** is a device at the top of the chain and at the bottom of some zippers to prevent the slider from becoming detached from the chain. For zipper constructions that are closed at both ends, the top stop is called a **bridge**. A bridge top stop forms an arch that holds both stringer tops permanently together. For zippers that separate, there is a **retainer box** in which the **insertion** or **retainer pin** is either removable or fixed and prevents the slider from detaching from the teeth.

Sliders are available in different styles with different functions depending on the intended use. Sliders can be categorized by size, material, function, pull-tab shape, and surface treatment. Zipper slider variations used in apparel products include automatic lock, semi-automatic lock, pin-lock, nonlock, and a reversible slider.

Automatic Lock Slider The lock pin inside the slider disengages with ease when force is applied to the pull-tab to open or close the zipper. When no force is present, the slider remains locked in place.

Semi-Automatic Lock Slider The lock pin inside the slider is disengaged as soon as the pull-tab is raised to allow the zipper to open or close. When the zipper tab remains in the down position (against the chain), the slider remains locked in place.

Pin Lock Slider Pull-tab of the slider can engage between two teeth, creating a locked position at any point on the zipper. Pull-tab must be lifted in order to disengage the slider lock for opening or closing the zipper.

Nonlock Slider Slider does not contain a lock pin, so it does not lock in any position.

Reversible Slider Pull-tab can be moved along a rail and operated from either side of the slider body for use in reversible garments.

Zippers can be manufactured in a wide range of sizes that are designated by the size of the teeth and then the length of the zipper. When the teeth are closed, the width of the chain is measured in millimeters that designate the **chain size** or **gauge**. Common zipper sizes are shown in Table 12.2.

Zipper length is measured from the uppermost edge of the top stop to either the lower edge of the bottom stop or bottom of the retainer box. Zippers are ordered by the piece and require a minimum number of identical units to be purchased. Minimums vary by distributor and can be for an order as small as 100 units or as large as 12,000 pieces.

Zippers can be manufactured from materials such as aluminum, brass, copper, nickel, nylon, polyester, or zinc. Types of zipper construction include metal, coil, and molded plastic.

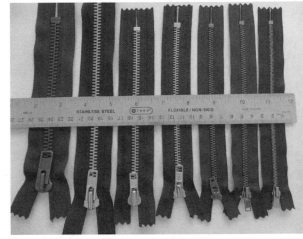

Standard zipper sizes (2, 3, 4.5, 5, 7, 8, 10)

TABLE 12.2
Zipper Sizes and Uses

Size	Chain Size or Gauge	Use
#2	2 mm	Lightweight pants, shorts
#3	3 mm	Lightweight coat linings, dresses, jackets, shorts, skirts
#4.5	4.5 mm	Medium weight dresses, pants, shorts
#5	5 mm	Medium weight jeans, jackets
#7	7 mm	Heavy duty jeans, jackets, pockets
#8	8 mm	Heavy duty jackets
#10	10 mm	Extra heavy duty jackets

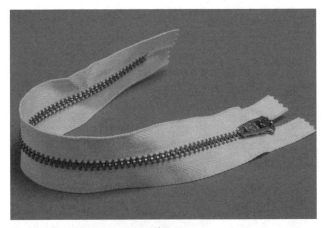

Metal zipper

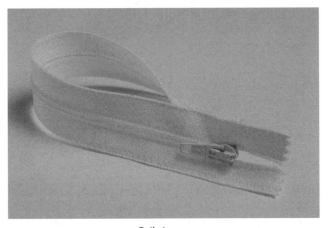

Coil zipper

Metal Zipper Chain elements constructed from individual metal teeth made from aluminum, brass, copper, nickel, or zinc are attached to the zipper tape. Metal zippers tend to be heavier and more rigid than others. Typical applications include

- Coveralls, jeans, and work wear
- Dresses and skirts
- Jackets and outerwear
- Trousers, shorts, and pants

Coil Zipper Chain elements are constructed from a continuous filament of extruded nylon or polyester that is attached to the zipper tape. Coil zippers are lightweight and very flexible. Typical applications include

- Dresses and skirts
- Jackets
- Trousers and pants

Molded Plastic Zipper (Vislon® Zipper) Chain elements are constructed from individual, injection-molded polyester teeth fused to the zipper tape for increased strength. Common apparel applications include placket and pocket closures on jackets, outerwear, and work wear.

Zippers are available in a variety of colors, materials, sizes, and styles. The weight of a zipper depends on the type of tape, the material used, and the structure. The type, chain gauge, length, and method of application for zippers selected depend on

- Garment style and design
- Garment type and use
- Garment construction
- Garment care
- Fabric type and weight
- Compatibility with fabric and the garment
- Opening type
- Type of garment finishing

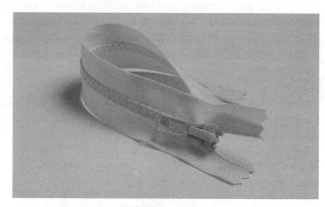

Molded plastic zipper

Zipper styles manufactured for apparel are classified by function. These include closed-bottom, invisible, separator, two-way separator, and bridge-top closed-bottom.

Closed-Bottom Zipper (Closed-End Zipper) Zipper constructed with metal, coil, or molded plastic teeth, 4 to 36 inches (10 to 90 cm) in length, open at the top and closed at the end by a bar spanning both tracks of teeth or coils called a bottom stop. Typical applications include

- Necklines openings
- Fly closures
- Bodices openings from the waistline upward
- Finished edges of fitted sleeves
- Center seams of a hood to convert the hood to a collar
- Underarm dress openings; long sleeve opening

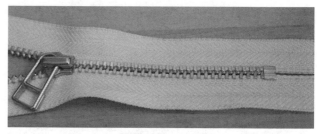

Closed-bottom zipper

Zippers for skirt or short neck openings are available in lengths from 4 to 10 inches (10 to 25 cm); for pants and trousers in lengths of 6, 9, and 11 inches (15.2, 22.9, and 28 cm); and for blouse, dress, and robe openings in lengths 16, 18, 20, 22, 24, 30, and 36 inches (40.6, 45.7, 50.8, 55.9, 61, 76.2, and 91.4 cm).

Invisible Zipper Chain is concealed beneath the zipper tape when it is zipped, leaving only the slider pull visible. This zipper produces a smooth, continuous seam line, making it useful where any other zipper application would detract from the garment appearance. An invisible zipper is constructed from a continuous filament of extruded nylon or polyester or metal elements. They are available for use in both top-weight and bottom-weight fabrics and available from 7 to 22 inches (18 to 56 cm). Typical applications include

- Fitted bodice openings from the waist to the neckline
- Neckline openings in the front or back of garments
- Back or side seam openings of dresses, skirts, shorts, pants, and trousers
- Lower edge openings of fitted sleeves

Invisible zipper

Separator Zipper Zipper constructed with metal or molded plastic teeth. The separator pin is inserted into the retainer box to secure the bottom of the zipper. When the slider is pulled, the elements lock together, joining the stringers together and closing the zipper. Separator zippers are selected for garments that require the front to open completely, to separate linings from dual-season coats and jackets, and horizontally, to add or remove a portion of a garment to increase or decrease lengths. Typical applications include front openings of parkas, coats, jackets, sweaters, and vests, and front or side openings of snowsuits and warm-up pants.

Separator zippers are available for application in top-weight and bottom-weight fabrics. Lengths for top-weight fabrics include 10 to 22 inches (25 to 56 cm). Lengths for bottom-weight fabrics include 14 to 24 inches (35 to 61 cm).

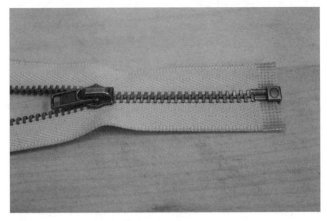

Separator zipper

Two-Way Separator Zipper Zipper constructed with metal or molded plastic teeth, two sliders, and a separator pin and retainer box that allows for opening or closing from both ends and separation at the bottom. Two-way separator zippers are selected for garments that require the ability to open the zipper from either end to provide access to garments layered underneath. Typical applications include

- Front openings on jackets and cardigan sweaters
- Openings on snowsuits, ski jackets and pants; skiwear
- Anywhere a separator zipper is used

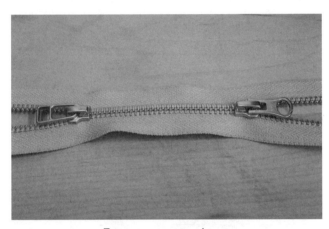

Two-way separator zipper

Bridge-top Closed-bottom Zipper Zipper 2 to 14 inches (5 to 35 cm) in length constructed with metal, coil, or molded plastic teeth, closed at the top by a bridge and closed at the bottom by a bar spanning both tracks of teeth or coils called a *bottom stop*. Typical applications include

- Garment seams that are closed at both ends of the placket opening
- Garments fitted at the waistline
- Underarm, side seam openings of blouses and dresses
- Openings extending into the neckline
- Pocket openings

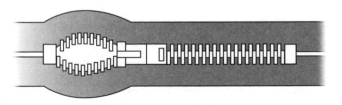

Bridge-top closed-bottom zipper

HOOKS

Hook and eye sizes

A **hook** is a metal fastener shaped into an engaging catch consisting of a bill and a base, designed with openings for attachment to a garment. Hooks can be paired with metal eyelets, loops, or eyes. Most hooks used in mass production are manufactured from metal, although some are made of plastic, such as a lingerie hook closure. Hooks can be used in conjunction with a zipper or lacing. They can also serve as functional and decorative closures. Hooks are used

- On fitted garments where there may be a strain on the clothing
- In a series to fasten an entire garment opening
- As a closure for camisoles, corsets, midriffs, and foundation garments

Hooks are sold either by the gross or great gross and are available in a variety of styles, sizes, and shapes. Various hooks and eyes are selected for specific uses. Hook styles used for apparel include hook and eye, covered hook and eye, gimp-covered hook and eye, or fur hook and eye, lingerie hook, sew-on hook and bar, no-sew prong hook and bar, and hook-and-eye tape. See Chapter 21 for the *ASTM D6193 Standard Practice for Stitches and Seams*, illustrating the stitch attachment for sew-on hook and eyes.

Hook and Eye Set of wire fasteners, one of which is shaped into a hook consisting of a bill and base, and the other an eye formed into a bar or loop and base. Hooks and eyes are available in brass, nickel, and enamel-coated metal (in black or white). *Straight eyes* are intended for use on *lap closures*, and *round eyes* are used on *abutted edges* (touching with no overlap). Sizes 00 to 3 are used for lightweight fabrics, and sizes 3 to 5 are used for heavier or coarse fabrics. Hook-and-eye closures are also used to secure the top of a zipper placket or waistband or at a single point of a garment opening such as a neckline.

Gimp-Covered Hook and Eye (Fur Hook and Eye)
Hook and eye covered with reinforced cord to conceal the metal. The size of hook is four times larger than the largest metal eye available. Gimp-covered hook-and-eye closures are used where a metal fastener would detract from the garment appearance.

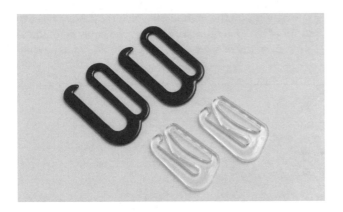

Lingerie Hook Flat metal or plastic plate, similar to an oblong rim buckle, designed with one open section, shaped to engage and hold a fabric loop. Fastening rims are made in a variety of widths to accommodate straps of different sizes. Lingerie hooks are used for

- Removable shoulder straps
- Secure closures on lingerie and swimwear

Sew-On Hook and Eye Set of shaped metal plates, one curved to form a broad hook or bill, the other a raised bar receptacle, both with openings for attachment to the garment. Bars are available with adjustable eye combinations. Sew-on hook and eyes are used on garments with lapped closures at the waistband such as of skirts, shorts, pants, and trousers, and those made from loosely woven fabrics.

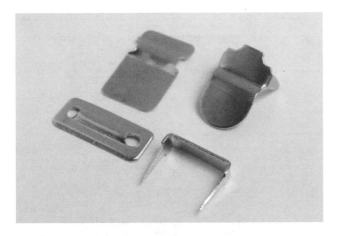

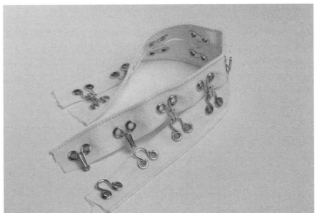

No-Sew Prong Hook and Eye Set of shaped metal plates, curved to form a broad hook or bill, the other a raised bar receptacle, both with prongs for attachment to the garment. No-sew prong hook and eyes are used on lapped closures of heavy bottom-weight fabrics; on waistbands of jeans, skirts, shorts, pants, and trousers; and for garments where there will be a maximum amount of strain.

Hook-and-Eye Tape Pair of tapes with hooks and corresponding eyes attached at regular intervals. Hook-and-eye tape can relieve the strain on the zipper when a garment is first closed and prevents the zipper from becoming disengaged or broken because of excess strain. Tapes are available in a variety of widths, with hooks and eyes in a variety of space intervals. Hook-and-eye tape is put up in 100-yard rolls and can be cut to specific lengths to conform to a garment section. It is designed for lap or centered applications. The base fastening of the hook and eye may be concealed by fabric. Hook-and-eye tape is used in areas where there is a lot of strain, such as on foundation garments.

DRAWSTRINGS, LACINGS, AND TIES

The functions of drawstrings, lacings, and ties are essentially the same, although the manner in which they are applied to garments differs. These fastenings are used to cinch in areas of a garment to aid in fitting or closure. They may be made of cord, braid, ribbon, a leather strip, or fabric tubing and are available in a variety of sizes and styles. Premade materials are put up in 100-yard rolls.

Drawstring Long, narrow strip that when pulled through a casing on the garment gathers or draws in the circumference. A drawstring is designed to be longer than the flattened casing or garment section. Drawstrings are planned to emerge on the inside or outside of the garment, from openings such as eye slits, buttonholes, machine-worked or metal eyelets, grommets, or seam openings. Drawstrings allow for flexibility and individual control of circumference adjustment. They can change the style effect by allowing the drawstring to manipulate the garment at the neckline, sleeve, and bodice waistlines to cinch or create a blouson. Drawstrings are used on

- Hoods
- Lower edges of sleeves or pants
- Lower or upper edges of camisoles
- Waistlines of upper or lower torso garments
- Empire, waistline, or hipline of one-piece garments
- Necklines of blouses
- Waistbands of casual pants, shorts, and skirts

Lacing Ribbon, cord, braid, or tubing in which two free ends are pulled alternately through opposing eyelets, grommets or buttonholes, or under hooks to cinch a garment or add a decorative design detail. Lacing is used on

- Belts, corsets, midriffs, and vests
- Leggings and pants

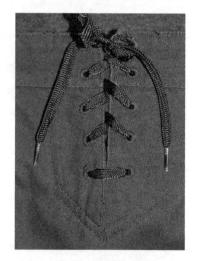

Ties Opposing pairs of ribbon, or fabric strips (self or contrasting), attached to a garment as a single pair, grouped, or in a series to hold garment fullness in place. Ties are used on

- Center front, center back, or side seams of blouses, jackets, dresses, pants, or swimwear
- Apron fastenings
- Lower edges of sleeves or pants
- Garments to fasten at the shoulder

BELTS AND BUCKLES

A **belt** is a flexible band used to secure a garment in place, or cinch or close a garment. Belts can be buckled, tied, or looped back through rings to secure them in place. Materials used for belts include leather, cording, fabric, elastic, metal, polyurethane, ribbon, webbing, or belt backing covered with fabric to create a *self belt* (made from the same fabric as the garment) or a combination of materials.

Belting is a stiff narrow band produced by bonding tightly woven fabric, buckram (stiff, coarsely woven cotton or linen material), and compressed fiber used as backing material for self belts. Belting is available in ½- to 3-inch (1.3 to 7.6 cm) widths and in premeasured lengths.

Belts can be made straight or contoured. A **straight belt** opens out flat, whereas a **contoured belt** is curved. On the body, a straight belt is perpendicular to the floor and sits squarely at the waist or on the hips. A contoured belt fits the curves of the body and is used with garments that sit lower on the waist, where the center front sits lower than the center back.

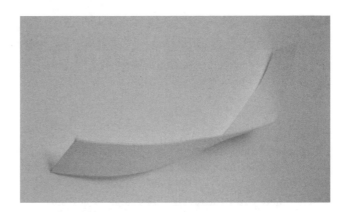

A **buckle** is an open rim having a single or central bar that may or may not contain one or more prongs used to secure a belt. Buckles can be manufactured out of common materials such as metal and metal alloys, plastic, polyester, urea formaldehyde, or wood. Belts and buckles are available in a variety of materials, finishes, sizes, shapes, and weights. Belts are used

- To define the waistline
- To secure a garment
- As a closure
- As a decorative detail
- To anchor free ends of tabs on sleeves, shoulders, and pockets

Types of buckles include anchor, clasp, concealed, covered, dog leash, overall, paired rings (D-rings), and ratchet.

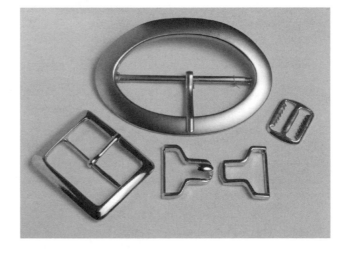

Anchor Buckle (Hook-and-Eye Buckle) Metal fastener consisting of a hook and opposing opening, both designed with an aperture for attaching it to the garment. Anchor buckles are used on

- The end of a belt or a tab
- Outerwear and sportswear for garment closure

Clasp Buckle (Interlocking Buckle) Pair of circular, square, or oblong shapes made of metal or plastic that interlock when one is slipped through the other. Clasp buckles are used on belts and tabs of coats and jackets.

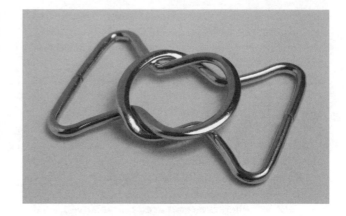

Concealed Hook Buckle Plate, in a variety of sizes and shapes, designed with a concealed hook or clip at one end and a bar through which the belt is attached at the other end. The face of the buckle may be designed or adorned in a variety of details and materials. Concealed hook buckles are used

- To close a belt
- To anchor free ends of a tab on sleeves, shoulders, and pockets
- As a garment closure design detail

Covered Buckle Two-piece buckle form or mold; the top section is covered with a ply or plies of fabric or other material and clamped into a corresponding base section. Buckles are available with or without one or more prongs. Covered buckles are used to

- Match or complement garment fabric or trim
- Accentuate or contrast garment fabric

Dog Leash Buckle (Swivel Hook or Swivel Snap Hook) Two-piece metal fastener consisting of a metal bar with a hooked end, closed by a spring clip to form a complete loop, and an opposing opening. Both are designed with an aperture for attachment to the garment. Dog leash buckles are used

- To close a belt
- In place of *toggles* on sportswear and rain gear
- To hold a belt to a belt loop or carrier
- In conjunction with a half-belt attached at the waistline of a garment

Overall Buckle Two-piece fastener composed of a metal rim, with one side designed for attaching to the garment and the other shaped to engage the shank of an opposing tack button. Fastening rims are made to accommodate straps of different widths. A strap-adjustment bar buckle is used in conjunction with the overall buckle. Overall buckles are used

- To fasten suspenders or straps of overalls to the bib section
- On shoulder straps of sportswear similar to overalls
- On aprons

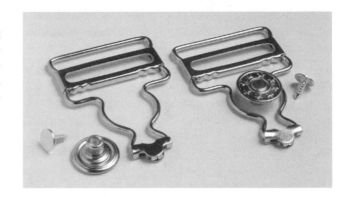

Ratchet Buckle (Spring-and-Hook-Type Buckle) Two-piece metal fastener consisting of a hinged spring clip and a hinged opposing plate. The hinged plate has one or more openings, any one of which allows the clip to pass through and snap back to secure the closure. Each piece of the fastener is designed with a prong for attachment to the garment. The plate may be designed with up to five openings for adjustability. A grommet opening may be used instead of the hinged opposing plate. Ratchet buckles are used as a functional or decorative fastener on

- Rain gear and slickers
- Active sportswear and outerwear

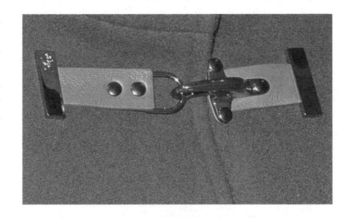

Paired Rings (D-rings) A pair of metal or plastic rings held together by a looped and stitched end of a belt. The rings function as a buckle when the free belt end is slipped through both and doubled back over the first and through the second. Paired rings are used on raincoats, trench coats, and sportswear to

- Tighten sleeve width
- Cinch the waist

OTHER FASTENERS

Some fasteners are related to other closure categories already discussed; however, they are different enough to list them separately.

Frog Two-piece closure consisting of loops and a Chinese ball button. The closure is formed by knotting, twisting, plaiting, interlocking or looping cord, soutache, or *bias fabric tubing* (strip of material cut on the bias, stitched, and turned to form a tube). Frog closures are available in a variety of styles and sizes and are sold by the gross. Frogs are used

- As a decorative closure
- To accentuate closure details
- To accentuate Asian-inspired garments

Frog closures

Fur Tack Two-piece fastener concealed within a decorative shell, consisting of a snap, clasp, or clip. Fur tacks are sold by the gross and are used to

- Hold a separate collar or fur piece to a coat or jacket
- Fasten opposing ends of a fur piece

Grommet Metal tube, in any variety of shapes and sizes, which when applied to a garment forms a flattering rimmed opening. Grommets are available in a variety of metals including brass and nickel and enamel-plated metal. They are sized by the inside diameter of the hole and sold by the gross. Common grommet sizes are shown in Table 12.3. Grommets are used

- To finish and strengthen punched openings
- To reinforce openings for drawstrings, lacings, and ties
- On nonoverlapping closures such as opposing ends of belts, midriffs, waist-cinchers, and corsets
- As an opening to accommodate a scarf, ribbon, or belt
- In conjunction with a ratchet buckle or hook
- On belts for wide or square buckle prongs
- As a decorative detail

TABLE 12.3
Grommet Sizes

Size	Diameter	Size	Diameter
#0	$9/_{32}$ inch (7 mm)	#3	$15/_{32}$ inch (12 mm)
#1	$13/_{32}$ inch (10 mm)	#4	$9/_{16}$ inch (14 mm)
#2	$7/_{16}$ inch (11 mm)	#5	$5/_{8}$ inch (15 mm)

Hook-and-Loop Fastener (Velcro® Fastener) Woven nylon hook-and-loop fastener consisting of two mating units, in a variety of sizes, shapes, and colors; one unit is designed with minute flexible hooks and the other with many soft loops. When opposing units are pressed together, the hooks engage the loops, forming a strong closure that opens when the units are peeled apart. Their attachment facilitates ease of dressing. Put-up is typically in 100-yard rolls. Velcro is used

- Instead of buttons, snaps, or hooks and eyes
- On detachable collars, cuffs, and trimmings
- On belts
- On wraparound garments

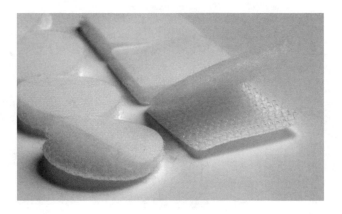

Hook-and-Loop Tape (Velcro Tape) Woven nylon hook-and-loop fastener that consists of two mating tapes: one tape designed with minute flexible hooks and the other with many small, soft loops. When opposing tapes are pressed together, they form a strong closure that opens when tapes are peeled apart. Put-up is typically in 100-yard rolls. Tapes are available in a variety of colors and widths. Velcro tape is used

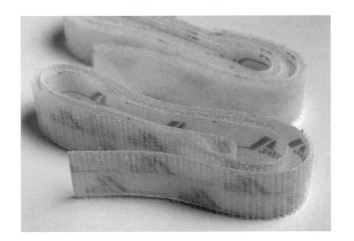

- To form an adjustable closure
- When a secure closure is desired
- On leg and neck wraps; belts
- On garment details such as detachable collars, cuffs, and trimmings

Mixture is a tape with the hooks and loops combined together on one tape rather than the hook tape and the loop tape. The hook-and-loop tape can be attached by means of sewing or adhesive hook-and-loop tape.

Lingerie Clasp Two metal or plastic plate fittings designed to interlock to form the closure when one is inserted into the other. Both sides are formed with a closed section to hold a loop of fabric. The overall height and width as well as the size of the opening will vary depending on the style and use. Manufacturers sell these closures by the gross. Lingerie clasps are used to close

- Front of a bra or other lingerie item
- Back of a swimsuit top or cover-up

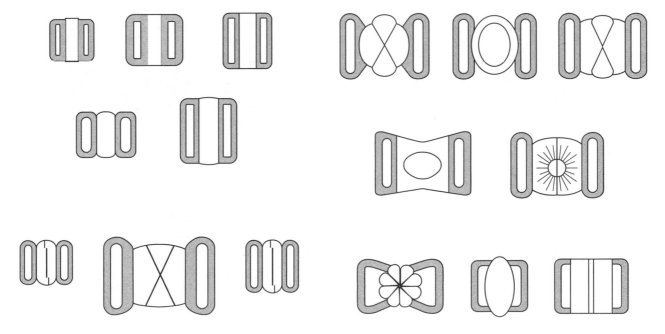

Lingerie clasps

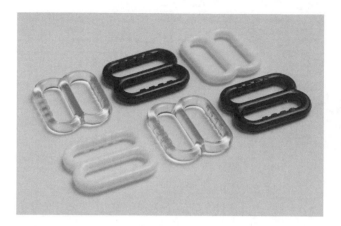

Lingerie Slider Flat metal or plastic plate designed with two closed ends for strap material to be woven through to adjust and hold strap in place. Sliders are made in a variety of widths to accommodate straps of different sizes and are sold by the gross. Lingerie sliders are used on bras, swimwear, tank tops, lingerie, and other garments designed with adjustable-length straps.

Lingerie Ring Small, flat or rounded metal or plastic ring designed for strap material to be woven through to adjust and hold strap in place. Lingerie rings are made in a variety of sizes to accommodate straps of different widths and are sold by the gross. Lingerie rings are used on bras, swimwear, tank tops, lingerie, and other garments designed with adjustable-length straps.

Metal Eyelet Round or square metal tube with an opening of approximately ¼ inch (6.4 mm), which when applied becomes a flattened, rimmed opening on a garment. Eyelets can be made of nickel, aluminum, or brass with a variety of finishes and are sold by the gross or great gross. Metal eyelets are used

- To make a reinforced opening
- To prevent openings from stretching out of shape
- To accommodate lacing
- On belts with pronged buckles
- In place of a metal eye for a hook closure

Rivet and Burr Metal reinforcement often used in place of a thread bar tack, or sometimes in addition to it. Rivets and burrs are manufactured in brass, stainless steel, steel, or metal alloy and are sold by the gross or great gross. Brand names, logos, and patterns can be cast or stamped into rivets. Rivets and burrs are used on jeans and work wear where reinforcement is needed.

Tab Decorative strip made of self fabric (garment fabric), folded tape, grosgrain ribbon, or strapping. A variety of designs may be made by twisting, plaiting, or looping cord from cut and sewn pieces of fabric or combinations. Tabs are used to secure or fasten a button, buckle, no-sew snap, or lacing.

References

American Efird Inc. (2010). *Thread recommendations for buttonsew, buttonholes & bar tacks.* Retrieved November 2, 2015, from http://www.amefird.com/wp-content/uploads/2010/01/Recommendations-for-Buttonsew-Buttonhole-Bartack-2-5-10.pdf

ASTM International. (2016a). D5497 Standard terminology relating to buttons. *2016 ASTM International standards* (Vol. 07.02). West Conshohocken, PA: Author.

ASTM International. (2016b). D123 Standard terminology relating to textiles. *2016 ASTM International standards* (Vol. 07.01). West Conshohocken, PA: Author.

ASTM International. (2016c). D2050 Standard terminology relating to subassemblies. *2016 ASTM International standards* (Vol. 07.01). West Conshohocken, PA: Author.

M&J Trimming (n.d.; a). *Button backing chart.* Retrieved November 15, 2015, from http://www.mjtrim.com/pdf/buttonchart.pdf

M&J Trimming (n.d.; b). *Button size chart.* Retrieved November 2, 2015, from http://www.mjtrim.com/pdf/buttons.pdf

Quality Zipper Supply. (n.d.). *About zippers.* Retrieved November 2, 2015, from http://qualityzipper.com/aboutzipper.php

Richard the Thread. (2015). Product catalog. Retrieved November 2, 2015, from http://www.richardthethread.com/index.php?src=gendocs&link=catalog&category=Main

Steinlauf and Stoller Inc. (2002). Products. Retrieved November 2, 2015, from http://www.steinlaufandstoller.com/products.htm

Universal Fasteners. (n.d.). *How the world buttons up.* Retrieved November 2, 2015, from http://www.universal-fasteners.com/buttons/

YKK. (2015). *Structure of a zipper.* Retrieved November 2, 2015, from http://www.ykkfastening.com/products/types/s_zipper.html

Garment Labels

Garment labels contain information required by law regarding fiber content, country of origin, manufacturer identification number, care instructions, and voluntary information identifying size and brand. Garment labels should be affixed and legible for the useful life of the apparel item. Labels are selected based on location of label (interior or exterior application); garment type and design; contact with the wearer's skin; intricacy or simplicity of label content (logo, graphic art, words, and so on); garment fabric, brand, quality, and price point; and information to be disclosed.

LABEL TYPES

Garment labels can be woven or printed. Woven labels are more durable and maintain their appearance and legibility longer than printed labels after repeated laundering or drycleaning. Materials used for sew-in labels include acetate, cotton, bamboo, polyester, leather, suede, PVC (polyvinyl chloride), silicone, or rubber.

Ribbon or **tape** refers to a narrow width of woven fabric put up on a continuous roll and available in ¼-, ½-, ¾-, 1-inch (0.6-, 1.3-, 1.9-, 2.5-cm), and larger widths.

Woven Label Material produced with a loom using damask, satin, twill, or plain weave construction with a minimum of two different-colored sets of yarns, wherein garment information is woven as part of the fabric's construction; solid-colored labels produced with a loom utilizing a plain, twill, or satin weave construction are printed with label content. Plain or twill woven labels are referred to as taffeta because they do not contain sheen. Woven labels can be affixed to the inside or outside of a garment. The tapes are cut into individual labels, finished, and sold in minimum put-ups of 1,000 pieces or by 100-yard or 100-meter rolls.

Printed Label Blank satin, twill, or plain weave or nonwoven fabric or tapes used for garment labels, wherein the label content is screen printed or rotary printed on the continuous roll. Printed labels are affixed to the inside of garments. The tapes are cut into individual labels and sold in minimum put-ups of 1,000 pieces or by 100-yard or 100-meter roll.

Tagless Label (Heat Transfer Label) Label information is thermally transferred directly to the inside of a garment rather than stitched. Tagless labels are soft against the skin and do not cause irritation like some sew-in labels.

Leather and Imitation Leather Label Leather or faux leather is embossed or printed with a brand name or logo, die cut into individual labels, and sold in minimum put-ups of 1,000 pieces. Leather and imitation leather labels are sewn to the inside or outside of a garment.

Suede and Imitation Suede Label Suede or faux suede is printed or embossed, die cut into individual labels, and sold in minimum put-ups of 1,000 pieces. Suede and imitation suede labels are sewn to the inside or outside of a garment.

Molded PVC, Rubber, and Silicon Labels Polyvinyl chloride, synthetic rubber, or silicone is injection molded to create a three-dimensional brand label where the surface can have embossed and depressed portions that form a brand name or logo. These labels are sewn to the outside of a garment and are cut into individual labels and sold in minimum put-ups of 1,000 pieces.

Rubber Tape Label Thin, clear film of synthetic rubber tape printed or embossed, cut into individual labels, finished, and sold in minimum put-ups of 1,000 pieces or by the 100-yard or 100-meter roll to be sewn into garments. Rubber tape labels are affixed to the inside of garments.

LABEL CUTS AND FOLDS

Garment labels can be cut and folded in a variety of ways, depending on the desired look, brand, quality desired, comfort of the wearer, and price point.

Die Cut *Metal die charge* (form with a sharp edge for cutting) pressure cuts leather, suede, and other fabrics into desired shapes and sizes for garment labels. Die cutting allows labels to be cut in unique shapes.

Fuse Cut Heat and pressure cut synthetic fiber fabrics or ribbons (tapes) into labels. Heat seals the edge of thermoplastic fibers and prevents the label from fraying during wear and refurbishment.

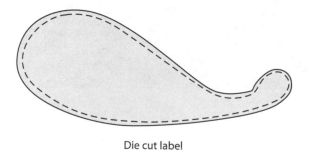

Die cut label

Fuse cut label

Straight cut label

Straight Cut Cutting and finishing a label by turning back all of the raw edges to prevent them from raveling during wear and refurbishment.

Ultrasonic Cut Cutting woven labels using sound wave vibrations provides a smooth soft edge but can be used to cut only one edge or side of a label.

Laser cut label

Laser Cut Cutting woven garment labels using a focused laser beam to allow for unique shapes to be cut. The raw edges are sealed to prevent fraying and raveling during wear or refurbishment.

Center Fold Label folded in half to form a loop in a vertical or horizontal orientation and stitched into a garment at the open end. Labeling information is woven in or printed on the front or both sides of the loop.

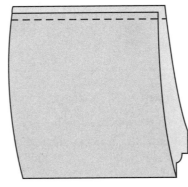

Center fold label

End folds on label

End Folds Woven label finished on the top and bottom edges with the raw edges at the right and left ends. The raw edges are folded back to lie under the body of the label, and stitched down at the left and right ends, or tacked at the four corners to affix the label to the garment and prevent fraying during wear and refurbishment.

Miter fold label

Miter Fold Woven label that is finished on the top and bottom edges with the raw edges at the right and left ends. The raw edges are folded back at right angles to form a U shape. The raw edges are stitched into the garment to prevent fraying during wear and refurbishment.

PRICE CLASSIFICATIONS FOR LABELS

Labels for garments are cues to quality and brand image. Price classifications for different types of labels include

Low Cost
- Taffeta plain woven and printed
- Taffeta twill woven
- Twill printed
- Satin printed
- Nonwoven printed
- Heat transfer

Moderate Cost
- Satin woven and printed
- Twill printed
- Imitation leather
- Imitation suede
- Rubber tape
- Nonwoven printed
- Heat transfer

Expensive
- Damask woven
- Leather
- Suede
- Molded PVC, rubber, and silicone

GOVERNMENT LABELING REGULATIONS FOR TEXTILE APPAREL PRODUCTS

In the United States, the Federal Trade Commission (FTC) has enacted laws regarding how apparel items must be labeled. The FTC enforces these labeling rules for all apparel products sold in the United States, whether manufactured domestically or imported. The Code of Federal Regulations (CFR) contains the following sections:

- 16 CFR 300: Rules and Regulations Under The Wool Products Labeling Act of 1939

- 16 CFR 303: Rules and Regulations Under The Textile Fiber Products Identification Act
- 16 CFR 423: Care Labeling of Textile Wearing Apparel and Certain Piece Goods as Amended
- 19 CFR 134: Country of Origin Marking

All labeling information should be presented in English. Some companies will provide an additional translation such as Spanish or French.

■ Fiber Content

Fiber content is the delineation of fiber types and weights listed in percentages on the front or back side of a garment label or in descriptions. Rules for listing fiber content are very specific in that any part of an apparel item made from fiber, yarn, or fabric must be disclosed on a label. Exceptions of garment components that do not have to be listed but are made of fiber, yarn, or fabric include linings (unless for warmth), trim, small amounts of ornamentation or decoration, and thread. The FTC defines trim as "collars, cuffs, braiding, waist or wristbands, rick-rack, tape, belting, binding, labels, leg bands, gussets, gores, welts, findings [including] elastic materials and threads added to a garment in minor proportion for structural purposes; and elastic material that is part of the basic fabric from which a product is made if the elastic does not exceed 20 percent of the surface area." (Federal Trade Commission & Bureau of Consumer Protection, 2015, p. 8). On a garment label, a 3 percent tolerance is allowed on all fibers, except for wool. The 3 percent provides for any slight inconsistencies that may occur during manufacturing of textile products. Rules for fiber content disclosure on garment labels include the following:

- All fibers must appear in the same font style or type and be of equal size, easily legible, and readily visible to the customer.
- Generic fiber names or trademark names accompanied by their generic equivalents, listed in numeric percentages in descending order with the largest percentages first, followed by the lowest. For example, "98% Cotton, 2% Lycra® Spandex."
- Fiber names cannot be abbreviated.
- Garments composed of only one fiber, such as 100 percent cotton, can be listed on the label as "All Cotton."
- Fibers composing 5 percent or more should be listed, while all others below 5 percent should be listed as "other." Exceptions to 5 percent rule:
  ○ When the fiber less than 5 percent serves a significant function, such as spandex for stretch or elasticity. The functional significance does not need to be disclosed on the label.
  ○ Wool fiber must always be revealed by name and percentage of weight, even when it is less than 5 percent. If the fiber has been recycled, it must be listed as "Recycled Wool."

- When several nonfunctionally important fibers are each less than 5 percent, the percentages of these fibers can be added together and listed as "other," even if their aggregate total is greater than 5 percent. For example, the fiber content may be listed as "80% Cotton, 10% Silk, 2% Spandex, 8% Other." In this situation, the *other* fibers are listed last even though their aggregate total is greater than the 2 percent spandex.
- "Exclusive of Decoration" can be used rather than disclosing fiber content when decorative designs integral to the fabric or decorative trim (e.g., embroidery, appliqué, overlay, or attachment) do not exceed 15 percent of the surface area of the garment. For example, "60% Cotton, 40% Polyester, exclusive of decoration."
- When decoration of 15 percent of the garment's surface area, fiber content must be disclosed. For example, "Body–100% Wool, Decoration–100% Silk."
- "Exclusive of Ornamentation" can be used rather than disclosure of fiber content when "any fibers or yarns imparting a visibly discernable pattern or design to a yarn or fabric" are not greater than 5 percent of the garment's fiber content (Federal Trade Commission & Bureau of Consumer Protection, 2015, p. 10).
- When ornamentation exceeds 5 percent of the garment's fiber weight, fiber content must be disclosed. For example, "Body–100% Wool, Ornamentation–100% Silk."
- When filling, lining, interlining, or padding is included in an apparel item for the purpose of adding structure, it does not have to be disclosed unless it contains wool fiber.
- When filling, lining, interlining, or padding is included in an apparel item for the purpose of adding warmth, fiber content must be disclosed. For example, "Shell: 90% Cotton, 10% Silk, Lining: 100% Polyester; Shell: 100% Nylon, Filling: 100% Polyester; Shell: 100% Cotton, Interlining: 100% Cotton."
- When garments are composed of sections having different fiber contents, each portion must be disclosed separately. For example, "Body: 60% Wool, 40% Mohair, Sleeves: 100% Wool."

- Fabrics containing pile must either disclose the fiber content of the whole product or list the pile fiber separate from the backing, but the ratio between the pile and backing must be disclosed. For example, "60% Polyester, 40% Rayon; 100% Rayon Pile, 100% Polyester Back (Back is 60% of fabric and pile is 40%)."
- Specific types of premium or luxury fibers can be disclosed, but specific percentages must be included. For example:
  - A garment made entirely of Egyptian cotton can be disclosed as "100% Cotton" or "100% Egyptian Cotton." If the garment contains only a portion of Egyptian cotton, it can be listed as "100% Cotton" or "60% Egyptian Cotton, 40% Cotton."
  - A garment made from the hair of an alpaca, Angora goat, camel, Cashmere goat, llama, or vicuna or fleece from a lamb or sheep can be disclosed as wool or labeled with the specialty fiber name. For example, "100% Wool"; "100% Cashmere."
  - When fur fiber is incorporated and is greater than 5 percent of the total fiber weight of the garment, the name of the animal can be used to disclose the content as long as the hair or fur fiber would not be classified as wool (see previous bullet). For example, "60% Wool, 40% Fur Fiber"; "80% Cotton, 10% Silk, 10% Angora Rabbit Hair."
- When reclaimed or recycled fibers are used, this must be disclosed. For example, "70% Recycled Wool, 30% Acrylic."

The FTC has designated specific names to be used for man-made or synthetic fibers. The International Organization for Standardization (ISO) lists some man-made fibers differently, and although they are not listed by the FTC, they are acceptable for use in compliance with fiber identification disclosure laws (Federal Trade Commission, 2015). Some examples include

- ISO uses Viscose or Modal; FTC uses Rayon.
- ISO uses Elastane; FTC uses Spandex.
- ISO uses Polyamide; FTC uses Nylon.
- ISO uses Polypropylene; FTC uses Olefin.
- ISO uses Metal Fibre; FTC uses Metallic.

■ Country of Origin

Country of origin must be identified in English to disclose where the product was produced and must appear on the front of the label (not be covered by any other label).

- Country of origin must be accessible, legible, and easily visible.
- If products are made in the United States from imported materials, the label must state this. For

example, "Made in the U.S.A. of imported fabric"; "Made in U.S.A. of fabric made in Italy"; "Fabric made in Italy, cut and sewn in U.S.A."
- Both portions of production must be disclosed if a product is processed or manufactured in the United States and another country. For example, "Assembled in the U.S.A. of imported components"; "Made in Costa Rica, finished in U.S.A."

GOVERNMENT LABELING REGULATIONS FOR TEXTILE APPAREL PRODUCTS (continued)

■ Manufacturer, Importer, or Dealer Identification Number

Garment labels must contain the company name or the **registered identification number (RN)** of the manufacturer, importer, or broker handling or distributing the merchandise. RN is found on either the front or backside of the label. **Wool products labeling (WPL)** numbers at one time were issued to companies that manufactured wool products. Although WPL numbers are no longer issued, they can still be seen today. The FTC is responsible for issuing and monitoring the use of RN numbers to U.S. companies involved in manufacturing, importing, distributing, and marketing textile products, including wool and fur. RN numbers are not issued to companies outside the United States. Rules for identifying the manufacturer, importer, or dealer on a garment label include the following:

- RN, WPL, or company name must be legible and easily visible.
- RN or WPL must appear immediately before the registered identification number.

- Only one RN number is issued to a company, and it cannot be transferred or reassigned.
- When a company name is used rather than a WPL or RN number, the full name by which the company conducts business must be stated on the garment label. "It cannot be a trademark, trade name, brand, label, or designer name—unless that name is also the name under which the company is doing business." (FTC & Bureau of Consumer Protection, 2015, p. 23).
- When a product is imported, the label can identify any one of the following:
  - Manufacturer's name
  - Importer's name or RN or WPL number
  - Wholesaler's name or RN or WPL number
  - Retailer's name or RN or WPL number

■ Care Label

A **care label** is required by law to be permanently affixed to the garment and legible for its useful life, to provide the customer with a guide to refurbishment without causing damage to the product. Manufacturers and importers are required to provide either drycleaning or washing instructions for textile apparel products. If damage can be caused to a product by using sensible cleaning procedures, warnings must be provided on the care label using words such as "Do not," "No," or "Only" to alert the customer. Warnings must be stated for sensible procedures to use in the routine refurbishment of laundered or drycleaned items. Reversible garments that do not contain pockets can be exempted from the requirement for the care label to be permanently affixed for the useful life of the garment. Nevertheless, the care instructions for the product must appear on a hang tag, packaging, or other easily visible place for the customer to view the refurbishment procedures prior to purchase.

ASTM International developed ASTM Standard D5489, Standard Guide for Care Instructions on Textile Products, which designates care symbols in the **ASTM Guide to Care Symbols** and outlines the order in which they should appear on garment labels. **Care symbols** are icons developed specifically to represent procedures used in cleaning textile and apparel products, to guide or instruct a person

how to safely refurbish a product. As of 2010, these symbols are not required by law to be used on labels but can appear in conjunction with written English terms or on their own.

Washing

Washing is a method for removing soil and stains from garments using water and detergent or soap and agitation. **Washing instructions** must include washing method and water temperature and can be accompanied by any modifications to the normal process. Washing warnings must also be included if damage can occur when routine sensible procedures are used. Washing instructions for apparel include

- Washing method
  - Hand wash or machine wash
  - Water temperature such as cold, warm, or hot. If the hottest water, up to 145 degrees Fahrenheit (63 degrees Celsius) will not harm the product, wash temperature does not have to be stated.
  - Wash modifiers include
    —Gentle/delicate cycle
    —Durable press cycle
    —With like colors

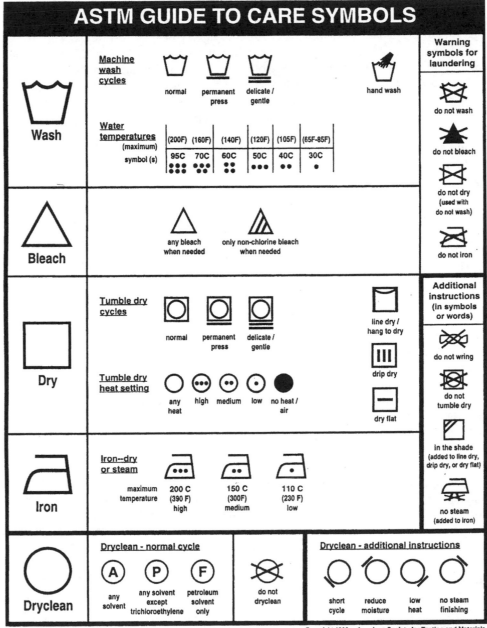

ASTM GUIDE TO CARE SYMBOLS

Reprinted, with permission, from
1997 Annual Book of ASTM Standards

Copyright 1996   American Society for Testing and Materials
100 Barr Harbor Drive   West Conshohocken, PA 19428-2959

—Wash separately
—Wash inside out
—Rinse temperature such as cold rinse or warm rinse
—Rinse thoroughly
—Wipe clean with damp cloth
—Spot clean
—Wash before wearing

• Washing warnings
  ◦ Do not wash
  ◦ Do not spin
  ◦ Do not wring
  ◦ Do not commercial launder
  ◦ To retain flame resistance, use detergent not soap

Bleaching

Bleaching instructions should include the type of recommended bleach accompanied by any warnings if damage could occur when routine sensible procedures are used. **Chlorine bleach**, available in liquid form only, is made of sodium hypochlorite and water. **Nonchlorine bleach** is an oxygen bleach available in liquid (hydrogen peroxide and water) or powder (sodium perborate or sodium carbonate) form. If no bleach is specified, the customer can use either type without causing damage to the garment. Bleaching instructions for apparel include

- Bleach method
  ○ Bleach when needed (used when all bleach types can be safely used without damaging the garment)
- Bleach warnings

  ○ Do not bleach
  ○ Nonchlorine bleach only

Drying

Drying removes remaining moisture contained in the garment fabric after it is washed. Moisture is evaporated through exposure to indoor or outdoor air or machine drying. **Drying instructions** must include the method and temperature and can be accompanied by any modifications to the normal process. Drying warnings must also be included if damage can occur when routine sensible procedures are used. Drying instructions for apparel include

- Drying method
  ○ Tumble dry
    —Drying temperature such as no heat, low, medium, high, durable press, or permanent press cycle
  ○ Drip dry
  ○ Dry flat
  ○ Line dry
  ○ Drying modifiers include
    —Remove promptly
    —Line dry away from heat
    —Reshape, dry flat
    —Dry until damp and then line dry, or dry until damp and then dry flat
    —Dry with three tennis balls (used to fluff filling in ski jackets and similar items that contain padding that can become matted during cleaning)
- Drying warnings
  ○ Do not dry
  ○ Do not machine dry
  ○ Do not tumble dry
  ○ No heat

Ironing and Pressing

Ironing and **pressing** remove wrinkles from garments using dry heat or heat and steam. **Ironing** or **pressing instructions** should include the temperature and any warnings if damage can occur when routine sensible procedures are used. Ironing or pressing instructions for apparel include

- Ironing or pressing method
  ○ Temperature, such as cool, low, warm, or hot
  ○ As needed
  ○ Iron damp
  ○ Steam press
  ○ Steam iron
- Ironing or pressing warnings

  ○ Do not iron
  ○ Do not iron decoration
  ○ Use press cloth
  ○ Iron on wrong side only
  ○ Do not steam
  ○ No steam
  ○ Steam only

Drycleaning

Drycleaning uses perchloroethylene, petroleum, or fluorocarbon solvents to remove soils and stains from textile wearing apparel. Moisture is commonly added to drycleaning solvent to achieve up to 75 percent relative humidity in order to remove water-soluble soil and stains. Once the garments are cleaned with the solvent, it is recovered through means of drying at temperatures up to 160 degrees Fahrenheit (71 degrees Celsius), followed by steam pressing or finishing. **Drycleaning instructions** should state dryclean, professionally dryclean, commercially dryclean, or leather clean and include any warnings if damage can occur when common solvents and routine sensible procedures are used. Drycleaning instructions for apparel include

- Dryclean, professionally dryclean, or leather clean
- Solvent type:
  ○ Perchloroethylene
  ○ Petroleum
  ○ Fluorocarbon
- Drying temperatures, such as cool or warm
- Drying method such as tumble dry or cabinet dry
- Drycleaning modifiers include
  ○ Short cycle
  ○ Minimum extraction
  ○ Reduced moisture

- Drycleaning warnings
  - Do not dryclean
  - No steam
  - Steam only
  - Do not use perchloroethylene solvent
  - Do not use petroleum solvent
  - Do not use fluorocarbon solvent
  - Do not tumble

Care Disclosure Requirements for Children's Sleepwear

The Consumer Product Safety Commission (CPSC) requires additional information to be disclosed on garment labels for children's sleepwear because of flammability regulations. These include the following:

- 16 CFR 1615: Standard for the Flammability of Children's Sleepwear Sizes 0–6X
- 16 CFR 1616: Standard for the Flammability of Children's Sleepwear Sizes 7–14

These standards for loose-fitting and tight-fitting children's sleepwear must be adhered to. If the care instructions are disclosed on the back of the label, the words "Care Instructions on Reverse" must be stated on the front of label. Care warnings must be stated on the garment label and permanently affixed for the useful life of the product and include "precautionary instructions to protect the items from agents or treatments which are known to cause deterioration of their flame resistance. If an item has been initially tested under §1615.4(g)(4) [or initially tested under §1616.5(c)(4) *Laundering*,] after one washing [and drying], it shall be labeled with instructions to wash before wearing (CPSC, 2015a, b, §1615.4(g)(4) and §1616.5(c)(4))."

Other common care labeling systems include ISO/GINETEX, JIS care labeling, Canadian care symbols, and Chinese GB/T 8685 labeling system.

Category	JIS L0001 :2014
Washing	
Bleaching	
Natural Drying	
Tumble Drying	
Wringing	
Ironing	
Commercial dry-cleaning	
Professional Textile Care	

JIS care labeling

GOVERNMENT LABELING REGULATIONS
FOR TEXTILE APPAREL PRODUCTS (continued)

Washing Process

Symbol	Washing Process
95	- maximum washing temperature 95°C normal process
70	- maximum washing temperature 70°C normal process
60	- maximum washing temperature 60°C normal process
60	- maximum washing temperature 60°C mild process
50	- maximum washing temperature 50°C normal process
50	- maximum washing temperature 50°C mild process
40	- maximum washing temperature 40°C normal process
40	- maximum washing temperature 40°C mild process
40	- maximum washing temperature 40°C very mild process
30	- maximum washing temperature 30°C normal process
30	- maximum washing temperature 30°C mild process
30	- maximum washing temperature 30°C very mild process
(hand)	- wash by hand maximum temperature 40°C
(crossed)	- do not wash

Bleaching Process

Symbol	Bleaching Process
△	- any bleaching agent allowed
⚠	- only oxygen / non-chlorine bleach allowed
✕	- do not bleach

Tumble Drying Process

Symbol	Tumble Drying Process
⊙	- tumble drying possible - normal temperature - maximum exhaust temperatue 80°C
⊙	- tumble drying possible - drying at lower temperature - maximum exhaust temperature 60°C

Natural Drying Process

Symbol	Natural Drying Process
I	- line drying
II	- drip line drying
—	- flat drying
=	- drip flat drying
I (shade)	- line drying in the shade
II (shade)	- drip line drying in the shade
— (shade)	- flat drying in the shade
= (shade)	- drip flat drying in the shade

Ironing Process

Symbol	Ironing Process
iron •••	- iron at a maximum sole-plate temperature of 200°C
iron ••	- iron at a maximum sole-plate temperature of 150°C
iron •	- iron at a maximum sole-plate temperature of 110°C without steam steam ironing may cause irreversible damage
iron ✕	- do not iron

Professional Textile Care Process

Symbol	Professional Textile Care Process
Ⓟ	- professional dry cleaning in tetrachloroethene and all solvents listed for the symbol F normal process
Ⓟ	- professional dry cleaning in tetrachloroethene and all solvents listed for the symbol F mild process
Ⓕ	- professional dry cleaning in hydrocarbons (distillation temperature between 150°C and 210°C, flash point between 38°C and 70°C) normal process
Ⓕ	- professional dry cleaning in hydrocarbons (distillation temperature between 150°C and 210°C, flash point between 38°C and 70°C) mild process
✕	- do not dry clean
Ⓦ	- professional wet cleaning normal process
Ⓦ	- professional wet cleaning mild process
Ⓦ	- professional wet cleaning very mild process
✕	- do not professional wet clean

ISO/GINETEX care symbols

Guide to Apparel Care Symbols

Wash / Do Not Wash

Machine Wash Cycles

Normal | Permanent Press | Delicate/Gentle | Hand Wash

Do Not Wring

Water Temperatures

(Maximum)	(200F)	(160F)	(140F)	(120F)	(105F)	(65F-85F)
Symbol(s)	95°C	70°C	60°C	50°C	40°C	30°C

Bleach / Do Not Bleach

Any Bleach When Needed

Only Non-Chlorine Bleach When Needed

Dry / Do Not Tumble Dry / Do Not Dry (used with do not wash)

Tumble Dry Cycles

Normal | Permanent Press | Delicate/Gentle | Line Dry/Hang to Dry | Dry Flat

Heat Setting

Any Heat | High | Medium | Low | No Heat/Air | Drip Dry | In the Shade

Iron / Do Not Iron or Press

Iron-Dry or Steam

200°C (390F) High | 150°C (300F) Medium | 110°C (230F) Low | No Steam (added to iron)

Professional Textile Care / Do Not Dry-clean / Do Not Wet-Clean

Dry-clean - Normal Cycle

(P) Any Solvent Except Trichloroethylene

(F) Petroleum Solvent Only

(W) Wet-Clean

Canadian care symbols

Symbol	Washing Process
95	- Maximum washing temperature 95°C - Normal process
70	- Maximum washing temperature 70°C - Normal process
60	- Maximum washing temperature 60°C - Normal process
60	- Maximum washing temperature 60°C - Mild process
50	- Maximum washing temperature 50°C - Normal process
50	- Maximum washing temperature 50°C - Mild process
40	- Maximum washing temperature 40°C - Normal process
40	- Maximum washing temperature 40°C - Mild process
40	- Maximum washing temperature 40°C - Very mild process
30	- Maximum washing temperature 30°C - Normal process
30	- Maximum washing temperature 30°C - Mild process
30	- Maximum washing temperature 30°C - Very mild process
(hand wash symbol)	- Hand wash - Maximum washing temperature 40°C
(crossed out symbol)	- Do not wash

Symbol	Bleaching Process
△	- Any bleaching agent allowed
⧄	- Only oxygen / non-chlorine bleach allowed
⧄	- Do not bleach

Symbol	Natural Drying Process
▯	- Line drying
▯▯	- Drip line drying
□	- Flat drying
▤	- Drip flat drying
◩	- Line drying in the shade
◩	- Drip line drying in the shade
◸	- Flat drying in the shade
◸	- Drip flat drying in the shade

Symbol	Tumble Drying Process
⊙⊙	- Tumble dry - Normal temperature - Maximum exhaust temperature: 80°C
⊙	- Tumble dry - Low temperature - Maximum exhaust temperature: 60°C
⊠	- Do not tumble dry

Chinese GB/T 8685 labeling

VOLUNTARY LABEL INFORMATION FOR TEXTILE APPAREL PRODUCTS

Not all information contained on garment labels is required by law. However, brand and size information provide valuable assistance to customers when making clothing purchases. See Table 13.1 for a summary of labeling content requirements for selected countries.

▪ Brand Designation

Disclosure of the brand name or logo on garment labels is important for identification, name recognition, and promotional purposes. Many customers shop and purchase specific apparel brands based on their knowledge of fit, quality level, garment design and construction techniques, status, or price point. These labels also serve as constant reminders of brands customers like and identify with, whether they are shopping, looking in their closet, or viewing a brand label on another person.

▪ Size Designation

Although there is no law requiring size to be disclosed on apparel labels, it is vital for consumers. **Size** designates the overall combination of garment component dimensions for various ages and figure types and groups them into particular categories. Body dimensions within individual garment sizes can range from one manufacturer to another. Size can be designated by numerals, letters, or words.

- XXS, XS, S, M, L, XL, XXL, XXXL
- XX-Small, X-Small, Small, Medium, Large, X-Large, XX-Large, XXX-Large
- One size fits all
- One size fits most
- *Women's* designates full figure adult females using even numbers followed by W. Sizes in this range typically include 14W to 24W.
- *Misses* uses even number sizes and typically includes 00 to 20.
- *Petite* (women under 5'5" [165 cm] in height) and *tall* (women over 5'6" [167.6 cm] in height) are additional size designations used for women's apparel.
- *Junior* sizing uses odd numbers, typically ranging from 1 to 17.
- *Men's* sizing is based on body measurements in inches. Suits and jacket sizes typically range from 32 to 50; pant sizes typically range from 28 to 40; tailored dress shirt sizes typically include neck circumference ranges from 14 to 18½ with sleeve lengths ranging from 30/32 to 34/36.
- *Short* (men under 5'7" [170.2 cm] in height), *regular* (men 5'8" to 5'11" [172.7 cm to 180.3 cm] in height), and *tall* (men 6' [183 cm] and over in height) are additional size designations used for men's apparel.
- See Chapter 4 for infant and children's sizing as well as bra sizing for women.

▪ Style Number

Once a design is adopted, a **style number** is assigned as a means of identifying the specific garment style so it can be tracked through the supply chain. The system for assigning style numbers depends on the company's product mix and the style numbering system it has developed. Product developers/designers, patternmakers, sample makers, materials and production sourcing, contractors, sales reps, and retailers all use these numbers to communicate information about a particular garment style. Style number is not required by law to be included on a sew-in garment label but is commonly found on the reverse side, or if multiple labels are stacked, it can be located on the front or back of the last one.

Style numbers can be configured using letters, numbers, or a combination of both. When only letters are used, they are referred to as a **style code**. For example, a girl's satin pajama pant, offered in three prints (i.e., cat, heart, and butterfly), could be coded as

- GSPJPCAT (**g**irl's **s**atin **p**ajama **p**ant in **cat** print)
- GSPJPHRT (**g**irl's **s**atin **p**ajama **p**ant in **h**ea**rt** print) and
- GSPJBFLY (**g**irl's **s**atin **p**ajama **p**ant in **b**utter**fly** print)

If this same pajama pant were offered in a different fabric, such as flannel, the style code would change to GFPJPBFLY (**g**irl's **f**lannel **p**ajama **p**ant in **b**utter**fly** print). This style code system is very simplified and can be confusing if people don't know what the letters stand for. If letters are used, there must be a standard system for designating what each letter or abbreviation means, and that system must be used consistently to avoid any confusion between styles.

The combination of letters and numbers can be used to designate style numbers. Once again, it is very important for every letter to consistently mean the same thing. For example, a long sleeve T-shirt that is the 105th design, offered in cotton for spring 2018, can be numbered as

- LST105CSP18 (**l**ong **s**leeve **t**-shirt, *105*, **c**otton, **sp**ring 20*18*)

Some companies incorporate the season and year into the style number, such as F for fall, H or Ho for holiday, R for resort, and SP for spring. However, it is more common to list this information below the style number on the sew-in label.

The best way to develop style numbers is strictly using a numbering system. Again, the numbering configuration will depend on the company and its product mix. Style numbers are typically composed of four to six numbers.

VOLUNTARY LABEL INFORMATION
FOR TEXTILE APPAREL PRODUCTS (continued)

TABLE 13.1
Summary of Garment Labeling Content Requirements for Selected Countries

Country	Language	Fiber Content	Origin (Country, Manufacturer, Importer, Trader, Retailer Identification)	Care	Size
Australia	English	Mandatory	Mandatory (Country)	Mandatory	Voluntary
Austria	German	Mandatory	Voluntary (Country)	Mandatory	Voluntary
Belgium	Official Language of Region*	Mandatory	Voluntary	Voluntary	Voluntary
Brazil	Portuguese	Mandatory	Mandatory	Mandatory	Mandatory
Bulgaria	Bulgarian**	Voluntary	Voluntary	Voluntary	Voluntary
Canada	English and French	Mandatory	Mandatory	Voluntary	Voluntary
China	Chinese	Mandatory	Mandatory	Mandatory	Mandatory
Cyprus	Greek	Voluntary	Mandatory	Voluntary	
Czech Republic	Czech	Mandatory	Mandatory (Country)	Mandatory	Mandatory
Denmark	Danish, Norwegian, or Swedish	Mandatory	Voluntary	Voluntary	Voluntary
Dominican Republic	Spanish	Mandatory	Mandatory	Mandatory	Voluntary
Estonia	Estonian	Mandatory	Mandatory	Mandatory	Mandatory
Finland	Finnish or Swedish	Mandatory	Mandatory	Voluntary	Voluntary
France	French	Mandatory	Voluntary	Voluntary	Voluntary
Germany	German	Mandatory	Voluntary	Voluntary	Voluntary
Hungary	Hungarian	Mandatory	Mandatory (Country)	Mandatory	Mandatory
India	English or Hindi	Mandatory	Mandatory	Voluntary	Mandatory
Indonesia	Indonesian	Voluntary	Voluntary	Voluntary	Voluntary
Ireland	Irish or English	Mandatory	Voluntary	Voluntary	Voluntary
Italy	Italian	Mandatory	Mandatory (Manufacturer or Importer)	Voluntary	Voluntary
Japan	Japanese (Country of Origin may be disclosed in English)	Mandatory	Mandatory	Mandatory	Voluntary
Latvia	Latvian	Mandatory	Voluntary	Voluntary	Voluntary
Lithuania	Lithuanian	Mandatory	Mandatory (Country)	Mandatory	Mandatory

TABLE 13.1

Summary of Garment Labeling Content Requirements for Selected Countries *(continued)*

Country	Language	Fiber Content	Origin (Country, Manufacturer, Importer, Trader, Retailer Identification)	Care	Size
Luxembourg	French or German	Mandatory	Voluntary	Voluntary	Voluntary
Malaysia	Bahasa Malay or English	Voluntary	Mandatory (Importer)	Voluntary	Voluntary
Malta	English or Maltese	Mandatory	Voluntary	Voluntary	Voluntary
Mexico	Spanish	Mandatory	Mandatory	Mandatory	Mandatory
Netherlands	Dutch	Voluntary	Voluntary	Voluntary	
Pakistan	English or Urdu	Voluntary	Mandatory	Voluntary	Voluntary
Philippines	English or Filipino	Mandatory	Mandatory	Mandatory	Voluntary
Poland	Polish	Mandatory	Mandatory	Mandatory	Mandatory
Portugal	Portuguese	Mandatory	Mandatory (Importer)	Voluntary	Voluntary
Romania	English or Romanian	Mandatory	Mandatory (Country)	Mandatory	Voluntary
Russia	Russian	Mandatory	Mandatory	Mandatory	Mandatory
Saudi Arabia	Arabic	Mandatory	Mandatory	Mandatory	Mandatory
Singapore	English	Voluntary	Voluntary	Voluntary	Voluntary
Slovak Republic	Slovak	Mandatory	Mandatory (Country)	Voluntary	Mandatory
Slovenia	Slovene	Mandatory	Mandatory (Country)	Mandatory	Mandatory
South Korea	Korean	Mandatory	Mandatory	Mandatory	Voluntary
Spain	Spanish	Mandatory	Mandatory (Importer)	Mandatory	Voluntary
Sweden	Swedish	Mandatory	Voluntary	Voluntary	Voluntary
Taiwan	Chinese	Mandatory	Mandatory	Mandatory	Mandatory
Thailand	Thai	Mandatory	Mandatory	Mandatory	Mandatory
United Kingdom	English	Mandatory	Voluntary	Voluntary	Voluntary
United States	English	Mandatory	Mandatory	Mandatory	Voluntary
Vietnam	Vietnamese	Mandatory	Mandatory	Mandatory	Voluntary

Note: Language specifies the language(s) required or acceptable for use on garment labels.
*Belgium requires labeling to be disclosed in the official language of the region where the product is sold (i.e., French, Dutch, German).
**English, German, and French languages are excepted.
Sources: http://web.ita.doc.gov/tacgi/overseasnew.nsf/d1c13cd06af5e3a9852576b20052d5d5/fad8900a6a29da2b8525789d0049ea04?OpenDocument
http://web.ita.doc.gov/tacgi/overseasnew.nsf/alldata/Belgium#Labeling
http://web.ita.doc.gov/tacgi/overseasnew.nsf/annexview/EU+Member+Labeling+Requirements

VOLUNTARY LABEL INFORMATION
FOR TEXTILE APPAREL PRODUCTS (continued)

Historically, the first number designates the market or gender. Therefore, style numbers starting with 1 designate men's wear, 2 signify women's wear, and 3 identify children's wear:

- 10000 series = Men's wear
- 20000 series = Women's wear
- 30000 series = Children's wear

This is not a hard-and-fast rule though. If an individual launches a children's line, that person may choose the first number to start with 1. The second number designates product:

- 11001 = Men's shirts
- 12001 = Men's shorts
- 13001 = Men's suits
- 14001 = Men's outerwear
- 15001 = Men's pants/trousers
- 16001 = Men's furnishings

The remaining numbers represent the incremental increase in the number of styles. For example, 14127 would represent men's outwear style 127. Style numbers can also be coded for fabrication if necessary. The last digit would represent the fabrication, such as

- 1 = cotton
- 2 = nylon
- 3 = merino wool
- 4 = cashmere

For example, 141273 would represent men's outwear style 127 offered in merino wool.

PLACEMENT OF LABELS IN WEARING APPAREL

Labels featuring information required by law must be securely affixed to the garment. The location of labels must be clearly marked and easy for the customer to find. All required and optional information can be contained in one label or in several labels attached to the garment.

Options for brand placement inside apparel items

Characteristics of labels placed in garments with a neck include the following:

- Brand labels are typically found at the inside center back of the neck. They can also be affixed to various locations on the outside of a garment.

- Country of origin labels must be attached to the inside center of the neckline or in close proximity to another label placed at the midpoint between the shoulders. If one label contains all of the required information, by law it must be attached in this area.
- Fiber content, manufacturer identification number, and care instructions can be attached to the side seam.

Labels placed in garments with a waist can be characterized as follows:

- **Garment labels** are found on the inside of the waistband or waist area.
- **Brand labels** are typically found on the inside of the waistband or waist area. They can also be affixed to various locations on the outside of a garment.

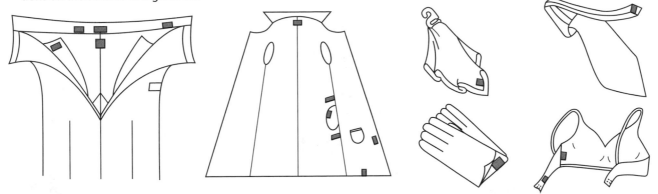

Placement of label information inside apparel items

References

ASTM International. (2016). *2016 ASTM International standards* (Vol. 07.02). West Conshohocken, PA: Author.

Avery Dennison. (2008). *Eco friendly woven labels.* Retrieved December 5, 2015, from http://www.ibmd.averydennison.com/products/documents/eco/ECO-WovenLabels_Tearsheet_lang-us-en_size-us.pdf

BCI. (2005). *Clothing labels.* Retrieved December 5, 2015, from http://www.bcilabels.com/index.html

Bureau of Customs & Border Protection. (2015, December 5). *Electronic code of federal regulations: 19 CFR 134: Country of origin marking.* Retrieved December 5, 2015, from http://www.ecfr.gov/cgi-bin/text-idx?SID=301c2ae310c9fb9f4dc57ed375a188da&mc=true&node=pt19.1.134&rgn=div5

Consumer Products Safety Commission. (2015, December 5; a). *Electronic code of federal regulations: 16 CFR 1615: Standard for the flammability of children's sleepwear sizes 0–6X.* Retrieved December 5, 2015, from http://www.gpo.gov/fdsys/pkg/CFR-2012-title16-vol2/xml/CFR-2012-title16-vol2-part1615.xml

Consumer Products Safety Commission. (2015, December 5; b). *Electronic code of federal regulations: 16 CFR 1616: Standard for the flammability of children's sleepwear sizes 7–14.* Retrieved December 5, 2015, from http://www.gpo.gov/fdsys/pkg/CFR-2012-title16-vol2/xml/CFR-2012-title16-vol2-part1616.xml

Federal Trade Commission. (2015, December 5; a). *Care labeling of textile wearing apparel and certain piece goods, as amended effective September 1, 2000.* Retrieved December 5, 2015, from https://www.ftc.gov/node/119456

Federal Trade Commission. (2015, December 5; b). *Electronic code of federal regulations: 16 CFR 300: Rules and regulations under the wool products labeling act of 1939.* Retrieved December 5, 2015, from http://www.ecfr.gov/cgi-bin/text-idx?SID=4d32f443901ac1d35f94e705e794f10b&mc=true&node=pt16.1.300&rgn=div5

Federal Trade Commission. (2015, December 5; c). *Electronic code of federal regulations: 16 CFR 303: Rules and regulations under the textile fiber products identification act.* Retrieved December 5, 2015, from http://www.ecfr.gov/cgi-bin/text-idx?SID=4d32f443901ac1d35f94e705e794f10b&mc=true&node=pt16.1.303&rgn=div5

Federal Trade Commission. (2015, December 5; d). *Electronic code of federal regulations: 16 CFR 423: Care labeling of textile wearing apparel and certain piece goods as amended.* Retrieved December 5, 2015, from http://www.ecfr.gov/cgi-bin/text-idx?SID=4d32f443901ac1d35f94e705e794f10b&mc=true&node=pt16.1.423&rgn=div5

Federal Trade Commission & Bureau of Consumer Protection. (2015, December 5). *Threading your way through the labeling requirements under the textile and wool acts.* Retrieved December 5, 2015, from https://www.ftc.gov/tips-advice/business-center/guidance/threading-your-way-through-labeling-requirements-under-textile

Intertek. (2014). *Care labeling: Caring about the consumers beyond the label.* Retrieved December 5, 2015, from http://www.intertek.com/uploadedFiles/Intertek/Divisions/Consumer_Goods/Media/PDFs/Services/Low%20Res%20CompleteCareLabelling.pdf

Thiry, M. C. (2008, October). Tagged. *AATCC Review: International magazine for textile professionals, 8*(10), 22–24, 26–28.

Woven Labels Clothing. (2015) *Woven labels glossary.* Retrieved December 5, 2015, from http://www.wovenlabelsclothing.com/2.html

Xpresa Labels. (2015). *Glossary for labels.* Retrieved December 5, 2015, from http://www.xpresalabels.com/glossary-for-labels/

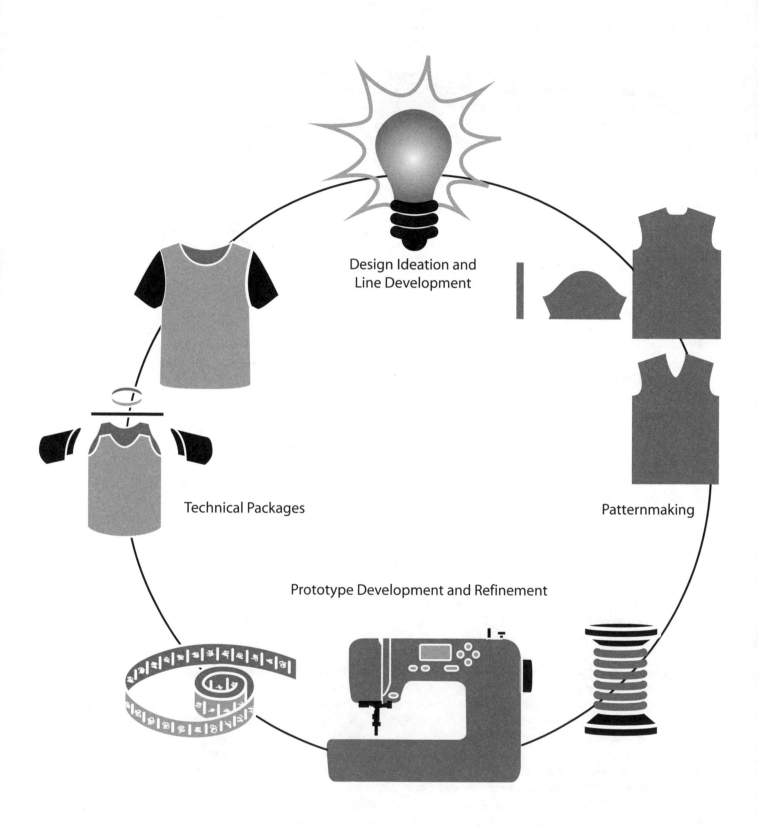

Design Ideation and
Line Development

Patternmaking

Prototype Development and Refinement

Technical Packages

Design Development
and Product Specifications

Designers and product developers play a critical role in creating product lines each season that are on trend and appropriate for the brand and the target customer. These tasks include everything from analyzing trend forecasts to determining appropriate styling, design details, and preproduction operations such as patternmaking, producing technical packages, and specifying stitches and seams for assembly. Part Three of this book will provide an overview of product design, patternmaking methods and tools, design details, garment openings, hem finishes, stitches and seams selection, as well as garment sizing and fit strategies used in the development of garments for mass production.

CHAPTER 14

Product Design (Product Development)

Design is a critical component in the development of fashion products. Apparel designers are influenced by trends and global events and are challenged with interpreting these into garment styles appropriate for the brand and target customer. Knowledge of one's target market is essential to the successful development and positioning of a product line. Development teams consider the customer at the core of all decisions made.

RESEARCH

Design of mass-produced apparel begins with research. This research includes evaluating environmental trends, consumer trends, and product trends. People who conduct **environmental trend research**, also known as **market and global trends research**, investigate current events that may have an impact on the development of products. This research involves the evaluation of variables businesses cannot control yet must consider, such as assessing the current economic situation, evaluating what has occurred in the past twelve months and projecting what may happen in the next year; and tracking economic trends, social and cultural trends, technological advances, and political influences on consumer behavior and spending.

Consumer trend research or **target market research** involves gathering demographic and lifestyle data for the existing target market, as well as potential customers. Analysis of this data allows for the creation of customer profiles or updates.

Demographic data includes

Age	Housing type
Gender	Ethnicity
Income	Marital status
Education	Occupation
Geographic area	Spending patterns
Family size	Religious affiliation

Lifestyle data includes social and psychological factors that motivate purchases, such as

Life stage	Personality
Reference groups (peers)	Attitudes and values
Cultural distinctions	Behavior
(preferences based	Generation group
on ethnic or cultural	(e.g., baby boomers,
influences)	gen X'ers, millennials)
Social class	

Target Customer (Core Customer) Individuals who are part of a brand's primary target market.

Potential Customer (Fringe Customer) Individuals who occasionally shop a brand but are not part of the primary target market. These individuals have potential to become core customers.

Trend board

Styling:
Juliette Sleeves, Zippered Pockets, Print and Graphic Mixing, Lots of Layers, Racer Back Tanks, Heavy Embellishment, Curvaceous Silhouettes, Graffiti Influence, Hip-Hop Styling

Fabric:
70/20 Cotton Spandex Lightweight Stretch Denim
100% Polyester Lightweight Sheer Plaid & Floral Woven
60/40 Cotton Rayon Jersey
100% 1x1 Rib Brushed Cotton

Territory Spring Summer '08 Color Palette

Cloud Sand Bonita Ocean Turquesa Gris Stone Salsa Tango Azteca Noir

Product developers continuously monitor and evaluate products in the marketplace. People who conduct **product trend research** investigate general market trends by exploring competing products, researching innovative products being developed or introduced, and evaluating trend forecasts. This analysis provides companies with information regarding ways to improve current product offerings as well as find new opportunities to expand business.

Trend Forecast Projected influences and trends that will impact fashion and product design. Forecasted trends include

- *Color*
- *Fibers and fabrics* (e.g., weave or knit structures influencing texture)
- Influences providing inspiration and conceptual focus
- *Silhouette*(s)
- *Design details* (e.g., pleats, trim, collar style)

DESIGN DEVELOPMENT

Trend forecasting services are important to the development of apparel product lines. Designers interpret trends for sales potential and appropriateness for the brand, target customer, and product line. Trend information is gathered through travel to key cities around the globe. Destinations vary depending on the merchandise category (e.g., activewear, sportswear, loungewear) and target market. Trends provide designers with inspiration to develop a line concept for the season.

Designers develop and refine ideas to meet the needs of the target market, brand, product line, budgeted costs, and production. Garment patterns and prototypes are created and tested for fit, function, and aesthetic appropriateness;

fabrics and trims are sourced; and preliminary costing is completed. Once garments for the product line are selected and perfected, final costing is completed, production yardage is ordered, and production begins.

Concept Development Design direction for a product line is based on the inspirational source, idea, or theme from trend forecasts that provides a path for a product line development. Conceptual images or mood boards visually communicate inspiration for the collection. Concept should convey

Mood or theme	Target market appropriateness
Brand image	Seasonal trends appropriate for
Product focus	target market and brand

Concept board

DESIGN DEVELOPMENT (continued)

Apparel silhouettes/garment silhouettes

Apparel Silhouette (Garment Silhouette) The garment outline by its overall shape and identified as

Natural	Tubular	Tent (Trapeze)
Hourglass	A-line	

Silhouettes can be further delineated into horizontal divisions of seams and overlays. Horizontal seam divisions include

- Empire (waistline seam, just under the bust and above the natural waist)
- Fit and flare (natural waistline)
- Dropped waist (below natural waist to high hipline)
- Long torso (hipline)

Horizontal overlay divisions include the tunic, which extends below the hipline to the knee, and tiers composed of a series of layers creating parallel rows.

Design Detail Style line or design feature within the silhouette of the garment that creates additional visual interest:

Collars	Pockets	Yokes
Necklines	Closures	Sleeves
Cuffs	Trimmings	

Design Ideation Exploration and development of design ideas for product line solutions. Styles are created, color palettes selected, and fabrics chosen or developed in-house or sourced from fabric mills.

Design Refinement and Selection Modifications, final adjustments, and selection of design ideas take place based on concept, fit and functionality, cost, production limitations, and merchandise plan; content of the product line is determined.

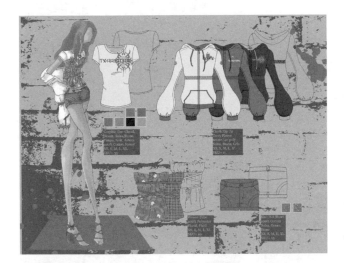

Storyboards

DESIGN DEVELOPMENT (continued)

Test Muslin (Muslin Proof) Muslin reproduction of the pattern, pinned, or stitched together in the form of the garment. Test muslins are used to

- Check the fit, balance, and proportion of the original draft
- Check fabric potential of a drafted design
- Adjust the fit of a new design on a dress form or fit model

A test muslin may be constructed as the right half only or as a complete garment.

Virtual Prototype Digital simulation created with software that converts a two-dimensional pattern into a three-dimensional garment. Virtual prototypes are used to evaluate aesthetic appeal on a figure while minimizing the number of physical samples needed to develop and refine a garment, saving time and resources. Some software programs evaluate the virtual prototype for fit, comfort, and functionality.

3D Printed Prototype Garment created using 3D modeling software to print three-dimensional articulated product samples from laser-sintered powdered nylon or plastic (TPU 92A-1 9, a thermoplastic polyurethane). This technology allows for samples to be quickly and efficiently produced, which is known as *rapid prototyping*. Three-dimensional prototyping requires less raw material, therefore producing less waste. Eli Bozeman, founder of Occom Group, a digital prototyping and development agency stated, "It's only a matter of time before all fashion products at least get their start this way. It's far more efficient and allows you to get something much sooner with fewer costly design iterations" (Dhani, 2013). This technology could change the way apparel is sampled and manufactured in the future.

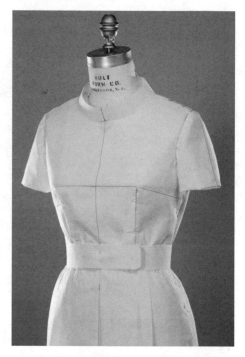

Muslin test

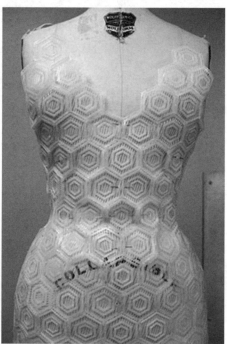

3D printed garment dress sample

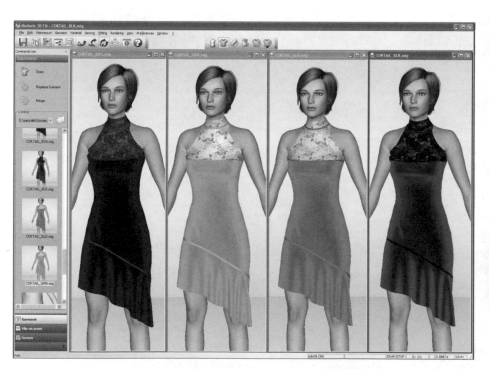

Virtual prototype

TABLE 14.1
ASTM Body Measurement Apparel Sizing Specifications

Size Range	Sample Size	ASTM Specification
Children Sizes		
Preemie to 24 months	3 to 6 months or 6 months	D4910
Girls Sizes		
2 to 20 and girls plus	10 Regular, Slim, Plus	D6192
Juniors Sizes		
0 to 19	7	D6829
Boys Sizes		
4H to 24 Husky	10	D6860/D6860M
8 to 14 Slim and 8 to 20 Regular	10	D6458
Misses Sizes		
00 to 20	8 or 10	D5585
00P to 20P	8P or 10P	D7878/D7878M
Maternity 2 to 22 (Includes variation from Misses Regular)	8 or 10	D7197
Women's Sizes		
Age 55 and older 0 to19 0P to 19P 00 to 20 00P to 20P 00T to 20T 14W to 32W	7 regular and petite 8 or 10 regular, petite, and tall 18W to 20W	D5586/D5586M
*P=Petite *T=Tall *W=Women's plus		
Men's Sizes		
Age 35 and older 34 to 52 Short, Regular, and Tall	34 for Bottoms 40 to 42 for Jackets Short, Regular, and Tall	D6240/D6240M

Note: See *2016 ASTM International Standards*, Volume 07.02, for specific body measurements under each designation. These body dimensions are available as a general reference guide. Manufacturers and product developers have the liberty to designate the specific body dimensions for their brands for each size within a designated range.

First Sample Original sewn prototype of a new design created from a drafted or draped pattern to test fit, function, and aesthetic appeal.

Production Sample Final sewn prototype that has been corrected, perfected, and tested for fit, function, and aesthetic appeal. It is sewn with the same construction methods and fabrics used for mass production.

Sample Size Manufacturer's designated size for dress forms, fit models, first pattern development, and prototypes (see Table 14.1). Most manufacturers use a size closest to the middle of the size range for better proportions when *grading*. Some premium or luxury brands do not grade patterns from a sample size; they create an original pattern for each size within the range.

References

ASTM International. (2016). *2016 International standards* (Vol. 07.02). West Conshohocken, PA: Author.

Bubonia-Clarke, J. & Borcherding, P. (2007). *Developing and branding the fashion merchandising portfolio.* New York: Fairchild Publications, Inc.

Dhani, M. (2013). *How 3-D printing could change the fashion industry for better and for worse?* Retrieved December 21, 2015, from http://fashionista.com/2013/07/how-3-d-printing-could-change-the-fashion-industry-for-better-and-for-worse#1

Noe, R. (2013, March 19). *Materialise launches new flexible and durable material for laser sintering.* Retrieved December 22, 2015, from http://www.core77.com/posts/24586/Materialise-Launches-New-Flexible-n-Durable-Material-for-Laser-Sintering

Rietveld. F. (2015). *3D printing: The face of future fashion?* Retrieved December 22, 2015, from http://tedx.amsterdam/2013/07/3d-printing-the-face-of-future-fashion/

Shapeways, Inc. (2015). *N12: 3D Printed bikini.* Retrieved December 22, 2015, from http://www.shapeways.com/n12_bikini

CHAPTER 15

Patternmaking Methods and Computer Technology

A **pattern** is a guide for cutting one or more

garments. It includes all the pieces needed

to make a garment. Patterns conform to

standard measurements, but interpretation of

the measurements for sizing varies by brand.

Patterns for garment styles are developed,

tested, and perfected to ensure accurate

design, function, and fit of an apparel line.

PATTERNMAKING STAGES

Block or Sloper Basic tag board pattern or digital pattern of a garment section that follows the natural contours of the body or dress form, with notches, having no style lines and may or may not include seam allowances; developed from specific measurements, a dress form, a live fit model, or brand specifications of a sample or given size. A block is used to develop original bodice, skirt, dress, pant, and sleeve designs, and to create first patterns of new or modified styles.

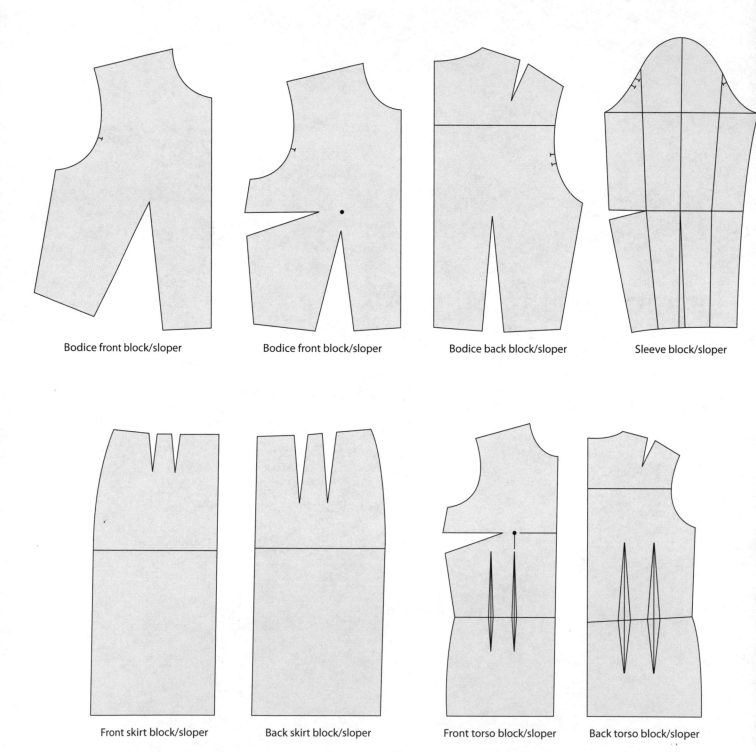

Bodice front block/sloper

Bodice front block/sloper

Bodice back block/sloper

Sleeve block/sloper

Front skirt block/sloper

Back skirt block/sloper

Front torso block/sloper

Back torso block/sloper

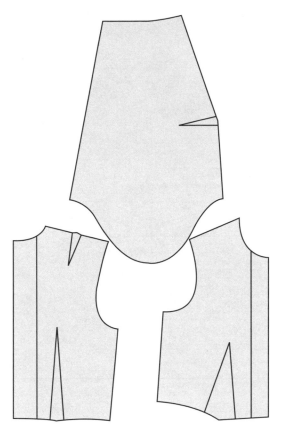

First pattern without seam allowances

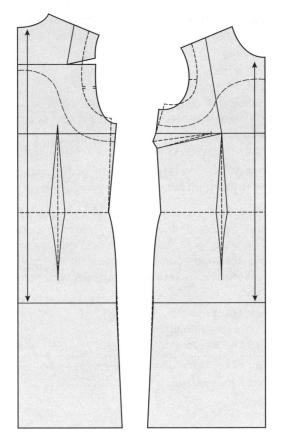

Working pattern

First Pattern Original or initial pattern developed for a design that includes seam and hem allowances.

Working Pattern Pattern in the revision stage of the process; work in progress.

Final Pattern Paper or digital pattern, consisting of individual garment sections, including trued seam lines, seam allowances, notches, grainlines, and pattern identification. A final pattern is used as the pattern for

• Physical muslin or virtual proof
• Cutting out a trial or sample garment

The final pattern is tested in muslin or fabric and corrected for the development of the sample or production pattern.

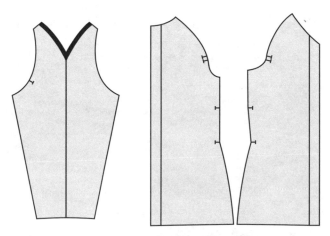

Final pattern without seam allowances

Pattern Card (Pattern Chart) Form containing information pertaining to a production pattern such as

- Style number
- Garment sketch
- Size range
- Color offerings
- Yardage needed for fabrics, lining, interfacing, and trims
- Size, amount, and description of findings
- List of all pattern pieces and number to be cut

The pattern card or chart is hung in front of the production pattern from a pattern hook.

Production Pattern Tag board or digital copy of the tested and perfected final pattern including specified seam allowances, perforations, notches, grainlines, and pattern identifications. Complete pattern set containing all of the pieces for a complete garment. Production patterns are used to

- Cut duplicate garments
- Grade sizes for size range
- Develop a marker for fabric layout

Production patterns include pattern pieces for both sides of the garment.

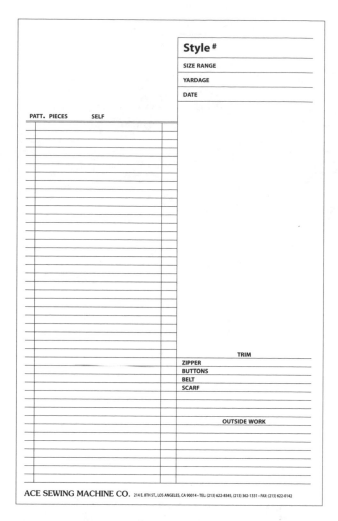

Pattern card/pattern chart

Production pattern

Graded Pattern Individual patterns of a particular garment or style proportioned to a set of standardized body measurements for each size within a range. Graded patterns are used to

- Cut duplicate samples
- Calculate yardage requirements
- Make a marker for fabric layout

A production pattern is increased and decreased to form graded patterns. Methods of grading differ according to the brand, garment type, and designated size range. Patterns are graded using specialized computer software for speed and accuracy. Some luxury brands create a new pattern for each size within the size range rather than grading, to ensure proper fit and proportion of garment components and design details on all sizes.

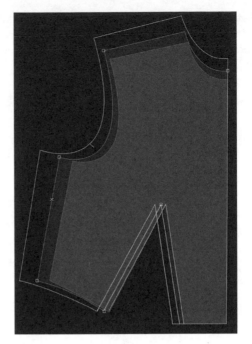

Graded pattern

PATTERN DEVELOPMENT

Patternmaking involves checking for interpretation of design and accurate fit, trueing, establishing *seam allowances*, and *marking* and identification. *Style ease*, which is part of the design, and *wearing ease* are built into the development of pattern pieces. Patternmakers or technical designers develop patterns through manual or digital methods of drafting, draping, or reverse engineering.

■ Drafting and Flat Pattern

Drafting or **flat pattern** design is manually or digitally manipulating the *block (sloper)* pattern or using designated measurements to achieve an original design. A set of blocks is drafted from measurements taken from a dress form, live model, or according to standardized or individual manufacturer's specifications. Using the block, pattern paper, and tools, the designer prepares a draft for translation into a final pattern.

Drafted Pattern Pattern developed through using measurements taken from the dress form or fit model from standardized or individual brand's specifications, created manually on a work table or directly on a computer using computer-aided design (CAD) software. This type of pattern is two-dimensional. Drafted patterns are used to

- Cut a test muslin
- Cut a sample garment

The pattern is developed through the *pivot method* or *cut and slash* or by a combination of both.

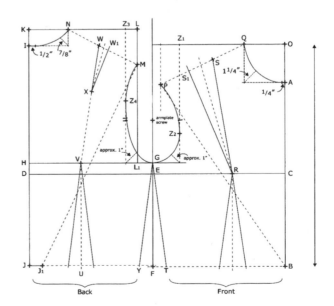

Drafted pattern

Flat Pattern Pattern developed through manipulation of drafted *blocks* manually on a work table or directly on a computer using CAD software. This type of pattern is two-dimensional. A flat pattern is used to

- Create a new style
- Cut a test muslin
- Cut a sample garment

The pattern is developed through the pivot method or cut and slash or by a combination of both.

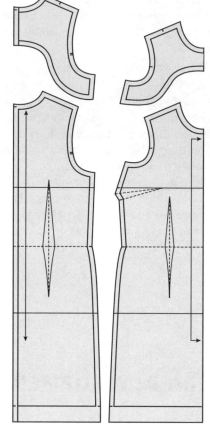

Flat pattern

Pivot Method (Pivot, Pivoting) Manual or digital rotation of the *block* or pattern, from a marked position toward a designated guide line during pattern development. The technique is part of the process of developing a new design or as an alternative to or in conjunction with the *slash and spread method* to manipulate the block. Pivoting is controlled from the *apex*, a perimeter point, or other designated point within the block.

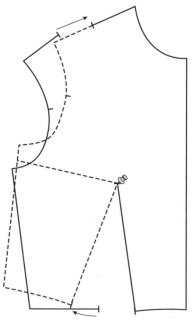

Pivot method

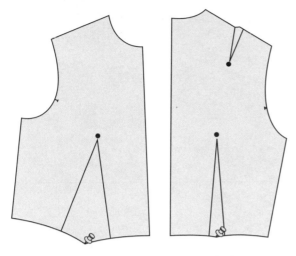

Pivot points on bodice patterns blocks

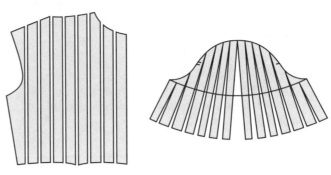

Slash and spread

Pivot Point Designated position on the *block* calculated to facilitate manipulation in the development of the desired design; predetermined by the design element of a garment section.

Slash and Spread Method for developing a new design or introducing fullness, by manually or digitally cutting or slicing a traced *block* along predetermined guide lines and opening or spreading apart the pieces to a designated measurement. The slash and spread method is an alternative to or used in conjunction with the pivot method to manipulate the block or pattern.

Apex of dart

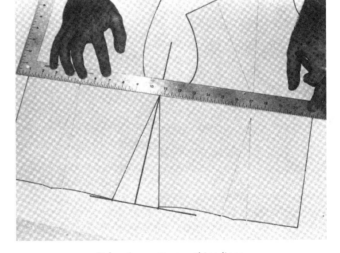

Balancing patternmaking lines

Apex of Dart Tapered point at the end of a dart. The apex of a dart is used

- As a pivot point on the block for rotation and for developing a new pattern
- To establish or foreshorten new darts

All front bodice darts converge towards the apex area. Temporary darts are planned towards the apex area, and princess lines are planned through the apex area.

Balance or Balancing Patternmaking Lines Process of matching or establishing grainlines or a common seam line on adjacent pattern sections. Balancing is used to

- True a pattern
- Shape seams of princess line or gored garments
- Shape side seams on skirts, pants, torso, and bodice
- Transfer common *grainlines* or guide lines

To maintain balance, the patternmaker extends or reduces common seam lines in equal amounts from the related guide, seam, or fitting lines.

Break Point Line Strategic markings or drawn lines placed on a pattern to indicate the point of change in the direction of a controlled turn, roll, or flare planned on the finished garment. Break point occurs on

- Shawl collars
- Two-piece notched collars
- Lapels and *revers* (turned back or reverse portion of a garment such as a facing of a lapel, collar, or cuff)
- Flares of gored skirts

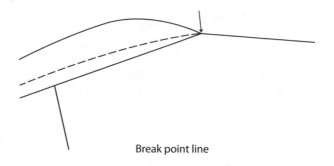

Break point line

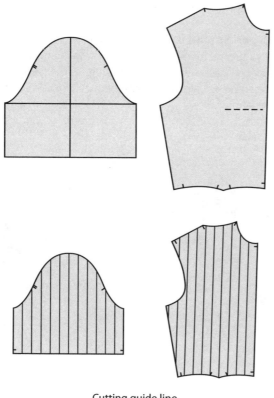

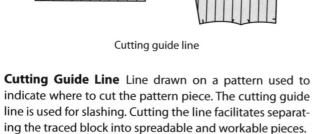

Cutting guide line

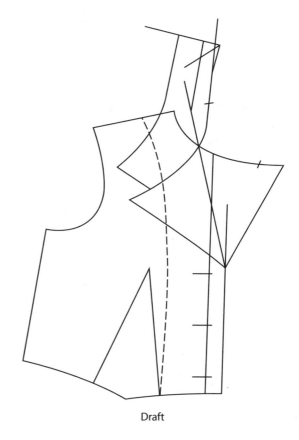

Draft

Cutting Guide Line Line drawn on a pattern used to indicate where to cut the pattern piece. The cutting guide line is used for slashing. Cutting the line facilitates separating the traced block into spreadable and workable pieces.

Draft Development of a pattern by measurements or through the pivot or slash and spread method, which includes all pertinent marks, lines, and information for completion of the final pattern. A draft is a base to establish style lines, roll lines, break points, and design features.

A draft does not include seam allowances.

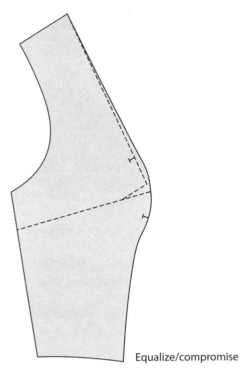

Equalize/compromise

Length grain

Cross grain

Grainline Indicator Arrows located on a straight line extending from edge to edge on a pattern piece to identify fabric grain. Arrows identify the line as the *grainline*. Grainline indicates how the garment will be cut, on *straight grain*, *bias*, or *cross-grain*. Grainline is indicated

- On draft, final, and production pattern pieces
- To determine placement of pattern piece on corresponding grain of fabric
- To align a pattern piece on corresponding fabric grain

The length of line is made with regard to the size of pattern piece. Grainline arrows on the pattern pieces are placed parallel to the selvage of the fabric.

Equalize (Compromise) To form a continuous line by correcting discrepancies in a seam or style line resulting from the pivot or slash and spread method of patternmaking. Equalizing is used to

- Preserve the symmetrical contour of a pattern line
- Eliminate irregularities while trueing corresponding seam or style lines of necklines; side seams of bodices, skirts, and pants; sleeve underarms; inseams of pants; midriffs and yokes

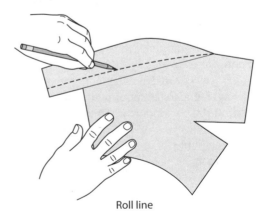

Roll line

Roll Line Where the exposed part of a collar or cuff turns toward the portion fastened to the neckline or sleeve of the garment. In patternmaking, it is designated by a drawn line.

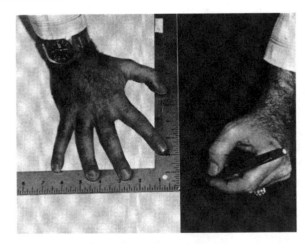

Squared line/right angle line

Squared Line (Right Angle Line) Line drawn perpendicular to another line or pattern fold. A squared line is used to establish

- Perpendicular line development of a *block*, or pattern draft
- Lower edge of a sleeve when developing sleeve variations from the block
- Crotch lines of pants

An L-square, T-square, or see-through ruler facilitates drawing squared lines.

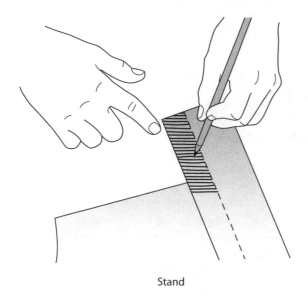

Stand

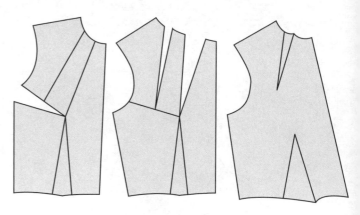

Temporary dart/working dart

Stand Collar area located close to the neck seam, which determines height and establishes roll of the collar. The stand may be planned for a portion of the collar front or back, or may be part of the entire collar.

Temporary Dart (Working Dart) Relocation of all or partial *dart pickup* (excess material taken in by a dart to fit a portion of a garment), placed at a right angle to the style detail being developed. Temporary darts are used to

- Develop a style featuring two or more parallel darts or dart substitutes
- Extend an area for gathers, tucks, or released tucks

In the process of developing a new style line or controlled fullness, a temporary dart is absorbed and is not part of the finished pattern.

■ Draping

Draping is manipulating cloth to conform to one or more curves of a dress form or fit model, in order to create a pattern. Draping allows a designer to visualize the garment as the pattern develops in three-dimensional form.

Using appropriate tools, designers select *muslin* or another appropriate fabric to prepare, pin, cut, and shape to achieve a garment pattern. When using CAD software to create a draped pattern on a virtual body, the designer inputs fabric specifications to digitally mimic how the material will drape in real life. Excess fabric may be absorbed or controlled by the use of darts, dart tucks, gathers, seams, or manipulation into flares. Once the pattern is draped, the designer transfers it to tag board to create a paper pattern or converts it into a two-dimensional digital pattern.

When a designer drapes, the length-grain of the fabric usually hangs vertically from the shoulder to the hem of a garment and from the shoulder to the hem of the sleeve. The length-grain allows fabric to fall subtly on the body. Cross-grain usually appears in the circumference of a garment. A garment designed on the bias molds when draped, allowing the fabric to skim or cling to the body.

Pattern pieces for symmetrical designs are developed representing only the right half of the garment and marked with bracketed symbols at the center front or center back to indicate a fold and alignment with the fabric's grainline.

Pattern pieces for asymmetrical and bias-cut designs are developed in their entirety and are marked with grainline symbols to indicate alignment with the grainline of the fabric.

Drape (Draping) *Cutting and blocking, pinning, slashing,* and *marking* of *muslin* or fabric to develop a pattern. This can be done manually on a dress form or digitally on a virtual body form.

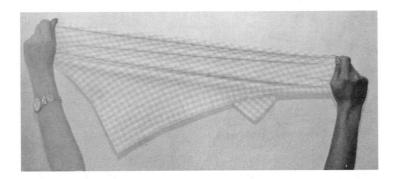

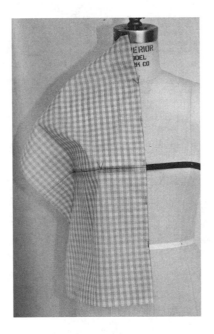

Cutting and Blocking—Preparation of a determined length and width of muslin or fabric to drape a garment section.

Slashing—Clipping of muslin or fabric toward the pinned perimeter of the area being draped to relieve fabric tension and facilitate subsequent draping procedure.

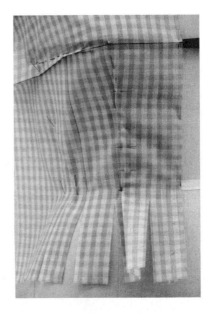

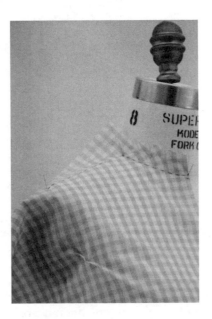

Pinning—Anchoring fabric to the dress form on structural guidelines and grainlines; the process of securing fabric while developing pattern shape, detail, and perimeter lines.

Marking—Recording, while the piece is on the dress form, the perimeter, intersecting lines, and pattern details in preparation for *trueing*. Marking is done by pencil or marker on muslin, or pins, *thread tracing* (marking using thread and a needle to stitch along a line), or chalk on fabric.

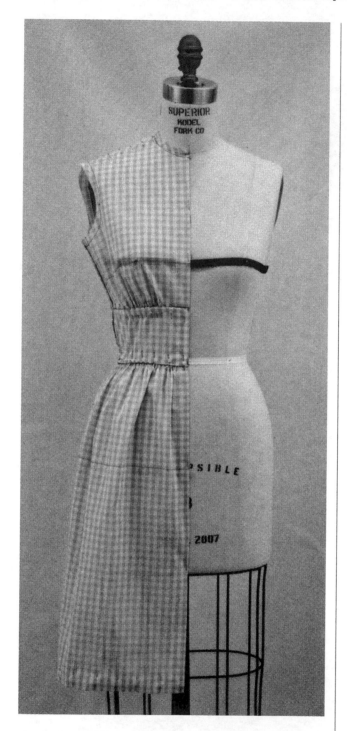

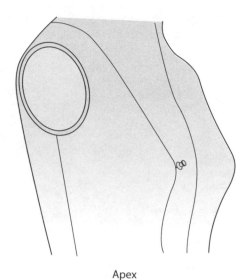

Apex

Apex Bust point; highest point on the bust on a dress form or fit model. The apex is used as a guide when establishing cross-grain position of a front bodice muslin.

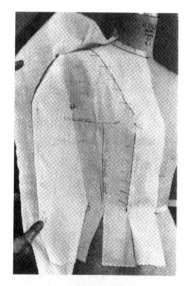

Balancing of a muslin

Draped Pattern Pattern developed by manipulating *muslin* or fabric on the model form or live model. Draped patterns are used when cutting a sample or test muslins. Patterns for knits are made of the same knit as the garment to ensure proper drape of the garment.

Balancing of a Muslin or Balance Matching the grains on adjacent pattern sections. Muslins are balanced

- To prepare sections, panels, or blocks for draping
- To match adjacent pattern sections and true a common seam

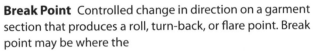

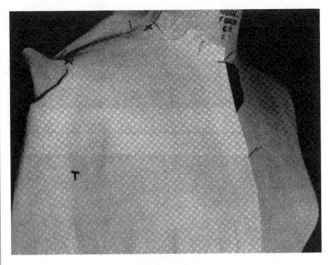

Cross marks

Break Point Controlled change in direction on a garment section that produces a roll, turn-back, or flare point. Break point may be where the

- Collar folds back to roll on the stand or garment
- Collar meets an extension
- Roll of the lapel folds back from the edge of the garment
- Seam begins to slope or flare outwardly on a gored skirt
- Flare starts to break away from the body to form a cone or to add fullness on a garment

Cross Marks Short lines indicating the intersection and juxtaposition of seam or style lines from the dress form to the muslin or fabric. Cross marks are used to

- Guide trueing of original seams, darts, and design lines
- Locate darts, dart tucks, and pleats or indicate position and extent of gathers
- Identify various garment parts such as front, back, or side
- Ensure matching of corresponding pattern sections such as sleeves, collars, cuffs, pockets, and yokes

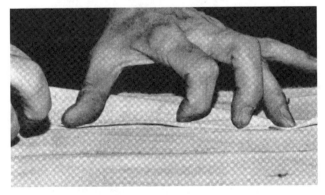

Crease

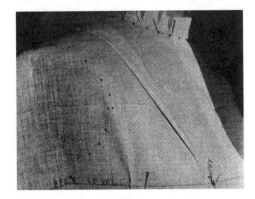

Dots

Crease Fold along a grain or structural line set by ironing or finger pressing. Creases are used

- To facilitate pinning muslin or fabric to a dress form
- To develop darts, dart tucks, or folds
- Along a seam or design detail to facilitate joining of seam lines or darts

Dots Marks made with a pencil, marker, or chalk on draped muslin fabric to record perimeter seam lines, style lines, and design details. Dots are used as a guide for trueing. A pin line or nonmarring chalk is used in place of dots when draping with fabric.

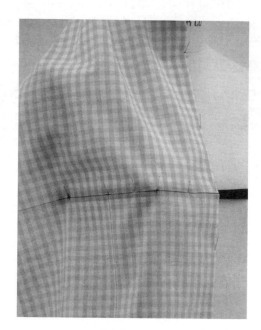

Fabric excess

Fabric Excess Fabric manipulated into darts, or formed into tucks or gathers, to conform to body shape and garment styling.

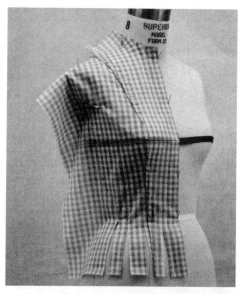

Fabric fold

Fabric Fold Fabric ply doubled back on itself along a creased edge forming an underlay. The fabric fold is used to

- *Drape pleats*, *flange darts*, *dart tucks*, extensions, or self facings
- Pin or join seam or dart lines

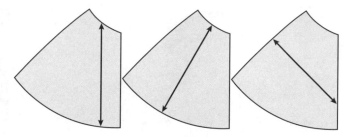

Grainline markings on muslin

Grainline Markings on Muslin Lines drawn on the length and cross-grains of muslin to indicate grain direction and guidelines for the finished pattern. Placement of grainline on the pattern affects how fabric will drape in the finished garment. Grainline markings are used to

- Facilitate development of original muslin patterns
- Align a pattern on corresponding fabric grain when planning a layout
- Indicate when grain transferring muslin onto a paper pattern, or block (sloper)

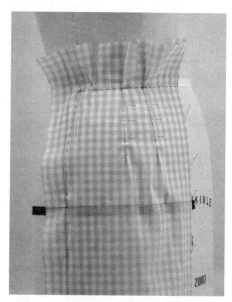

Guidelines on muslin

Guidelines on Muslin Lines drawn on the prepared muslin to facilitate draping. Guidelines are used to

- Indicate level apex, hiplines, shoulder blades, sleeve biceps, and sleeve elbow, as well as center of darts
- Control grain placement
- Indicate center front, center back, extensions, and *fold lines*
- Indicate side seams when developing side seams of a basic skirt, pants, shift, and torso

Panel A determined measure of muslin or fabric planned for developing a design that features vertical style lines. Panels are used to produce a multiseamed or gored garment.

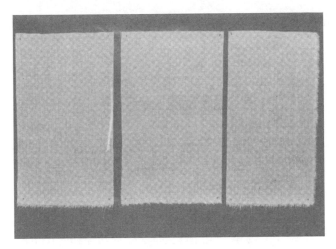

Panel

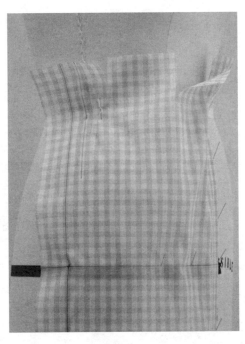

Slash

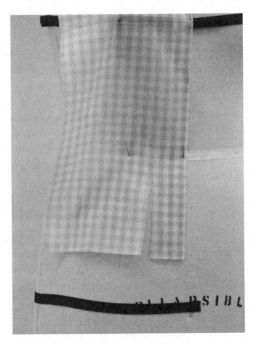

Slash for design detail

Slash Cut or cuts made on muslin or fabric, from the perimeter toward the style or seam line, while draping on the dress form or live fit model. A slash is used to relieve tension in muslin or fabric draped around curves or to fit a body contour.

Slash for Design Detail Straight cut, from a free edge to a designated point, in the body of a draped muslin or fabric garment section. A slash can be used to

- Produce sharp corners
- Allow insertion of a gusset or godet
- Prepare placement of placket
- Open excess or fold of a dart, allowing the garment section to conform to a body contour
- Drape dart slash design details

■ Digital Patternmaking

Patternmakers can use specialized **vector-based** CAD software to create patterns directly on the computer using drafting and flat pattern techniques or draping methods on a virtual figure. Vector-based software uses **paths** to define lines with start and end points rather than pixels to form shapes. Paths can be straight or curved, circles or ovals, squares or rectangles, or polygon shapes that are used to create garment patterns. This technology increases accuracy and reduces the amount of time it takes to create or modify a pattern and to grade it into the designated sizes.

Two-dimensional garment patterns can easily be translated into three-dimensional virtual prototypes using specialized CAD software. The ability to view a prototype on a virtual body reduces the number of samples needed to perfect the garment style, therefore reducing time and resources.

Digital Pattern Two-dimensional pattern created with specialized CAD software, from drafting or flat pattern techniques or draping on a virtual figure. Digital patterns are used to create

- Block patterns
- New styles
- Virtual prototypes

When existing digital patterns are modified, the seam allowances and grading files are automatically updated.

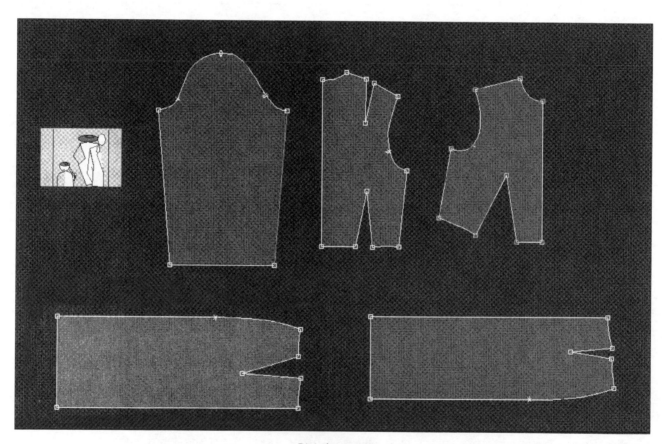

Digital pattern

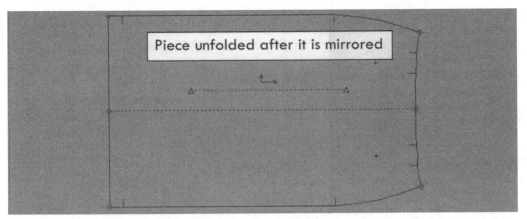

Fold CAD function that allows designers to view a pattern piece folded at center front or center back. The software automatically adjusts any modifications made on both sides of the pattern piece to maintain symmetry.

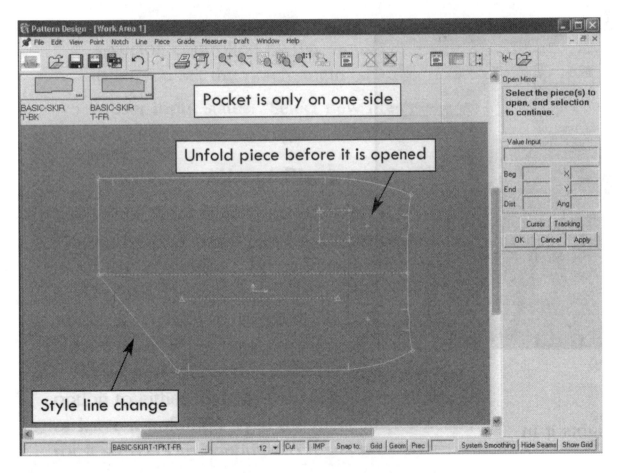

Unfold CAD function that allows designers to view a pattern piece unfolded at the center front or center back, in order to check the shape and contour of seam lines. This function is used for

- Necklines
- Hemlines
- Waistbands
- Yokes

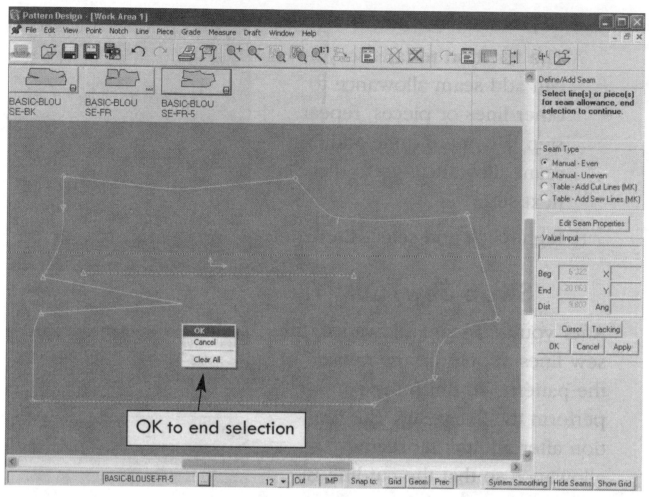

Line segment

Line Segment Line created in CAD by the placement of points; a beginning point and ending point may have points in between. Line segments can be straight or curved.

Merge or Join CAD function that joins lines or points together.

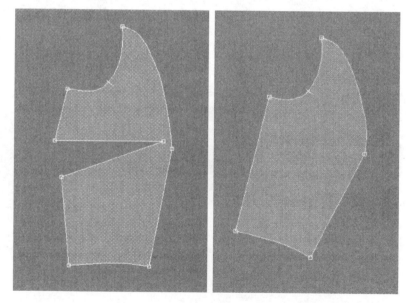

Merge or join

Mirror CAD function that generates a duplicate reverse of a pattern piece to create one symmetric piece. Mirroring helps maintain symmetry on both sides of the pattern piece. The mirror function may be used on the center front or center back of a pattern or another area where symmetry is desired.

Points Dots used to create line segments in vector-based CAD software programs.

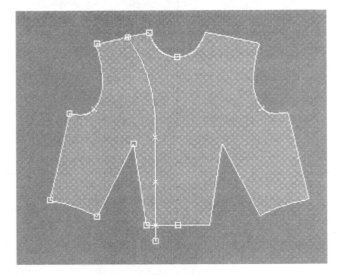

Mirroring

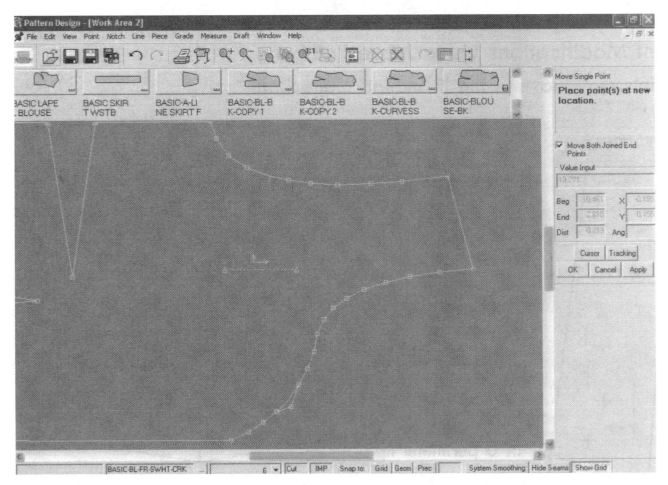

Points

Plot Pattern pieces sent to a plotter for printing.

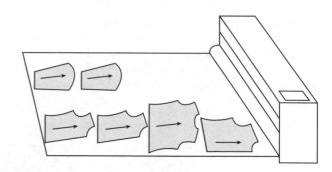

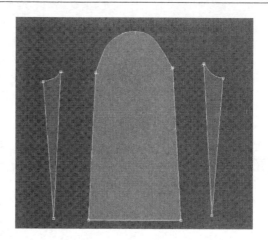

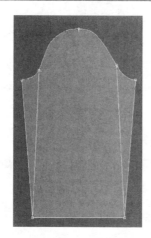

Split CAD function that separates a line into two or more segments.

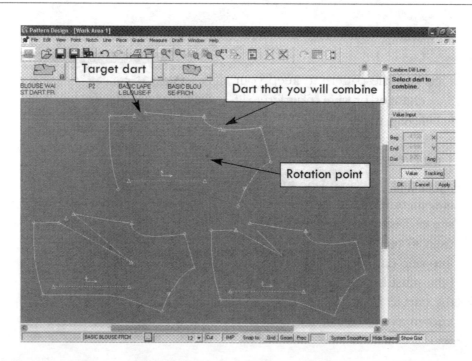

Rotation Point Designated position on the digital block calculated to facilitate manipulation in design development, which is predetermined by the design element of a garment section. It is equivalent to the pivot point in manual pattern drafting and flat pattern. A rotation point may occur at the apex, on the perimeter, or from a given point within the block.

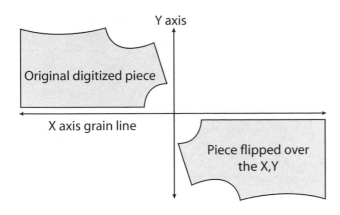

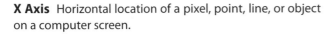

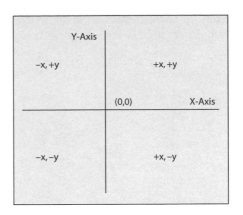

X Axis Horizontal location of a pixel, point, line, or object on a computer screen.

Y Axis Vertical location of a pixel, point, line, or object on a computer screen.

■ Reverse Engineering

A patternmaking process that begins with a finished product; the garment is deconstructed to reveal the pieces used to create the item. These pieces are used to create a pattern.

Reverse Engineered Pattern Paper or digital pattern of an existing garment design. This method is commonly used for creating knock-offs.

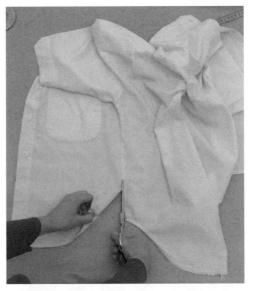

Deconstruct To take apart; to remove the stitching and seams that hold all the garment components together.

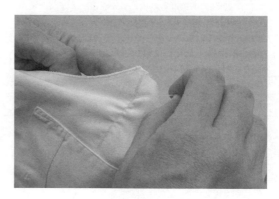

Deconstruct

GENERAL PATTERNMAKING TERMS AND MARKINGS

Terms that concern establishing and identifying style features, garment sections, seam lines, and seam allowances apply to various patternmaking methods. **Markings** are construction symbols transferred from the pattern to the garment section after cutting. These symbols can be made on the face, inside, or through (when using thread for marking). Markings or tracings indicate the position of points of construction, design detail, grainlines, and center lines. Pattern markings on fabric are guides for various means of fitting and sewing. The method of tracings and transfer markings selected depends on

- Fabric type and weight
- Fabric color
- Placement of marking

- Method of construction
- Methods of fitting
- Methods of production

Blend or Blending To round, shape, and smooth angular lines to create a continuous seam; matching corresponding style and seam lines. Blending is used

- On seams of sleeves, armholes, princess lines, waist-lines, gored skirts, fitted or contoured side seams, and fitted or contoured darts
- To equalize discrepancies of marks or lines made on a muslin or pattern draft

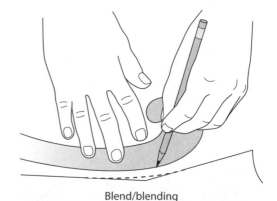

Blend/blending

Chalked Marking Marking one or two fabric plies on the seam, style, or detail lines with tailor's chalk or wax or a marking pencil over a pin or pins positioned in the fabric. Chalked marking is used

- On the face of fabric for marking details such as pockets, trimmings, and pleats
- To mark bonded or laminated fabrics
- When draping directly with fabric

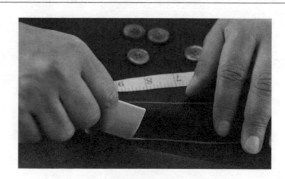

Chalk marking

Color Coding System for Patternmaking Predetermined colors to mark pattern pieces to distinguish which pieces will be cut from fabrics other than the *self fabric* for the garment or component. A standard color coding system identifies the following colors and use:

- Pencil or black ink to identify self fabric
- Blue, brown, purple, and pink to identify contrasting fabric used in addition to self fabric
- Red to identify lining fabric
- Green to identify interfacing

Some manufacturers have their own color coding systems for labeling patterns.

Converge Lines on a muslin or pattern from a given point of calculated measurement that end at a juncture to form a point or points, shaped seam line, or roll line.

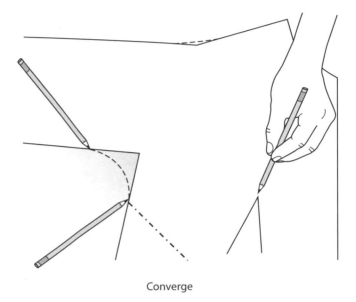

Converge

Cupping To roll or fold a pattern section so the portion being trued or pinned lies flat. Cupping is used to allow corresponding lines to conform without distortion.

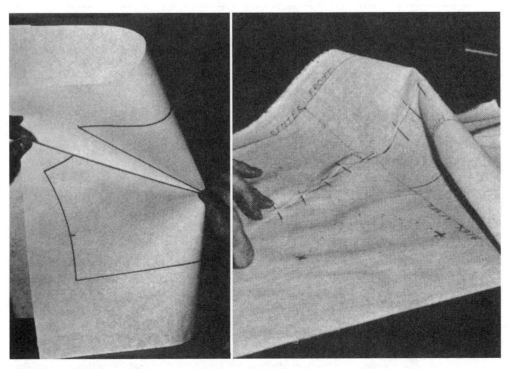

Cupping

Dart Manipulation Establishing dart placement from a variety of dart positions; from a basic one- or two-dart concept to a creative design.

Dart Substitution (Dart Variation) Manipulating and distributing dart pickup from one or two darts into a flange dart, dart tucks, tucks, release tucks, gathers, seams, or flares.

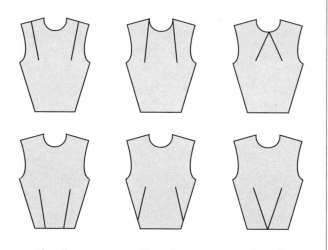

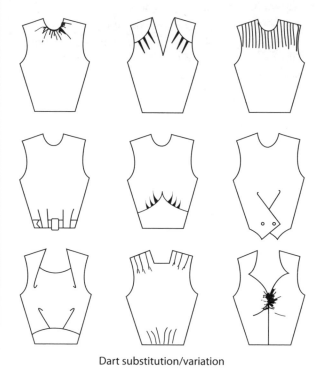

Dart manipulation

Dart substitution/variation

Fold Line Design line formed on a drafted pattern or muslin to indicate a fold. The fold line is used on the finished pattern section to indicate a creased edge, which forms a *pleat*, *dart*, *dart flange*, *dart tuck*, extension, or *self facing*, or to indicate self facing or self hem.

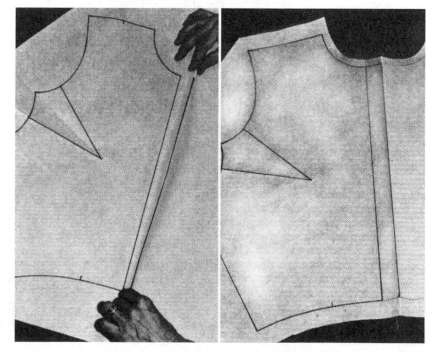

Fold line

Garment Section Portion of a garment delineated by a seam or style lines forming a pattern piece; identified as front and back bodice, front and back skirt, yoke, midriff, princess panel, band and insert, sleeve, collar, and pocket.

Jacket

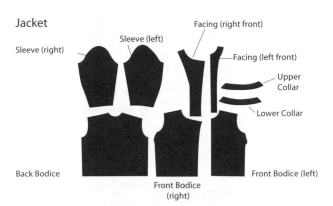

Dress

Garment section

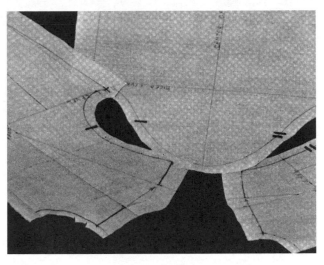

Notches

Notch or Notches Mark or set of marks placed on the perimeter of a block (sloper), or across a seam line on the muslin, paper, or digital pattern; a cut in the edge of a pattern or piece of a garment to mark seam allowances, hem allowances, center lines, darts, pleats, tucks, placement of a zipper, waistline, and adjoining pattern or garment pieces to be matched and sewn together. Notches are used

- On patterns to ensure the garment seams and sections will be placed in proper alignment
- Singly or in groups as an aid to identify various garment parts such as the front, back, and sides
- To position *darts*, *tucks*, *gathers*, and other design features
- To indicate position and extent of *ease*, gathers, *ruching*, *French shirring*, or *smocking*
- To match corresponding pattern areas such as sleeves, collars, cuffs, pockets, and yokes
- To fit a larger drawn-in section to a smaller corresponding one

Pattern Identification Words, numbers, and symbols placed on individual sections of the final pattern. Used to identify

- Pattern piece
- Pattern size and style number
- Number of pattern pieces to cut out of fabric, interlining, or interfacing
- Quantity of individual pattern pieces required to complete the garment

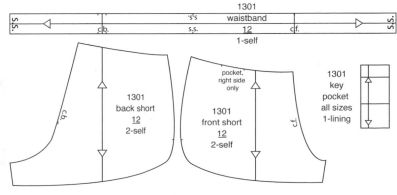

Pattern identification

Punch Holes (Circles) Small circles on patterns or holes made in fabric to mark

- Dart points
- Curved darts
- Pocket placement
- Where to end stitching for stitched pleats

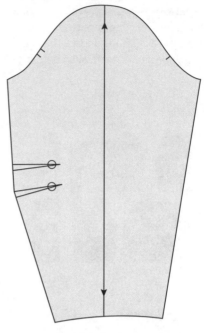

Punch holes/circles

Seam Allowance Portion extending a specified amount from the seam line to the edge of the pattern. Seam allowances vary according to

- Development of the first pattern, muslin, final, or production pattern
- Seam position and type
- Fabric type and weave
- Garment type and purpose
- Specifications
- Garment intended price point

Seam allowance is also the distance from the seam stitching to the edge of the fabric. Basic seam allowances include

- ¼ inch for curved seams at necklines, sleeveless armholes, facings, extreme curved seams, and enclosed seams
- ½ inch for center seams, side seams, waistlines, and style lines
- ¾ to 1 inch for seams with zippers, hems for shirts, full skirts, and jeans
- 1½ to 2 inches for hems on skirts, jackets, trousers

Seam allowances on draped patterns and test muslins are planned wider for straight and nearly straight seams, and narrow for curved seams and small details.

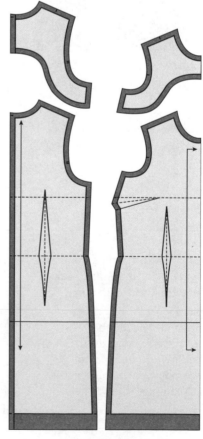

Seam allowance

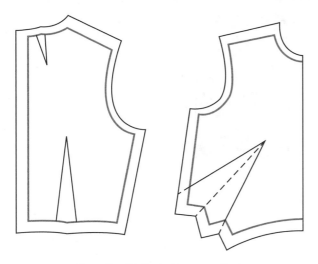

Seam line (indicated by green line)

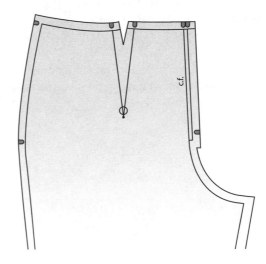

Jog seam

Seam Line Line established on a pattern, indicating where garment sections are joined. A seam line designates the functional or decorative stitching of two or more garment parts. Seam lines may be marked by chalk, pencil, or wax or left unmarked.

Jog Seam Change in the width of a seam allowance on a pattern or garment. A jog seam is used on seams with a zipper, vent, or slit.

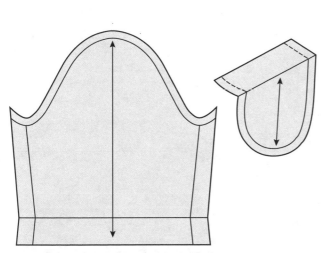

Directional seam line

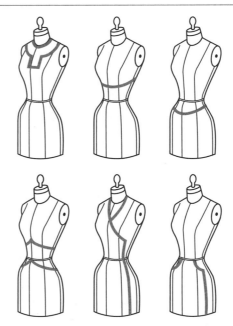

Style line

Directional Seam Line Portion of a seam allowance or hem that when folded back is traced to correspond to the shape or angle of the pattern piece or section. A directional seam line is used to

- Prevent distortion of a turned seam when joined to corresponding garment section
- Allow the turned-up hem to fit the circumference of the garment section

Style Line A delineation representing a design line, seam line, or finished edge. Style lines are indicated

- By line on the pattern draft
- With style tape on a dress form
- With markings on muslin or fabric pattern during or after draping

Sweep Circumference measurement of a garment's hem edge. The sweep is used to describe the circumference of a

- Finished garment
- Hem edge of a finished pattern or garment sections such as upper and lower torso garments, and sleeves

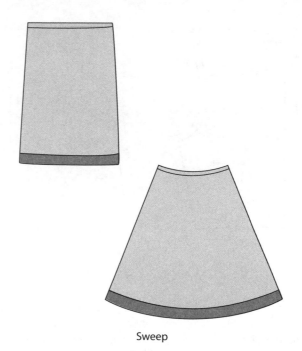

Sweep

Transferring To trace a trued seam line or detail marking to another ply of muslin, fabric, or paper. Transferring is used to

- Balance grain
- Duplicate the shape of the pattern section or outline

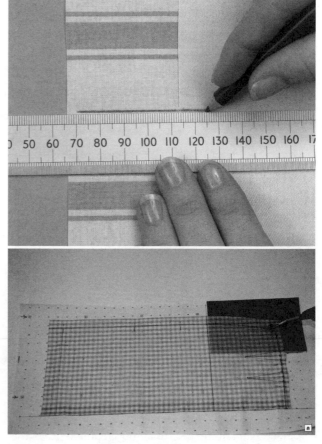

Transferring

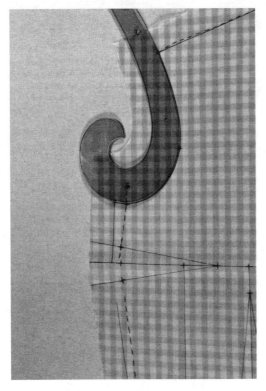

Trueing

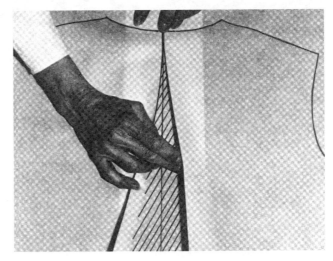

Underlay

Underlay Pattern portion constituting the inside or underside of the design or fold line or dart pickup. Formed when establishing

- Darts, dart tucks, and flange darts
- Pleats
- Closures and extensions
- Fold back of a seam, directional seam, or hem

Trueing Establishing corrected seams or style lines by blending markings, dots, or cross marks made during pattern development. Trueing is used to

- Establish continuous seam or style lines
- Establish darts, dart variations, and dart substitutions
- Equalize pattern discrepancies

Verifying the form

Verifying the Form Aligning and balancing the shoulder-side seam relationship on a dress form. A dress form is verified

- Prior to draping or measuring the dress form for pattern development
- To find correct placement of lower torso, shoulder, and underarm side seams
- To ensure proper drape of muslin or fabric

Alignment may necessitate changing the shoulder or underarm seam by establishing new working lines.

CHAPTER 16

Patternmaking Tools

Pattern development and garment construction processes require marking tools and equipment. These tools vary depending on the patternmaking method used, such as drafting, draping, reverse engineering, or digital pattern drafting.

Patternmakers use drafting and flat-pattern tools to manually develop a *block* (sloper) from measurements and to create patterns from a block. Each tool or piece of equipment serves as a basis for line placement or line transfer, and each suits a particular situation. A combination of two or more tools may help simplify and accomplish the desired results. Patternmakers select tools and equipment for drafting and draping, measuring, and marking with consideration for

- Use and efficiency
- Type of line or curve desired
- Placement of a line or curve
- Method required for truing or transferring

Awl Metal rod tapering to a needle point, approximately ⅛ inch (3.2 mm) in diameter by 3 to 8 inches (8 to 20 cm) in length, with a wooden or plastic handle. Typical uses include

- Punching dart ends on blocks or patterns
- Marking placement of pockets, trimmings, or bands on patterns
- Marking punch-hole placement in fabric

Awls

Circle Template Plastic or metal stencil with round die-cut holes. Diameters range in size from ¹⁄₁₆ inch to 2 inches plus corner radii in inches (and millimeters). Typical uses include

- Drawing placement and spacing of buttons and snaps on patterns
- Indicating placement of circular trimming, appliqué, embroidery, screen printing, or design on fabric or a garment pattern

The size, arrangement, and template shapes vary with each manufacturer and intended use. Templates are also available in other shapes such as squares, rectangles, ovals, and triangles.

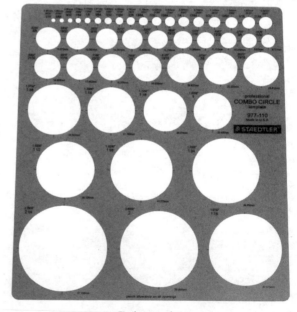

Circle template

Compass Instrument consisting of two arms, one sharply pointed and the other equipped with a drawing tip, joined at the top by a pivot or center wheel to provide adjustable measurement. Typical uses include

- Measuring spacing between buttons or buttonholes
- Establishing parallel style and seam lines
- Duplicating curves such as scallops, cascades, loops, and flounces
- Duplicating circles for patterns of embroidery and placement of trimming or beading
- Drawing curves or circles

Some compasses have two sharply pointed tips.

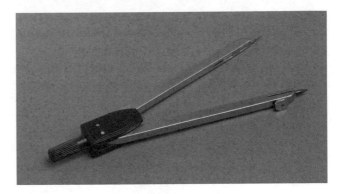

Compass

Combination Ruler and Curve All-in-one, clear plastic straight-edged ruler, hip curve, and armhole curve. A slot parallel to the straight edge is helpful to form parallel lines or for control when tracing seam lines (the wheel is inserted into the slot). Typical uses include

- Measuring straight lines
- Establishing, marking, and trueing darts, seam lines, necklines, and armhole curves, and around gently curved areas such as yokes, waistlines, hiplines, and princess lines
- Establishing lines of shaped bodices
- Forming or drawing scallops and stylized lines

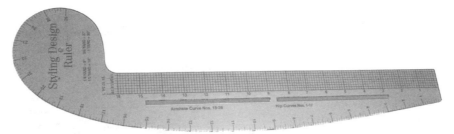

Combination ruler and curve

Curve Stick Metal curved 24-inch ruler marked in inches or centimeters and fractional segments. Typical uses include

- Establishing and trueing curves for lapels, elbows, hiplines, and wherever a special contour is desired
- Establishing and blending waistline and hipline contours on skirt, dress, pant, and trouser patterns

- Establishing and trueing curved seams and style lines
- Shaping seam lines to establish flares on gored garment pattern panels
- Trueing shaped and contoured darts

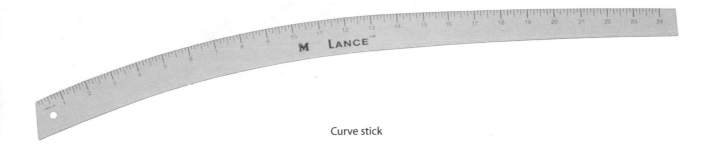

Curve stick

Vary Form Curve Metal ruler with a curved end marked in inches or centimeters and fractional segments. Typical uses include

- Establishing and blending waistline and hipline contours on skirt, dress, pant, and trouser patterns
- Establishing and trueing variable curves of seams on a pattern such as necklines, lapels, yokes, armholes, elbows, waistlines, princess lines, hems, and style lines

- Shaping seam lines to establish flares on gored garment pattern panels
- Trueing shaped and contoured darts
- Trueing hemlines of curved, flared, or circular garment patterns
- Forming and altering sleeve caps

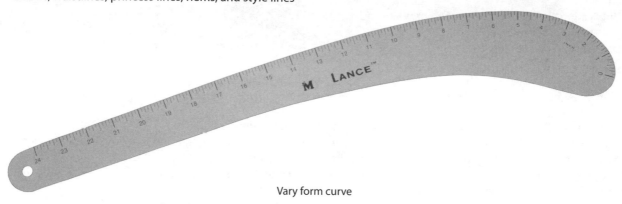

Vary form curve

Dietzgen # 17 Curve Plastic guide, 10 inches in length (25.4 cm), with a edge spiral curve. Typical uses include

- Drawing curves of lapels and crotch seams
- Establishing and trueing shaped and contoured darts and variable curves of pattern seams
- Shaping and trueing edges of necklines and armscyes
- Developing the cap and rounded sleeve seams of sleeves

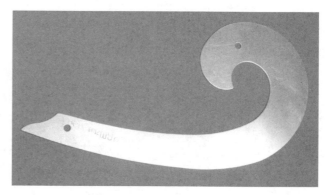

Dietzgen # 17 curve

French Curve Clear plastic template having a variety of curved edges. These are available in a variety of shapes and sizes such as 6¾-, 12½-, 13-, 15½-, 24-inch lengths. Typical uses include

- Shaping and trueing edges of curved darts, collars, necklines, and armscyes
- Establishing crotch curved lines
- Forming lines of lapels, pockets, collars, and cuffs
- Forming body contour lines of skirts and slacks
- Establishing and trueing variable curves of pattern seams such as necklines, armholes, elbows, waistlines, and princess lines
- Developing cap and rounded sleeve seams

French curves

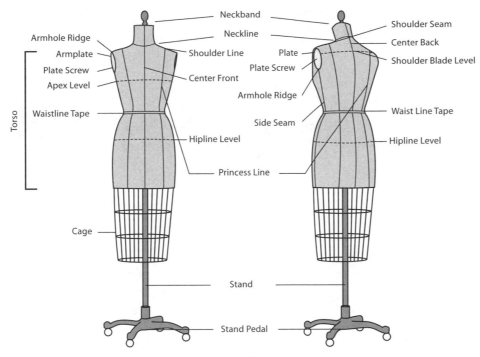

Parts of dress forms front and back

Labels (front form): Neckband, Neckline, Armhole Ridge, Armplate, Shoulder Line, Plate Screw, Center Front, Apex Level, Waistline Tape, Hipline Level, Princess Line, Torso, Cage, Stand, Stand Pedal

Labels (back form): Shoulder Seam, Center Back, Plate, Shoulder Blade Level, Plate Screw, Armhole Ridge, Side Seam, Waist Line Tape, Hipline Level

Dress Form (Body Form or Model Form) Standardized representation of a human form, from the neck to torso or neck to ankle, padded with cotton and covered in canvas, set on a moveable, height-adjustable stand. Typical uses include

- Measuring and establishing the block
- Developing original patterns
- Developing garments from draping fabric
- Fitting sample garments
- Altering garments
- Establishing garments hemlines

Dress forms are available in a range of standard sizes in men's, women's, children's, and infants, and in height and figure types petite, tall, half sizes, and maternity. Companies can customize forms according to measurements of a particular size and figure type for a product line or brand.

The dress form is designed and shaped according to the type and category of garment:

- Standard form with straight skirt or neck to ankle
- Slacks form 4 inches above the waist to ankle
- Brassiere and panty forms
- Swimsuit form
- Strapless or evening forms available in neck to knee or neck to ankle with more defined bust and shaped buttocks

Forms are created for the current idealized fashion figure and are replaced when brands and manufacturers change their sizing. Dress form features can include collapsible shoulders, removable shoulder caps, arm forms, straight skirt or shaped buttocks, or more defined bust.

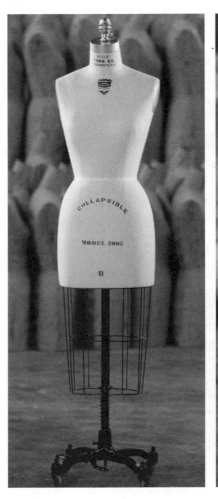

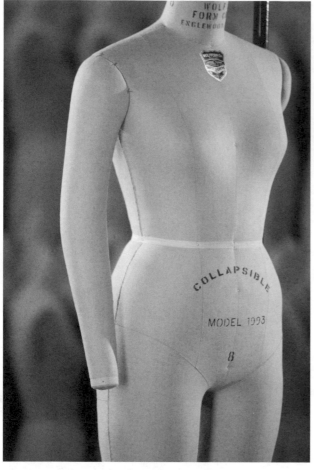

Arm form

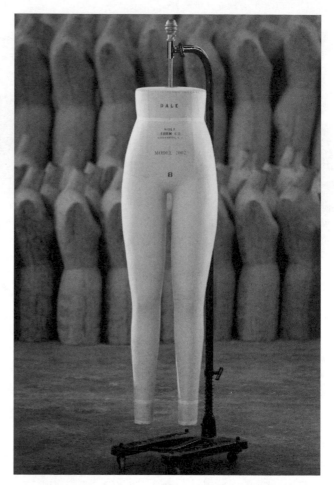

Leg form

Arm Form Removable cotton, padded, canvas-covered representation of the human arm, from shoulder to extended wrist, made to attach to a dress form. Typical uses include

- Draping sleeves
- Developing dropped-shoulder or off-the-shoulder styles
- Draping capes

Leg Form Cotton padded canvas-covered representation of the human body form from about 4 inches above the waist to the ankle. Typical uses include

- Measuring and establishing a pant block
- Developing original or first patterns
- Developing garments draped from fabric
- Fitting and altering sample garments
- Establishing garment hemlines

Shoulder Cap Permanent or removable cotton, padded, canvas-covered simulation of upper arm to assist in fitting fullness and armscye ease of a pattern or garment.

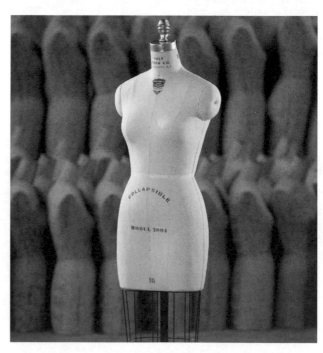

Shoulder cap

Style Tape Smooth, narrow adhesive tape in red or black, available in ⅛-inch widths. Typical uses include

- Delineating style lines on the dress form or muslin while draping
- Holding or controlling excess fabric while establishing gathers or fullness

Twill tape or a narrow flat ribbon can also work.

Style tape

Long-Reach Stapler Stapler with a 12-inch reach for stapling patterns. It takes standard 210 staples.

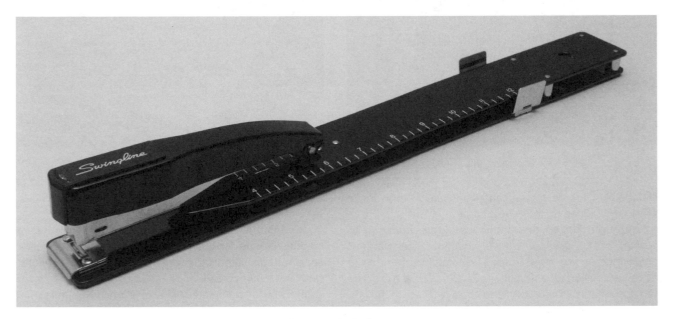

Long-reach stapler

Notcher Punching tool for producing U-shaped notches ¼ inch deep by ¹⁄₁₆ inch wide. Typical uses include marking items on patterns such as

- Seams allowance
- Dart legs
- Center front and center back
- Hem allowance
- Pleats, gathers, and tucks

Singly or in groups, notching can identify various parts of the garment, such as the front, back, and sides.

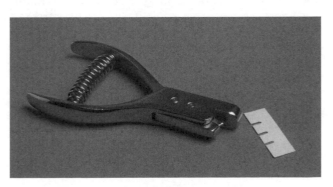

Notcher

Soft muslin

Medium muslin

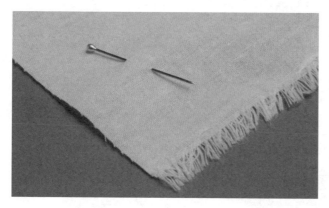

Coarse muslin

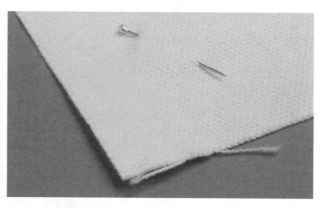

Canvas muslin

Muslin A 100-percent cotton plain-weave fabric made from unbleached or bleached carded yarns that vary in weight, from fine to heavy, and in texture, from soft to coarse. With muslin, designers drape original patterns or designs on the dress form and experiment with and develop a design idea. Quality and hand of muslin are chosen according to the texture and characteristics of the fabric planned for the garment.

Soft Muslin—Simulates draping quality of natural and synthetic silk, woven, and fine cotton fabrics.
Medium Muslin—Simulates draping quality of wool and medium-weight cotton.
Coarse Muslin—Simulates draping quality of heavyweight wool and heavy cotton.
Canvas Muslin—Simulates draping of heavyweight fabric, fur, and imitation-fur garments.

Marker Paper (Guide Marking Paper or Dotted Marking Paper) White paper marked with a grid pattern of dots or letters and numbers at 1-inch intervals with yard markings, available in 45-, 60-, and 66-inch widths and 500-foot rolls. The most common use is for creating paper markers for cutting samples or for production.

Marker paper

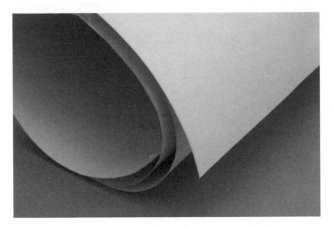

Tag board

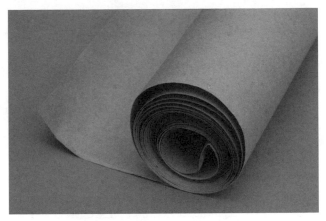

Pattern paper

Tag Board (Oak Tag or Manila Paper) Strong, firm, pliable paper that is lighter than cardboard. Typical uses include making

- Blocks or production patterns
- Templates and guides
- Patterns for pleating fabric

Tag board is available in 48-inch widths on 120- to 150-yard rolls.

Pattern Paper (Kraft Paper or Brown Paper) Strong paper, in white or brown, available in a variety of weights on rolls 45 and 60 inches wide. Typical uses include

- Drafting a pattern
- Developing production patterns
- Covering work tables and floors under dress forms to provide a clean, smooth work surface and to prevent garments and fabrics from soiling

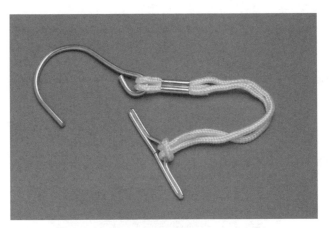

Pattern hook

Pattern punch

Pattern Hook Braided nylon 10-inch cord with a hook affixed to one end and a T-bar at the other. Typical uses include hanging

- Blocks
- Sets of block patterns for filing
- Production patterns

Pattern Punch Metal hand tool with a lever and a ¾-inch-diameter circular die cutter. Patternmakers use these tools to make a hole in a pattern to facilitate hanging and storing.

Pattern Shears Heavy-duty scissors with an extra long shank for cutting tag board and heavy materials.

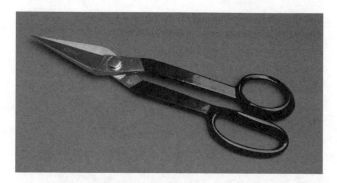

Pattern shears

Bent-Handle Dressmaker's Shears Cutting instrument with offset blades, one with a sharp point, the other rounded or at a blunt angle. The offset lower blade rests flat on the cutting surface. Blades are joined by an adjustable bolt or screw and designed with equally sized ring handles. Shears range from 7 to 10 inches (18 to 25.4 cm) long. The bent handle helps prevent work from lifting away from the cutting surface. Typical uses include cutting

- Fabrics, skins, paper, and pattern paper
- Drafted patterns
- Sample garments
- Muslin for draped patterns

Bent-handle dressmaker's shears

Push Pin Thumb tack with a ½-inch point and a plastic or aluminum drum-shaped head. Typical uses include

- Holding oak tag block or pattern pieces on a pattern work table with a self-healing cork surface
- Holding pivot points of a pattern in place when designing
- Transferring style lines and draped muslin to a paper pattern

Push pins

Center-Finding Ruler Metal, wooden, or plastic ruler marked in inches and fractional segments, with the zero point at the center and numbers increasing toward both ends of the rule. Typical uses include

- Measuring from the center to either edge
- Determining placement of buttons and buttonholes, multiple fasteners, appliqué, trimming, and inserts, pockets and cuffs, and fasteners on double-breasted garments
- Finding centers of darts, pleats, and cuffs

Center-finding ruler

Clear Plastic Grid Ruler A 1- or 2-inch-wide, clear plastic straightedge imprinted with a grid in inches or centimeters and fractional segments in the length and width directions; available in 6-, 12-, or 18-inch lengths. (C-Thru is a popular brand.) Typical uses include

- Establishing grainlines and seam allowances on patterns
- Marking style lines and parallel lines of seams and such details as pleats and tucks
- Establishing and marking the position of buttonholes and set-in pockets
- Establishing, marking, or measuring bias strips
- Measuring small garment sections

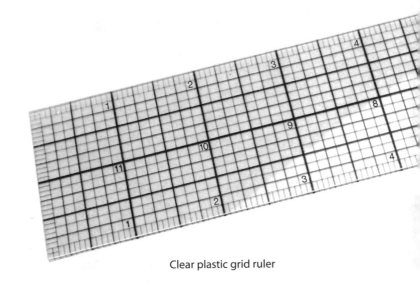

Clear plastic grid ruler

See-Through Ruler Clear plastic 15-inch (38 cm) ruler with cutout slots at 1, ¼, ½, ⅝, and ¾ inch (2.54, .63, 1.27, 1.59, and 1.90 cm). Slots help the patternmaker control the tracing wheel when outlining seam lines and drawing parallel lines. The transparent plastic allows for an unhampered view of the object. Typical uses include

- Marking seam allowances on patterns
- Locating grainlines on muslins, patterns, or fabrics
- Marking or adjusting lines on muslin or paper patterns
- Establishing and marking bias strips
- Measuring and marking tucks or pleats, and establishing and marking buttonhole and button placement on patterns

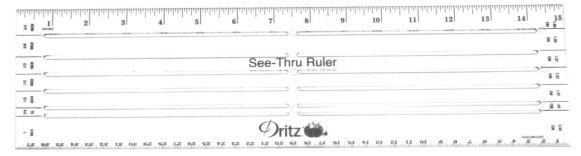

See-through ruler

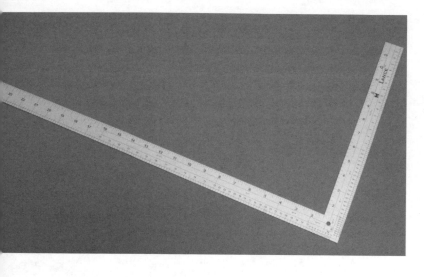

L Square (Tailor's Square) Metal, wooden, or plastic rule having two extensions of different lengths meeting at a right angle; marked in inches or centimeters and fractional segments. Typical uses include

- Drafting block patterns from measurements and establishing length and grainlines on muslin, block, or pattern
- Squaring off corners of muslin, block, or pattern sections in order to continue subsequent operations of pattern development
- Establishing perpendicular lines, reference points, and levels for pattern development
- Measuring crotch depth on a pants model form or fit model and establishing crotch depth and length for muslin or drafted pattern development
- Preparing muslin or fabric for draping

Scaled to include inch and millimeter segments: 1/32 inch (0.8 mm), 1/16 inch (1.6mm), 1/8 inch (3.2 mm), 1/4 inch (6.4 mm), 1/2 inch (12.7 mm), 1/12 inch (2.1 mm), 3/16 inch (4.2 mm), and 1/3 inch (8.5 mm).

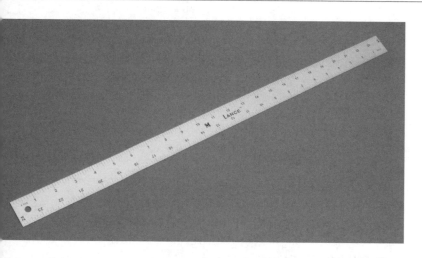

Straight Rule Straight metal ruler available in 12-, 24-, 36-, 48-, and 72-inch lengths, marked in inches and centimeters and fractional segments. Typical uses include

- Measuring and marking straight lines and seam allowances on patterns
- Measuring fabric yardage
- Checking and establishing garment lengths on a dress form or live model from the floor
- Marking placement of trimmings
- Establishing placement of grainlines from pattern to muslin and checking grainlines when laying out a pattern

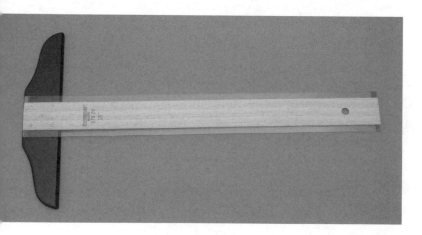

T-Square Straight-edged rule having a short crossbar centered and fixed perpendicularly at one end of a long bar. Inches, centimeters, and fractional segments are indicated on the long bar or on both bars. A typical use is locating grainlines and trued intersecting grainlines on patterns, blocks, or fabrics. T-squares are available in metal or clear plastic.

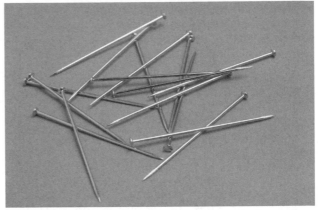

Screw Punch Small wooden-handled hole punch with a screw and mechanism to fit a variety of steel bit sizes: 5/64 inch (2 mm), 3/32 inch (2.5 mm), 1/8 inch (3.2 mm), 5/32 inch (4 mm), and 13/64 inch (5 mm). With this tool, the pattern-maker can easily cut holes in tag board, leather, and fabric with downward pressure and a turning motion. Pattern-makers use this tool to mark punch-hole placement in patterns and fabrics.

Straight Pins *Satin pins* in size #17. Typical uses include

- Anchoring muslin fabric to a dress form while draping
- Holding muslin sections together for balancing and trueing
- Fastening muslin or fabric sections together to test accuracy of a completed pattern and to test shape on a dress form

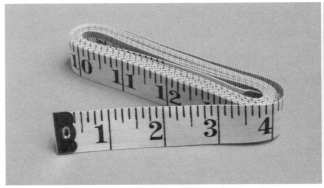

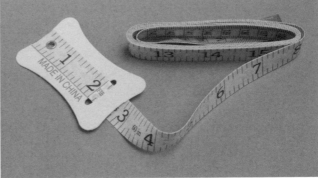

Tape Measure A ¼-, ½-, ⅝-, or ¾-inch wide flexible tape 60 to 120 inches in length imprinted with measurements in inches on one side and centimeters on the reverse; fractional segments are included. Some tape measures come with a bone-shaped plastic crotch piece for measuring inseams. Typical uses include

- Measuring circumference, length and width of a dress form, body parts, garment sections, pattern pieces, muslin, or fabric
- Measuring around circles with ease (on its edge)
- Transferring body measurements to muslin or paper

EQUIPMENT AND SUPPLIES (continued)

Tailor's Chalk, Tailor's Wax, or Tailor's Crayons A roughly 1½-inch square piece of white or colored chalk or wax, tapered to a fine edge on two ends. Typical uses include

- Drawing lines on garments
- Marking fabric for construction (chalk rubs off and wax melts into the fabric)
- Transferring drafted patterns onto fabric
- Marking the wrong side of fabric or garment pieces for identification

Tailor's chalk works well on fabrics made of cotton, linen, silk, wool, or manufactured fibers. Tailor's wax is used only on wool fabrics, as it leaves a grease mark on other fabrics.

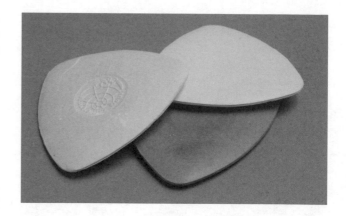

Transparent Tape Clear plastic strip having an adhesive surface on one side only that can be written on directly. Typical uses include

- Extending paper size
- Mending tears in a pattern
- Holding slashed-style lines in place when drafting patterns

Tracing Wheel (Pattern Tracer) Smooth-edged, needle-pointed, or serrated metal disk mounted on one end of a wooden or plastic handle. Typical uses include

- Transferring markings from a muslin pattern or garment onto paper
- Transferring balanced seam lines of one pattern piece to another
- Marking sheer, white, or lightweight fabrics (leaving an imprint only)

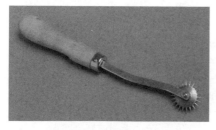

Needle-Pointed Wheel (Pounce Wheel)—Used to transfer trued areas of entire pattern markings onto paper or tag board or to trace deconstructed garment parts in reverse engineering.

Small Serrated Wheel—Used on woven and nonwoven fabrics.

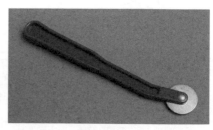

Smooth-Edged Wheel—Used on fine and lightweight fabrics.

Triangle A right-triangle-shaped tool whose hypotenuse is marked with degree angles. Typical uses include

- Establishing and marking bias lines on patterns
- Squaring a corner
- Drafting lines at right angles

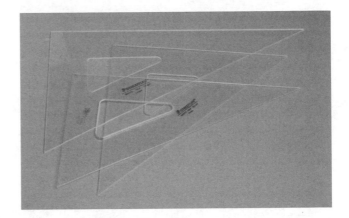

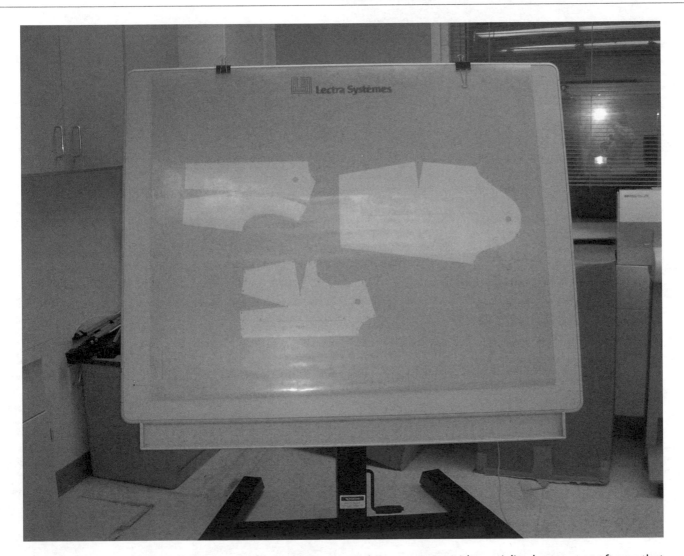

Digitizer Equipment for tracing a paper pattern or deconstructed garment parts with specialized computer software that allows the patternmaker to transfer them into a digital format. With digitizers, patternmakers can create an electronic copy of a block or pattern or develop a pattern from an existing garment.

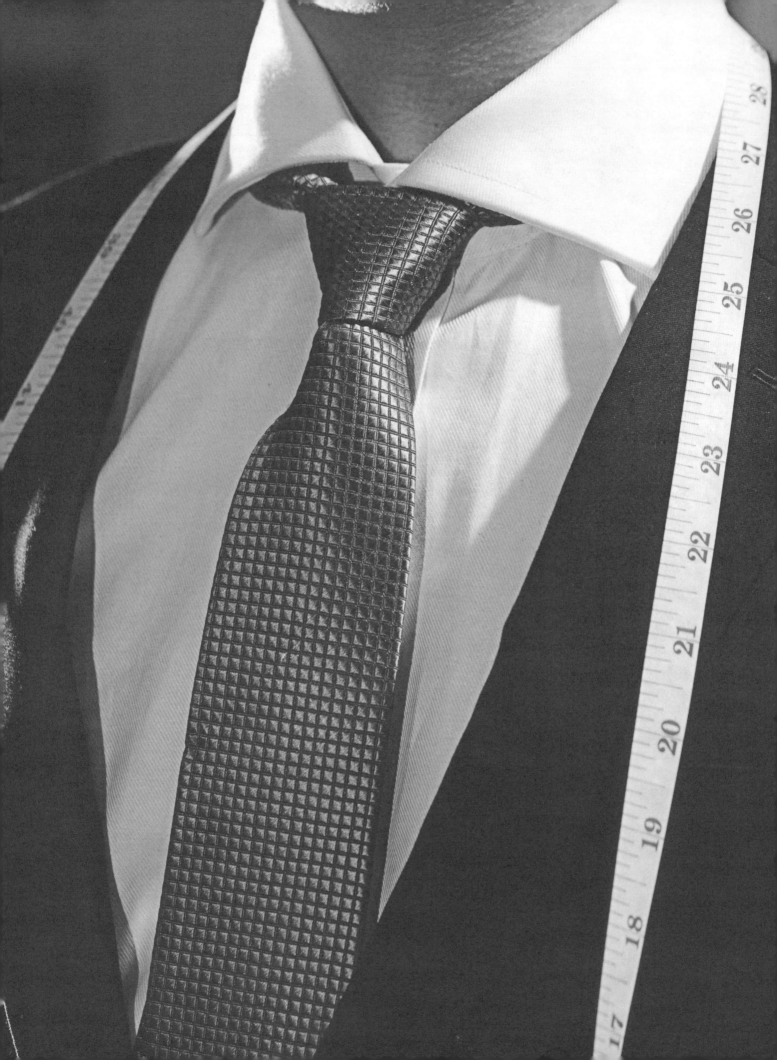

CHAPTER 17

Sizing and Fit

Fit is an important aspect that makes many customers loyal to particular brands. Some brands label garments as smaller sizes than their measured dimensions. This practice is referred to as **vanity sizing** in women's wear and **manity sizing** for the men's wear industry. This technique makes customers feel good about themselves and the brand because they can wear a "smaller" size. While customers may like this, it creates size confusion and frustration as customers shop for apparel items from different brands. Fashion companies establish sets of measurements that correspond to the size designations they offer. This is why measurements for similarly styled size 8 garments can vary from brand to brand. **Size designations** for apparel products correspond to a body size that is specified by a letter code or number on a garment label to assist consumers with making purchases.

Numeric Sizing System for designating size based on specific body measurements or product dimensions measured in centimeters or inches. Body or product dimensions relate to one or more key measurements such as the waist (*primary measurement*) and length (*secondary dimension*).

Primary Dimension or Primary Measurement Main body mass measurement used to define the size of an apparel item such as the waist for a pair of pants or the bust/chest for a jacket or shirt.

Secondary Dimension or Secondary Measurement Ancillary body measurement used in conjunction with the primary dimension to distinguish the size of an apparel item such as sleeve length or pant inseam.

Letter Code Sizing System for designating size of a garment by means of one or more letters or characters. This type of sizing covers two to three numeric sizes and is used for casual garments that are designed with more ease and do not require a precise fit. Common letter code sizes include

- XXS
- XS
- S
- M
- L
- XL
- XXL

SIZING STANDARDS

Many brands are now available around the globe, which is becoming a greater challenge to provide apparel items that fit many different body types and measurement configurations. Voluntary size standards are available from a variety of organizations in an effort to provide designers, product developers, and manufacturers with anthropometric body measurements and figure type data for men, women, and children that reflect current populations. Even though international size standards exist, apparel brands are not required to follow them. Therefore, purchasing apparel that fits well can be frustrating for many customers whether shopping in store or online. For some individuals, apparel purchases are followed by visits to a tailor to modify the garments so they fit the body correctly. Some organizations offering size standards include

- ASTM International
- ISO (International Organization for Standardization)
- JIS (Japanese foreign standard)
- EN (European Standard)
- BS EN (British foreign standard represented in European CEN)
- DEN EN (German foreign standard represented in European CEN)
- SS EN (Swedish standard represented in European CEN)

This data can be used to

- Adapt sizing for different body types and measurement configurations
- Create a sizing system
- Develop garment patterns
- Improve garment fit
- Modify a size range
- Reduce size confusion and inconsistencies among brands

Anthropometric Data Information resulting from measuring human populations to determine variations and commonalities in body dimension and shape for use in standardizing sizes of apparel items.

Sizing System Body measurements classified by gender, age, and garment type (when applicable) to provide size classifications for mass-produced apparel products.

The relationship between the size and styling of an apparel product and the body is known as **fit**. Fashion trends influence decisions designers make that affect the aesthetic appearance, style, ease, and fit of the garment. There are different design details or methods for fitting garments to the body such as darts, seams, gathers, tucks, and pleats. In addition, designers must consider the amount of design ease and functional ease necessary to achieve the desired style while maintaining comfort and performance of the garment. The direction of fabric grain can also be used to contour a garment to the curves of the body. All of these concepts are covered in Chapter 18, "Design Details."

Although fashion trends evolve from season to season and year to year, which impact a designer's selection of design details and garment styling, it is critical for sizing and fit to be consistently maintained. Characteristics of well-fitting garments include

- Appropriate garment to body proportion
- Fabric falls easily on the body
- No presence of pulls or unintended folds
- Garment design and cut are appropriate for the figure type
- Smooth appearance of the garment

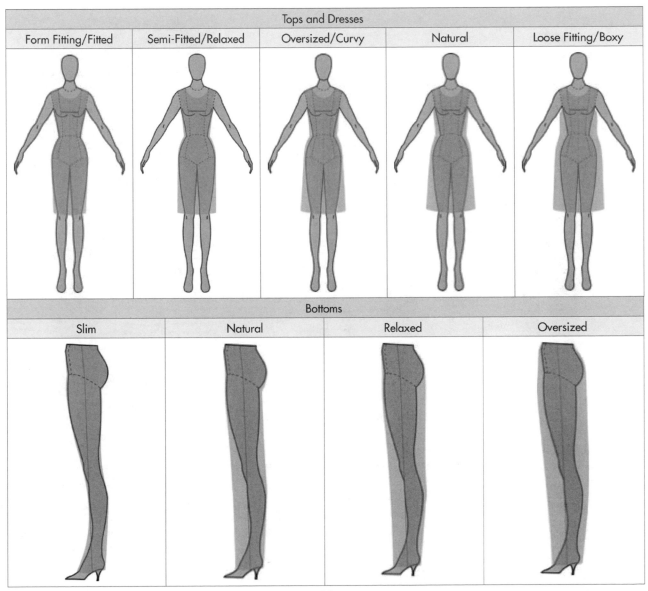

Apparel fit types

Fit type distinguishes the level of ease between the garment and the body to create a silhouette. There are a variety of fit types for apparel items. Fit types for tops and dresses include

- Fitted or Form fitting or Slim
- Semi-fitted or Relaxed
- Oversized or Curvy
- Natural
- Boxy or Loose Fitting

Fit types for bottoms include

- Slim
- Natural
- Relaxed
- Oversized

Break, another form of fit for bottoms, refers to the intentional fold in a pant leg near the hem where it hits the instep of the foot or shoe. This affects the overall length and appearance of pants and trousers. There are three types of break: no break, half-break or medium break, and full-break.

No Break The trouser or pant leg falls straight at the hem with no folds and barely touches the top of the shoe. The hem opening is cut at an angle with the front slightly higher than the back to accommodate the contour of the top of the foot. This style of break is best for shorter individuals to create more visual height.

Half-break / Medium Break The trouser or pant leg falls with a single fold that appears across the front at the ankle. The hem rests lightly on top of the shoe in front and covers the highest point of the shoe in the back. This style of break is considered traditional for men's wear and suiting.

Full-break The trouser or pant leg falls with a fold that runs all the way around the ankle. The hem rests completely on top of the shoe and often touches the top of the sole in the back. This style of break is more casual and can often convey a less polished appearance.

Properly fitted garments should hang smoothly on the body with no visible folds or pulls in the fabric. The key to achieving proper fit is to match the garment's three-dimensional volume to the body's contours while reflecting the proper location of body mass. The bust measurements for two different brands can be the same, but body type may be different. For example, the sample size bust measurement for Brands X and Y is 36 inches or 91 centimeters. How this measurement is distributed around the body can differ depending on where the body mass resides. For Brand X, the target customer has small breasts and a wide back. The front torso dimension will be smaller while the rear portion is larger to accommodate a broader back. Brand Y's target customer has a full bust line and narrow back; therefore, the front torso dimensions will be larger than the back in order to achieve the proper fit for this figure type. Technical designers are trained to recognize fitting issues so they can be corrected during the prototype stage before garments are sent to production. Keep in mind, while the technical designer's goal is to create proper garment fit, mass-produced apparel may still require minimal tailoring after purchase to enhance the fit for individual customers. Fitting problems can be seen on garments in the form of drag lines, folds, and flaring.

Drag lines Undesirable diagonal or horizontal pulls or folds in a garment that are not planned as part of the design; they visually indicate fit problems that need to be resolved. These lines show where the fabric is being pulled or stressed and point to or radiate from the areas where the fitting issues are present. Drag lines occur in areas of garments that are too tight, meaning there is not enough volume or ease within the garment sections to match the contours or body mass. Areas within a garment where drag lines typically occur include

- Bustline
- Buttock
- Crotch
- Thigh
- Shoulder blades
- Upper sleeve

Drag lines

Folds Fabric excess causing undesirable vertical or horizontal creases or wrinkles to an area of a garment.

Horizontal Folds—Creases or wrinkles formed across the body that indicate the length is too long and needs to be adjusted.

Vertical Folds—Creases or wrinkles formed in an up and down direction that indicate there is too much fabric in the circumference of the garment that needs to be removed.

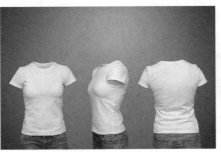

Horizontal folds

Vertical folds

Flaring When the horizontal balance line of a garment is not level, causing it to hang improperly. For example, when a garment portion unintentionally tilts away from the body, causing the side seam to fall at a slight angle. The back of the garment may hang too far away from the body and the front too close or vice versa. The garment should hang symmetrically on the body from side to side and front to back.

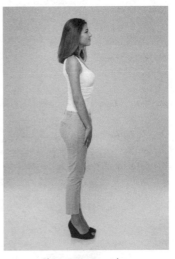

Flaring on pant leg

Flaring on shirt

Design Details

Fashion trends and styling determine the

type and amount of shaping or fullness that

become the design element of the garment.

A designer achieves silhouette, style, and

proportion through the placement of fabric

grainlines, design lines, and the manipulation

of excess fabric.

The designer forms the silhouette or style lines of a garment by molding, shaping, and releasing fabric to conform to body contours for functional or decorative purposes. A designer can use bias-cut fabric to mold over the body contour to fit or add fullness to the garment. **Style** is the essential characteristic of a garment with regard to silhouette, design details, proportion, color, and fabric. **Proportion** is the harmonious interrelationships between silhouette, design details, style lines, and fabric grainline in a given design with regard to the target consumer. Functional and decorative features for design control, shaping, and fit may be planned vertically, horizontally, or diagonally according to garment design or effect desired.

The type and shape of design control selected depends on

- Desired silhouette
- Garment design and style
- Garment type
- Garment use
- Fabric type, weight, and care
- Size range and figure types

FABRIC GRAIN

The three basic grainlines of woven and knitted fabrics are straight grain, bias grain, and cross-grain. The direction of the fabric's grain can affect the overall fit and appearance of a garment. The alignment of the fabric's yarns determines whether it is *on-grain* or *off-grain*. Off-grain or skewed fabrics can cause problems as garments are worn and cleaned.

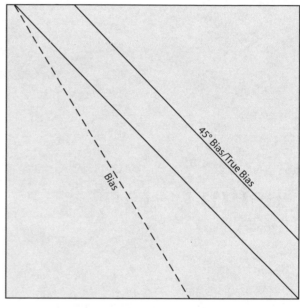

Bias grain

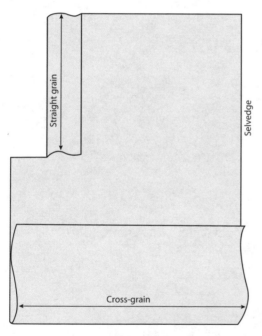

Straight grain

Straight Grain Runs in the warp direction for woven fabrics (wale direction for knits), parallel to the selvage. A straight grain is the most stable because warp yarns are stronger than weft. Most garments are cut on straight grain to provide a crisp appearance.

Bias Grain Grainlines that do not run parallel to the warp (wale) or filling (course) yarns. True bias runs at a 45° angle from the intersection of straight- and cross-grains. Designing a garment on bias grain allows fabric to conform to curves of the body to achieve fit. Bias grain

- Achieves body-skimming silhouettes, with soft, lightweight, and loosely woven fabrics
- Creates a softer drape or silhouette for garments cut from heavyweight or closely woven fabrics
- Emphasizes geometric fabric prints, sheen and light refraction, or metallic yarns
- Provides stretch in woven garments
- Emphasizes an area of the garment or body. Minimize matching of plaids on garment components. Majority

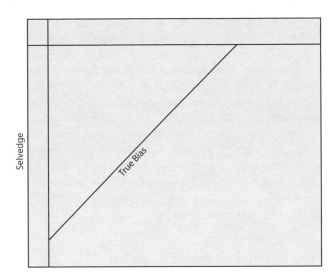

True bias

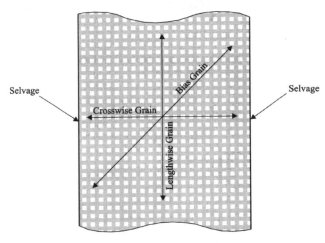

Cross-grain

of the garment is cut on straight grain and small details are cut on the bias, or vice versa. Examples of bias-cut details include yoke, tab, epaulette, cuffs, waistband, self belt, collar, pockets, and placket.

- Creates a chevron effect when a stripe, plaid, or check fabric is cut on the bias and seamed together to create a V or inverted V on a garment.

Cross-Grain Runs in the filling direction of woven fabrics (courses direction for knits), perpendicular to the selvage. Cutting a garment on cross-grain is common with *border print* fabrics. Since the border is printed parallel to the fabric's selvage, pattern pieces need to be laid out on cross-grain to showcase the pattern along the hemline of a garment.

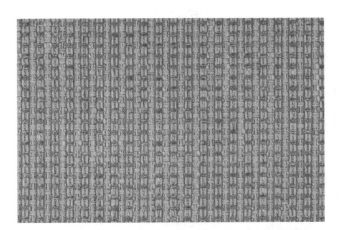

On-Grain Warp (wales) and filling (courses) yarns in a fabric meet at right angles.

Off-Grain Warp (wales) and filling (courses) yarns in a fabric are skewed and do not meet at right angles. The garment will not hang correctly and will appear twisted. This torque typically becomes worse with refurbishment and cannot be corrected.

Cut on the Bias (Bias Cut) Fabric for a garment is planned on the bias to affect the controlled fullness and conform to the curves of the body. Bias cut

- Creates body-skimming silhouettes on garments made of soft, lightweight, and loosely woven fabrics
- Produces crisp silhouettes that stand away from the body on garments made of heavyweight or closely woven fabrics
- Emphasizes geometric fabrics, sheen, light refraction, or glitter of novelty fabrics

Bias-cut garments rely on seams for fitting, emphasizing design detail, or extending fabric width.

Cut of the Garment (Flare) The result of manipulating fabric, without darts, pleats, or gathers, to conform to a body contour, seam, or style lines to control fullness at the lower edge of the garment. Fabric can be manipulated to include both straight grain and bias within the same portion of a garment, for example, in a circular skirt. By a garment's cut, the designer develops skirts, trapeze tops or capes, swing coats, bell or cap sleeves, and flared pants.

The introduction of pleats or gathers into a flared garment section can add fullness, design emphasis, or style variation. Fullness at the lower edge of a garment may be minimal or exaggerated depending on the fabric, silhouette, or desired design effect.

Bias cut

Flare cut

TYPES OF EASE

Ease is the amount of fabric allowed in a pattern design to accommodate body movement; the variance between the finished product measurements and body measurements for the intended size (dimensions of garment minus body dimensions equal ease). Ease allows the garment to fit the body while allowing for movement and comfort, making it an important component of garment design, pattern development, and garment construction. Designers also rely on ease to achieve style and aesthetic appeal. Even distribution of fullness at a seam or style line controls a minimal amount of fabric excess without forming gathers, tucks, or darts. Ease may

- Replace a dart in a fitted sleeve or skirt, on back shoulder seams, across shoulder blades, the bust, or hipline; at the waistline of a bodice, sleeve cap, pants, and skirts
- Join a larger garment section to a smaller one
- Shape seams of a princess line bodice over apex areas

It is easier to ease and mold knit, stretch, and loosely woven fabrics than firmly woven fabrics.

Functional Ease (Wearing Ease) Fullness added to a pattern's body or dress form measurements in the length and width directions to allow for body movement.

Design Ease (Garment Ease or Style Ease) Fullness added to a pattern's body or dress form measurements and functional ease to achieve the desired garment design.

DARTS AND SEAMS

Darts and seams are a means of shaping fabric to fit the figure. Darts allow for extra fabric to be taken up and molded around curves of the body. A variety of darts fit a garment to the body while providing a smooth, subtle look or design detail. Seams attach garment parts together and provide a smooth or textured appearance depending on the treatment of the garment parts being joined. Designers can plan darts and seams horizontally, vertically, or diagonally, to provide design detail in addition to function.

Dart Excess fabric taken up at the edge of a garment converges to a diminishing point, to contour fabric to the body. Darts formed to fit body contours vary in shape and size and may result in straight, concave, or convex converging pattern lines. Straight darts are commonly placed at the bust, elbow, waist, hip, neck, and shoulder areas. *Concave darts* curve in toward the body. They are used above the waist

in the midriff area to the apex (bust) line. The greater the curve, the closer the fit. *Convex darts* curve outward away from the body. These darts are for areas where the body curves outward; the bust, abdomen, and hip areas. They can also replace a side seam or shape gores of a skirt from the hip to the waist area. Convergent lines on the finished garment indicate the dart's shape. Darts may shape fabric

- Over the bust on a front bodice section
- Over the upper shoulder and allow ease over the shoulder blades at the back neck or back shoulder seams
- To the waistline at the back bodice waist
- At the elbow for movement of long, fitted sleeves
- To the waistline and allow ease over the hips on dresses, skirts, pants, and shorts
- To the waistline and allow ease over the hips on the side front and side back panels of a dress or gored skirt

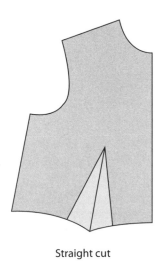

Straight cut

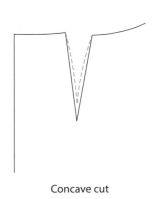

Concave cut

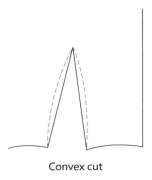

Convex cut

Decorative dart

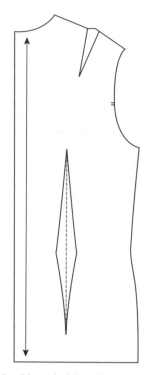

Double ended dart/double dart

Decorative Dart *Dart* on the face of the garment to create a design effect and emphasize a style line. These darts may be stitched with the same, contrasting, or buttonhole twist thread or emphasized with cording insert or stiffening.

Double-Ended Dart (Double Dart) *Dart* that begins at the apex level and extends to the hip to shape or contour fabric to curves of the body. Double-ended darts fit one-piece dresses, coats, or long jackets at the waistline. Double darts may vary in size and length and result in straight, concave, or convex converging pattern lines.

Flange Dart *Dart* released at one end to form a pleat on a front or back pattern piece or at the intersection of the shoulder and armhole seam. Flange darts can create an illusion of wider shoulders or create ease across the chest, back, and upper armhole.

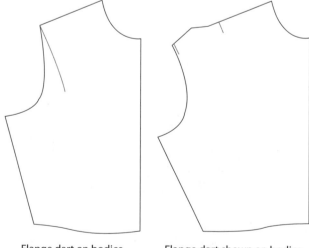

Flange dart on bodice

Flange dart shown on bodice pattern piece

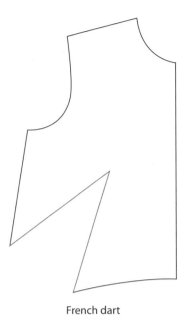

French dart

French Dart Diagonal darts originating from any point between the hipline to 2 inches above the waist at the side seam and tapering to the bustline.

Dart Slash Fitted dart constructed to contour the bust, shoulder, or hip. A dart slash

- Introduces design fullness for style effect
- Used horizontally gives a yoke effect at the hip or shoulder
- Used horizontally creates a midriff or band effect
- Creates variation in sleeve silhouette

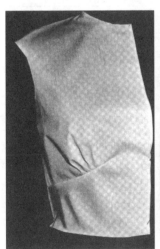

Dart slash

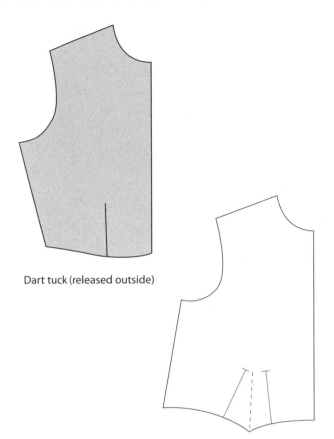

Dart tuck (released outside)

Dart tuck (released inside)

Dart Tuck The take-up of excess fabric, of a determined amount, that converges to a point or points of release, at the edge of the garment. A dart tuck

- Releases fabric to conform to body contours at the waistline, shoulder, or center front
- Allows ease over the hip and abdomen at the waistline of skirts, pants, or shorts
- Releases fullness above and below the fitted area on one-piece garments
- Fits the wrist on full sleeves
- Creates a softer design effect than other dart options

Fabric excess may be distributed into two or more dart tucks. A dart tuck is formed by partially stitching the dart along its convergent lines releasing the fullness.

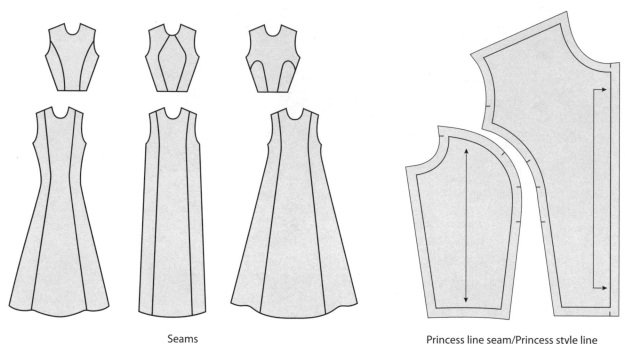

Seams   Princess line seam/Princess style line

Seams Eliminating fabric excess by manipulating two or more panels to conform to the style line and body contour; the place where garment parts are sewn together. Seams

- Fit the garment to the body in lieu of darts, tucks, or gathers
- Form fitted princess line garments
- Form gored skirts or garments from the shoulder to the hem as shifts, tent dresses, capes, coats, and jackets

Princess Line Seam (Princess Style Line) Seam line intersecting the apex and extending to the shoulder or armhole, depending on the desired effect. Bodice princess style lines can originate and end at any perimeter point on the front bodice and cross the apex area, resulting in two or more panels with corresponding seams. Princess line seams may

- Fit a garment through the bust, waist, and hip areas
- Create gores on a dress or skirt
- Provide fit and flare on a skirt

Side Panel Garment section that provides fit and shape in place of a side seam. Seam lines of the panel run vertically on the body and run a few inches from the apex, in contrast to the princess line seam, which runs through it. Side panels may replace side seams on jackets, coats, activewear tops, and pullovers while adding subtle shape to a garment.

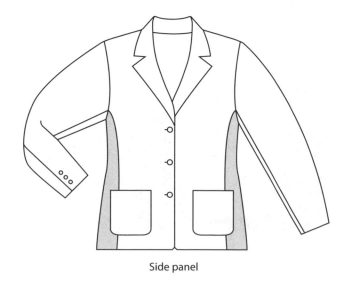

Side panel

Gores Panels in a skirt or skirt portion of a dress created by dividing the skirt into vertical sections. Flare can add fullness to a garment. The number of panels dictates the number of gores. The number of gores in the front and the back of the skirt do not have to be identical, but they can be:

- Four gore—Gore lines located at center front, center back, and side seams to create four panels.
- Six gore—Gore lines located at the front and back princess line seams and at the side seams to create six panels.
- Ten gore—Gore lines located at the front and back princess line seams, at side seams, and seams that equally divide the space between princess line panels and side seams to create ten panels.

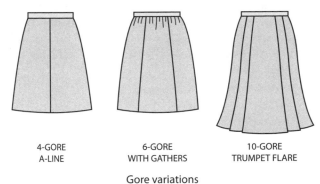

4-GORE
A-LINE

6-GORE
WITH GATHERS

10-GORE
TRUMPET FLARE

Gore variations

GATHERS, PLEATS, AND TUCKS

Gathers, pleats, and tucks introduce fullness to clothing. Fullness may be drawn in to a desired width by elastic or drawstring enclosed in a casing, or by elastic stitched directly to the garment. Pleats are parallel folds in fabric that add fullness and motion to a garment. They create a vertical line design and facilitate ease of body movement and action.

Pleats are designated as flat or dimensional. **Flat pleats** may be folded and left unpressed, creased, or stitched to a designated length. They may be planned singly, in groups, or in an evenly spaced series. **Dimensional pleats** are permanently set into a pattern of creased ridges or fluting. Flat and dimensional pleats may be shaped or controlled to fit body contour. Crease lines of pleats follow the grainline

of the fabric, with the exception of sunburst pleats, which have radiating lines. Firm and closely woven fabrics hold creases better than soft or loosely woven fabrics or knitted fabrics. Specific machines help professional pleaters to permanently set pleats on prepared panels of predetermined length and width, with regard to designer's specifications.

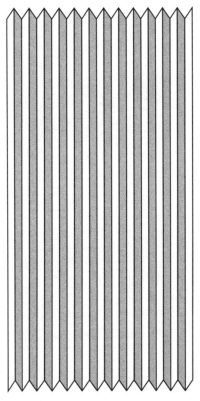

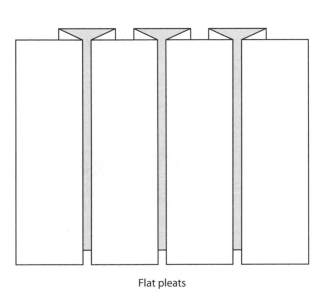

Flat pleats

Dimensional pleat

Gathering (Shirring) Fullness of a predetermined amount, drawn in to form soft folds corresponding to smaller adjoining seam lines or specified body measurements. The seam line conceals stitches forming gathers. Gathering can be created by drawing in one, two, or three parallel rows of machine-gathering stitches, or by specialized industrial machines. Gathering evenly distributes fullness on

- A yoke or midriff
- Necklines and waistlines
- Sleeve caps to create a puff
- Lower edges of sleeves, skirts, or pants legs
- *Ruffles, ruching,* and *jabots* (ruffle on the front of a blouse)

Gathering/Shirring

Elastic Shirring Multiple rows of parallel stitching with elastic cord or thread that control fullness to produce expansion and contraction in garment section. Shirring forms a decorative design detail visible on the face of the garment. The amount of control is determined by the length of the stitch, type and expandability of elastic, number and spacing of parallel rows of stitching, and their interrelationship with the fabric. This effect can be created with elastic thread in the bobbin of a *lockstitch* or *zigzag machine*, elastic thread as a chain stitch, or by encasing elastic cord in a zigzag stitch. Elastic shirring may

- Accommodate more than one size or body configuration
- Control fullness
- Form tube or halter tops and dresses

Elastic shirring (face of garment)

Elastic shirring (inside of garment)

French shirring/French gathering

French Shirring (French Gathering) Drawing up three or more parallel rows of machine-gathering stitches that are produced on multineedled industrial machines. The number of rows of shirring depends on location on the garment, body contour, and design detail desired. Stitching may be made with matching, contrasting, buttonhole twist, or decorative thread. A stay beneath shirring reinforces it. When completed, shirring is fixed and lacks give or elasticity. French shirring may

- Create a yoke effect at the shoulder or hip
- Create a band effect at the lower edge of a sleeve
- Release fullness above and below the stitching

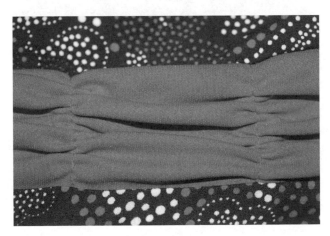

Ruching

Ruching Predetermined fullness gathered to correspond to a parallel gathered seam or to release gathers on both sides of a seam. Soft folds are created horizontally or vertically on the body whenever evenly distributed fullness in the form of draped folds are designed into a garment. Ruching can also take the form of a strip of fabric or ribbon that is stitched and gathered in a repeating pattern to create a scalloped or ruffled effect on trim. Ruching can provide a decorative detail to a yoke or midriff, or at the lower edge of a sleeve, cuff, or hem.

Waffle Shirring A grid of *elastic shirring* that produces two-way expansion and contraction in a garment section. The amount of control is determined by the length of stitch, type and expandability of elastic, number and spacing of grid rows of stitching, and their interrelationship with the fabric. Waffle shirring is made on the length- and cross-grains of the fabric. Waffle shirring may

- Provide two-way stretch on garments such as bodysuits, swimwear, and activewear
- Accommodate more than one size or body configuration
- Control fullness of an entire bodice, partial bodice, midriff, or hip area
- Form tube or halter tops
- Detail or trim small areas
- Form a decorative design detail on the face of the garment

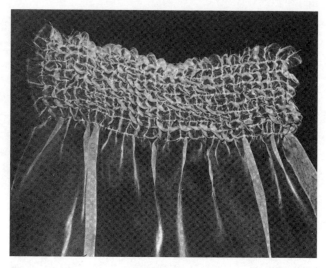

Waffle shirring

Pleat The take-up of excess fabric at the edge of a garment by means of doubling the fabric ply upon itself, producing a fold and forming an underlay of ⁵/₈ inch to 2 inches (15.875 to 50.8 mm). Pleats can be used singly or in a series. A series of pleats may be planned to face in one direction or toward each other. A softened effect can be created at points of release. Pleats may create a design detail

- At the waist, shoulder, or hipline
- Below a yoke line
- At the lower edge of a sleeve to fit it to a cuff
- At the cuff or hem
- At sleeve caps
- On a blouse, bodice, or jacket, releasing fullness over the apex or across the shoulder

Pleats

Accordion pleat

Accordion Pleat Evenly spaced pleats, creating a raised and recessed pattern permanently set by an industrial pleating machine. Panels for a garment are cut and hemmed prior to pleating. The unhemmed edge of a pleated panel is controlled to fit body circumference or style line. Accordion pleats may give garments a straight or cylindrical silhouette on shifts, skirts, sleeves, and shirtwaist-styled garments.

Box pleat

Box Pleat Evenly spaced folds in a fabric ply doubled over to face away from each other. The depth of the underlay producing the box pleat does not need to be equal to the width of the box. A box pleat may be unpressed, pressed in place, or particularly stitched. They may be grouped or designed to fill circumference of the garment on skirts, blouses, bodices, and one-piece garments, and below hip or shoulder yokes.

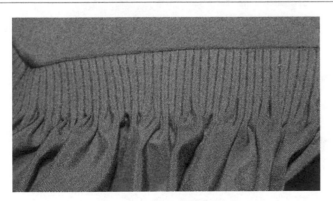

Cartridge pleating (gauging)

Cartridge Pleating (Gauging) Three or more rows of evenly spaced running stitches drawn up to a controlled, predetermined fullness that corresponds to a smaller adjoining seam, specified body measurement, or garment area. Small, even folds formed by the gauging pattern are visible on the face of the garment. Every row of stitching must line up exactly with the rest. Running stitches may vary from ⅛ to ⅜ inch (3.175 to 9.525 mm) in length. Cartridge pleating emphasizes drawing up fullness in the garment style, as, for example, in academic and clerical robes. It may also emphasize geometric patterns of fabric.

Crystal pleating

Inverted pleat

Crystal Pleat Series of narrow accordion-like creased folds creating an evenly spaced pattern. Pleats can be set into a partial length of fabric in a garment section to create a novelty effect. Panels for a garment are cut and may be hemmed prior to pleating or after to create a ruffled effect. Designers use crystal pleats to create design details on

- Garments where a straight or cylindrical silhouette is desired
- Evening or bridal wear
- Shifts, skirts, sleeves, and shirtwaist-styled garments
- Flounces and ruffles

Inverted Pleat Two folds in a fabric ply, a measured distance apart, doubled under to meet each other at a central point on the face of the fabric. Designers may use inverted pleats to create a design detail

- At the center front, center back, or side seam of skirts and pants
- At the center back of men's shirts and jackets to allow arm movement
- On gored skirts and princess line garments to increase circumference
- At the center back of coats and jackets to provide sitting ease

Kick Pleat An inverted or side pleat released at knee level or below. A kick pleat may be planned as a single side pleat, as a double pleat, or with a separate underlay. Kick pleats can increase the circumference of narrow garments to allow for walking ease at the center front, center back, or side seam.

Kick pleats

Knife Pleat A pleat doubled upon itself in a series of folds forming underlays of ⅝ inch (15.875 mm) or less; permanently pressed to lie in one direction. A knife pleat is not applicable to stretch, bulky, or napped fabrics. This type of pleat may be planned in groups or as an evenly spaced series filling the circumference of a garment. Knife pleats can work as an inserted panel or in conjunction with fitted yokes on skirts, blouses, bodices, and one-piece garments.

Knife pleats

Side Pleat (Single or Multiple) One or more pleats contoured to fit the body. The underlay can range from ⅝ inch to 2 inches (15.875 to 50.8 mm). Side pleats can be repeated to form a series all facing one direction. They may be folded and left unpressed, creased, or partially stitched down to fit the body contour. Side pleats

- Allow for arm movement below shoulder and hip yokes
- Accommodate sitting and walking ease on coats and jackets at the princess line
- Increase circumference on gored skirts, princess line garments, lower sleeve edges, and sleeve caps
- Release fullness over the apex or across the shoulders

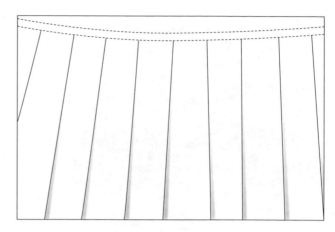

Side pleats

Sunburst Pleat Series of radiating pleats creating a raised and recessed pattern on sheer and lightweight fabrics. Garment panels are cut to predetermined size prior to pleating. Pleats are permanently set by an industrial pleating machine. The hemline and hem finish of garments are established after the garment is completed. The narrow part of pleat formation appears at the waist or shoulder line, or sleeve cap of the garment. Sunburst pleats may create

- Flared or circular silhouette
- Full silhouette without bulk at the waistline
- Interest on flounces and ruffles

Sunburst pleat

Pin Tucks Evenly spaced parallel folds, ⅛ inch (3.175 mm) or less, stitched at a designated length from the pattern edge or area to be fitted. Pin tucks may be evenly spaced either individually or by group and planned to start at a seam line or within a garment section. Pin tucks construct a creased fold on the face of a garment to create a limited amount of design fullness.

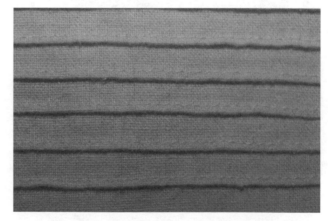

Pin tucks

Release Tucks (Outside and Inside) Evenly spaced parallel folds, ¼ to ⅝ inch (6.35 to 15.875 mm) partially stitched down to fit an area of a garment and then released to produce a desired amount of fullness. Folds may lie on the face or inside of the garment. They may all be turned to face one direction, turned toward or away from the center of a garment, or turned toward or away from each other in groups. Tucks directing fullness may be evenly spaced individually or in a group. Release tucks can be stitched with matching, contrasting, or buttonhole twist thread, or corded to produce a raised effect. They may be planned as vertical or horizontal design elements that start at a seam line or within a garment section. Release tucks

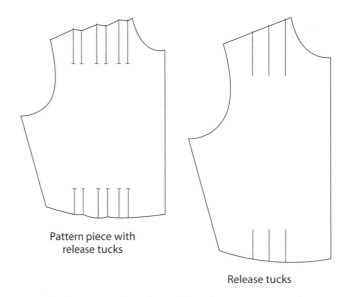

Pattern piece with release tucks

Release tucks

- Used vertically form a yoke at the shoulder or hip, releasing fullness below the stitching line
- Used horizontally form a yoke releasing fullness into a sleeve
- Create a midriff in a one-piece garment, releasing fullness above and below stitching
- Create a band at the end of a full sleeve

Release tucks

CASINGS

A **casing** is a fold-over edge or applied strip that encloses a drawstring or elastic to draw in the garment circumference to fit corresponding body areas. Casings are established at the edge of garments or span seam or style lines and may be constructed on unfitted or one-piece garments.

Designers use them on garments intended to accommodate more than one size or as a design detail. A casing is planned ¼ inch (6.4 mm) wider than the elastic or drawstring. On higher-priced apparel, a ⅛-inch (3.2 mm) header is planned at the top of the casing to provide stabilization for the elastic and finish the edge. Additionally, vertical stitches through the side seams of the casing help secure and stabilize the elastic. Elastic may be ribbon, or rib-type, or webbing. The type or method of application for casings selected depends on

- Garment style and design
- Garment use
- Garment care
- Fabric type and weight
- Type and width of the elastic or drawstring

Drawstring Casing Drawstring inserted into the casing, to allow the wearer to control garment circumference for body comfort and fit. The drawstring may be cord, braid, ribbon, leather strip, or fabric tubing. It may be planned to emerge on the inside or outside of the garment; from openings such as eye slits, buttonholes, metal eyelets, grommets, or seam openings. When the designer uses contrasting fabric, the casing can become a focal point of a garment. A drawstring casing may cinch in predetermined fullness on waistlines of skirts, pants, shorts, blouses, and jackets. It can also change the style effect by allowing drawstring manipulation at necklines, sleeves, hems, the waistline area of one-piece garments, and the waistline of upper-torso garments.

Drawstring casing

Elastic Casing Elastic is inserted into the casing. Elastic may be *ribbon*, *rib* type, *webbing*, or *clear*. It is available in various widths. Elastic casing may

- Facilitate ease of dressing
- Support a garment on a figure with no waistline indentation
- Eliminate the need for a placket or band on the waistline of garments made of knit or stretch fabrics
- Provide support on the upper edge of strapless garments; on waistlines of skirts, pants, or shorts; or blouson bodice
- Allow adjustable-style effects on necklines, lower sleeve edges, and pants legs
- Provide snug leg openings of swimwear and leotards

Elastic casing

Casing with Heading Casing established at a measured distance from the finished edge of the garment. An edging is formed when elastic or the drawstring is enclosed. Width of the heading and casing are determined by garment design and desired effect. A casing with a heading may create a ruffled edge on necklines, waistlines, hems, and hoods of garments made from sheer light- and medium-weight fabrics.

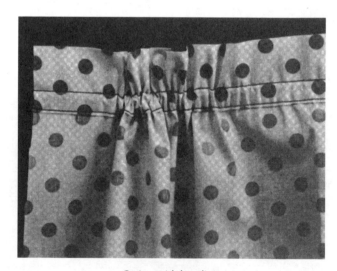

Casing with heading

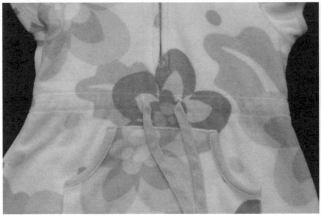

Inside applied casing (exterior view)

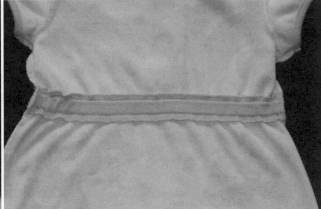

Inside applied casing (interior view)

Inside Applied Casing Separate strip of fabric applied to the inside of the garment either at an edge or a seam or style line. The strip may be ribbon, bias tape, *self* (garment material), or lighter-weight contrasting fabric. Inside applied casings may

• Replace a self casing on garments made of thick, bulky fabrics or on curved edges
• Create a ruffle, flounce, or peplum a measured distance from the edge of the garment
• Encase boning

Outside applied casing

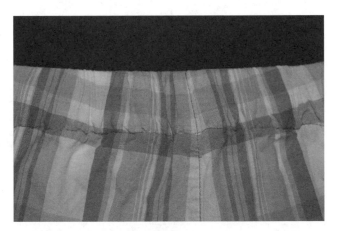

Self casing

Outside Applied Casing Separate strip of fabric applied to the face of the garment either at an edge or span of a seam or style line. The strip may be ribbon, bias tape, or self or contrasting fabric. An outside applied casing is used to emphasize a design element at a measured distance from the edge of the garment to create a ruffle, flounce, or peplum.

Self Casing A fold-over, machine-stitched finish at the edge of a garment section. Width of self casing is determined by garment design and desired effect. A self casing works well on sheer, light, or medium-weight fabrics for

• Straight edges and shallow curves
• Waistlines of skirts, pants, shorts, blouses, and jackets
• Edges of sleeves, pants legs, and hoods

WAISTLINE TREATMENTS

Waistbands and waistline finishes hold garments in proper position on the body. Style ease, which is part of the design, and wearing ease are included in the development of the pattern for waistband and waistline finishes. Waistlines on garments may be designed without an opening or may be planned with a lapped or centered opening at center front, center back, side seam, or princess line according to the garment design and function. Garments designed with horizontal seams joining upper and lower portions of the garment are designated as having seamed waistlines or inserts. Waistlines may be established on an all-in-one garment by a casing, elastic, or gathering to draw in the excess fabric to fit the body. The type of waistband or waistline finish selected depends on

- Garment style and design
- Garment use
- Garment care
- Fabric type and weight
- Fabric design
- Production and construction procedures

Seamed Waistline Upper and lower sections of a garment joined by a horizontal seam or seams. Horizontal design lines designating waistlines are identified as

Empire waistline—Just below the bust
Raised waistline—Slightly above the natural waist
Natural waistline—At the actual body waistline
Lowered waistline—Slightly below the natural waist
Long torso—Around the hip area

The joined seam may include

- Insertion of cording, piping, or trimming
- Application of decorative band, ribbon, or trimming

Unseamed Waistline Waistline spans the body above and below the waist area, not delineated by horizontal seams or bands. An unseamed waistline may be part of a sheath, shift, A-line, or tent silhouette when other methods of drawing in fullness would restrict body movement.

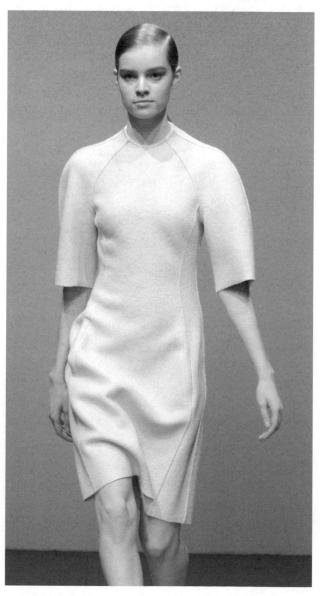

Built-up waistline

Built-up Waistline Garment part rising above the natural waistline and shaped by darts or panels to fit the body. Interfacing or boning strengthens the built-up section, which is finished with a shaped facing or lining. A built-up waistline can provide an alternative to a horizontal seam line produced by an added waistband.

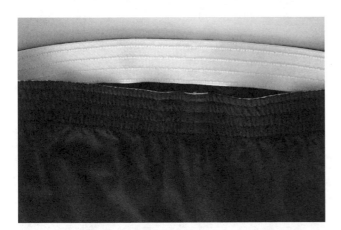

Elasticized waistline

Elasticized Waistline Elastic applied in any of a variety of methods to a waistline edge or a waistline area. A variety of elastic webbing widths and degree of elasticity produce differences in flexibility or design effect. An elasticized waistline may

- Provide ease of dressing
- Draw in an unfitted waistline
- Provide greater comfort

Faced waistline

Faced Waistline Garment component of the same shape as the waistline area and edge applied. A facing is usually applied to lie flat on the inside of the garment but may be applied to lie on the face as a decorative finish. A faced waistline may be desirable where other waistline applications would interfere with the design element of the garment or restrict body movement.

Bias-Faced Waistline Bias strip of the self, contrasting, or lighter-weight fabric, shaped to fit the contour of the garment's waistline. A bias-faced waistline may reduce bulk by providing a flatter finish than other facing types that would detract from the garment's appearance.

Bias-faced waistline

Ribbon-Faced Waistline Grosgrain, twill, or satin ribbon shaped to fit the contour of the garment waistline, producing a flat finish. This waistline treatment provides a smooth appearance on eyelet, openwork, or lightweight fabrics where facings would show through to the face of the garment. A ribbon-faced waistline can also allow for greater flexibility than wider facings that are more restrictive.

Ribbon-faced waistline

Insert Waistline (Inset Waistline) Shaped or straight band, made of self or contrasting fabric or ribbon, attached between the bodice and lower garment sections to emphasize the waistline. Width and shape of the insert varies depending on design. The insert can be designed to imitate a belted garment, to lie above or below the natural waist, or to span the waistline.

Insert waistline/Inset waistline

Contoured waistband

Contoured Waistband Band formed to fit the body's curve between the midriff and hip. Contoured waistbands may be interfaced, stiffened, or boned according to the amount of support desired. It may be decoratively shaped along either or both edges, and of uniform or graduated width. Contoured waistbands require a separate facing shaped to match. This waistband may provide a band finish for special design features such as low-rise or raised waistlines.

Straight waistband

Straight Waistband Band, 2 inches (5.1cm) or less in finished width, of two or more plies attached at the waistline. The band may have a seamed or fold-over upper edge and may be finished flush with one end of the garment, concealing an extended underlay. It can be planned with a pointed or rounded extension for lapped openings. This waistband may open at center front, center back, side seam, or princess line. A straight waistband may

- Provide a stable finish to the garment edge
- Support garments covering the lower torso such as trousers, shorts, or skirts
- Anchor garments covering the upper torso such as jackets or blouses

Elastic-backed straight waistband

Elastic-Backed Straight Waistband Elastic completes the inside of a waistband of a single-ply band of self-fabric, 2½ inches (6.4 cm) or less in finished width. An elastic-backed straight waistband is used on knit fabrics to provide a nonroll waistband compatible with the garment fabric's extendibility.

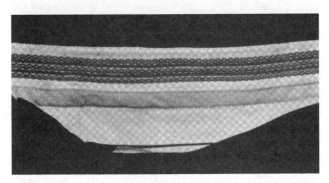

Non-slip-backed waistband

Non-Slip-Backed Waistband Waistband curtain having woven rows of rubber yarn on one surface or embossed or printed silicone adhered to an inner waistband material to produce a nonslip surface on the waistband that is attached to complete the inside of a single-ply waistband of self fabric. Non-slip-backed waistbands are used on trousers and skirts to hold tuck-in blouses and shirts in place.

Ribbon-Backed Straight Waistband *Self* fabric band, 2 inches (5.1 cm) or less in width, backed with grosgrain or twill ribbon to complete the inside waistband. A ribbon-backed straight waistband may

- Eliminate bulk on garments made of heavy, coarse, or nubby fabrics
- Add body and stability to garments made of sheer and loosely woven fabrics
- Prevent garment fabric from coming into direct contact with the body and causing irritation

Ribbon-backed straight waistband

Stretch Waistband Separate waistband or casing enclosing applied elastic cut the same length as the garment waist seam. A placket may be needed for garments made of knit fabrics with limited stretch. A stretch waistband may provide ease of dressing for knit pull-on pants, skirts, and shorts.

Stretch waistband

Trouser Waistband (Curtain Waistband) Waistband with a self fabric face supported by a reinforced, commercially prepared bias strip constructed with an additional bias strip designed to hang below the waistline seam. Waistband support is attached to a self fabric ply at the upper edge only. Available in widths ¾ inch to 2 inches (1.9 to 5.1 cm). This waistband adds support to tailored trousers.

Trouser waistband/curtain waistband

Waistline with Casing A fabric strip applied to a waistline edge, or to span a waistline area or folded edge constructed to enclose a drawstring or elastic. The *casing* may be applied to the face of the garment for decorative purposes. The width of the casing and elastic or drawstring affects the silhouette of the garment. Width of the elastic, degree of elasticity, and method of application produces a difference in flexibility or design effect. A waistline with a casing allows for an unfitted waistline to be drawn in for individual control of circumference adjustment.

Waistline with casing

MISCELLANEOUS DESIGN DETAILS

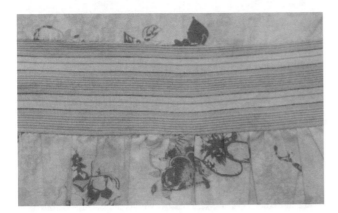

Band/banding

Band or Banding A strip of self or contrasting fabric cut on straight grain, bias, or shaped, inserted or topstitched to a garment ply. A band may

- Finish the edge of a garment or garment section
- Extend a garment edge such as on a hemline of a jacket, blouse, sleeve, dress, skirt, or pants
- Serve as a facing

Eye slit

Eye Slit Clean-finished vertical or circular opening made by the application of a stitched, slashed, and turned strip or patch. An eye slit may

- Provide a decorative opening for a drawstring or belt
- Create open-slit buttonholes
- Hold a decorative scarf or tie

An opening seam, buttonhole, eyelet, or grommet may work as an eye slit.

Chevron/mitering

Chevron (Mitering) Decorative "V" design produced at the seam line when adjoining pattern pieces of geometric design fabric or trim are cut and sewn at the same angle. Patterns are placed for cutting so that sizes and colors of bands will produce identical chevrons.

Flounce Circular cut piece of fabric sewn smoothly into an adjoining seam line. A flounce enhances a hem or cuff.

Flounce

Godet Triangular or rounded piece inserted into a slashed opening or seam in a garment section or sections. Length, width, and shape of the godet will vary according to the garment style or desired effect. A godet may

- Enhance the lower portion of skirts, pants, sleeves, tops, jackets, coats, and capes; petticoats, slips, lingerie, robes, and aprons
- Create a flounce effect
- Create a fuller silhouette

Godet

Gusset Diamond-shaped piece inserted into a slashed opening on a larger garment section. Gusset may be planned using one, two, or four pieces. A gusset allows for freedom of movement when set into a fitted sleeve, crotch area of pants or trousers, thermal underwear, intimate apparel, and activewear.

Gusset

Ruffle Gathered or pleated single- or double-ply strip of fabric drawn up on one side to a predetermined fullness and sewn into a smaller adjoining seam line. A ruffle enhances hems, cuffs, plackets, and necklines.

Ruffle

Smocking Elastic shirring with an overlay pattern of decorative stitches applied to the face of the fabric. Decorative patterns vary according to stitch or stitch groups. Degree of stretch varies according to the type and expandability of elastic thread or cord, length of stitch, and number and spacing of parallel rows of stitching. Machine smocking is completed on fabric or garment sections prior to construction. Smocking

- Creates an expandable or contractible decorative-patterned effect
- Simulates handwork in mass-produced garments where hand smocking would be too expensive
- Forms the effect of a yoke, midriff, band, or cuff
- Accommodates more than one size or body configuration
- Releases fullness above and below the stitching

Smocking

Underlay Strip of self or contrasting fabric or ribbon measured to accommodate the area to be backed and constructed to lie beneath a folded, faced, or abutted seam. An underlay may

- Create a separate ply to complete a pleat
- Stabilize the under portion of pleats where panels of princess line or gored garments are joined
- Stabilize the under portion of an inverted pleat when planned at the center front or center back
- Support a free-hanging strip behind a slashed opening at the lower edge of shirts or pants
- Introduce color or fabric contrast to inverted or kick pleats, behind butted plackets or seams, laced or hooked openings, frog or loop, and button plackets or openings
- Protect an undergarment or body from zipper teeth abrasion

Underlay

Full Fashioned Two-dimensional garment pieces shaped as they are knitted on a flat bed machine and emerge ready to assemble. Trim components are attached to the garment through **linking (looping)**. This process requires joining them together by matching each stitch along the garment panel with each stitch along the trim edge. In comparison to cut-and-sew knits, full fashion garments

- Require minimal seaming to construct the garment
- Provide better fit
- Offer higher-quality construction but are more expensive to produce

Full fashioned

Knit-and-Wear (Seamless) Three-dimensional pre-shaped garments knitted to fit the shape of the body require minimal operations for finishing. Products emerge from knitting machines ready to wear. This knitting process eliminates preproduction and assembly operations such as cutting, bundling, sewing, and linking. Seamless garments are available within each price classification and may vary in design, fit, and styling complexity. Knit-and-wear garments may include

- Hosiery
- Leggings
- Sweaters
- Undergarments

Knit-and-wear machine

Knit-and-wear

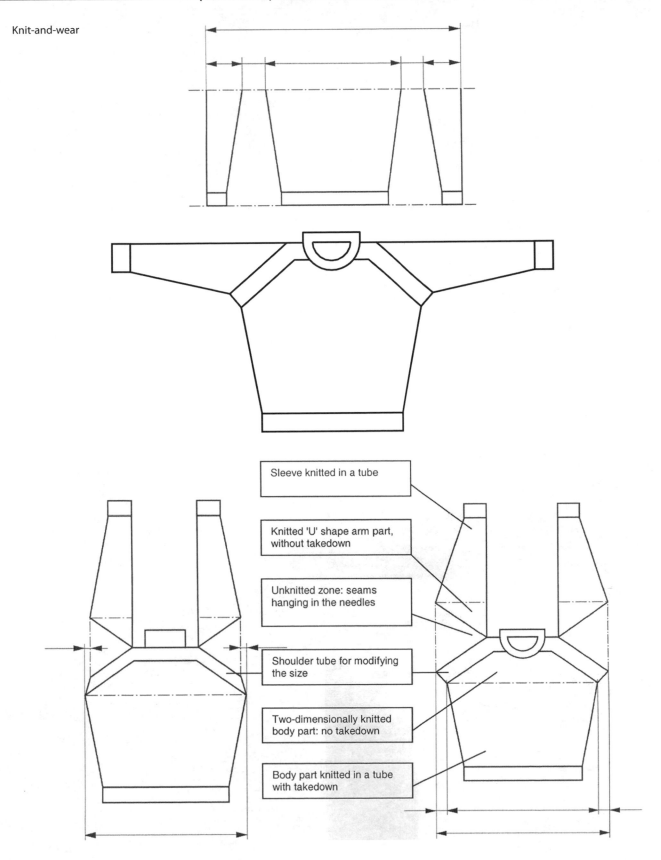

Sleeve knitted in a tube

Knitted 'U' shape arm part, without takedown

Unknitted zone: seams hanging in the needles

Shoulder tube for modifying the size

Two-dimensionally knitted body part: no takedown

Body part knitted in a tube with takedown

Garment Openings

When designers develop apparel lines, they consider the overall aesthetic appeal in relation to how each garment will function. A **garment opening** is carefully planned to provide a means for putting an apparel item on the body or taking it off. Functional openings are designed to provide access when dressing and can be fastened closed with various types of closures depending on the desired effect.

The type of garment opening selected depends on

- Garment design and style
- Garment type and use
- Purpose and placement

- Method of application
- Fabric type and weight
- Garment care

PLACKET

A **placket** is a finished opening in a garment section. It should be designed and styled in sufficient lengths to permit ease and convenience of dressing. Placket openings on sleeves allow expansion of the narrow end and provide room when the cuff is opened. They may replace a zipper on front or back neckline openings. Plackets are planned as extensions for the placement of buttonholes, snaps, and other closures. The type and length of a placket selected depends on

- Placement of the placket
- Function of the placket
- Garment design and style
- Garment use
- Fabric type and weight
- Care of garment
- Method of construction

Band Placket or Tab Placket Two finished strips of equal width that produce a lapped closure where the overlap strip is visible on the face of the garment. A tab placket design may be extended to include an all-in-one facing, combining both the neck and placket bands. Tab strip ends may be incorporated into the seam allowance of the opening to produce a square finish across the bottom. The lower end of the tab may be planned with a pointed or rounded extension for decorative purposes. The extension may hang freely or be topstitched to the garment. The closure may be planned with or without fasteners. A band placket emphasizes openings at the neck, sleeve, and hem areas of dresses, skirts, pants, slacks, and shorts. Additionally, it can create a focal point on garments designed without full-length openings such as pullover jackets, shrugs, and ponchos.

Band placket or tab placket

Bound Placket An opening that does not overlap, formed by a fabric strip applied, slashed, turned, and finished as a bound seam. The strip may be made of bias or straight-grain fabric of self or contrasting fabric. A bound placket may

- Form an opening where no seam is planned
- Accent neck or sleeve openings that close with a loop closure or ties
- Provide an edge finish for a slit on tops, skirts, pants, or shorts
- Allow ease at lower hem edges of blouses, skirts, pants, or shorts to allow ease or as a decorative design detail

Bound placket

Continuous Lap Placket Finished opening formed by one strip of bias or straight-grain fabric that encases the raw edges of the slash. A continuous lap placket may

- Conceal the opening
- Permit hands and feet to fit through sleeve, cuff, and hem openings
- Provide an alternative opening for necklines and sleeves

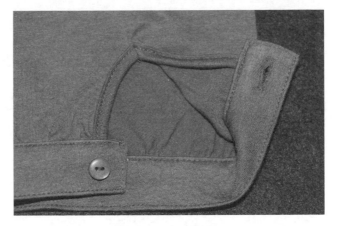

Continuous lap placket

Continuous Lap Placket Placed in a Seam Finished opening that encases the raw edges of the seam at the placket opening. A continuous lap placket placed in a seam may be applied

- In place of a zipper in a seam opening
- When an opening is needed in a seamed section of the garment
- To reinforce seams for buttons, snaps, and hook-and-eye fasteners

Continuous lap placket placed in a seam

Faced-Slashed Placket Clean-finished opening with no overlap, produced by a facing turned inside of a garment. Faced-slashed plackets are applied where garment edges meet rather than overlap on

- Sleeves and necklines where no seam is planned
- Neck or sleeve openings that close with a loop fastener or ties
- Lower hem edges of blouses, skirts, and shorts to allow ease

Faced-slashed placket

CHAPTER 19: GARMENT OPENINGS

Hemmed-Edge Placket Horizontal, hemmed garment section that lies between the ends of an applied band. When the band is fastened, the hemmed edge forms a pleat. A hemmed-edge placket provides an economical and simple construction method on bulky or loosely woven fabrics.

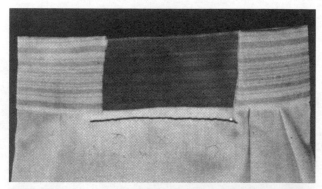

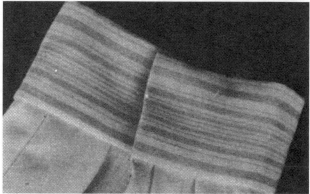

Hemmed-edge placket

Tailored Placket or Shirtsleeve Placket Two strips of unequal widths that enclose raw edges of an opening. The wider, topstitched strip overlaps and conceals the narrower binding strip to the unfinished edge. The topstitched placket section shows on the face of the garment. The placket produces a strong, flat-finished opening. Tailored plackets emphasize openings with overlapping closures on sleeves and skirts.

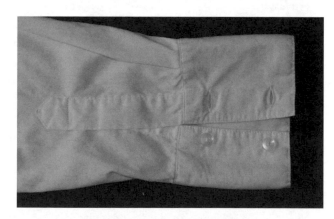

Tailored placket or shirtsleeve placket

Zipper applications vary depending on the garment design and closure function. Zippers allow a garment section to open and close, but they can also be decorative.

Centered Zipper Insertion (Slot Zipper Insertion) Two seam edges of the garment are folded, abutted, or faced over the center of the zipper chain and stitched approximately ¼ to ½ inch (6.4 to 12.7 mm) parallel to the finished seam line. Center zipper insertion applications include

- Center back plackets in skirts, slacks, and shorts
- Princess seams of dresses and gored skirts
- Center front and center back opening of blouses and dresses
- Fitted sleeve openings
- Plackets of parkas, snowsuits, boating jackets, and other sportswear
- Hoods of coats and jackets
- Pocket openings

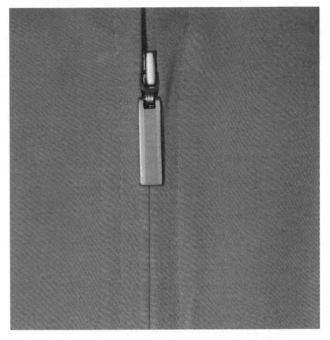

Centered zipper insertion/Slot zipper insertion

Exposed Zipper Insertion Decorative zipper with enlarged teeth and wide tape that show on the face of the garment. A pull tab may be designed as a decorative pendant. The zipper tape and teeth may contrast. It may be a *separating zipper*, *closed bottom*, or *bridge top closed bottom* zipper. Exposed zipper insertion applications include

- Plackets and pocket closures of parkas, snowsuits, boating jackets, and other sportswear
- Hoods of coats and jackets
- Activewear and industrial garments for easy accessibility

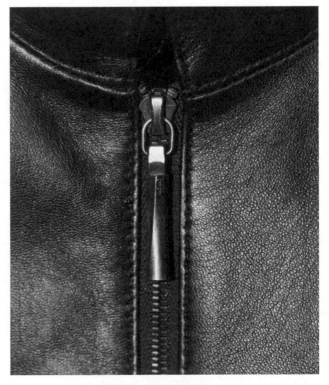

Exposed zipper insertion

Fly-Front Concealed Zipper Insertion One side of a zipper tape stitched to a facing that is turned back and stitched a measured distance from the folded edge to extend beyond the garment closure line. This extension conceals the other half of the zipper, which is aligned and stitched to close at the center of the lap. Fly-front concealed zipper insertion applications include

- Center or asymmetrical garment closures on coats, jackets, rain or snow weather gear, and sportswear
- Winter garments, in conjunction with other fasteners
- Garments where other fasteners or zipper applications would detract from the appearance
- Garments where the extended lap is part of wearing and design allowance

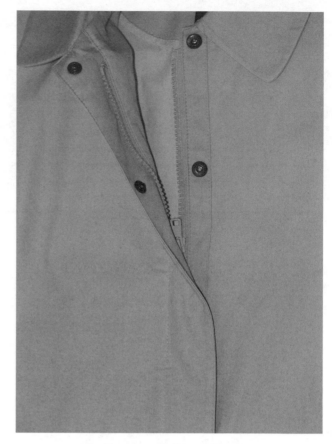

Fly-front concealed zipper insertion

Lap Zipper Insertion Folded seam edge of a garment section stitched along the stitching guideline on the zipper tape. The folded edge of the second garment section, when stitched ¼ to ½ inch (6.4 to 12.7 mm) from the folded edge, forms a tuck concealing the entire unit. When completed, only one line of stitching is visible. Lap zipper insertion applications include

- Left side seam openings of dresses, skirts, and pants
- Skirt and dress plackets
- Center front and center back opening
- Concealed primary closures on outerwear and sportswear fastened with buttons, toggles, and snaps
- Fitted sleeve openings

Lap zipper insertion

Invisible Zipper Insertion Insertion into a seam in which the chain is concealed when the zipper is closed. Stitching does not show on the face of the garment, producing a smooth, continuous seam. Invisible zipper insertion applications include

- Fitted sleeve openings
- Neckline openings
- On back or side seam openings of dresses, skirts, pants, and trousers

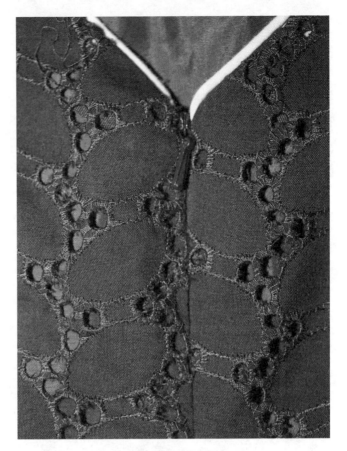

Invisible zipper insertion

Trouser fly zipper insertion

Trouser Fly Zipper Insertion One side of the zipper tape is double-stitched to a facing that is turned back and stitched 1½ inches (3.8 cm) from the folded edge to conceal the other half of the zipper, which is stitched to an underlay extending beyond the center front line. In addition to trousers, trouser fly zipper insertion applications are popular on pants and jeans.

CHAPTER **20**

Hem Finishes

Hems are the finished lower edges of garments that prevent raw edges of material from fraying or tearing. Hems may be turned to the back or inside of the garment, made on the face of the garment as a decorative finish, or left unturned and finished with a decorative stitch pattern.

HEMS

A **hemline** is the designated line along which the hem is to be folded, faced, or finished. Hems may be stitched or held in place or finished with bonding agents. Bonding agents expedite garment construction by replacing machine stitching. Different stitches are designed to duplicate the stitch pattern and appearance of handwork. Blind stitching may be done in a variety of stitch configurations not visible on the face of the garment. Machine-stitched hems may be made to show on the face of the garment for functional or decorative purposes. Hem type or finish selection depends on

- Fabric type and finish
- Fabric weight and hand
- Garment, style, and design
- Garment type
- Garment care
- Current methods of production and manufacturing

Band Hem A shaped, bias, or straight-grain double-ply strip of fabric, folded or seamed, applied to a garment edge. A band may be applied to enclose the garment ply in order to produce a clean finish. Band hems may introduce color or textural contrast to a garment edge or increase the length of a garment.

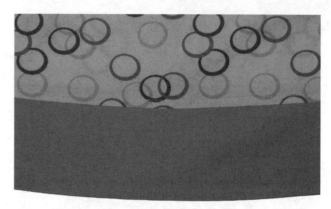

Band hem

Blind-Stitched Hem A folded hem secured by a series of interlocking loop stitches that are not visible on the face of the garment. The type of blind-stitch machine used is determined by the type of fabric, placement of the hem, use of the garment, type of thread, and count of loop stitch required. Blind-stitched hems are applied between the bottom edges of the fabric and the garment ply. They can be applied with or without a tape or binding.

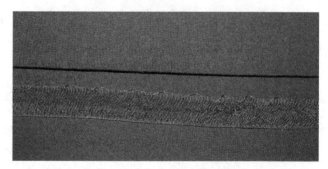

Blind-stitched hem

Book Hem Raw edge folded under and secured to the garment ply by concealed *blind stitches*. Stitches may be made with thermoplastic thread, which bonds the hem to the garment when activated by heat, steam, or pressure. Book hems finish the bottom edges of unlined dresses, skirts, trousers, jackets, and coats. These are selected for garments where exposed stitches would detract from the appearance of the garment or raw edges would be subject to abrasion.

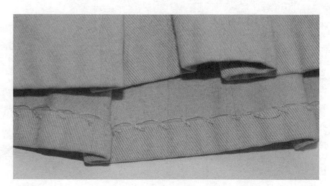

Book hem

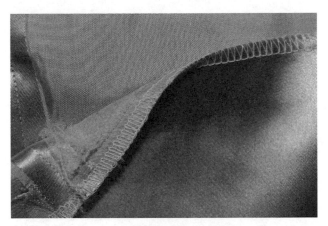

Bonded hem

Bonding agent strip

Bonded Hem Strip of bonding agent placed between the fold of the hem and the garment and fused with heat. Bonded hems are suitable for woven and knit fabrics. Bonding strip is available in a variety of widths: ¾, 1½, 5, and 18 inches (1.9, 3.8, 12.7, and 45.7 cm). Bonded hems provide a smooth look where any stitch would detract from the appearance of the garment or where hem stitches would show.

Bound hem

Bound hem

Bound Hem (Hong Kong Finish or Welt Finished Edge) Bias strip of self or contrast fabric applied to conceal and bind the raw hem edge. Bound hems are applied as a decorative detail or when a flat hem finish is desired on garments made from thick material, which may fray.

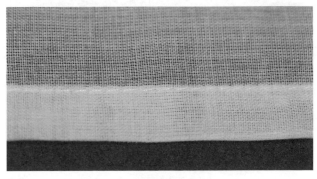

Double-fold hem

Double-Fold Hem Straight-grain edge finish characterized by two full hem-depth folds to add weight and body to the lower edge of the garment. Double-fold hems are common with transparent and lightweight fabrics where the garment needs a deeper, heavier hem. They provide durability when applied to rugged wearing apparel that is laundered frequently.

Double-Stitched Hem Two rows of machine hemming stitches, one row applied midway along the hem depth and the other along the upper edge. Double-stitched hems provide security to an edge finish so it will not fall out if one row of stitching is broken. They are ideal on bulky and heavyweight fabrics and can hold a weighted hem.

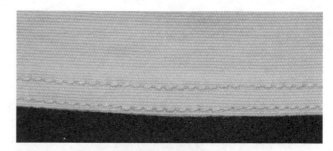

Double-stitched hem

Edge-Stitched Hem Straight-grain hem in which the initial raw edge is turned under, ¼ inch (6.4 mm), and machine-stitched prior to final hemming. Edge stitched hems

- Prevent the edge from raveling
- Provide body to a limp hem
- Produce a strong edged finish for machine-washable garments

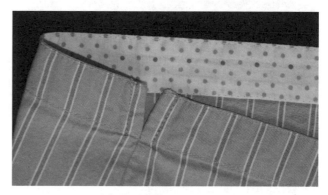

Edge-stitched hem

Faced Hem Clean-finished hem produced on a shaped edge by stitching a similarly formed section of fabric on the face of the garment and then reversing the piece to the inside. Faced hems

- Maintain a curved edge
- Reduce bulk on garments made of heavy fabrics
- Provide support and maintain the shape of scalloped edges
- Lengthen a hemline

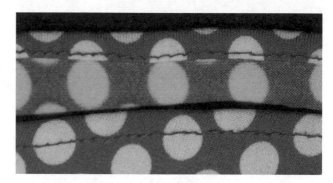

Faced hem

Flat Hem (Plain Hem or Turned Flat Hem) Blind hem produced by a turned-up fold with an unfinished edge void of visible stitching on the face of the garment. Flat hems produce a hemline free of bulk and ridges. This hem requires fabrics that will not unravel.

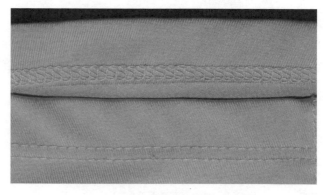

Flat hem/Plain hem/Turned flat hem

Glued Hem A turned-up fold with an unfinished edge glued to the body of the garment. Glued hems are applied to garments made from leather, suede, and other skins, as well as felt and other matted fabrics where machine stitching is undesirable.

Glued hem

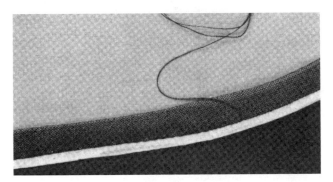

Horsehair Hem A stiff, transparent woven bias braid with a heavy thread along one edge to facilitate shaping is placed between the fold of the hem and the garment. Horsehair adds body to the hem, producing a billowing affect at the lower edge, and allows for controlled fullness. Horsehair hems may

- Provide flare on lower edges of sleeves, wide collars, capes, dresses, and gowns
- Shape bouffant silhouettes created in lightweight or sheer fabrics
- Stabilize the hem in heavy fabrics

Horsehair hem

Interlined Hem (Interfaced Hem) An additional strip of reinforcement for shape retention placed between the fold of the hem and the garment. Interlined hems

- Add body and crispness
- Prevent softening and wrinkling
- Act as a base for the hem
- Alter the silhouette of the garment hemline

Interlined hem/Interfaced hem

Machine-Stitched Hem Hem held in place by means of one or more parallel rows of machine stitching, penetrating all plies, and visible on the face of the fabric. Machine-stitched hems are found on garments subjected to increased wear and frequent washings such as work and play clothes. This type of hem produces a flat finish to the edge of garments made from firmly woven or bulky fabrics.

Machine-stitched hem

Mitered Hem Hem that in turning a corner is seamed at an angle bisecting that corner. Mitered hems

- Eliminate bulk at corners
- Achieve a flat look at corners or points
- Square the corner of faced and other hems
- Produce a continuous fitted look when a band or trimming is placed on the outside hem area of garments; form smooth, finished corners in slashed designs

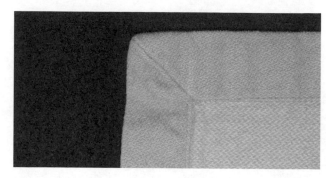

Mitered hem

Over-Edged Hem Clean finish on a raw edge by means of interlocking thread loops. Over-edged hems

- Create an edge finish to an unturned raw edge
- Prevent edges from raveling
- Produce a lettuce edge finish on knit and stretch fabrics

Padded Hem A piece of thick, soft fabric inserted between the hem and the garment. The additional piece typically extends beyond the hem area ¼ inch (6.4 mm) to ½ inch (12.7 mm) and is doubled at the hem fold to provide a soft hemline. Padded hems

- Prevent a sharp crease on hem folds
- Eliminate ridges on hems of heavy fabrics
- Produce roundness to lower edges
- Add weight and body

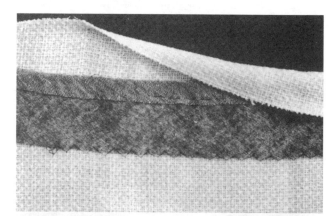

Over-edged hem

Rolled hem

Rolled Hem A narrow double-folded hem, $\frac{1}{8}$ inch (0.2 mm) depth, in which the raw edge is fed through an attachment to complete the folding and stitching in one operation. Rolled hems provide a narrow, lightweight edge finish on very full garments made of sheer and lightweight fabrics.

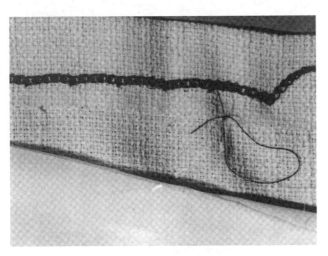
Weighted hem

Weighted Hem A metal chain (in assorted lengths, widths, and metals), a square or round lead disk (maybe covered in fabric), or lead pellets (uncovered or encased in fabric) are added or attached to the inside of the hem portion of the finished garment. Weighted hems

- Control the drape of the hem
- Help the hem fall evenly
- Keep the hem straight
- Hold the hem detail in place
- Prevent the hem areas from shifting or riding up on the body
- Add body to the hem of lightweight fabrics

This type of hem is common on the lower edge of pleats and slashed openings and on the front corner of hems and facings of coats and jackets.

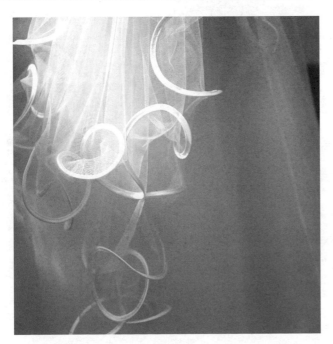
Wired hem

Wired Hem Plastic monofilament or wire placed into the fold of a narrow hem to produce a stiffened edge. Wired hems

- Add body to hem areas without weight
- Billow or stand out
- Create structural detail to ruffles and trimmings
- Produce a lettuce edge on sheer and lightweight fabrics

CHAPTER 21

ASTM and ISO Stitch Classifications

A **stitch** is a loop formation made by interlocking one or more threads by machine or hand to produce seams or surface decoration. The process of forming a series of stitches is known as **stitching**.

Stitch length is measured in millimeters (mm) or can be designated using the number of **stitches per inch (SPI)** or **stitches per centimeter (SPC)**. Stitches may be concealed within or may show on the face of the garment. Stitch types are referred to in terms that describe their configuration or effect.

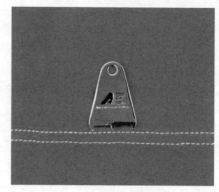

Stitch counter measuring 9 stitches per inch

The relationship among threads that form the stitches is known as **thread tension**. When **balanced thread tension** is used, the stitching has a smooth appearance, and the threads interlock in the middle of the fabric layers. If tension is not properly adjusted, it can cause **unbalanced thread tension**, which appears on the face or inside of the stitch line as a bead or loop(s) of thread formed between the stitches. When stitch tension is too loose, seam grin occurs when stress is placed on the seam, causing the stitches to show at the seamline. If stitch tension is too tight, puckering will be visible along the stitch line, and when tension is applied, it may cause the thread to break.

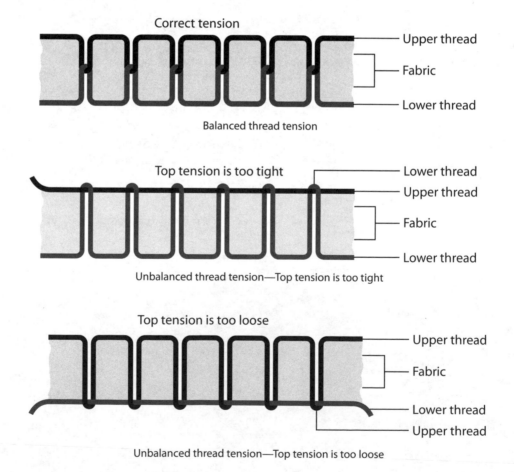

Production engineers require a numbered specification to avoid confusion in production operations. The industry follows **ASTM D6193 Standard Practice for Stitches and Seams**, formerly Federal Standard 751a, or **ISO 4915 Standard Practice for Determining Ticket Numbers for Sewing Threads** to classify stitches. These standards divide stitches into six classifications. Each **stitch class** is identified by the first digit of a three-digit number, 100 through 600. Individual stitches are further identified by a second and third digit denoting their concatenation (series of thread configurations). Each of ISO's stitch class numbers is accompanied by a name. ASTM and ISO stitch classifications include

Class 100 Chain Stitches
Class 200 (Originated as hand stitches)
Class 300 Lockstitches
Class 400 Multithread Chain Stitches
Class 500 Overedge Chain Stitches
Class 600 Covering Chain Stitches

The ASTM D6193 standard also includes an appendix: Sewn Applications for Buttons/Snaps/Hook and Eye Attachments, Buttonhole Stitching, Bartack/Reinforcement Stitching, Tacking, Specialty Stitching/Seams and Guide to Count Stitches Per Inch.

Industrial sewing machines are typically designed to produce one type of stitch. Machines are equipped with numbered stitch size regulators that can be set to sew a selected number of *stitches per centimeter (SPC)* or *stitches per inch (SPI)* or **stitch density**. The set number is an approximate indicator of stitches per centimeter or inch. The setting is a starting point and is tested for accuracy and performance. Factors that influence stitch performance include

- Fabric type and weight
- Number of plies being sewn
- Thread size
- Machine type
- Stitches per centimeter or inch
- Thread tension

Zigzag, buttonhole, and hem stitch machines, as well as special attachments that operate with a side-to-side motion of the needle, produce **stitch bite**. Bite indicates the width of the track or stitching pattern. Blind stitch machines produce a variety of stitch configurations that hold garment plies together without visible stitching on the face of the garment. The type and size of machine stitches selected depends on

- Garment design and style
- Garment use and function
- Garment care
- Garment life
- Fabric type and weight
- Placement of stitch
- Construction technique
- Method of production
- Quantity of garments produced

100 CLASS CHAIN STITCHES

A category of stitches in which a single thread passes through a ply or plies of fabric and interloops with itself on the opposite surface. This loop formation produces a flexible stitch. Single-thread stitches can unravel if they are broken or cut, and can be removed by pulling on an unlocked thread end. A sewing operator can regulate the stitch length.

Single-thread stitches are used for

- Blind hems of skirts, pants, jackets, and dresses
- Light construction

- Attaching trim
- Basting
- Stay chains to anchor linings or form belt carriers

The 100 class contains stitch types 101 through 105. The most commonly used stitches for apparel within this class are

103 Blind stitch
104 Saddle stitch

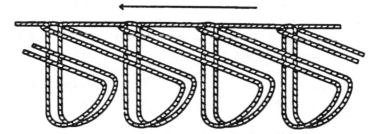

DIRECTION OF SUCCESSIVE STITCH FORMATION

NOTE 1—This type of stitch shall be formed with one needle thread, which shall interloop with itself on the top surface of the material. The thread shall be passed through the top ply and horizontally through portions of the bottom ply without penetrating it the full depth.

Stitch Type 103

ASTM stitch type 103 Blindstitch formation

FACE VIEW AS SEWN

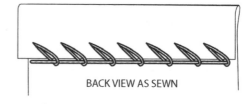

BACK VIEW AS SEWN

ASTM 103, ISO 103 (Face view as sewn; Back view as sewn)

ASTM 103, ISO 103 Blindstitches face view

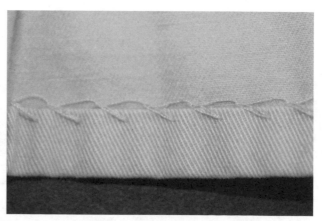

ASTM 103, ISO 103 Blindstitches back view

D6193 – 11

DIRECTION OF SUCCESSIVE STITCH FORMATION

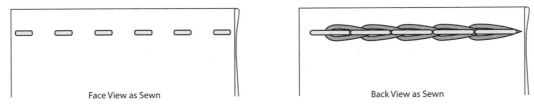

NOTE 1—This type of stitch shall be formed with one needle thread which shall interloop with itself on the undersurface of the material.

Stitch Type 104

ASTM stitch type 104 Blindstitch formation

Face View as Sewn

Back View as Sewn

ASTM 104, ISO 104 Blindstitches (Face view as sewn; Back view as sewn)

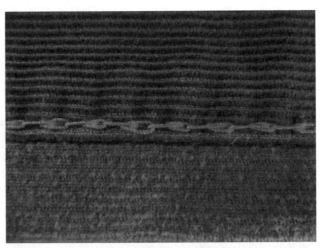

ASTM 104, ISO 104 Blindstitches (Face view)

ASTM 104, ISO 104 Blindstitches (Back view)

200 CLASS (ORIGINATED AS HAND STITCHES)

A category of stitches created by hand or by machine to imitate handwork. One or more needle threads pass through a ply or plies of fabric as a single line of thread that interloops on itself or is secured by passing in and out of the material to show alternately on the face and reverse of the garment. Hand stitches are very labor-intensive and expensive, so their use is quite limited in mass-produced apparel. Machine-imitated hand stitches require special equipment. In mass production, hand stitches are more common for decorative purposes than functional main seaming.

Simulated hand stitches are used for decorative stitches that show on the face of the garment.

The 200 class contains stitch types 201 through 205. The most commonly used stitches within this class are

202 Backstitch or prick stitch
203 Decorative chain stitch
204 Catch stitch or herringbone stitch
205 Running stitch or saddle stitch

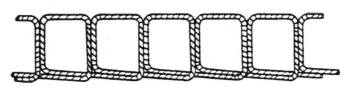

NOTE 1—This type of stitch shall be formed with one needle thread, which shall be passed through the material brought forward two stitch lengths, passed back through the material and brought back one stitch length before being passed through the material a third time.

Stitch Type 202

ASTM stitch type 202 Hand stitch formation

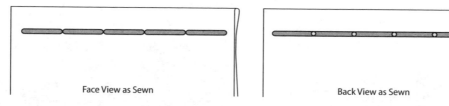

ASTM 202, ISO 202 Hand stitches (Face view as sewn; Back view as sewn)

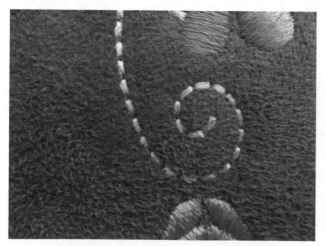

ASTM 202, ISO 202 Hand stitches (Face view)

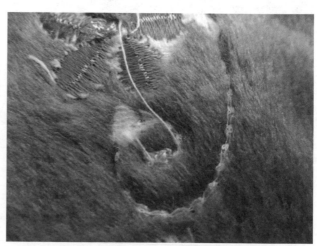

ASTM 202, ISO 202 Hand stitches (Back view)

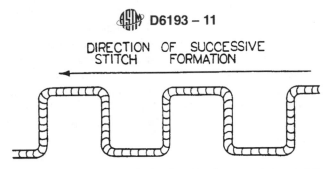

DIRECTION OF SUCCESSIVE
STITCH FORMATION

NOTE 1—This type of stitch shall be formed with one or more needle threads and has for a general characteristic that the thread does not interloop with itself or any other thread or threads. The thread is passed completely through the material by means of a double pointed center eye needle and returned by another path. This class of stitch simulates hand stitching.

Stitch Type 205

ASTM stitch type 205 Hand stitch formation

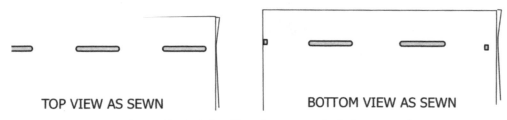

TOP VIEW AS SEWN | BOTTOM VIEW AS SEWN

ASTM 205, ISO 205 Hand stitches (Face view as sewn; Back view as sewn)

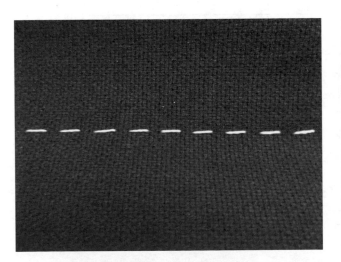

ASTM 205, ISO 205 Hand stitches (Face view)

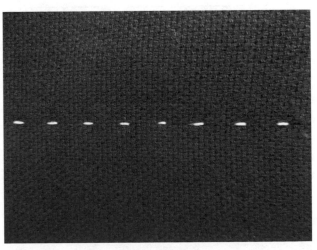

ASTM 205, ISO 205 Hand stitches (Back view)

300 CLASS LOCKSTITCHES

A category of stitches in which single- or double-needle threads and the bobbin thread interlace midway between the surface of the fabric ply or plies as they are fed through the machine to provide the same appearance on the top and bottom surfaces. Double needles may be spaced from $1/16$ to $1/2$ inch (1.6 to 12.7 mm) apart. Some in the industry consider lockstitches to be the standard or regular machine stitch. Length of the stitch can be regulated from 4 to 30 per inch, depending on the individual machine. Lockstitches can be formed in a straight line or a zigzag pattern. Zigzag lockstitches are formed through the combined action of the needle, moving from side to side, and the fabric feeding through the machine whereby the needle and bobbin threads interlace. A narrow bite is used for sewing seams, and a deep bite is used for finishing raw edges. Different industrial machines produce a wide variety of stitch patterns. Two stitches in the same direction and two stitches in the opposite direction form two-stitch zigzag stitches. Three-stitch zigzag stitches are formed by three stitches in one direction and three stitches in the opposite direction.

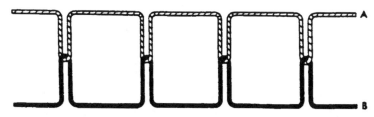

NOTE 1—This type of stitch shall be formed with two threads: one needle thread, A, and one bobbin thread, B. A loop of thread A shall be passed through the material and interlaced with thread B. Thread A shall be pulled back so that the interlacing shall be midway between surfaces of the material or materials being sewn.

Stitch Type 301

ASTM 301, ISO 301 stitch type 301 Lockstitch formation

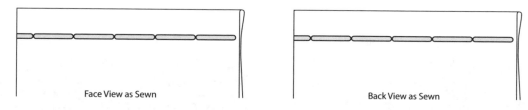

Face View as Sewn

Back View as Sewn

ASTM 301, ISO 301 Lockstitches (Face view as sewn; Back view as sewn)

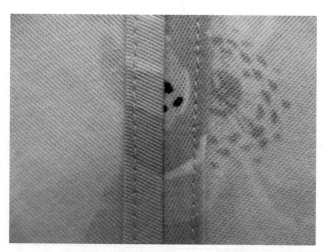

ASTM 301, ISO 301 Lockstitches (Face view)

ASTM 301, ISO 301 Lockstitches (Back view)

Lockstitches are used for

- Sewing straight stitches or seams
- Joining two or more plies of fabric
- Stitching a single ply of fabric
- Embroidering
- Attaching trim
- Top stitching
- Stitching back tacking
- Attaching belt loops
- Attaching buttons
- Stitching buttonholes
- Finishing raw edges
- Applying elastic
- Joining elastic fabric

The 300 class contains stitch types 301 through 316. The most commonly used stitches for apparel within this class are

301 Lockstitch
304 Zigzag lockstitch

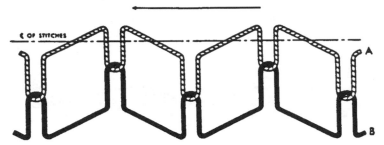

DIRECTION OF SUCCESSIVE STITCH FORMATION

NOTE 1—This type of stitch shall be formed with two threads: one needle thread, A, and one bobbin thread, B. This stitch type is exactly the same as stitch type 301 except that successive single stitches form a symmetrical zigzag pattern.

Stitch Type 304

ASTM 304 stitch type 304 Lockstitch formation

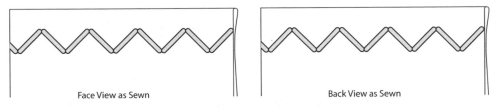

Face View as Sewn   Back View as Sewn

ASTM 304, ISO 304 Lockstitches (Face view as sewn; Back view as sewn)

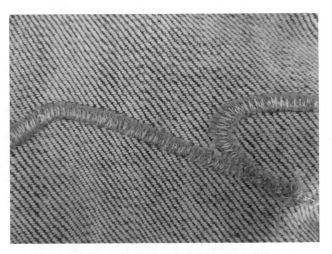

ASTM 304, ISO 304 Lockstitches (Face view)   ASTM 304, ISO 304 Lockstitches (Back view)

400 CLASS MULTITHREAD CHAIN STITCHES

A category of stitches in which single- or double-needle threads and the bobbin thread interlace and interloop between the surface of the fabric ply or plies as they are fed through the machine, to provide the appearance of a lockstitch on the top and a chain-stitch formation on the bottom surface. Double needles may be spaced from 1/16 to 1/2 inch (1.6 to 12.7 mm) apart. This loop formation of the chain produces a flexible stitch, making 400 class stitches the strongest and most elastic of all stitch classes. Stitches do not unravel as easily if they are broken or cut because they are formed with two or more threads, unlike chain stitches, which are categorized in the 100 class. Stitch formation, size, bite, and spacing vary according to different machines. The stitch length can be regulated.

Multithread chain stitches are used for

- Sewing straight stitches or seams
- Joining two or more plies of fabric

DIRECTION OF SUCCESSIVE STITCH FORMATION

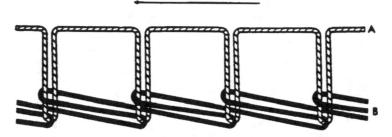

NOTE 1—This type of stitch shall be formed with two threads: one needle thread, A, and one looper thread, B. Loops of thread A shall be passed through the material and interlaced and interlooped with loops of thread B. The interloopings shall be drawn against the underside of the bottom ply of material.

Stitch Type 401

ASTM stitch type 401 Multithread chain stitch formation

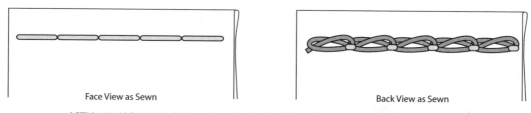

Face View as Sewn

Back View as Sewn

ASTM 401, ISO 401 Multithread chain stitches (Face view as sewn; Back view as sewn)

ASTM 401, ISO 401 Multithread chain stitches (Face view)

ASTM 401, ISO 401 Multithread chain stitches (Back view)

- Stitching main seams
- Hemming knit garments (with a double needle)
- Embroidering
- Attaching trim
- Creating permanent creases
- Attaching elastic

The 400 class contains stitch types 401 through 411. The most common stitches for apparel within this class are

401 Two-thread or multithread chain stitch (single or twin needle can be used)
402 Cording stitch
406 Two-needle bottom coverstitch

NOTE 1—This type of stitch shall be formed with three threads: two needle threads A and A′ and one looper thread, B. Loops of threads A and A′ shall be passed through the material and interlaced and interlooped with loops of thread B. The interloopings shall be drawn against the underside of the material.

FIG. 28 Stitch Type 402

ASTM stitch type 402 Double/twin needle multithread chain stitch formation

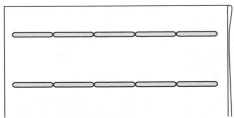

Face View as Sewn

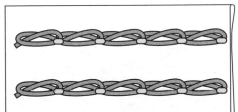

Back View as Sewn

ASTM 402, ISO 402 Double/twin needle multithread chain stitches (Face view as sewn; Back view as sewn)

ASTM 402, ISO 402 Double/twin needle multithread chain stitches (Face view)

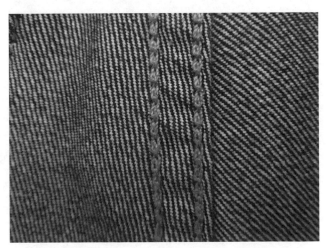

ASTM 402, ISO 402 Double/twin needle multithread chain stitches (Back view)

400 CLASS MULTITHREAD CHAIN STITCHES (continued)

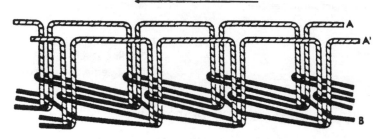

DIRECTION OF SUCCESSIVE STITCH FORMATION

NOTE 1—This type of stitch shall be formed with three threads: two needle threads, A and A' and one looper thread, B. Loops of threads A and A' shall be passed through the material and interlaced and interlooped with loops of thread B. The interloopings shall be drawn against the underside of the material.

Stitch Type 406

ASTM stitch type 406 Double/twin needle bottom cover stitches formation

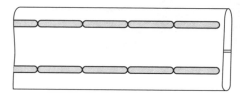

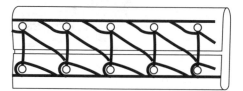

Face View as Shown

Back View as Shown

ASTM 406, ISO 406 Double/twin needle bottom cover stitches (Face view as sewn; Back view as sewn)

ASTM 406, ISO 406 Double/twin needle bottom cover stitches
(Face view)

ASTM 406, ISO 406 Double/twin needle bottom cover stitches
(Face view)

500 CLASS OVEREDGE CHAIN STITCHES

A category of stitches produced by interlocking one or more threads whereby threads enclose the raw edges of the fabric ply or plies. Stitch formation, size, bite, and spacing vary according to different machines and the type of fabric or effect desired. Overedge machine stitches may be used for purl edging and lettuce edging. Lettuce edging is a frilled, unturned edge, similar in appearance to lettuce leaves and is produced by stretching a knit fabric as it is fed into an overedge machine. A safety stitch is produced by simultaneously sewing two parallel independent rows of stitches. One row of lockstitches or multithread chain stitches is positioned at a specified distance from the overedge stitch formation. This combination of stitches provides strength and security or reinforcement should the lockstitch become cut or broken. Overedge stitches provide strength, durability, and elasticity. An increased seam allowance affords a measure of protection against seam slippage, which can be a problem if the thread tension is not set properly.

Overedge stitches are used for

- Sewing main seams
- Finishing an edge
- Preventing fraying, raveling, or rolling of a seam or hem edge
- Joining garment seams of knit and stretch fabrics
- Joining elastic to a garment edge
- Joining a finished exposed seam made on the face of the garment for decorative or styling purposes

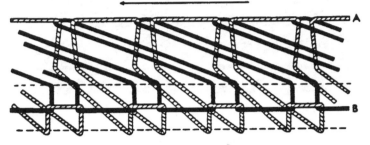

Note 1—This type of stitch shall be formed with two threads: one needle thread, A, and one looper thread, B. Loops of thread A shall be passed through the material and brought to the edge where they shall be interlooped with thread B. The loops of thread B shall be extended from this interlooping to the point of needle penetration of the next stitch and there interlooped with thread A.

Stitch Type 503

ASTM stitch 503 Two-thread overedge chain stitch with single purl on edge formation

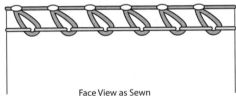

ASTM 503, ISO 503 Two-thread overedge chain stitch with single purl on edge stitches (Face view as sewn; Back view as sewn)

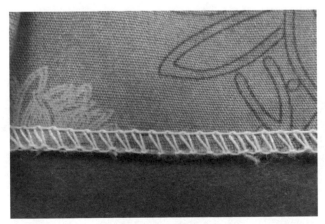

ASTM 503, ISO 503 Two-thread overedge chain stitch with single purl on edge stitches (Face view)

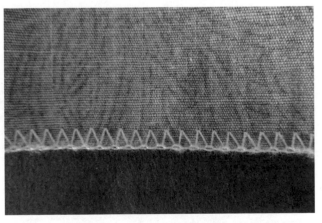

ASTM 503, ISO 503 Two-thread overedge chain stitch with single purl on edge stitches (Back view)

- Finishing decorative hems
- Finishing edges of collars, pockets, scarves, and ruffles

The 500 class contains stitch types 501 through 522. The most frequently used stitches for apparel within this class are

503 Two-thread overedge stitch (single purl on edge)
504 Three-thread overedge stitch
514 Four-thread overedge stitch
516 Five-thread overedge safety stitch

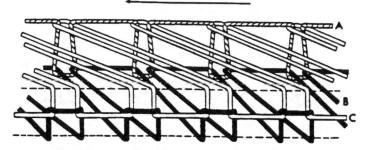

DIRECTION OF SUCCESSIVE STITCH FORMATION

NOTE 1—This type of stitch shall be formed with three threads: one needle thread, A; one looper thread, B; and one cover thread, C. Loops of thread A shall be passed through the material and interlooped with loops of thread B at the point of penetration on the underside of the material. The loops of thread B shall be extended to the edge of the material and there interlooped with loops of thread C. Loops of thread C shall be extended from this interlooping to the point of needle penetration of the next stitch and there interlooped with thread A.

Stitch Type 504

ASTM stitch 504 Three-thread overedge chain stitch formation

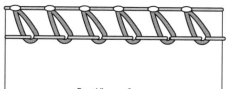

Face View as Sewn

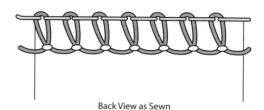

Back View as Sewn

ASTM 504, ISO 504 Three-thread overedge chain stitches (Face view as sewn; Back view as sewn)

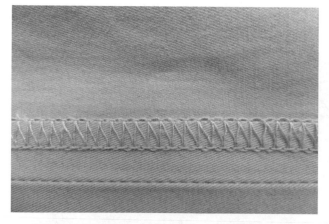

ASTM 504, ISO 504 Three-thread overedge chain stitches
(Face view)

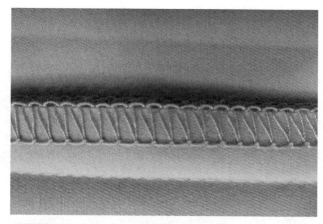

ASTM 504, ISO 504 Three-thread overedge chain stitches
(Back view)

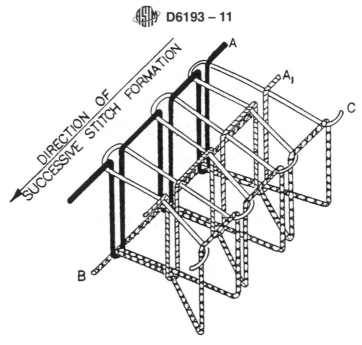

D6193 – 11

NOTE 1—This type of stitch shall be formed with four threads: two needle threads, A and A'; one looper thread, B; and one cover thread, C. Loops of threads A and A' shall be passed through the material where they shall be interlooped at the lower point of penetration with lops of thread B. The loops of thread B shall be brought around the edge of the material and interlooped with loops of thread C. The loops of thread C shall be extended to the point of needle penetration of threads A and A' at the next stitch where they shall be entered by loops of these threads.

Stitch Type 514

ASTM stitch 514 Four-thread overedge chain stitch formation

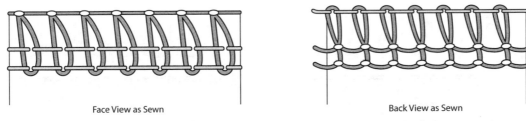

Face View as Sewn   Back View as Sewn

ASTM 514, ISO 514 Four-thread overedge chain stitches (Face view as sewn; Back view as sewn)

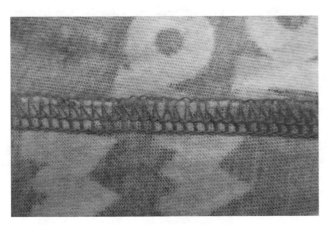 

ASTM 514, ISO 514 Four-thread overedge chain stitches
(Face view)

ASTM 514, ISO 514 Four-thread overedge chain stitches
(Back view)

D6193 – 11

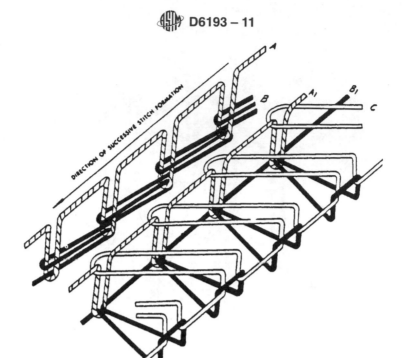

NOTE 1—This type of stitch shall be formed by simultaneously sewing one row of stitch type 401 a specified distance from the edge of the material, and one row of stitch type 504 on the edge of the material.

Stitch Type 516

ASTM stitch 516 Five-thread overedge safety stitch formation

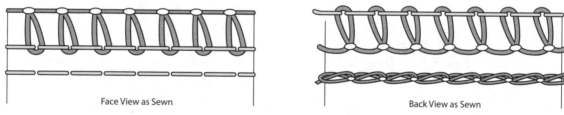

Face View as Sewn

Back View as Sewn

ASTM 516, ISO 516 Four-thread overedge chain stitches (Face view as sewn; Back view as sewn)

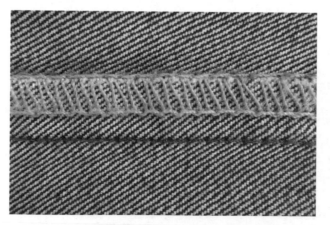

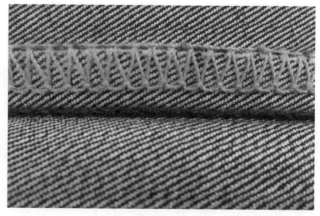

ASTM 516, ISO 516 Four-thread overedge chain stitches
(Face view)

ASTM 516, ISO 516 Four-thread overedge chain stitches
(Back view)

A category of stitches produced by interlooping two or more groups of threads whereby two of the groups of threads enclose the raw edges of both surfaces of the fabric plies. Threads are cast on the surface of the material and then interlooped with loops of thread formed on the backside of the fabric. Stitch formation, size, bite, and spacing vary according to different machines and the type of fabric or effect desired.

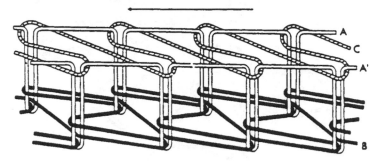

DIRECTION OF SUCCESSIVE STITCH FORMATION

NOTE 1—This type of stitch shall be formed with four threads: two needle threads, A and A′; one looper thread, B; and one cover thread, C. Loops of threads A and A′ shall be passed through loops of thread C already cast across the top surface of the material, and then through the material where they shall be interlooped with loops of thread B on the underside.

Stitch Type 602

ASTM stitch 602 Two-needle four-thread cover stitch formation

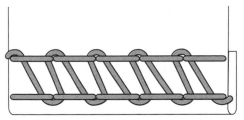
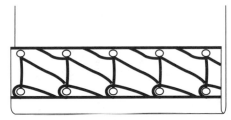

Face View as Shown

Back View as Shown

ASTM 602, ISO 602 Two-needle four-thread cover stitches (Face view as sewn; Back view as sewn)

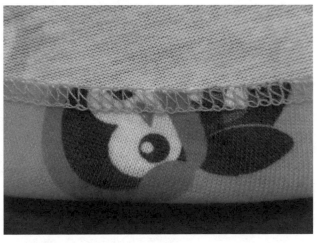

ASTM 602, ISO 602 Two-needle four-thread cover stitches
(Face view)

ASTM 602, ISO 602 Two-needle four-thread cover stitches
(Back view)

600 CLASS COVERING STITCHES (continued)

Cover stitches are used for

- Main seaming on knitted garments
- Decoration

- Main seaming on tight-fitting garments such as swimwear, shapewear, thermal underwear, and athletic apparel
- Sewing *flat seams*

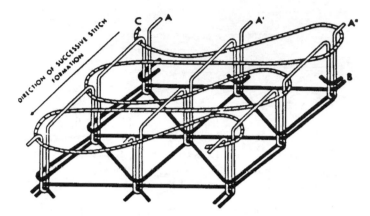

NOTE 1—This type of stitch shall be formed with five threads: three needle threads, A, A′, and A″; one looper thread, B; and one cover thread, C. Loops of threads A, A′, and A″ shall be passed through loops of thread C already cast on the top surface of the material and then through the material where they shall be interlooped with loops of thread B on the underside.

Stitch Type 605

ASTM stitch 605 Three-needle five-thread cover stitch formation

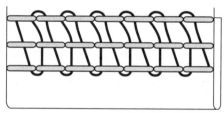

Face View as Shown

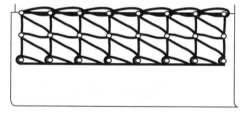

Back View as Shown

ASTM 605, ISO 605 Three-needle five-thread cover stitches (Face view as sewn; Back view as sewn)

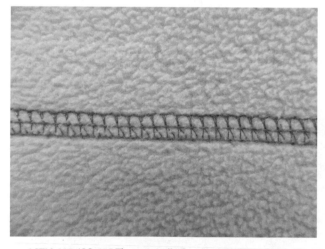

ASTM 605, ISO 605 Three-needle five-thread cover stitches
(Face view)

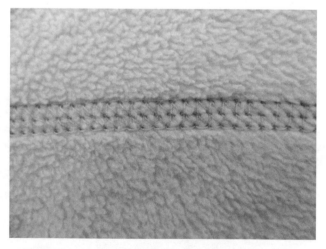

ASTM 605, ISO 605 Three-needle five-thread cover stitches
(Back view)

The 600 class contains stitch types 601 through 610. The most commonly used stitches for apparel within this class are

602 Two-needle four-thread cover stitch
605 Three-needle five-thread cover stitch
607 Four-needle five-thread cover stitch

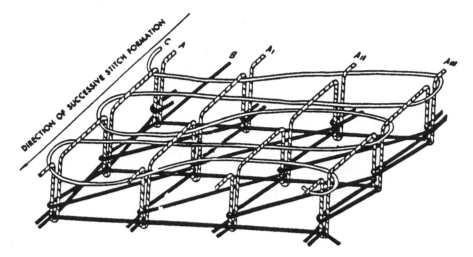

NOTE 1—This type of stitch shall be formed with six threads: four needle threads, A, A', A″, and A‴; one looper thread, B; and one cover thread, C. Loops of threads A, A', A″, and A‴ shall be passed through loops of thread C already cast on the surface of the material, and then through the material where they shall be interlooped with loops of thread B on the underside.

Stitch Type 607

ASTM stitch 607 Four-needle five-thread cover stitch formation

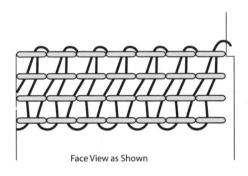

Face View as Shown

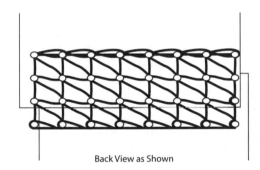

Back View as Shown

ASTM 607, ISO 607 Four-needle five-thread cover stitches (Face view as sewn; Back view as sewn)

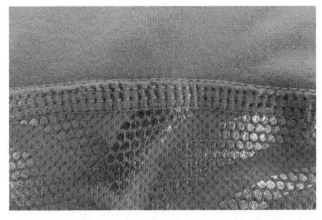

ASTM 607, ISO 607 Four-needle five-thread cover stitches (Face view)

ASTM 607, ISO 607 Four-needle five-thread cover stitches (Back view)

BUTTONHOLE STITCHING

Stitched buttonholes are formed using purl or whip stitching. *Purl stitching* provides a range in appearance from very fine to coarse, depending on the thread Tex selected. *Buttonhole gimp* or *reinforcement cord* is used for eyelet buttonholes to maintain shape and provide structure. Purl stitching is formed by a single-needle thread that passes through the center of the buttonhole where the bobbin thread becomes entangled as the needle position moves from side to side. *Whip stitching* is a zigzag lockstitch formed by a single-needle thread and a bobbin thread that interlace as the needle thread position moves from side to side. The stitch density is much higher for purl stitched buttonholes. The style of buttonhole can vary from straight, eyelet-end, no-eye, or imitation (mock). Regardless of the buttonhole style, all ends must be tacked to avoid stitches from pulling out.

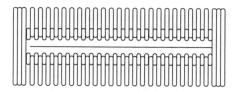

Straight buttonhole with purl stitching

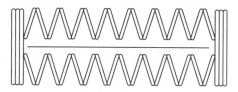

Straight buttonhole with whip stitching

Buttonholes are classified into two cut type constructions: cut-before or cut-after stitching. *Buttonholes cut-before stitching* commonly range in length from ½ inch (1.27 cm) to 1¾ inches (4.45 cm). This method produces a high-quality buttonhole that is very clean and consistent in appearance because the stitching covers raw edges of the cut fabric. Buttonholes cut-before stitching are more expensive to produce, and utilization is limited to bridge and designer priced garments sewn with fusible interlinings that provide enough stability to maintain their shape during stitching.

Buttonholes cut-after stitching typically range in length from ½ inch (1.27 cm) to 2 inches (5.08 cm). This method is the most common type of construction used for budget, moderate, and better-priced garments and can be used on any knitted or woven fabrics regardless of softness, firmness, or interlining type. Buttonholes cut-after stitching do not always provide a clean, smooth appearance and can sometimes show threads severed during the cutting process or yarns from the fabric that remain in the opening of the buttonhole due to a dull knife blade or improper machine settings.

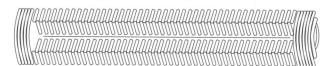

Straight buttonhole with flat, square tacked ends

No-eye buttonhole with straight finished end

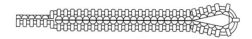

No-eye buttonhole with fly bar tacked end

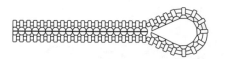

Eyelet-end buttonhole with fly bar tacked end

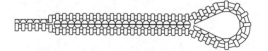

Eyelet-end buttonhole with straight finished end

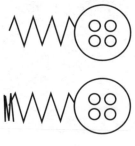

Imitation buttonhole

STITCH CONFIGURATIONS FOR ATTACHING BUTTONS, SNAPS, AND HOOKS AND EYES

The number of stitches used for attaching buttons, snaps, and hooks and eyes varies from 6, 8, 12, 16, 24, or 32 stitches. The most commonly used stitch densities are 8, 16, or 32 stitches. Fabric weight and the number of holes in the button, snap, or hook and eye determines the number of stitches used to attach it to the garment. See Table 21.1 for commonly used stitch densities by fabric weights.

TABLE 21.1
Commonly Used Stitch Densities by Fabric Weights

Fabric Weight	Stitch Densities
Extra light weight 1 to 3 oz/sq/yd (33.91 to 101.72 g/m²)	• 6 or 8 stitches for hooks, eyes, snaps, and two hole or four hole flat or shank buttons
Light weight 4 to 6 oz/sq/yd (135.62 to 203.43 g/m²)	• 8 stitches for hooks, eyes, snaps, and two-hole flat or shank buttons • 16 stitches for four-hole flat buttons
Medium weight 7 to 9 oz/sq/yd (237.34 to 305.15 g/m²)	• 16 stitches for hooks, eyes, snaps, and two-hole or four-hole flat or shank buttons
Heavy weight 10 to 12 oz/sq/yd (339.06 to 406.87 g/m²)	• 16 stitches for hooks, eyes, snaps, and two-hole or four-hole flat or shank buttons
Extra heavy weight 14 to 16 oz/sq/yd (474.68 to 542.49 g/m²)	• 16 stitches for hooks, eyes, snaps • 16 or 32 stitches for two-hole or four-hole flat or shank buttons

A **crossover stitch** is a single stitch that appears on some four-hole flat buttons that are continuously stitched in one operation. The crossover stitch is taken in order to move from one stitching area of the button to another. Crossover styles include C, S, and Z. The most commonly used stitch configurations for buttonhole, snap, and hook and eye attachments include

- Two-hole vertical or horizontal stitching
- Four-hole parallel stitching with or without a crossover stitch
- Four-hole X pattern stitching with or without a crossover stitch
- Shank button with or without a stay button
- Button with neck-wrapped thread shank

Two-hole flat button with horizontal stitching

Four-hole flat button with parallel stitching

Four-hole flat button with parallel stitching and C-style crossover

Four-hole flat button with parallel stitching and S-style crossover

Four-hole flat button with parallel stitching and Z-style crossover

Four-hole flat button with X-pattern stitching

Four-hole flat button with X-pattern stitching and vertical crossover

Hook and eye stitching

Snap with parallel stitching

Shank button with a stay button

Shank button without a stay button

Button with neck-wrapped thread shank

REINFORCEMENT STITCHING

Reinforcement stitching provides increased security and strength in specific areas of garments. Two common types of reinforcement stitching include backstitching and bartacking. **Backstitching** is produced by reversing the stitch direction a minimum of three stitches at the beginning and ending of a stitch line to prevent stitches from unraveling causing *run-back* and to provide additional strength. **Bartacks** are formed by a series of *whip stitches* used at the beginning or ending of stitch lines for attaching and securing belt loops or straps and for reinforcing pocket openings, side seams, fly closures, or buttonholes. Bartack applications may consist of 14, 21, 28, 36, 42, 56, or 64 stitches and can be formed using a W, X, Z pattern.

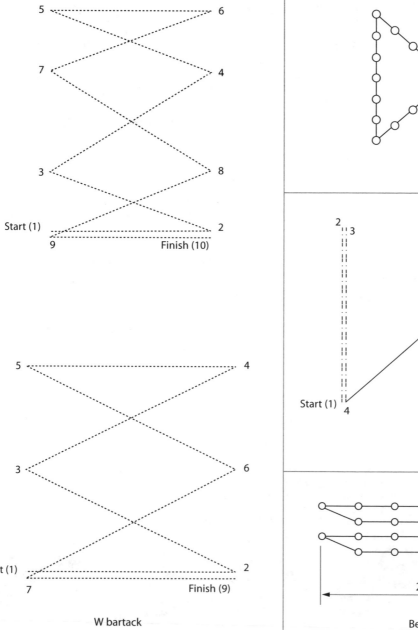

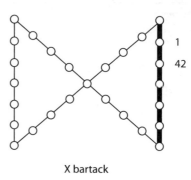

X bartack

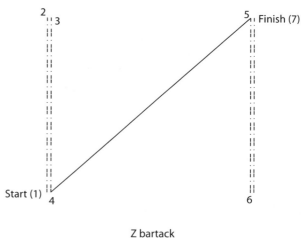

Z bartack

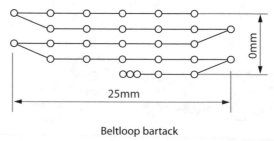

Beltloop bartack

PRODUCTION SEWING EQUIPMENT

Garment production requires a variety of machines to produce different types of stitches, seam constructions, and stitching details. Industrial sewing machines are characteristically designed to produce one type of stitch.

Bartacking Machine Sewing machine that produces tightly packed zigzag stitches to reinforce areas of garments that need extra strength. Bartacking machines are used for securing

- Belt loops
- Pocket openings
- The base of fly front closures on jeans

Bartacking machine

Buttonhole Machine Sewing machine that produces a stitched buttonhole. Buttonhole machines can produce

- Stitched buttonholes
- Keyhole buttonholes
- Stitched eyelet holes

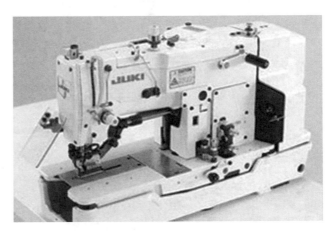

Buttonhole machine

Button Sewing Machine Sewing machine that stitches a button or sew-on snap to a garment.

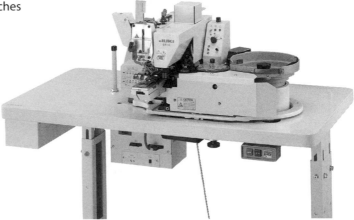

Button sewing machine

Chain-Stitch Machine Sewing machine that produces stitches formed either by one looper thread or by a looper thread and needle threads. Varieties of chain stitch machines include

- Blind stitch
- Single-needle chain-stitch basting
- Flat-bed two-needle double chain stitch
- Feed-off-the-arm lapseamer
- Feed-off-the-arm double chain stitch
- Feed-off-the-arm four-needle double chain stitch
- Feed-off-the-arm four-needle flatseamer

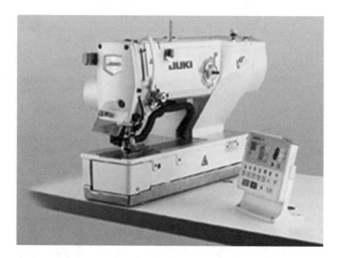

Cover Stitch Machine Sewing machine that produces stitches formed by a looper thread and multiple needle threads that joins two plies of fabric while covering the raw edges.

Lockstitch Machine Sewing machine that produces a series of straight stitches formed by interlocking a bobbin thread and needle thread. A twin needle can be inserted to create parallel rows of stitching simultaneously. Varieties of lockstitch machines include

- Single-needle lockstitch
- Double-needle lockstitch
- Single-needle zigzag lockstitch

Overlock Machine Sewing machine that forms stitches over the edge of a seam. When the fabric is passed through the machine, it stitches over the raw edges. Some machines are equipped with a knife blade that cuts the unneeded seam allowance away and then stitches over the cut edge.

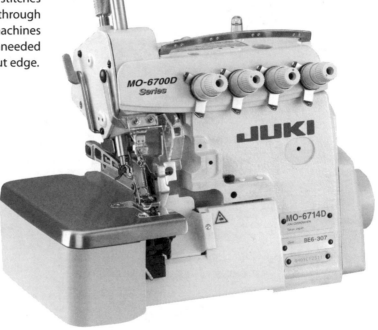

References

ASTM International. (2016). *D6193 ASTM International standards* (Vol. 07.02). West Conshohocken, PA: Author.

International Organization for Standardization (ISO). (1991). *International Standard 4915, Textiles—Stitch Types—Classification and Terminology*. Switzerland, 1–48.

ASTM and ISO Seam Classifications

A seam is the result of joining together two or more pieces of fabric by means of stitching or thermal bonding. Seams are functional and may be used for decorative purposes. Lines and design features are expressed through seams in garments. A **seam line** is the designated line along which the seam is to be joined. A **seam allowance** is the distance from the fabric edge to the stitching line farthest from the edge. Technical designers plan seam allowance according to the width needed for the type of seam, seam finish, or garment design. Most seams are constructed on the inside, or wrong side, of the garment.

Production engineers require numbered specifications for seams to avoid confusion in production operations. The industry follows **ASTM D6193 Standard Practice for Stitches and Seams** or **ISO 4916 International Standard for Textiles—Seam types—Classification and terminology**. ASTM D6193 divides seams into six classifications. Each **seam class** is identified by two or more uppercase letters that classify the seam, followed by one or two lowercase letters identifying the type of seam within the class, and one or more numbers indicating the number of rows of stitching within the seam. ISO 4916 divides seams into eight classifications. Each seam class is identified by a numeric sequence containing five digits. The first number identifies the seam class (1 to 8) and is followed by a period. The second and third double-digit numerals (01 to 82) designate differences in fabric configurations that relate to the number of components within the seam and are followed by a period. The fourth and fifth double-digit numerals (01 to 12) distinguish the needle position and penetrations or passages through the fabric to create the seam.

ASTM D6193 seam classes include

> SS Superimposed Seams
> LS Lapped Seams
> BS Bound Seams
> FS Flat Seams
> OS Ornamental Seams
> EF Edge Finish Seams

ISO 4916 seam classes include

Seam Class 1	Seam Class 5
Seam Class 2	Seam Class 6
Seam Class 3	Seam Class 7
Seam Class 4	Seam Class 8

The type of seam selected depends on

- Fabric type
- Garment use
- Seam placement or position
- Retail price point
- Garment care

SUPERIMPOSED SEAMS (SS CLASS) AND CLASS 1 SEAMS

A category of seams in which two or more plies of fabric are overlaid, one on top of the other with raw edges aligned, and sewn together at a designated distance from the raw edge, with one or more rows of stitching. Seams within this class are produced in a single- or two-step operation. When seams are constructed in a single operation, the fabric plies are superimposed with raw edges aligned and stitched on the designated seam line. For seams constructed using a two-step process, known as an *enclosed seam*, the raw edges are folded and concealed within the layers of material that compose the seam. When the seam allowance of a superimposed seam is pressed open, it is referred to as a *booked seam*. The ISO Class 1 seams are primarily superimposed, although there are a few lapped and flat seams included as well. Superimposed and Class 1 seams are the most common for apparel construction. ASTM and ISO stitch classifications commonly used in the construction of superimposed seams include

> 100 Class Chain Stitches
> 300 Class Lockstitches
> 400 Class Multithread Chain Stitches
> 500 Class Overedge Chain Stitches

There are 55 superimposed seam configurations and 26 Class 1 seam variations. Superimposed and Class 1 seams are used for

- Main seaming in dresses, blouses, shirts, skirts, jeans, trousers, pants, shorts, jackets, coats, and pajamas
- Garments containing a lining
- Cut and sew sweaters and knit garments
- Outer edges of collars, cuffs, necklines, waistbands, and waistlines
- Attaching interlinings
- Attaching buttonhole strips
- Garments made of sheer fabrics such as chiffon, organza, georgette, and organdy where the seam finish may show

Several types of superimposed seams are frequently used in garment construction. Their ISO seam class equivalencies include

- SSa Seam Type = 1.01 Seam Type
- SSh Seam Type = 4.03 Seam Type
- SSk Seam Type = 1.12 Seam Type
- SSab Seam Type = 1.23 Seam Type
- SSae Seam Type = 1.06 Seam Type
- SSag Seam Type = 4.10 Seam Type
- SSaw Seam Type = 2.19 Seam Type

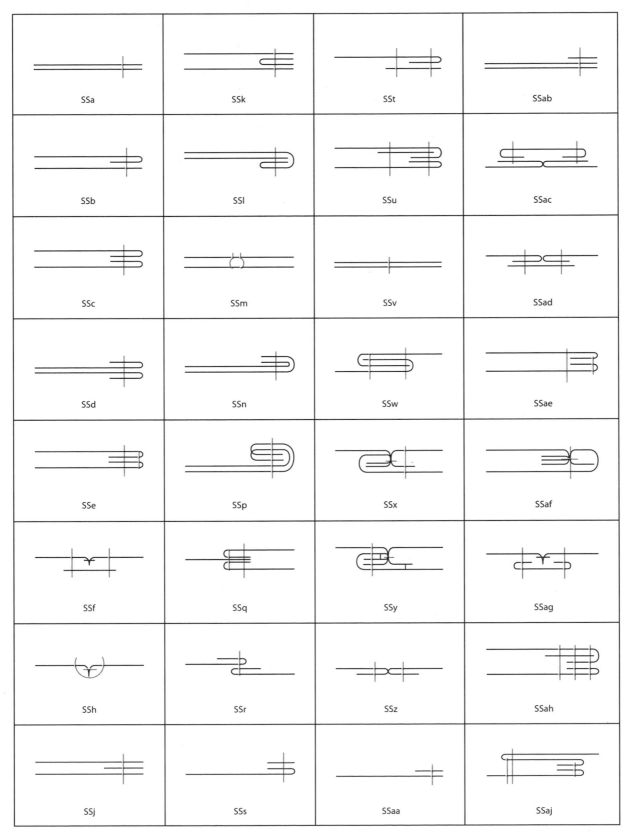

ASTM designated superimposed seams

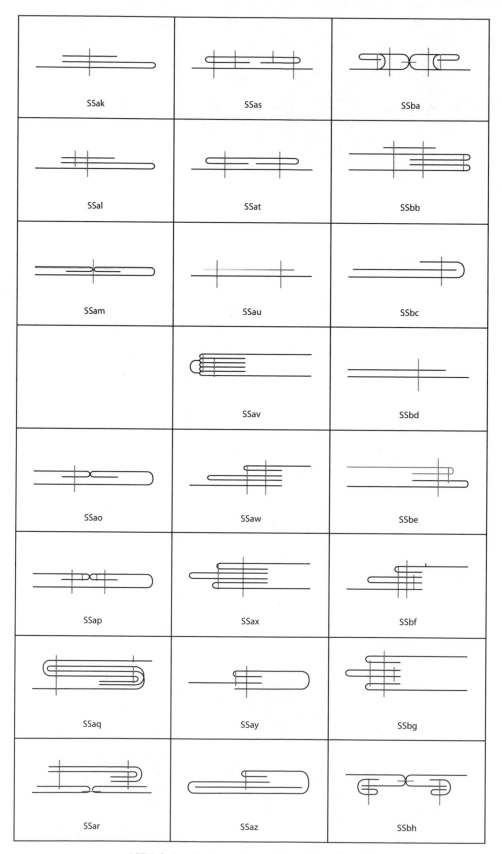

ASTM designated superimposed seams (continued)

SSa and 1.01 Seam Types Plain seams, the most commonly used within this classification, are selected for general seaming on straight or curved areas.

ASTM SSa seams

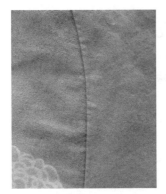

ASTM SSa Single-row stitching with raw edge face view

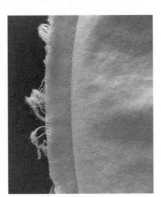

ASTM SSa Single-row stitching with raw edge back view

ASTM SSa Overedge face view

ASTM SSa Overedge back view

ASTM SSa Overedge with seam pressed open face view

ASTM SSa Overedge with seam pressed open back view

ASTM SSa Safety stitch face view

ASTM SSa Safety stitch back view

SSh and 4.03 Seam Types Narrow seams used on garment main seams such as sweatshirt side seams. SSh and 4.03 seams are constructed; then the seam allowance is pressed open and stitched again with a cover stitch.

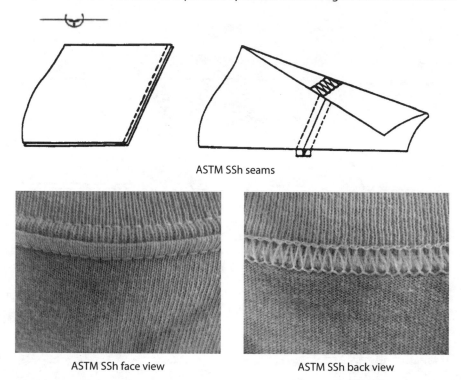

ASTM SSh seams

ASTM SSh face view   ASTM SSh back view

SSk and 1.12 Seam Types Piped seams that add decorative detail to a garment. Piping or cording inserted into the seam as an additional ply during construction.

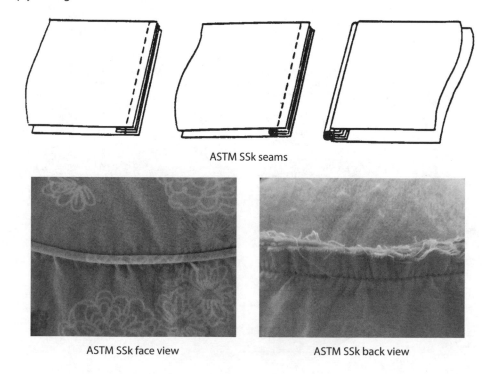

ASTM SSk seams

ASTM SSk face view   ASTM SSk back view

SSab and 1.23 Seam Types Taped seams employ twill tape, clear elastic tape, or shell (self) fabric at necklines, shoulder seams, and waistlines of garments to add stability and reinforcement.

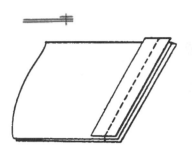

ASTM SSab seams

ASTM SSab face view

ASTM SSab back view

SSae and 1.06 Seam Types French seams, essentially constructed as a seam encased within a seam, are used for straight main seaming within a garment to enclose the raw edges of lightweight or sheer fabrics prone to raveling.

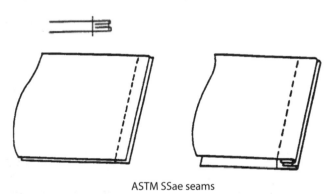

ASTM SSae seams

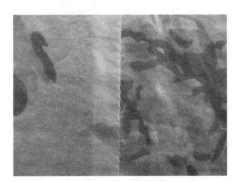

ASTM SSae face view

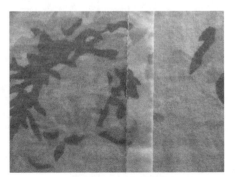

ASTM SSae back view

SSag and 4.10 Seam Types Bias tape reinforces shoulder seams of knitted garments and conceals the raw edges of seams in unlined jackets in strapped seams.

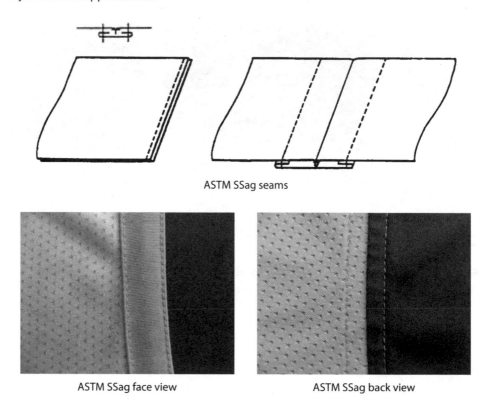

ASTM SSag seams

ASTM SSag face view

ASTM SSag back view

SSaw and 2.19 Seam Types Piping or cording inserted into the seam.

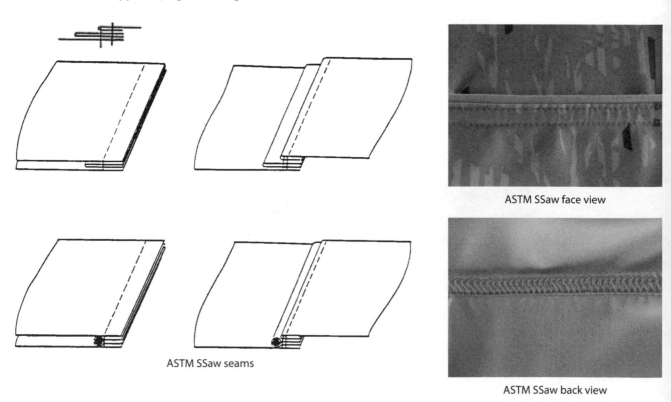

ASTM SSaw face view

ASTM SSaw seams

ASTM SSaw back view

Common production operations utilizing ASTM and ISO stitches and ASTM Superimposed Seams and ISO Class 1 seams are outlined in Table 22.1.

TABLE 22.1

Common ASTM and ISO Stitch and Superimposed Seam (SS) and Class 1 Seam Operations for Production

Production Operation	ASTM & ISO Stitches	ASTM Seams	ISO Seams
General seaming for wovens and knits	301, 401, 512, 514	SSa	1.01
Seaming and coverseaming knits	504 followed by 405	SSh	4.03
Seaming with piping inserted	301, 401 504	SSk	1.12
Seaming with stay tape	301, 401, 504	SSab	1.23
Edge stitching, attaching facings, and French seaming	301	SSae*	1.06.03*
Seaming, then taping neck and shoulders of knits	301, 401	SSag*	4.10.02*
Seaming and piping edges of yokes in shirts, dresses, and jackets	301, 401	SSaw	2.19

(American Efird, 2006; ASTM International, 2016; ISO, 2015)
*Two operations are required for construction.

LAPPED SEAMS (LS CLASS) AND CLASS 2 SEAMS

A category of seams in which two or more plies of fabric are overlapped with the raw edges exposed (for fabrics resistant to raveling), or the seam allowance is folded under and stitched with one or more rows of stitching. Common ASTM and ISO stitch classifications in the construction of lapped seams include

300 Class Lockstitches
400 Class Multithread Chain Stitches

This class includes 101 lapped seam configurations and 46 Class 2 seam variations. Lapped and Class 2 seams are used for

- Main seaming of denim jackets, jeans, and overalls
- Fabrics that will not ravel such as leather, suede, Melton, felt, lace
- Unlined garments

- Side seams of shirts
- Joining lace to another fabric
- Attaching patch pockets
- Joining garment sections such as a yoke, gusset, or godet to other garment sections
- Seams where stitching is desired as a decorative finish

Frequently used lapped seams in garment construction and their ISO equivalencies include

- LSc Seam Type = 2.04
- LSd Seam Type = 5.31
- LSq Seam Type = 2.02.03
- LSbm Seam Type = 2.02

Common production operations utilizing ASTM and ISO stitches and ASTM Lapped Seams and ISO Class 2 seams are outlined in Table 22.2.

TABLE 22.2

Common ASTM and ISO Stitch and Lapped Seam (LS) and Class 2 Operations for Production

Production Operation	ASTM & ISO Stitches	ASTM Seams	ISO Seams
Felled seams on wovens	2- or 3-needle 401	LSc	2.04
Setting patch pockets, flaps, facings	301	LSd	5.31
Seaming and topstitching on wovens	301, 401	LSq*	2.02.03
Seaming side seams of jeans, chino pants, jackets	1- or 2 needle 301 or 401	LSbm*	2.02*

(American Efird, 2006; ASTM International, 2016; ISO, 2015)
*Two operations are required for construction.

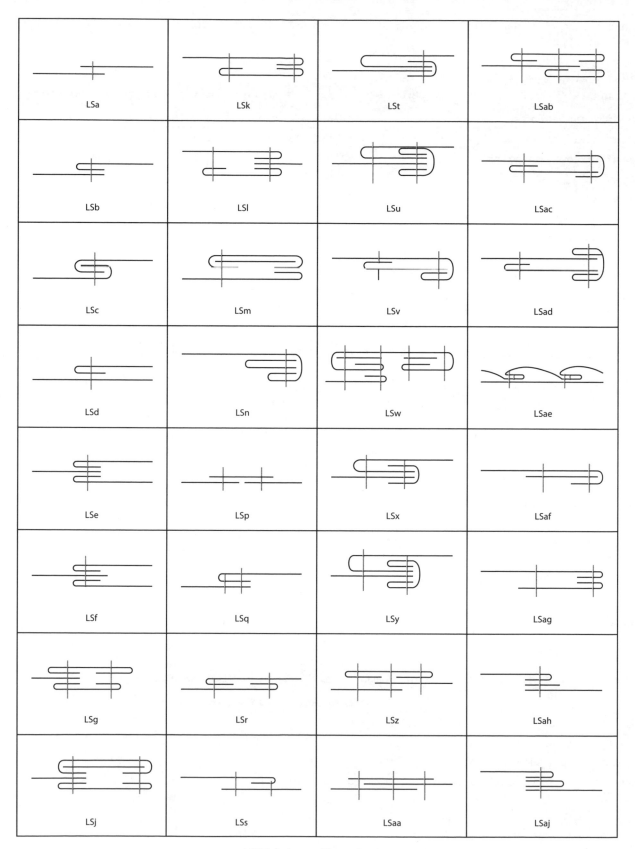

ASTM designated lapped seams

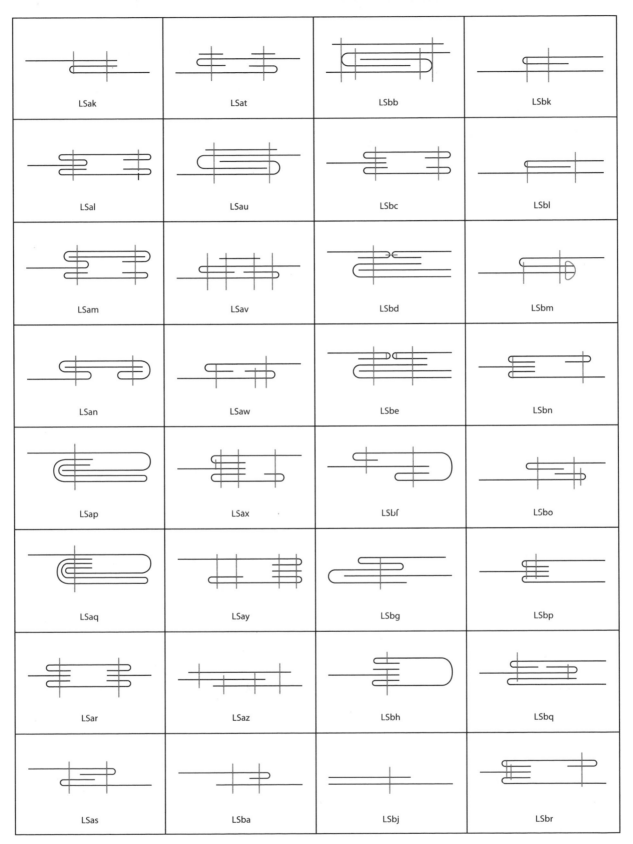

ASTM designated lapped seams (continued)

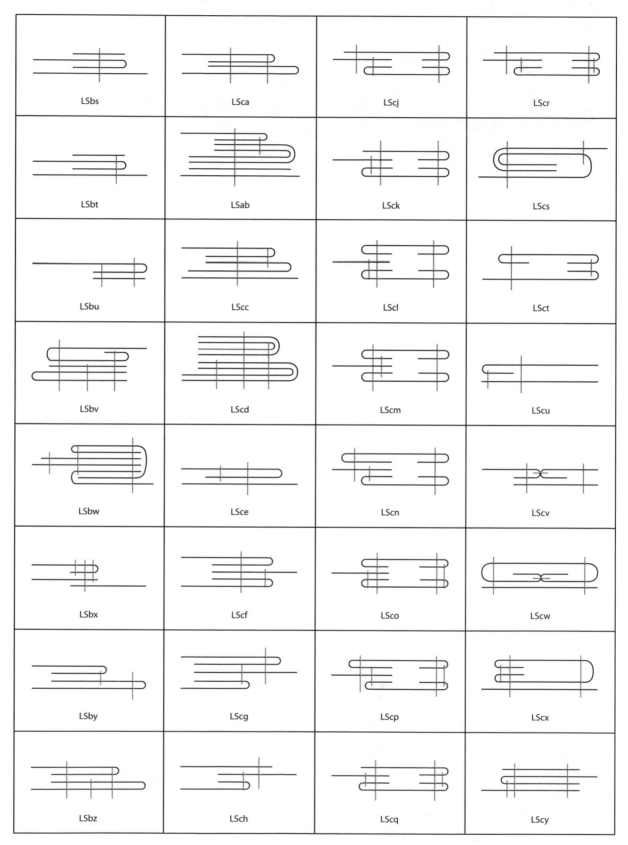

ASTM designated lapped seams (continued)

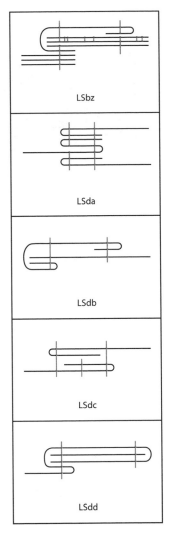

LSbz

LSda

LSdb

LSdc

LSdd

ASTM designated lapped seams (continued)

LSc and 2.04 Seam Types Flat felled seams encase all raw edges inside the seam and are used for straight main seaming of garments where strength and durability are desired.

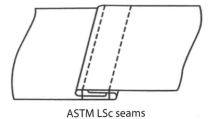

ASTM LSc seams

ASTM LSc Two rows of stitching face view

ASTM LSc Two rows of stitching back view

LSd and 5.31 Seam Types Patch pocket seam application.

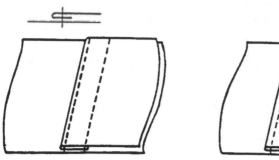

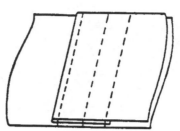

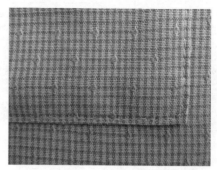

ASTM LSd seams

ASTM LSd One row of stitching face view

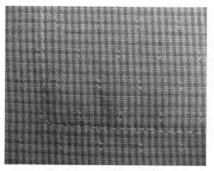

ASTM LSd One row of stitching back view

ASTM LSd Two rows of stitching face view

ASTM LSd Two rows of stitching back view

LSq and 2.02.03 Seam Types Welt seams do not encase all raw edges in the seam and are constructed using an SSa seam that is turned back and secured with one or more rows of stitching. Welt seams provide the appearance of a flat felled seam on the face of the garment but have raw edges that show on the back side.

ASTM LSq face view

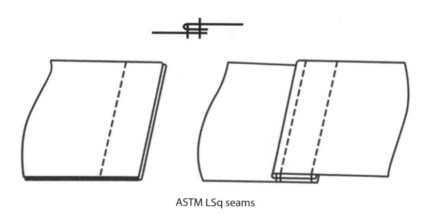

ASTM LSq seams

ASTM LSq back view

LSbm and 2.02 Seam Types Similar to LSq seams, the welt seam does not encase all raw edges in the seam and is constructed using an SSa-2 seam and one row of overedge stitches and is turned back and secured with one or more rows of stitching. Welt seams provide the appearance of a flat felled seam on the face of the garment but have raw edges covered with overedge stitches that show on the back side.

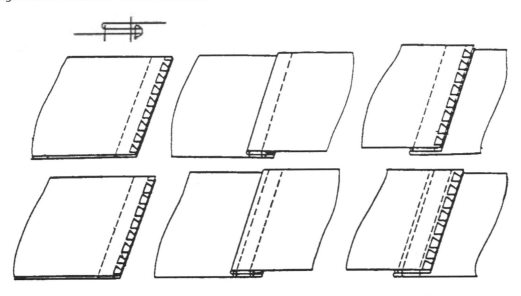

ASTM LSbm Seams

ASTM LSbm One row of stitching face view

ASTM LSbm One row of stitching back view

ASTM LSbm Two rows of stitching face view

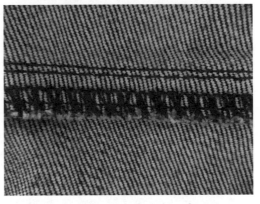

ASTM LSbm Two rows of stitching face view

BOUND SEAMS (BS CLASS) AND CLASS 3 SEAMS

A category of seams in which the raw edges of the seam allowance, of one or more plies of fabric, are covered with a bias binding and stitched with one or more rows of stitching. The ASTM and ISO stitch classifications commonly used in the construction of lapped seams include

300 Class Lockstitches
400 Class Multithread Chain Stitches

There are 18 bound seam configurations and 46 Class 3 seam variations. Bound and Class 3 seams are used for

- Finishing necklines, sleeve hems, or inside waistbands of trousers and pants
- Finishing seams of unlined jackets and coats
- As a design or decorative detail
- Finishing raw edges
- Continuing the motif design of lace

Within these classifications, a few types of bound seams are frequently used in garment construction. Their ISO equivalents include

- BSa Seam Type = 3.01
- BSb Seam Type = 3.03
- BSc Seam Type = 3.05
- BSm Seam Type = 7.40

Common production operations utilizing ASTM and ISO stitches and ASTM Bound Seams and ISO Class 3 seams are outlined in Table 22.3.

TABLE 22.3

Common ASTM and ISO Stitch and Bound Seam (BS) Class 3 Operations for Production

Production Operation	ASTM & ISO Stitches	ASTM Seams	ISO Seams
Setting collar and sleeve bindings on knits	602 or 605	BSa	3.01
Setting collars and binding leg and fly openings on knits	406	BSb	3.03
Setting sleeve facings (clean finish*) and piping on outerwear edges	301 or 401	BSc	3.05
Taping the back neckline (clean finish*) of knitted shirts	301	BSm	7.40

(American Efird, 2006; ASTM International, 2016; ISO, 2015)
*Clean finish = No raw edges of the fabric show.

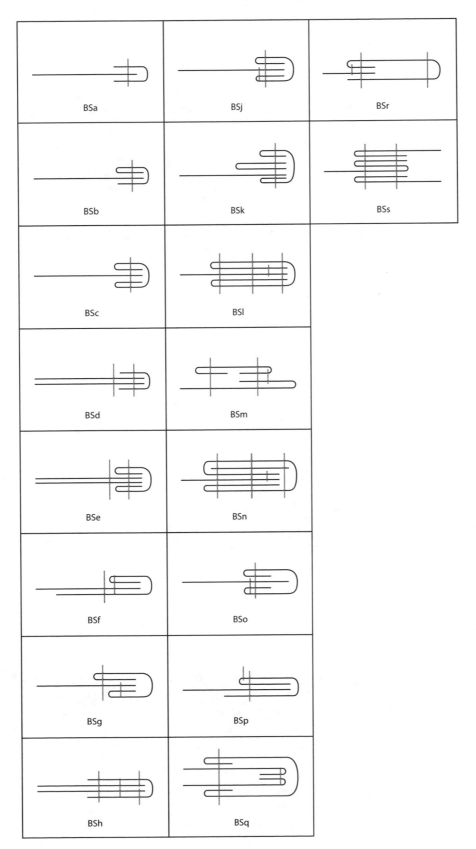

ASTM designated bound seams

BSa and 3.01 Seam Types Bound seam finish used for attaching single-fold braid, leather or suede, or bias binding to a fabric edge.

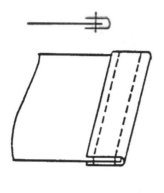

ASTM BSa seams

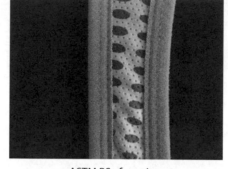

ASTM BSa face view

ASTM BSa back view

BSb and 3.03 Seam Types Bound seam finish used to attach bias binding. The edge of the binding on the face of the garment is folded under and stitched down to conceal the raw edge, but the raw edge is exposed on the inside of the garment.

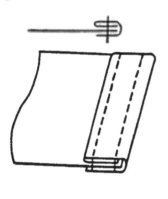

ASTM BSb seams

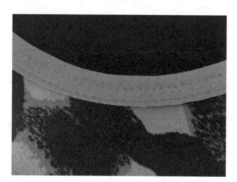

ASTM BSb face view

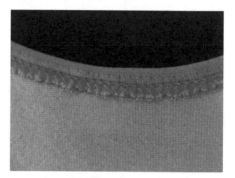

ASTM BSb back view

BSc and 3.05 Seam Types Bound seam finish used for attaching double-fold bias binding. The binding edges are folded under and all raw edges are concealed.

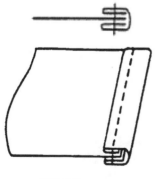

ASTM BSc seams

ASTM BSc face view

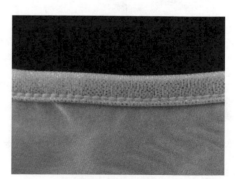

ASTM BSc back view

BSm and 7.40 Seam Types Taping the back neckline of knitted shirts to provide stabilization to prevent distortion. This provides a clean finish to the back neckline.

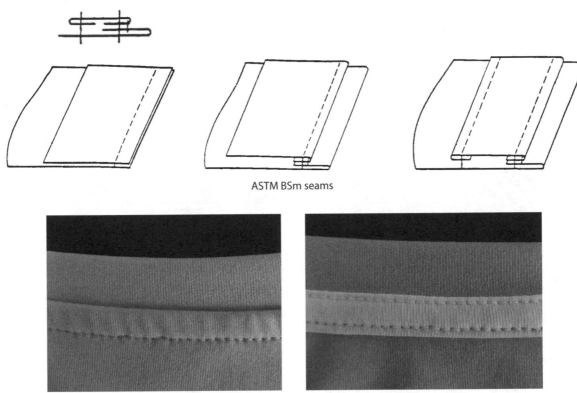

ASTM BSm seams

ASTM BSm face view

ASTM BSm back view

FLAT SEAMS (FS CLASS) AND CLASS 4 SEAMS

A category of seams in which the raw edges of the fabric plies are abutted or just slightly overlapped and joined together with stitching that covers the joint. Flat seams do not contain seam allowances, reducing fabric usage but increasing thread quantity. The ASTM and ISO stitch classifications used in the construction of flat seams are

　300 Class Lockstitches (zigzag variation)
　400 Class Multithread Chain Stitches (zigzag variation)
　600 Class Covering Chain Stitches

There are 6 flat seam configurations and 14 Class 4 seam variations. Flat and Class 4 seams are used for

- Close-fitting garments where the seam allowance may put pressure on the body
- High-stretch fabrics
- Athletic apparel, shapewear, undergarments, lingerie, thermal underwear, swimwear, and sweatshirts with side panels or with raglan sleeves
- Eliminating bulk at seams
- Seaming pelts of fur

Within this classification, the flat seams used most frequently in garment construction are **FSa** and **4.01 seam types**, a flat seam used to join garment parts together and form a low-profile seam.

Common production operations utilizing ASTM and ISO stitches and ASTM Flat Seams and ISO Class 4 seams are outlined in Table 22.4.

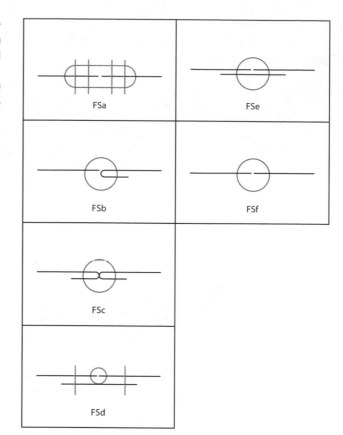

ASTM designated flat seams

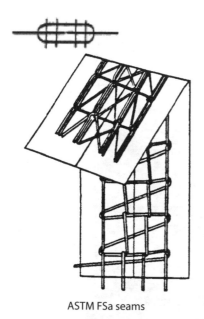

ASTM FSa seams

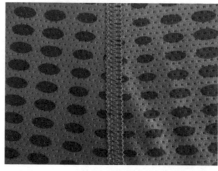

ASTM FSa face view

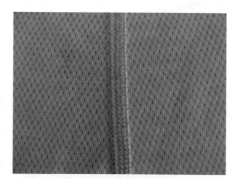

ASTM FSa back view

TABLE 22.4

Common ASTM and ISO Stitch and Flat Seam (FS) Class 4 Operations for Production

Production Operation	ASTM & ISO Stitches	ASTM Seams	ISO Seams
Seaming knits	607	FSa	4.01

(American Efird, 2006; ASTM International, 2016; ISO, 2015)

ORNAMENTAL SEAMS (OS CLASS) AND CLASS 5 SEAMS

A category of seams that add ornamentation to one or more plies of fabric by creating straight or curved lines or a designated design. The ASTM and ISO stitch classifications commonly used in the construction of ornamental seams are

100 Class Chain Stitches
200 Class (Originated as Hand Stitches)
300 Class Lockstitches
400 Class Multithread Chain Stitches

There are 8 ornamental seam configurations and 45 Class 5 seam variations. Ornamental seams are used for

- Adding a design detail
- Cording, piping, tucking, and welting
- Box or inverted pleating
- Decorative stitching

Ornamental seams and their ISO seam equivalents frequently used in garment construction include

- OSa Seam Type = 5.01 and 5.02
- OSe Seam Type = 5.32
- OSf Seam Type = 5.45

Common production operations utilizing ASTM and ISO stitches and ASTM Ornamental Seams and ISO Class 5 seams are outlined in Table 22.5.

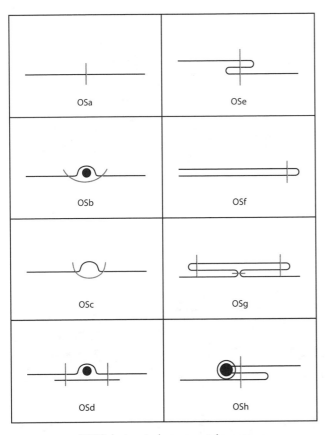

ASTM designated ornamental seams

TABLE 22.5
Common ASTM and ISO Stitch and Ornamental Seams (OS) Class 5 Operations for Production

Production Operation	ASTM & ISO Stitches	ASTM Seams	ISO Seams
Decorative stitching	607201, 202, 203, 204, 205, 301, 304, or 404	OSa	5.01, 502
Sewing tucks	301	OSe	5.32
Sewing darts	301	OSf	5.45

(American Efird, 2006; ASTM International, 2016; ISO, 2015)

OSa, 5.01 and 5.02 Seam Types Decorative straight rows of stitching.

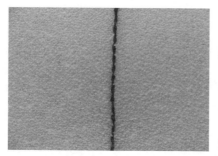
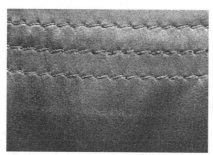

ASTM OSa seams

ASTM OSa One row of stitching face view

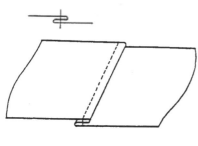
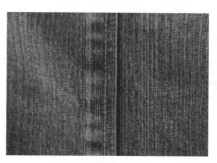

ASTM OSa One row of stitching back view

ASTM OSa Three rows of stitching face view

ASTM OSa Three rows of stitching back view

OSe and 5.32 Seam Type Tucks formed by folding the fabric and stitching it in place.

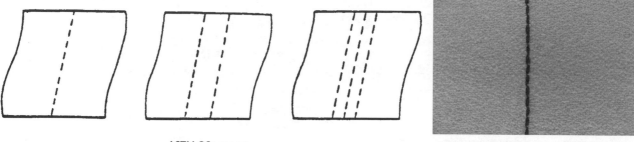

ASTM OSe seams

ASTM OSe face view

ASTM OSe back view

OSf and 5.45 Seam Types Stitched creases formed by stitching close to the folded edge of the fabric.

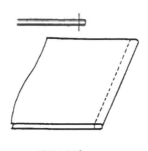

ASTM OSf seams

ASTM OSf face view

ASTM OSf back view

EDGE FINISH SEAMS (EF CLASS) AND CLASS 6, 7, AND 8 SEAMS

A category of seam constructed with one or two plies of fabric used to finish the edge of a garment or item. There are three finishing types within this classification. The first secures a folded edge to the shell fabric by stitching, either on the face or back. For the second type, stitching is used at the edge or to cover the raw edges, and may or may not be folded. The third type applies a binding on a single ply of a seam allowance to finish the raw edges. For the most commonly used Class 7 (7.40) seam, see ASTM's BSm. The

ASTM and ISO stitch classifications commonly used in the construction of edge finishing are

- 100 Class Chain Stitches
- 200 Class (Originated as Hand Stitches)
- 300 Class Lockstitches
- 400 Class Multithread Chain Stitches
- 500 Class Overedge Stitches

Common production operations utilizing ASTM and ISO stitches and ASTM Edge Finish seams and ISO Class 6, 7, and 8 seams are outlined in Table 22.6.

TABLE 22.6
Common ASTM and ISO Stitch and Edge Finish Seams (EF) Class 6, 7, and 8 Operations for Production

Production Operation	ASTM & ISO Stitches	ASTM Seams	ISO Seams
Hemming wovens	301 or 401	EFa	6.02
Hemming knits	2-needle 406	EFa	6.02
Hemming wovens with a clean finish*	301	EFb	6.03
Blind hemming knits	503	EFc	6.06
Finishing the raw edges	503, 504, or 505	EFd	6.01
Sewing flat shoulder straps	503, 504, or 505 followed by 401	No ASTM equivalent	8.02.01
Sewing flat shoulder straps	301, 401, or 402	EFh	8.03
Sewing spaghetti straps, drawstrings, or garment ties with raw edges concealed	301, 302 401, or 402	EFu*	8.06*

(American Efird, 2006; ASTM International, 2016; ISO, 2015)
*Clean finish = No raw edges of the fabric show.

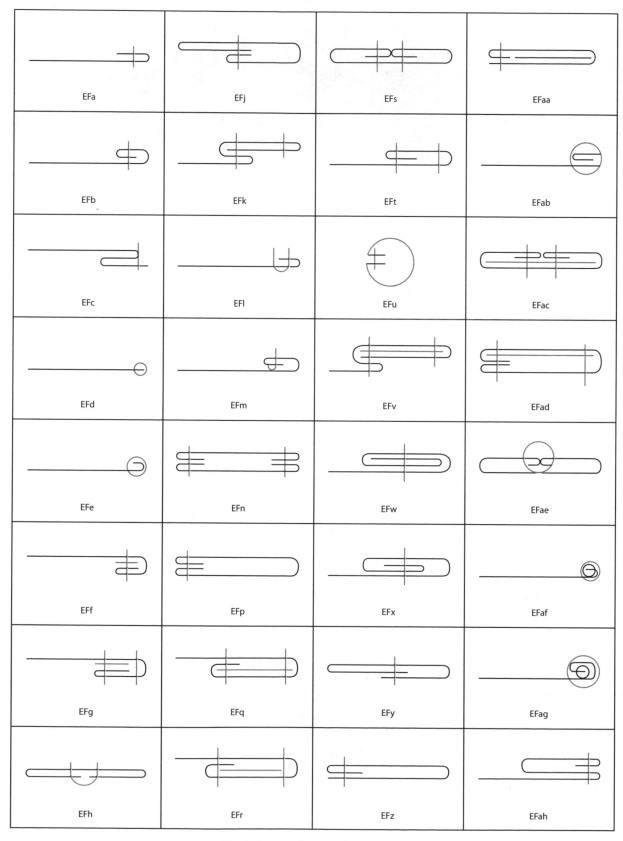

ASTM designation for edge finishing seams

There are 32 edge finish seam configurations, 8 Class 6, 82 Class 7, and 32 Class 8 seam variations. Edge finish seams are used for

- Hems
- Facings
- Seaming shoulder straps
- Seaming belt loops, belts, and drawstrings

Within these seam classifications, common edge finish seams include

- EFa Seam Type = 6.02
- EFb Seam Type = 6.03
- EFc Seam Type = 6.06
- EFd Seam Type = 6.01
- No ASTM equivalent = 8.02.01
- EFh Seam Type = 8.03
- EFu Seam Type = 8.06

EFa and 6.02 Seam Types Hem constructed from a single fold at the edge of the garment that is stitched in place.

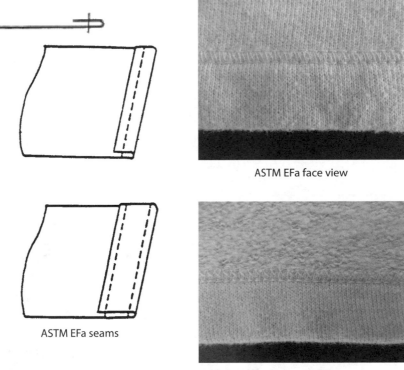

ASTM EFa face view

ASTM EFa seams

ASTM EFa back view

EFb and 6.03 Seam Types Shirttail hem folded twice and stitched close to the edge of the garment.

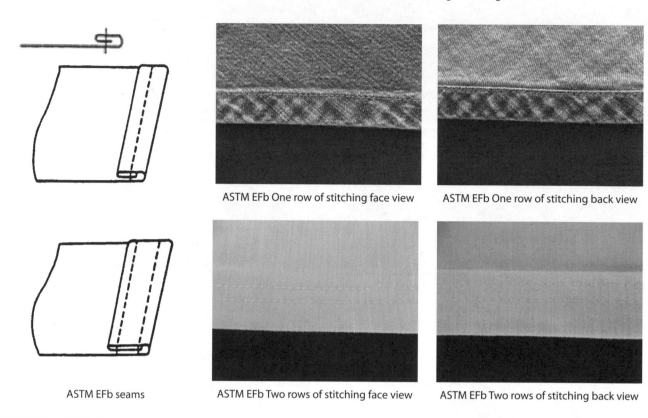

ASTM EFb One row of stitching face view

ASTM EFb One row of stitching back view

ASTM EFb seams

ASTM EFb Two rows of stitching face view

ASTM EFb Two rows of stitching back view

EFc and 6.06 Seam Types Blind hem where the fabric is turned back on itself and stitched at the edge to partially penetrate the folded edge. When laid flat, the stitching is barely visible on the face of the garment.

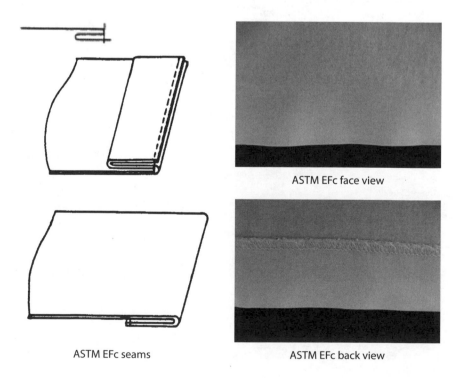

ASTM EFc face view

ASTM EFc seams

ASTM EFc back view

EFd and 6.01 Seam Types Hem created by stitching directly over the edge of the fabric.

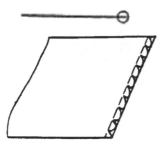

ASTM EFd seams

ASTM EFd face view

ASTM EFd back view

8.02 Seam Type Flat shoulder strap created with a narrow strip of fabric stitched on both sides with 500 overedge chain stitches to cover the raw edges. The second step in creating this seam is to fold the raw edges toward each other (close but not touching) in the center of the back of the strap. Each side is stitched independent of the other. There is no ASTM equivalent seam.

ISO 8.02.01 face view

ISO 8.02.01 back view

EFh and 8.03 Seam Types Flat shoulder strap created with a narrow strip of fabric folded with the raw edges touching or slightly overlapping in the center of the back and then stitched to cover the raw edges.

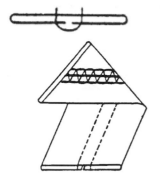

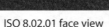

ASTM EFh seams

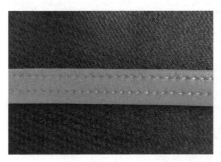

ASTM EFh face view

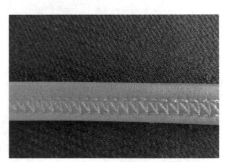

ASTM EFh back view

EFu and 8.06 Seam Types Spaghetti strap, drawstring, or garment tie created by stitching a tube of fabric and turning it right side out to conceal the raw edges and stitching.

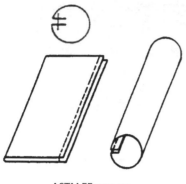

ASTM EFu seams

ASTM EFu face view

ASTM EFu back view

ALTERNATIVES TO STITCHED SEAMS

Seamless garments provide an alternative to cut and sew garments such as knit-and-wear, discussed in Chapter 18, "Design Details." This technology provides a smoother appearance and increased comfort for the wearer because there are no seams to apply pressure on the body and the bulkiness of the seam and seam allowance is eliminated. While seamless garments are currently limited for use in undergarments, shapewear, and performance athletic apparel, it is expected the industry will move forward with use in producing general wearing apparel. Another alternative to cut-and-sew garments include **stitchless garments**. When seams are required for producing a garment but sewn stitches are not desired, stitchless technologies

such as thermal bonding, laser welding, and ultrasonic sealing offer increased comfort and wearability, with the benefits of seamless garments. Stitchless garment technologies are currently limited in the assembly of undergarments, performance athletic apparel, and outerwear but have the potential of becoming more economical and environmentally friendly through reducing waste, reducing labor costs, and making lighter-weight garments than apparel assembled using stitched seams. While these technologies have great potential for application in general wearing apparel and provide great benefits, they require investment in new equipment, training, and time to master the techniques and methods for producing high-quality seams.

Thermal Bonding Thermoplastic film adhesives are used to glue seam components together in undergarments, outerwear, and performance athletic apparel. This seam construction can be used on cellulose, protein, and synthetic fiber fabrics. Film adhesive materials used for thermal bonding include

- Polyvinylchloride (PVC)
- Polyurethane (PU)
- Polyethylene (PE)
- Polypropylene (PP)

Benefits of thermal bonded seams can include

- Flat construction for added comfort
- Garment weight reduction up to 15 percent
- Greater stretch and recovery of seams
- Labor cost reduction

Seamless garment

Laser Welding Infrared laser and a laser-absorbing fluid technology are used to melt and seal seams of waterproof and performance wear garments made from specific thermoplastic fiber materials that can absorb infrared radiation in the near-infrared range. Benefits of laser-welded seams can include

- Clean seam finish
- Flat construction for added comfort
- Protection against penetration of liquids or gasses at the seams
- Strong flat seams that can accommodate curves better than thermal bonding

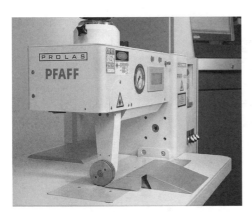

Laser welding machine

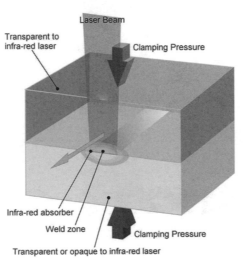

Laser welding diagram

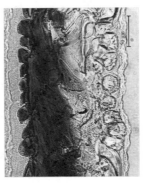

Laser welding melting of fibers

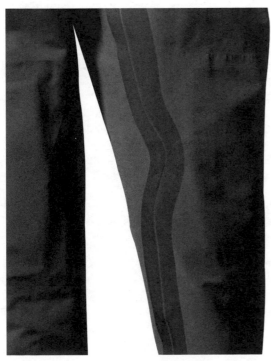

Laser-welded seam

Laser-welded garment

Ultrasonic Sealing Pressure and high-frequency sound waves (deployed at frequencies of 20,000 Hz) cause friction between fibers due to the vibration, which melts and fuses the seams of garments and waterproof and performance wear made from thermoplastic fiber materials. Benefits of ultrasonic sealed seams can include

- Clean seam finish
- Flat construction for added comfort
- Labor cost reduction
- Protection against penetration of liquids at the seams

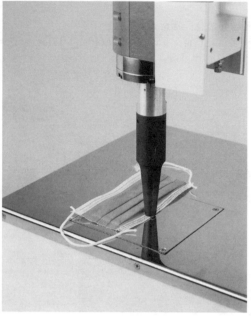

Ultrasonic welding equipment

Ultrasonic Slitting Vibration of high-frequency sound waves and pressure are used simultaneously with ultrasonic sealing to cut and seal raw edges of a seam or single layer of thermoplastic material. This technology produces a clean, smooth cut edge to prevent raveling and will not cause a hard bead to form during the slitting process.

Ultrasonic slitting

References

American Efird. (2006). Seams Drawings—Index. Retrieved January 8, 2016, from http://www.amefird.com/wp-content/uploads/2009/10/Seam-Type.pdf

ASTM International. (2016). D6293 Standard practice for stitches and seams. *2016 ASTM International standards* (Vol. 07.02). West Conshohocken, PA.

Bemis Associates Inc. (2007). *An intro to Sewfree® bonding*. Retrieved January 8, 2016, from http://www.bemisworldwide.com/products/sewfree

Bubonia, J. (2014). *Apparel quality: A guide to evaluating sewn products*. New York, NY: Bloomsbury Publishing.

Emerson Industrial Automation. (2015). *Textile and film processing Equipment*. Retrieved January 8, 2016, from http://www.emersonindustrial.com/en-US/branson/Products/plastic-joining/ultrasonic-plastic-welders/textile-and-film-processing/Pages/default.aspx

Hohenstein Textile Testing Institute. (2011, August 8). *Mechanically and visually perfect seams: New absorber systems to improve the quality of laser welded seams on technical textiles*. Retrieved January 8, 2016, from http://hohenstein.de/en/inline/pressrelease_8464.xhtml

International Organization for Standardization (ISO). (2015). *International Standard 4916 Textiles—Seam Types—Classification and Terminology*. Switzerland, 1–64.

Jones, I. (2007). Ec Contract Coop-CT-2005-017614 ALTEX. *Automated laser welding for textiles*. Cambridge, UK: TWI Ltd. Retrieved January 8, 2016, from http://cordis.europa.eu/documents/documentlibrary/121406901EN6.pdf

StreetInsider.com. (2015, August 5). *Bemis Associates' latest collections provide seamless construction and Sewfree® products for athleisure and natural fiber garment designs*. Retrieved January 8, 2016, from http://www.streetinsider.com/Press+Releases/Bemis+Associates'+Latest+Collections+Provide+Seamless+Construction+and+Sewfree®+Bonding+Products+for+Athleisure+and+Natural+Fiber+Garment+Designs/10783289.html

Textile Exchange. (2012). *Fabric welding*. Retrieved January 2, 2016, from http://www.teonline.com/knowledge-centre/fabric-welding.html

Walzer, E. (2011, May/June). The glue guys: Bemis takes bonded tech to the limit. *Textile Insight*. Retrieved January 8, 2016, from http://www.fibre2fashion.com/bemisworldwide/images/Bemis%20100%20Textile%20Insight%20May_2011.pdf

CHAPTER 23

Apparel Production Product Costing

Companies are in business to make a profit and generate revenue. **Profit** is monetary excess acquired through the sale of merchandise after the cost to produce the product has been subtracted. **Revenue** is the income generated from the sale of products during a specified time frame. Designers, manufacturers, merchandisers, marketers, and retailers must determine the costs associated with saleable products. **Cost** is defined as the associated expenses incurred when producing a product.

TYPES OF COSTING

Costing is the method for determining or approximating the total cost of resources and associated expenditures for a particular garment style or product. The process of costing outlines a detailed estimate of

- Garment component costs
- Labor costs
- Packaging costs
- Finishing
- Shipping costs
- Tariffs if applicable
- Factory overhead
- Wholesale markup
- Retail markup
- List price

Many costs are associated with manufacturing apparel. The **cost of goods** includes all variable and fixed costs incurred during the production of a product or garment style.

Variable Costs Long-term expenditures (investments) in labor, materials, and manufacturing plants. Costs fluctuate in direct proportion to the number of units produced. Variable costs may include

- Labor for construction
- Garment components and materials
- Packaging
- Freight

Nonvariable Costs (Fixed Costs) Short-term expenditures that essentially do not change and are not affected by an increase or decrease in volume, because the investment in labor and the manufacturing plant has already been made. Costs that are not affected by an increase or decrease in the number of units produced. Nonvariable costs may include

- Utility bills
- Lease payments
- Taxes
- Employee benefit expenses
- Labor costs for personnel (other than direct)

Overhead (Manufacturing Overhead) All costs incurred by a contractor or manufacturer for a plant to manufacture and make delivery of goods. Overhead costs may include

- Utilities
- Facilities maintenance and depreciation
- Machine and equipment maintenance and parts
- Property taxes for plant
- Workforce other than direct labor

Direct Costs Expenditures made to add value to the product during production. See Table 23.1.

Direct Labor Cost Wages for workers involved in the actual production of garment styles. Direct labor wages for

- Line supervisors
- Cutters
- Sewers
- Other employees who perform tasks to manufacture garments

Indirect Costs Expenditures that do not specifically add value to the product during production but are necessary for the operation of the factory. Indirect costs include

- Factory overhead
- Occupancy overhead
- Workers that do not add value to the product during manufacturing

Indirect Labor Cost Wages of workers who are essential to running and maintaining the factory but are not involved in the actual production of the garments. Indirect wages pay for

- Equipment repair technicians
- Maintenance staff
- Materials handlers
- Security

Bill of Materials A comprehensive list of materials compiled to produce a prototype of one garment style. The bill of materials is created prior to sample construction and submission of bids.

Bid Package A document containing garment style specifications provided to potential contractors in order for them to estimate:

- Plant capacity for production
- Technology required to produce the garment style at the specified quality level
- Production cost for the garment style
- Production time
- Delivery

Price Quote Written document submitted by a contractor in response to a bid package that includes the estimated price to produce a garment style or product.

Wholesale Price List price of a garment minus all discounts and allowances. This is the price the retailer actually pays a manufacturer for a product.

TABLE 23.1
Direct Manufacturing Costs

Materials Required to Produce Product	Labor Required for Production
Fabric	Cutting
Support materials and devices	Shade marking and bundling
Findings	Sewing
Thread	Wet processing
Trim	Finishing
Labels	First line supervisors
Packaging	Inspectors of Quality Control

Markup Predetermined percentage added to the whole-sale price of a garment style to get the retail price.

Keystone Markup Fifty percent markup.

List Price Product's suggested retail price.

Contribution Margin (Gross Margin Contribution) Product price minus the variable costs or cost of goods.

Gross Margin (Profit Margin) Cost of manufacturing subtracted from a product's net sales.

					BILL OF MATERIALS COST						
	Design #	SUIT0032	Prod. Group	Quelque Choses		Season	Spring	Status		Quote	
	Division	Martin RTW	Office	New York		Year	2016	Create Date		23 Feb 2016	
	Dept.	Womens	Prod. Desc.	Light spring suit consisting of jacket, blouse &straight skirt				Revise Date		1 March 2016	
	Line	Aprés Demain						Prod. Date		15 July 2016	

BOM Variation #	BOMWM0032	Var. Desc.	Bom using substitue fabric		
Sample #	WM0032	Sample Desc	Sample using production methods w/ substitute fabric		
Comments	Note this is a substitute fabric. Real fabric will be different weight, same fiber content.			Set Component	Skirt
BOM Status	Pending Approval		ESTIMATED	ESTIMATED	

Materials	Description	Gr. Usage	Net Qty	Price/Unit	Total	Gr. Usage	Net Qty	Price/Unit	Total
Type	Placement	Waste	UoM			Waste	UoM		
Conceptual	100% Wool Crepe	1.25	1.225	$5.95	$7.44	1.2	1.18	$5.95	$7.14
Suiting	Main Fabric	2%	Yards			2%	Yards		
LIN12348	100% Acetate	1.10	1.08	$3.47	$3.82	1.10	1.08	$3.47	$3.82
Lining	Fully lined	1.5%	Yards			1.5%	Yards		
Comments	Note that the Crepe being used is a substitute. Real fabric will be a heavier weight.								
Trimming	Description	Gr. Usage	Net Qty	Price/Unit	Total	Gr. Usage	Net Qty	Price/Unit	Total
Type	Placement	Waste	UoM			Waste	UoM		
INVZIP06	Plastic invisible 6" zipper	1	1	$0.25	$0.25	1	1	$0.25	$0.25
Zipper	Center back waist		Each				Each		
BU24L4H	Plastic 4 hole with rim- 24 ligne	1	1	$0.75	$0.75	1	1	$0.75	$0.75
Button	Center back waistband		Each				Each		
Comments									
Label	Description		Net Qty	Price/Unit	Total		Net Qty	Price/Unit	Total
Type	Placement		UoM				UoM		
CADRYC1232	Dry Clean only care label		1	$0.15	$0.15		1	$0.15	$0.15
Care Label	At waist, back right side		Each				Each		
ABFASH454	Aprés Demain Label		1	$0.21	$0.21		1	$0.21	$0.21
Brand Label	At waist, back right side		Each				Each		
Comments									
Packaging	Description		Net Qty	Price/Unit	Total		Net Qty	Price/Unit	Total
Type	Placement		UoM				UoM		
HANG248	Plastic Skirt Hanger		1	$0.50	$0.50		1	$0.55	$0.55
Skirt Hanger	Hang from waist side to side		Each				Each		
PLASTIC2	Plastic Cover		1	$0.02	$0.02		1	$0.02	$0.02
Plastic Cover			Each				Each		
Comments									

Comments	Sub-Total for Fabric	11.26	Sub-Total for Fabric	10.96
	Sub-Total for Trimming	1.00	Sub-Total for Trimming	1.00
	Sub-Total for Labels	.36	Sub-Total for Labels	.36
	Sub-Total for Packaging	.52	Sub-Total for Packaging	.52
	TOTAL ESTIMATED	$13.14	TOTAL ESTIMATED	$12.99

karat/pdm

Karat Manufacturing Company

1 March 2016
Page 5 of 7

Bill of materials

COSTING METHODS

Three common costing approaches are absorption costing, activity-based costing, and direct costing.

Absorption Costing (Whole Cost Method) Estimate of the variable costs associated with garment components (materials, trims, and findings), labor for product assembly, and a fixed factory overhead rate that is calculated as a percentage of the direct labor cost. The *overhead application rate* is the factory overhead total divided by the direct labor cost total for a specified period of time. Absorption costing method can recover overhead costs from the production of other items due to the overhead application rate.

Activity-Based Costing Estimate of all direct and indirect production expenditures required to manufacture a garment style. All costs are treated as variable in relation to the specific garment style's needs. Activity-based costing more accurately reflects costs associated with a specific garment style than other costing methods.

Direct Cost Estimate (Direct Costing or Variable Costing) Estimate of variable costs associated with garment components (materials, trims, and findings), labor for product assembly, and factory usage. These are the only factors that determine the cost of a product. The direct costing strategy is more effective for firms that produce basic goods or those that manufacture their goods in their own factories versus using contractors or outside shops. The following nonvariable costs are calculated per unit as fixed costs as part of gross margin or as part of the percentage of the targeted gross margin:

- Administrative and general business costs
- Factory overhead
- Design/product development costs
- Marketing/promotion costs

COSTING PROCESS

Costing at various stages of a product's development and production is important. The first stage of costing is to estimate the preliminary cost of a sample garment, followed by production costing, and lastly determining the actual costs during production. Accurately determining the cost of a garment style is essential to determine

- If a design can be produced at a targeted price point or within a specified price range
- Profit potential for a garment style
- Viability of the garment style for the product line

   Shipping charges and tariffs (*duty*) must be included as part of the garment costing equation. Costs associated with shipping include ocean freight and inland transportation costs known as **drayage**.

Free on Board (FOB) Ownership is transferred from the exporter or offshore contractor when the goods are loaded onto a ship for transporting from the country of origin. Charges incurred by the exporter that are incorporated into the price of the goods include

- Duty charges at point of export
- Quota charges if applicable
- Drayage (inland transportation from the factory to the port)
- Handling charges for loading goods onto the ship

Free on Board (FOB) Destination Ownership is transferred from the exporter or offshore contractor when the goods reach the retail store or distribution center. The goods are loaded onto a ship for transporting from the country of origin. Charges incurred by the exporter that are incorporated into the price of the goods include

- Duty charges at point of export
- Quota charges if applicable

- All drayage (inland transportation from the factory to the port at origin and from the destination port to the retail store or distribution center)
- Handling charges for loading and unloading goods during shipping

Cost, Insurance, Freight (CIF) Cost of merchandise, insurance, and transportation to the port of shipment. The manufacturer or exporter is responsible for clearing and paying all of the costs, including insurance, associated with delivery of the goods to the port of shipment (not destination). Once the merchandise is loaded onto the vessel, the buyer is responsible for

- Loss or damage to the goods
- Claiming the goods at the destination port
- Transportation costs to the distribution center, store, or warehouse

Duty Tariff or tax on imported goods.

Harmonized Tariff Schedule of the United States (2016)
Annotated for Statistical Repor ting Pur poses

XI
62-5

Heading/ Subheading	Stat. Suf- fix	Article Descr iption	Unit of Quantity	Rates of Duty		2
				1		
				Gener al	Special	
6201 (con.)		Men's or boys' overcoats, carcoats, capes, cloaks, anoraks (including ski-jackets), windbreakers and similar articles (including padded, sleeveless jackets), other than those of heading 6203: (con.)				
		Overcoats, carcoats, capes, cloaks and similar coats: (con.)				
6201.13		Of man-made fibers:				
6201.13.10	00	Containing 15 percent or more by weight of down and waterfowl plumage and of which down comprises 35 percent or more by weight; containing 10 percent or more by weight of down (653)	doz. .... kg	4.4%	Free (AU, BH, CA, CL, CO, IL, JO, KR, MA, MX, OM, P, PA, PE, SG)	60%
6201.13.30		Other: Containing 36 percent or more by weight of wool or fine animal hair............................	....	49.7¢/kg + 19.7%	Free (AU, BH, CA, CL, CO, IL, JO, KR, MA, MX, OM, P, PA, PE, SG)	
	10	Men's (434)	doz. kg			52.9¢/kg + 58.5%
	20	Boys' (434)	doz. kg			
6201.13.40		Other..	....	27.7%	Free (AU, BH, CA, CL, CO, IL, JO, KR, MA, MX, OM, P, PA, PE, SG)	
		Raincoats:				
	15	Men's (634)	doz. kg			90%
	20	Boys' (634)	doz. kg			
		Other:				
	30	Men's (634)	doz. kg			
	40	Boys' (634)	doz. kg			
6201.19		Of other textile materials:				
6201.19.10	00	Containing 70 percent or more by weight of silk or silk waste (734)	doz. .... kg	Free	Free (AU, BH, CA, CL, CO, E*, IL, JO, KR, MA, MX, OM, P, PA, PE, SG)	35%
		Other..	....	2.8%		35%
	10	Subject to restraints (334)	doz. kg			
	20	Subject to wool restraints (434)	doz. kg			
	30	Subject to man-made fiber restraints (634)	doz. kg			
	60	Other (834)	doz. kg			
6201.19.90 cotton						
6201 (con.)		Men's or boys' overcoats, carcoats, capes, cloaks, anoraks (including ski-jackets), windbreakers and similar articles (including padded, sleeveless jackets), other than those of heading 6203: (con.)				
		Anoraks (including ski-jackets), windbreakers and similar articles (including padded, sleeveless jackets):			Free (AU, BH, CA, CL, CO, IL, JO, KR, MA, MX, P, PA, PE, SG)	58.5%
6201.91		Of wool or fine animal hair:				
6201.91.10	00	Padded, sleeveless jackets (459)	doz. .... kg	8.5%	1.7% (OM)	
6201.91.20		Other..	....	49.7¢/kg + 19.7%	Free (AU, BH, CA, CL, CO, IL, JO, KR, MA, MX, P, PA, PE, SG) 9.9¢/kg + 3.9% (OM)	52.9¢/kg + 58.5%
	11	Men's (434)	doz. kg			
	21	Boys' (434)	doz. kg			

Duty costs

Estimated Landed Cost (ELC) Total product cost for garment components, labor, packaging, factory usage, shipping costs, and duty charges before wholesale and store markups are added.

Landed Duty Paid Landed value of a product plus any import duties, such as shipping, duty, delivery, insurance, and customs clearance costs. The supplier is responsible for paying landed duty.

Landed Cost Overall expenditure for completed products including domestic drayage to retail stores or distribution hubs. See Table 23.2.

TABLE 23.2
Cost of Goods

Variable Costs	Fixed Costs
Machine parts and oil	Depreciation of equipment and facilities
Sewing needles	
Cutting blades	Insurance
Plastic film for automated cutting	Property taxes
Machine and equipment costs	Rent
Maintenance and repair of equipment	Compliance regulation costs
Marker paper	Security
Materials management and handling*	General operating expenses
Utilities*	Materials management and handling*
	Utilities*

*Some items can be classified as a portion of both categories depending on the level of productivity of the plant at various times of the year (i.e., peak periods require more resources).

Preliminary Cost Estimate (Precosting or Quick Costing) During the design development stage of product design, an estimate of the cost of garment components (materials, trim, findings), labor, factory markup, packaging, finishing, shipping, tariff rate (if applicable), and wholesale markup to determine the retail price of the garment style is calculated.

COSTING PAGE - 1:1 - BLOUSE								
Design #	001232	. Group	Active	Season	Spring	Status	Costing	
Division	Casual	Office	Chamonix Intl	Year	2016	Create Date	Aug 13 2016	
Dept.	Womens	Prod. Desc.	Floral Top			Revise Date	Aug 14 2016	
Fabrication						In store Date		

STYLE INFORMATION					COSTING DETAILS			
Target Retail Price	Est. Retail Price	Target Mark Up	Est. Mark Up	Costing Type	Internal		Quote Requested	Aug 13 2016
28.00	28.00	% : 35.00%	% : 66.88%	Quote Request			Quote Received	Aug 13 2016
Garment Qty UoM	Min. Qty. UoM	Color Min. UoM	Pattern Min. UoM	Quote #	1		Quote Status	Others
500.00 Each	100.00 Each	50.00 Each	50.00 Each	Prod Set Comp	Blouse			

Comments	Assuming a quantity of 500 with a minimum of 100	Comments	Preliminary costing

QUOTE INFORMATION			COSTING WORKSHEET ORIGINAL COST			
				Material	Usage	UoM
Quote Variation						
Construction Var.	1	Basic	Material	3.75	1.50	yards
BOM Variation	1	Basic	Material	1.50	0.50	yards
Size Category	MIS Missy (001 XS - 4XL)			Target Cost	Estimated Cost	Est. Country
BOL Variation				Original: USD - Estimated: Not Defined @1		Not Defined @1
Request Ship Date	Actual Ship Date	01-15-2012				
			Fabric Cost	6.38	1.91	0.00
Comments	Needed for mid January		Trim Cost	4.00	5.50	0.00
			Label Cost	0.55	0.55	0.00
			Packaging Cost	1.00	0.75	0.00
VENDOR & FACTORY INFORMATION			Labor Cost	1.55	0.00	0.00
Office/Agent	Excellent Clothing Commission %	6.00%	Finishes	1.16	0.00	0.00
Contact	Robert		Coosting	1.00	0.00	0.00
Vendor	Accessories International		Free Spot 7	0.00	0.00	0.00
Contact	Jay		FOB	15.64	8.71	0.00
Facility			Duty %	0.07	0.04	0.00
Contact			Ship (Load)	1.11	0.00	0.00
FOB Point	USA		Commissions	0.94	0.52	0.00
Origin of Goods	USA		Quote Fees	0.45	0.00	0.00
HTS	100.1938.47657 Duty %	0.45%	Free Spot 8	0.00	0.00	0.00
Duty of Category	Duty 1		Free Spot 9	0.00	0.00	0.00
TRANSPORTATION INFORMATION			Landed Cost	18.20	9.27	0.00
Air/Ocean/Land	Land		Mark Up %	35.00%	66.88%	0.00%
Cost	1.25 per UoM	Ounces Ounces	Retail Price	28.00	28.00	0.00
Wght. of garment	18.00 UoM	Ounces Ounces	Out of Balance	0.00		
Company						
Contact						

Produced by Freeborders CPM Design, ©Freeborders 2016   Page   1 of 1

Preliminary cost estimate/Precosting/Quick costing

Production Costing (Final Cost Estimate) After the sampling stage of the product development process, a more detailed estimate is calculated to determine the retail price of the garment style with regard to the number of units to be produced. Production costing includes

- Cost of garment components (materials, trim, findings)
- Labor
- Factory markup
- Packaging and finishing

- Shipping and tariff rate (if applicable)
- Wholesale markup

Final cost estimates include *landed costs*.

COSTING PAGE - 1 : BLOUSE

freeborders	Design #	001232	. Group	Active	Season	Spring	Status	Costing
	Division	Casual	Office	Chamonix Intl	Year	2017	Create Date	Aug 13 2016
	Dept.	Womens	Prod. Desc.	Floral Top			Revise Date	Aug 14 2016
	Fabrication						In store Date	

STYLE INFORMATION				COSTING DETAILS			
Target Retail Price	Est. Retail Price	Target Mark Up	Est. Mark Up	Costing Type	Import	Quote Requested	Aug 14 2016
28.00	28.00	% : 35.00%	% : 33.92%	Quote Request	QR4000058	Quote Received	Aug 14 2016
Garment Qty UoM	Min. Qty. UoM	Color Min. UoM	Pattern Min. UoM	Quote #		Quote Status	Others
500.00 Each	150.00 Each	100.00 Each	0.00 Each	Prod Set Comp	Blouse		
Comments	Costs for each item is needed			Comments	Final Costing		

QUOTE INFORMATION			COSTING WORKSHEET ORIGINAL COST			
Quote Variation	1	[Q2]- Final		Material	Usage	UoM
Construction Var.	1	[Q2]- Basic	Material	3.75	1.50	yards
BOM Variation	1	[Q2]- Basic	Material	1.50	0.50	yards
Size Category	MIS Missy (001 XS - 4XL)			Target Cost	Estimated Cost	Est. Country
BOL Variation				Original: USD - Estimated: Not Defined		Canada CAN
Request Ship Date		Actual Ship Date	01-15-2012	1		1.3 5
Comments	Needed for mid December			Fabric Cost	6.38	1.91	2.58
				Trim Cost	4.00	5.50	7.43
				Label Cost	0.55	0.55	0.74
				Packaging Cost	1.00	0.75	1.01
VENDOR & FACTORY INFORMATION				Labor Cost	1.55	2.00	2.70
Office Agent	Excellent Clothing	Commission %	11.00%	Finishes	1.16	0.75	1.01
Contact	Robert			Coosting	1.00	0.55	0.74
Vendor	Knits & Wovens 4 U			Free Spot 7	0.00	1.00	1.35
Contact	onnie			FOB	16.75	13.01	17.57
Facility				Duty %	0.08	0.06	0.08
Contact				Ship (Load)	0.94	3.50	4.73
FOB Point	USA			Commissions	1.94	1.43	1.93
Origin of Goods	USA			Quote Fees	0.45	0.50	0.68
HTS	100.1938.47657	Duty %	0.45%	Free Spot 8	0.00	0.00	0.00
Duty of Category	Duty 1			Free Spot 9	0.00	0.00	0.00
TRANSPORTATION INFORMATION				Landed Cost	18.20	18.50	24.98
Air Ocean Land	Air			Mark Up %	35.00%	33.92%	34.92%
Cost	0.25	per UoM	Ounces Ounces	Retail Price	28.00	28.00	37.80
Wght. of garment	14.00	UoM	Ounces Ounces	Out of Balance	-1.85		
Company							
Contact							

Produced by Freeborders CPM Design Freeborders 2016	Page	2 of 3

Production costing/Final cost estimate

Actual Cost Monitoring and calculation of real costs occurs during the production phase to be sure they do not exceed the final cost estimate.

References

Agility Logistics. (2009). *CIF: Cost, Insurance and Freight. . .(named port of destination).* Retrieved December 23, 2015, from http://www .agilitylogistics.com.au/CIF.aspx

Glock, R. E., & Kunz, G. I. (2005). *Apparel manufacturing: Sewn product analysis.* Upper Saddle River, NJ: Pearson Prentice Hall.

Keiser, S. J., & Garner, M. A. (2012). *Beyond design: The synergy of apparel product development* (3rd ed.). New York: Bloomsbury Publishing.

Rosenau, J. A., & Wilson, D. L. (2014). *Apparel merchandising: The line starts here.* (3rd ed.). New York: Bloomsbury Publishing.

CHAPTER 24

Product Specifications

Different aspects of materials manufacturing,

design development, and apparel

production take several types of standards

and specifications. Specifying standards

for materials and garment components is

important to achieving the desired quality

level and performance of a finished product.

APPAREL MANUFACTURING SPECIFICATIONS

Material specifications provide performance expectations required for all materials that will be used to complete a garment style. These specifications include

- Color standard specifications (see Chapter 6)
- Thread specifications (see Chapter 8)
- Fabric, trim, and finding specifications (see Chapters 7, 11, and 12)

The styling details, design features, and characteristics of an apparel product in relation to aesthetic appeal are known as **design specifications**. Design specifications assist patternmakers in creating prototypes that maintain the integrity of the designer's or product developer's vision for a garment style. **Product specifications** provide standards for intrinsic components of a completed product such as

- Size and fit specifications
- Garment assembly specifications
- Finishing specifications

- Labeling specifications
- Packaging specifications
- Quality and performance specifications

These product specification forms are found in a **specification package**, also known as a **technical package (tech pack)**, which includes information regarding

- Technical drawings of the front, back, and detail views with callouts
- Grade rules
- Bill of materials for all garment components (materials and findings)
- Construction details
- Packaging and labeling
- Fit history and comments

Bill of Materials Listing of all garment component part descriptions including fiber content, placement within the garment, size, width, weight, finish, quantities needed, and *colorway* information.

XYZ Product Development, Inc.
Bill of Materials

PROTO# MWB1720		**SIZE RANGE:** Womens 4-18		
STYLE#		**SAMPLE SIZE:** 8		
SEASON: Fall 2017		**DESIGNER:** Moni van Deusenberg		
NAME: Missy Woven Pant		**DATE FIRST**		
FIT TYPE: Natural		**SENT:** 1/7/2016		
BRAND: XYZ, Missy Casual		**DATE REVISED:**		
STATUS: Prototype-1		**FABRICATION:** 9 oz denim		

ITEM/ description	CONTENT	PLACEMENT	SUPPLIER	WIDTH / WEIGHT / SIZE	FINISH	QTY
Indigo denim, 32/2x32/2, 116x62	96% cotton 4% spandex	body	Luen Mills UFTD-9002	58" cuttable, 9oz	enzyme wash, 30 min.	--
Pocketing	65 polyester 35 cotton, 45dx45d, 110x76	HAND POCKETS	K. Obrien Company	58"	pre-shrunk	--
interfacing, non-woven fusible	100% poly	waistband, fly	PCC	style 246	--	--
Zipper 3CC (CH), DA F-type drop pull	invisible	side seam	YKK Tokyo	6 1/2"	See below	1
thread-DTM body	100% spun polyester	join & overlock	A & E	tex 30	--	--
thread-DTM LABEL	100% spun polyester	back pocket	A & E	tex 30	--	--
thread-CONTRAST	100% spun polyester	topstitch	A & E	tex 90	--	--

COLORWAY SUMMARY

color #	main body color	zipper tape	zipper finish	topstitching	
477	wash black--enzyme	580	coil	A-448	
344B	dark denim--enzyme	560	coil	R-783	

Callout Description of a garment detail in a technical sketch to provide further information or explanation of an attribute.

Comment Important notation made on a specification sheet for use in production.

Component Sheet A listing of all elements used to assemble the garment such as findings, interlining, and trim. The lot or style number and location of each component within the garment are delineated to avoid confusion during production. Specifications for each of these components are found on the *trim sheet*.

Construction Details Cutting and assembly instructions for the garment. Construction details include stitch type, stitches per inch (SPI) with +/– tolerances, seam type and finish, hem type, top-stitching details, interlining type and area of garment for attachment, instructions for matching fabrics (such as patterns, plaids, stripes), closure details and method for attachment, and instructions for placement and sewing of labels into the garment.

XYZ Product Development, Inc. CONSTRUCTION PAGE	
PROTO# MWB1720	**SIZE RANGE:** Womens 4-18
STYLE#	**SAMPLE SIZE:** 8
SEASON: Fall 2017	**DESIGNER:** Moni van Deusenberg
NAME: Missy Woven Pant	**DATE FIRST SENT:** 1/7/2016
FIT TYPE: Natural	**DATE REVISED:**
BRAND: XYZ, Missy Casual	**FABRICATION:** 9 oz denim
STATUS: Prototype-1	

Cutting information: 1 way, lengthwise

Match Horizontal: NA

Match Vertical: NA

Match, other: NA

Stitches per inch (SPI) 11 +/- 1 for joining, 8 +/- 1 for topstitching

AREA	DESCRIPTION	JOIN STITCH	SEAM FINISH	TOPSTITCH	INTER-LINING
back rise, front rise	join & TS	5Tsafe	5Tsafe	1/16	--
back yoke	join & TS	5Tsafe	5Tsafe	1/4	
front waist facing	join & TS	SN-L	2N-L	1/4	--
side seams	join	5Tsafe	5Tsafe	1/16 (partial)	--
Bartacks	see detail sketches	--	--	--	--
hand pocket, side front	palm side, shell to pkt bag	1/4" 2N-T&B-CvS		--	--
hand pocket bag	French seam across bottom	SN-L	--	1/4"	--
bottom opening	hem	blind hem		at 1 1/2"	--
CLOSURES					
side zipper	join	SN-L, inv zip method			

Finishing Specifications Details regarding the processes for creating the product's completed appearance, such as

- Pressing or steaming
- Trimming thread ends
- *Wet processing* to alter the appearance. Finishing specifications for wet processing may include color standard or abrasion tolerances, equipment settings, and compounds used.

Fit History Record of measurements' modifications during the sampling process as they relate to measurements specified in the spec package.

Grade Rules Instructions for proportionately increasing or decreasing the garment sample size pattern pieces at specific locations by designated amounts to produce all of the sizes within the range for production.

Packaging Specifications Details regarding shipping and merchandise packaging for products. Packaging specifications might include

- Method of attachment and placement of hangtags
- Instructions for blocking, folding, or hanging a garment
- Packaging materials and sizes
- Number of garments per shipping container
- Labeling of shipping cartons or containers

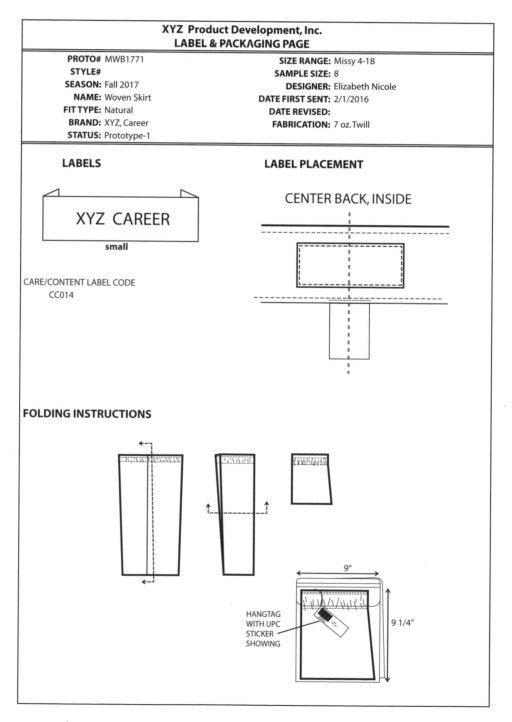

XYZ Product Development, Inc.
LABEL & PACKAGING PAGE

PROTO# MWB1771
STYLE#
SEASON: Fall 2017
NAME: Woven Skirt
FIT TYPE: Natural
BRAND: XYZ, Career
STATUS: Prototype-1

SIZE RANGE: Missy 4-18
SAMPLE SIZE: 8
DESIGNER: Elizabeth Nicole
DATE FIRST SENT: 2/1/2016
DATE REVISED:
FABRICATION: 7 oz. Twill

LABELS

XYZ CAREER

small

CARE/CONTENT LABEL CODE
CC014

LABEL PLACEMENT

CENTER BACK, INSIDE

FOLDING INSTRUCTIONS

9"

9 1/4"

HANGTAG
WITH UPC
STICKER
SHOWING

Product Lead Sheet or Design Sheet Cover sheet for a technical package that provides introductory information about the garment style for production such as

- Brand
- Company name and contact information
- Garment style number
- Season and year
- Color offerings/assortment
- Garment images/technical flats
- Information specific to materials used
- Size range
- Stitch and seam types, SPI/SPC, and locations
- Delivery dates and details

Information from the product lead sheet is carried over onto all other sheets that follow in the technical package.

Specification Library Company's database or paper filing system of specification packages developed for past and present products that can be used for new designs.

Trim Sheet Details trim specifications for garment production that is part of a technical package. Depending on the specific component, the following information may be included:

- Fiber content
- Type of material (i.e., buttons, snaps, zippers, etc.)
- Construction
- Size or width
- Quantity in the unit of measure
- Area of garment and method of attachment
- Color standards for manufacturing and matching
- Performance requirements
- Method and specifications for proper adhesion for interlinings

SIZE SPECIFICATIONS

Specification Buying or Specification Ordering Written communication provided to a manufacturer regarding product specifications, performance requirements and tolerances, and quality expectations.

An important aspect of garment design and production is the specification of garment dimensions. **Size specifications** are accurate standard measurements of a garment that are taken at various measurement points. **Anthropometric measurements** are those gathered from researching the body dimensions, sizes, and shapes of humans to draw comparisons. ASTM International publishes standard tables of body measurements for men, women, and children based on anthropometry. See Table 24.1.

TABLE 24.1

ASTM Size Tables Based on Anthropometry

Designation	ASTM Standard Tables of Body Measurements for
ASTM D 4910-078	Children, Infant Sizes—Preemie to 24 Months
ASTM D 5585-95	Female Misses Figure Type, Sizes 2–20 (Reapproved 2001) This standard was withdrawn in 2010 with no replacement.
ASTM D 5586M-10	Women Aged 55 and Older (All Figure Types)
ASTM D 6192-11	Girls, Sizes 2 to 20 (Regular and Slim) and Girls Plus
ASTM D 6240-98	Men's Sizes Thirty-Four to Sixty (34 to 60) Regular (Reapproved 2006)
ASTM D 6458-99	Boys, Sizes 8 to 14 Slim and 8 to 20 Regular (Reapproved 2006)
ASTM D 6829-02	Juniors, Sizes 0 to 19 (Reapproved 2008)
ASTM D 6860M-09	Boys, Sizes 6 to 24 Husky
ASTM D 6960-04	Women's Plus Size Figure Type, Sizes 14W–32W
ASTM D 7179-06	Misses Maternity Sizes Two to Twenty-Two (2–22)

(ASTM, 2011)

ASTM International standard size tables are available for brands, manufacturers, and retailers to use or modify for their fit and sizing needs. **SizeUSA**, developed by [TC]² (which specializes in solutions for improving supply chain management and technology development), is also available for use and is a compilation of anthropometric data gathered by scanning the bodies of 11,000 adults across the United States to determine common body shapes and sizes.

Size specifications are included on **specification sheets**, also referred to as **spec sheets**. Spec sheets include information regarding

- Garment style (including description, style number, season, size range, size category, sample size, fabrication, colors, knit stitches, trim, findings, accessories)
- Grading information for all sizes in range
- Technical drawings of the front, back, and detailed views of a garment style
- Scale of technical drawings
- Specific measurement points and garment measurements

A **technical designer** writes size specifications based on the garment design, fit, manufacturer, or brand size requirements and grade rules, sizes offered, and production needs.

Basic specification terms are defined in this chapter. For further reading on in-depth information regarding specific garment specifications and how they are measured, refer to one of these sources: *Technical Sourcebook for Designers* by Lee and Steen, *Complete Guide to Size Specification: Technical Design* by Myers-McDevitt, or *The Spec Manual* by Bryant and DeMers.

■ Size Specification Terms

Center Back (CB) Vertical midpoint of the back of a garment.

Center Front (CF) Vertical midpoint of the front of a garment.

Code Number or combination of numerals and letters to identify the measurement on a spec sheet and technical sketch that corresponds with instructions for measurement found in a company's measurement manual.

Extended Measurement Dimension of a designated garment area measured by stretching to full capacity.

Fully Graded Specification Product specification sheet containing measurement data for all sizes in the range.

High Point of Shoulder (HPS) Highest point of the shoulder; where the shoulder and the base of the neck meet.

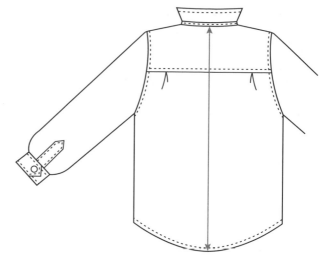

Center back (CB)

Center front (CF)

Measurement Manual Guidebook of codes with corresponding instructions for accurately measuring specific areas on a garment.

Method of Measurement Brief explanation of how a measurement is taken.

Point of Measure (POM) Indicates the exact position where a measurement will be taken.

Relaxed Measurement Dimension of a designated garment area measured without applying tension.

Side Seam (SS) Portion of a garment where its front and back panels are joined at the side.

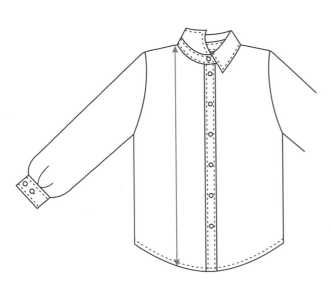

High point of shoulder (HPS)

Side seam (SS)

Size Category Classification of a size group found in men's, women's, or children's in which size ranges are found.

Size Range Assortment of sizes a garment will be manufactured in.

Sweep Total bottom edge opening or hem measurement.

Technical Design Analysis and evaluation of garment specifications regarding design, pattern development, fit, and production.

Tolerance Acceptable amount of deviation from an exact measurement specified in a +/– range.

Total Measurement (TM) Measurement of the circumference; a point of measurement that includes the front and back measurements of a designated garment area.

Sweep

References

ASTM International. (2016). *ASTM International standards* (Vol. 07.02). West Conshohocken, PA: Author.

Bryant, M. W., & DeMers, D. (2006). *The spec manual* (2nd ed.). New York: Fairchild Publications, Inc.

Johnson, M. J., & Moore, E. C. (2001). *Apparel product development* (2nd ed.). Upper Saddle River, NJ: Prentice Hall.

Keiser, S. J., & Garner, M. A. (2012). *Beyond design: The synergy of apparel product development* (3rd ed.). New York: Fairchild Books.

Lee, J., & Steen, C. (2010). *Technical sourcebook for designers*. New York: Fairchild Publications, Inc.

Myers-McDevitt, P. J. (2009). *Complete guide to size specification and technical design* (2nd ed.). New York: Fairchild Publications, Inc.

[TC]² (2016). *SizeUSA*. Retrieved January 10, 2016, from http://www.tc2.com/size-usa.html

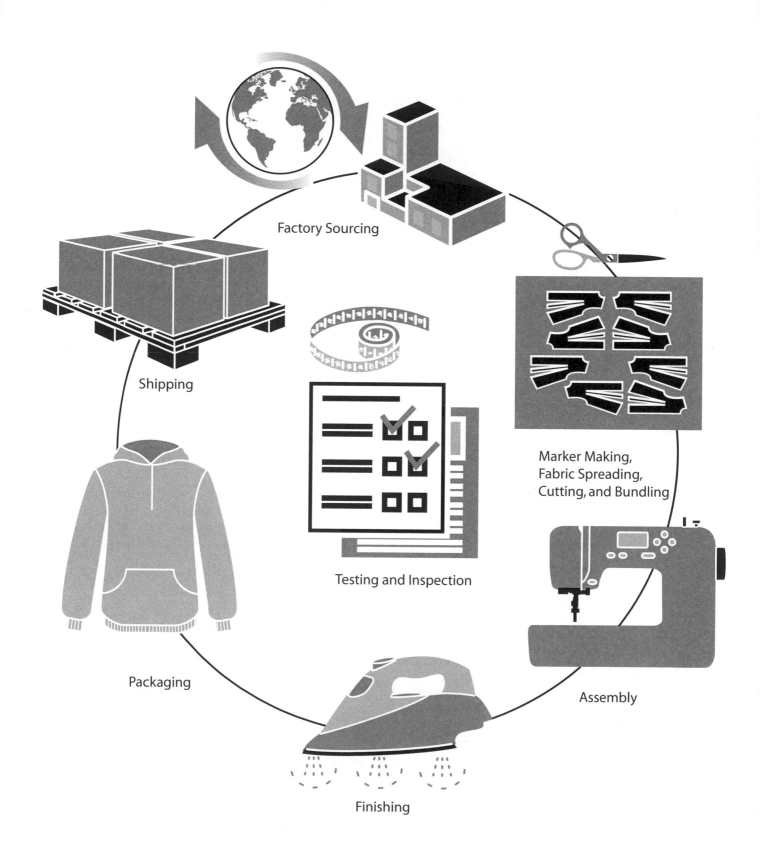

Factory Sourcing

Marker Making,
Fabric Spreading,
Cutting, and Bundling

Testing and Inspection

Assembly

Shipping

Packaging

Finishing

PART FOUR

Production and Quality Control

Once products are designed, production prototypes and technical packages finalized, and materials and factories sourced, production begins. Preproduction operations such as marker making, cutting, shade marking, and bundling take place in preparation for assembly. The type of manufacturer and production system selected will depend on the volume, styling, and quality requirements for the apparel items. Maintaining the desired quality level starts with design and continues through assembly, finishing, packaging, and distribution to the sales venue. Quality control, testing, and inspection are integrated throughout in an effort to verify specification standards are being met, to eliminate safety hazards, to reduce the number of defects and amount of rework, and to provide customers with a product that meets or exceeds their expectations. Part Four of this book will provide an overview of manufacturing and production systems for garment assembly, finishing, quality assurance, product testing, and inspection as well as packaging materials for mass-produced apparel.

CHAPTER 25

Production and Quality Control

Production, also known as manufacturing, is the process of converting raw materials into products for sale to the end consumer. **Production planning** requires factories to coordinate and schedule the manufacturing of goods based on demand and resources available, including anticipated or projected volume required, factory capacity, product requirements to produce the style, and start and end ship dates.

Factory selection is a critical component of production. Apparel is produced all over the world, and sourcing directors are challenged with determining where garments will be manufactured at the desired price and quality level. When goods are sourced internationally, tariffs are imposed on those products, which must be cleared through customs at the port of entry.

APPROACHES TO PRODUCTION

When manufacturers produce goods based on anticipated consumer demand, it is called **push through** or a **push system**. A **pull through** or **pull system** is based on the needs and wants of the consumer. As consumers demand faster flow of new fashion goods, companies look to streamline design, production, and distribution processes to move products through the supply chain at faster rates. According to Kristine Miller of Forbes.com (2006), "Topshop generates as many as 300 new designs a week. These retailers introduce new designs to the racks two to three times per week versus just ten to 12 times per year in traditional stores."

Fast Fashion, Speed to Market, or Quick Response Reducing the time needed to process goods through the supply chain, from the mill to manufacturer to retailer to the consumer. Response times are reduced by increased efficiency of design communication, manufacturing, and distribution of goods. This process allows for flexibility in manufacturing by limiting volume or stopping production of slow-selling merchandise and replacing it with fast-selling products. Companies such as Topshop, H&M, and Zara focus on delivering value-priced trendy merchandise, in limited quantities, to meet the changing needs of their target customers. In a Fast Fashion workshop, Ken Watson, director of the Industry Forum in London, explained that Zara trains its designers to develop products at a faster pace by making design decisions quickly and minimizing modifications in order to speed the development process so production can begin. This vertically integrated company works closely with its mills to match color standards, allowing fabrics to be prepared and cut for production at a much quicker rate.

Flexible Manufacturing Ability to manufacture small quantities of an assortment of product styles within a short period. Flexible manufacturing makes fast fashion possible by providing short lead times for small volume orders.

Long-Term Production Quantities manufactured based on anticipated demand or projected sales for an item.

Short-Term Production Quantities manufactured based on consumer demand for an item.

Production Standard The specific time required to manufacture a particular product style.

Standard Allowed Minutes (SAM) The time in minutes and seconds required for a worker to finish one operation with a specific machine and technique. SAM is commonly used in North and South America.

Standard Allowed Hours (SAH) A conversion from standard allowed minutes (SAM) to hours, which indicates the time in hours required for a worker to finish a dozen units. SAH is used when firms calculate cost by the dozen rather than by a single unit.

Standard Minute Value (SMV) or Standard Time The consistent allocation of time assigned to complete a specific task rather than measuring completion time based on minutes and seconds alone. Standard minute value is based on predetermined measures of time to complete a task but takes into account the necessary hand movements for handling materials and parts as well as sewing sequence. SMV is commonly used in Europe and Asia.

Factory Capacity Prospective volume of goods a manufacturing plant is able to produce at a particular quality level, within a specific time period. Capacity is determined by

- Available machinery
- Factory layout
- Labor intensity of the product to be produced
- Sewing and finishing needs of the particular product to be produced
- Production system
- Plant facilities and allocated space
- Skill and productivity of workers
- Time
- Volume

Available Factory Capacity Total number of hours available for scheduling the production of goods, within a specific time frame.

Committed Factory Capacity Total number of hours devoted to production of products that have already been scheduled for manufacturing during a specific time frame.

Demonstrated Factory Capacity Total quantity of component parts or finished products a machine or manufacturing plant is able to produce at a particular quality level, within a specific time period.

Required Factory Capacity The mandatory total output quantity of component parts or finished products needed from a machine or manufacturing plant, produced at a particular quality level, within a specific time period.

Throughput Time Actual time in hours, minutes, and seconds for a product to move through production, starting at the point of cutting and concluding at the point of shipment.

Throughput Volume Actual quantity of products produced within a specific time frame.

Work in Progress or Work in Process (WIP) Amount of raw materials or number of garments that are not yet complete at any given time during manufacturing.

Direct Labor Workers within a factory who are directly responsible for producing finished products; individuals who contribute to making the product. Direct labor includes

- First-line supervisors
- Fabric spreaders and cutting operators
- Shade markers and bundlers
- Materials handlers
- Sewing operators
- Finishing workers

Factory manager

Factory Managers Leaders within a factory who are responsible for managing workers and providing direction and organization for plant operations and facilities. Examples of factory managers include

- Engineers
- Plant managers
- Line supervisors
- Production managers

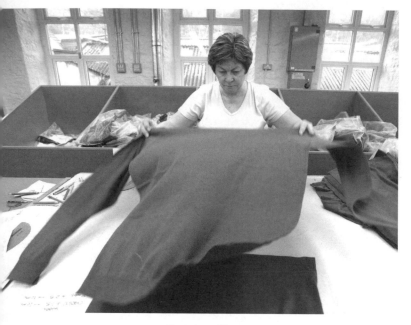

Factory staff

Factory Staff Workers who provide support to managers or work in tandem with direct laborers on the products produced. Examples of factory staff include

- Administrative staff
- Machine mechanics
- Quality control personnel

Value-Added Each individual handling the product during production increases value of the product through streamlining manufacturing processes. For example, when a sewing operator sets a sleeve or attaches buttons to a shirt placket, value is added to the product. To increase efficiency, garment components are handled only by sewing operators who will bring the product closer to completion.

SOURCING

The process of procuring resources to acquire materials or apparel products manufactured by domestic or offshore factories is known as **sourcing**. A **sourcing mix** includes all of the resources a company uses to manufacture a given product. To meet demand for a quick flow of goods, many companies follow a **multiple sourcing strategy**, meaning they contract production to several different factories. Companies create a timeline known as a **sourcing calendar** to designate deadlines and track the progression of design, product development, production, distribution, and delivery to the retail venues in which the products will be sold.

Logistics Distribution and warehousing processes within the *supply chain*.

Domestic Sourcing Hiring manufacturers located within the same country to produce product.

Off Shore Production of apparel products takes place in a different country than where the goods will be distributed and sold.

Near Shore The manufacturing country is located in close geographic proximity to the country goods will be distributed and sold.

Importer Firm that sources products from a foreign country for import into the domestic country for sale, processing, or re-export.

Private Brand Importer Retail firm that sources private label and store brand products in foreign countries for the purpose of importing them into the domestic country.

International Sourcing Hiring manufacturers offshore to produce product.

Sourcing Agent An individual hired to consult sourcing managers on offshore trade regulations, factory capabilities for production, and product quality, and to act as a liaison between the manufacturing plant and sourcing managers.

Field Inspector An individual hired to monitor domestic manufacturing and product quality.

	Milestone	Primary Owner/UserGroup	Mens XYZ Brand Fall/Holiday (7,8,9,10,11,12) 2018		Mens XYZ Brand Spring/Summer (1,2,3,4,5,6) 2019	
			Start Date	End Date	Start Date	End Date
1	Initial RM Meeting with Design	Design	4/24/17	4/24/17	8/28/17	9/1/17
2	Creative Trend and Color Direction	Creative Services	6/19/17	6/19/17	10/23/17	10/23/17
3	Initial Financial Plan	Finance	6/26/17	7/3/17	10/30/17	11/3/17
4	Create BDD	Design	6/26/17	6/30/17	10/30/17	11/3/17
5	Initial Line Plan	Merchandising	7/7/17	7/7/17	11/6/17	11/6/17
6	Line Plan Approval	Merchandising	7/7/17	7/7/17	11/10/17	11/10/17
7	Initial Line Plan Finalized	Merchandising	7/10/17	7/10/17	11/13/17	11/13/17
8	Season Kick-off	Merchandising	7/10/17	7/10/17	11/13/17	11/13/17
9	Color Palette to Colorist	Design	7/12/17	7/13/17	11/15/17	11/16/17
10	RM Meeting with Design	Design	7/14/17	7/14/17	11/16/17	11/16/17
11	Color Palette to Agent/Mfr	Product Development	7/14/17	7/14/17	11/16/17	11/16/17
12	Merch Sign-off	Design	8/7/17	8/7/17	12/11/17	12/11/17
13	Raw Materials Sign-off	Design	8/11/17	8/11/17	12/15/17	12/15/17
14	Order Sample Materials	Raw Materials	8/11/17	8/14/17	12/15/17	12/18/17
15	Sourcing Strategy	Product Development	8/14/17	8/14/17	12/18/17	12/18/17
16	Mfr to Send Mock-up's (for Board Review)	Product Development	8/21/17	8/21/17	12/26/17	12/27/17
17	Board Review	Merchandising	8/28/17	8/30/17	1/2/18	1/3/18
18	Post Board Review	Merchandising	8/31/17	8/31/17	1/4/18	1/4/18
19	Design Week	Design	8/28/17	9/1/17	1/2/18	1/5/18
20	Dev Collab	Design	9/6/17	9/14/17	1/8/18	1/19/18
21	Send Development Tech Pack/Prototype	Product Development	9/11/17	9/29/17	1/15/18	2/9/18
22	Prototype Tech Pack conf call with Vendors	Product Development	9/13/17	10/2/17	1/17/18	2/13/18
23	New Brand Creative Initiatives	Merchandising	10/31/17	10/31/17	3/18/18	3/18/18
24	1st Prototype/Cost/Min Order Quantity Due (Cost/MOQ, Prototype)	Product Development	10/31/17	11/3/17	3/12/18	3/16/18
25	1st Prototype/Cost Review w/Merchandising	Product Development	11/6/17	11/10/17	3/17/18	3/22/18
26	Buy Meeting	Merchandising	11/13/17	11/17/17	3/26/18	3/30/18
31	Post Buy Meeting	Merchandising	11/14/17	11/17/17	4/18/18	4/20/18
27	Item Set-up	Merchandising	11/14/17	12/1/17	3/28/18	4/16/18
28	Buy Meeting Prep	Merchandising	11/20/17	12/1/17	4/4/18	4/16/18
29	Review Line	Merchandising	12/1/17	12/1/17	4/16/18	4/16/18
30	Buy Meeting Sign-Off	Merchandising	12/4/17	12/8/17	4/16/18	4/20/18
32	Buy Mtg Recap (send to Mfr)	Product Development	12/6/17	12/11/17	4/18/18	4/23/18
33	1st Fit Review	Technical Design	12/13/17	12/20/17	4/27/18	5/2/18
34	Update Complete	Product Development	12/15/17	12/15/17	4/27/18	4/27/18
35	New Brand Creative Sign-off	Merchandising	12/11/17	12/11/17	4/23/18	4/23/18
36	Pre-Prod Tech Pack Send	Product Development	12/11/17	1/12/18	4/23/18	5/18/18
37	Receive/Review Orders	Merchandising	12/15/17	12/15/17	4/27/18	4/27/18
38	Updated Demand Plan to Agent/Mfr (Bulk)	Production Planning	12/17/17	12/19/17	4/30/18	4/30/18
39	Item Maintenance (if needed)/Orders Finalized in System	Merchandising	12/18/17	12/20/17	4/30/18	5/2/18
40	Final Orders Due (Style/Color/Size)	Merchandising	12/22/17	12/22/17	5/4/18	5/4/18
41	Final Demand Plan to Agent/Mfr (Style/Color/Size)	Production Planning	12/27/17	12/27/17	5/8/18	5/8/18
42	Buy Meeting Results Final	Merchandising	12/29/17	12/29/17	5/11/18	5/11/18
43	Request for Photo Sample for Direct/Mktg	Product Development	1/5/18	1/5/18	5/14/18	5/14/18
44	Receive Final Costing from Agent/Mfr	Product Development	1/23/18	1/23/18	5/28/18	5/28/18
45	PD-Final Costing Review	Product Development	1/24/18	1/29/18	5/30/18	6/1/18
46	2nd Sample Due	Product Development	2/5/18	2/5/18	6/4/18	6/4/18
47	Review Final Cost with Merch	Product Development	2/5/18	2/7/18	6/4/18	6/6/18
48	New Brand Creative All Brand & Flex Updates Due	Creative Services	2/12/18	2/12/18	6/11/18	6/11/18
49	PD to Handoff Final Cost to PP	Product Development	2/12/18	2/13/18	6/11/18	6/12/18
50	Final CTT Complete	Product Development	2/14/18	2/14/18	6/13/18	6/13/18
51	Final Fit Approved	Product Development	3/5/18	3/5/18	7/2/18	7/2/18
52	Production Orders Approved	Production Planning	3/12/18	3/12/18	7/9/18	7/9/18
53	PP Sample Due	Product Development	3/26/18	3/26/18	7/23/18	7/23/18
54	Prod Tech Pack Send	Product Development	4/9/18	4/13/18	8/6/18	8/10/18
55	Production Start	Production Planning	4/23/18	4/27/18	8/20/18	8/24/18
56	TOP Receive/Approve	Product Development	5/7/18	5/11/18	9/3/18	9/7/18
57	Goods at Consol	Production Planning	6/18/18	6/22/18	10/15/18	10/19/18
58	Carrier Pick-up	Production Planning	8/20/18	8/24/18	12/17/18	12/21/18
59	1st In-Store	Production Planning	9/7/18	9/7/18	1/4/19	1/4/19

Sourcing calendar

Outward Processing Arrangement (OPA) Customs procedure for the provisional export of goods within one's customs territory that allows for goods to be sent out for further processing or manufacturing in another country, with the intent to re-import the goods and pay a portion or be granted total exemption from paying tariffs.

Transshipment An illegal practice used to evade paying tariffs, in which goods are manufactured and shipped to another country, or are transferred to another vessel, where they are relabeled for export from a country other than the one goods were produced in; no value is added to the product.

World Trade Organization (WTO) The group that governs trade regulation rules around the world.

Tariff Tax paid on imported products.

Quota Regulation of quantities traded internationally. Textile quotas were abolished on January 1, 2005.

HARMONIZED TARIFF SCHEDULE OF THE UNITED STATES

The **Harmonized Tariff Schedule of the United States (HTSUS)** is a document published by the United States International Trade Commission that classifies imported products by fiber type, product type, and customer (infants, women and girls, or men and boys), and the **duty rates** or taxes assessed (see Table 25.1). The **U.S. Customs Service** is the body that governs international trade regulation rules by means of the Harmonized Tariff Schedule of the United States. The Harmonized Tariff Schedule of the United States is divided into 22 sections composed of 99 chapters. Section XI applies to Textile and Textile Articles and includes Chapters 50 to 61.

TABLE 25.1

Harmonized Tariff Schedule of the United States, Section XI Textile and Textile Articles

Chapter	Classification
50	Silk
51	Wool, fine or coarse animal hair; horsehair yarn and woven fabric
52	Cotton
53	Other vegetable textile fibers; paper yarn and woven fabric of paper yarn
54	Man-made filaments
55	Man-made staple fibers
56	Wadding, felt, and nonwovens; special yarns, twine, cordage, ropes and cables, and articles thereof
57	Carpets and other textile flooring coverings
58	Special woven fabrics; tufted textile fabrics; lace, tapestries; trimmings; embroidery
59	Impregnated (infused), coated, covered, or laminated textile fabrics; textile articles of a kind suitable for industrial use
60	Knitted or crocheted fabrics
61	Other made up textile articles; sets; worn clothing and worn textile articles; rags

(United States International Trade Commission, 2016)

Customs Broker Individual hired to assist in clearing goods through customs for an importer, exporter, freight line, or trade authority. U.S. customs brokers are licensed by U.S. Customs and Border Protection and must ensure shipments in and out of the United States meet federal requirements. Brokers are responsible for knowing

- Entry procedures
- Tariff rates
- Requirements for admission of goods
- Classification and valuation of goods

Customs The government agency responsible for overseeing the flow of imported and exported goods at ports of entry. Customs agents collect tariffs, monitor quotas for nontextile products, and inspect shipments and paperwork for compliance with trade regulations.

Customs Clearance (CCL) Process whereby customs agents inspect shipment documentation of imported or exported goods for compliance with federal regulations. Once clearance is obtained, the goods may continue toward their destination point.

References

Fiber2fashion.com. (2009, September 17). *Fast fashion: Fast thinking and fast changing*. Retrieved January 21, 2016, from http://www.fibre2fashion.com/industry-article/22/2114/fast-fashion-fast-thinking-and-fast-changing1.asp

Glock, R. E., & Kunz, G. I. (2005). *Apparel manufacturing: Sewn product analysis* (4th ed.). Upper Saddle River, NJ: Pearson Prentice Hall.

Jana, P. and Collyer, P. (2008, October 1). Operator skill: Single or multi? *Stitch World*.

Keiser, S. J., & Garner, M. B. (2012). *Beyond design: The synergy of apparel product development* (3rd ed.). New York: Fairchild Books, Inc.

Lezama, M., Webber, B., & Dagher, C. (2005). *Sourcing practices in the apparel industry: Implications for garment exporters in commonwealth developing countries*. London, UK: The Commonwealth Secretariat.

Miller, K. (2006, August 12). *Fashion's fast lane*. Retrieved January 21, 2016, from http://www.forbes.com/2006/09/13/leadership-fashion-retail-lead-innovation-cx_ag_0913fashion_print.html

United Nations. (2004). *International merchandise trade statistics: Compilers Manual, Annex B*. New York: Author.

United States International Trade Commission. (2016). *Harmonized tariff schedule of the United States* (2016 HTSA Basic Edition). Retrieved January 21, 2016, from https://hts.usitc.gov/current

U.S. Customs and Border Protection (2016). *Becoming a customs broker*. Retrieved January 21, 2016, from http://www.cbp.gov/trade/programs-administration/customs-brokers/becoming-customs-broker

CHAPTER 26

Manufacturers, Factory Layouts, and Production Systems for Assembly

Apparel manufacturing is the process of cutting and sewing garments from purchased fabrics, or the combination of mill and production functions.

MANUFACTURERS

An apparel or textile production facility or factory, owned and operated by one company that completes all aspects of apparel design and assembly in-house, is known as a **traditional manufacturer**. Not all companies design and manufacture the goods they sell; some outsource to contractors. A **contractor** is an independent business hired to provide production services to manufacture entire garments, product lines, or partially complete component parts. Apparel manufacturers, government agencies, and retail manufacturers all employ contractors. A **retail manufacturer** develops private-label goods that contractors produce for distribution and sale in their retail stores, catalogues, or online. Sourcing options for consideration range from contracting simple assembly of garments or components to comprehensive design and production of apparel items. There are three factory-direct sourcing options, which include CMT, OEM, and ODM. Other contractor categories include jobbers and specialty contractors also known as subcontractors.

Cut, Make, Trim (CMT) Contractor that completes all aspects of production to manufacture the garment. This type of contractor receives uncut, raw materials and produces the product by cutting, sewing, and finishing.

Specialty Contractor (Subcontractor) Independent contractor hired by a manufacturer to complete a portion of production of a garment that requires special skills and equipment not provided by other contractors. Some services provided by specialty contractors include

- Belt making
- Covering buttons
- Pleating
- Printing
- Quilting

Jobber Independent contractor hired by a manufacturer to outsource production of entire garments or partially complete component parts. Jobbers purchase raw materials and either send them directly to CMT contractors for production or send cut garment components to contractors for production.

Inside Shop Traditional manufacturer that designs and produces apparel in its own factories.

Outside Shop Independent contractor hired by a manufacturer to outsource one or more aspects of garment production. Outside shops include cut, make, trim (CMT); jobbers; and specialty contractors (subcontractors).

Original Equipment Manufacturing (OEM) or Full-Package Manufacturing Services provided by contractors that finance and source materials and component parts, assembly, finishing, packaging, and delivery of apparel products to retail destinations based on contracted specifications from designers, product developers, and retail manufacturers.

Original Design Manufacturing (ODM) or Full Package Supplier Independent contractor capable of completing all aspects of design, patternmaking, cutting, assembly, packaging, and is financially responsible for the procurement of materials and production costs. When ODM contractors are responsible for distribution of apparel products, they are called landed duty paid suppliers.

Manufacturing plants, also known as factories, are places where garment components are prepared and assembled into saleable goods. The physical arrangement of space within a manufacturing plant is the **factory layout**, which contains areas for production, administration, raw materials storage, and employee service. Efficiency of movement of materials and construction processes are important to the productivity and profitability of a plant. Within manufacturing plants, there are two types of production layouts. Many factories have both product and process layouts, although some rely on only one.

Product Layout (Line Layout) Spatial arrangement of manufacturing equipment according to the sequential order of garment assembly, not a specific garment style. Product layouts, also known as assembly lines, are efficient for manufacturing large volumes of identical merchandise.

Process Layout (Skill Center Layout) Spatial arrangement of manufacturing equipment grouped and placed into work areas according to the operations needed to produce a specific garment style. Bundles of component parts are grouped by assembly operation, and production equipment is arranged by each of the procedures to be completed. Process layouts are effective for manufacturing smaller volumes of a variety of garment styles.

PRODUCTION SYSTEMS

A **production system** is the combination of resources and work flow sequencing needed to manufacture finished, saleable garments. **Work flow** refers to the specific movement of garment component pieces and materials during the production process from the beginning to the end. **Work in process** or **work in progress** is the quantity of incomplete products in the course of assembly. Factories must be attentive to **materials handling**, which is the efficient flow of materials and garment components as they progress through the manufacturing process. A production system includes

- Handling of materials, garment component parts, and findings
- Labor force
- Production and assembly equipment and machinery
- Logical sequence for movement of materials and garment components during assembly

The four types of production systems in factories include make-through or whole garment production system, progressive bundle system, unit production system, and modular production system.

■ Make-Through Production System or Whole Garment Production System

A production method where each highly skilled individual is responsible for assembling a garment from start to finish. This system offers great flexibility and is used for producing the highest price, highest quality of small production runs of exclusive apparel items.

PRODUCTION SYSTEMS (continued)

■ Progressive Bundle System

A production method where garment component parts are *bundled* according to the sequential order of garment assembly. Factory workers complete the same operation day after day and become highly efficient.

Bundle Garment component parts grouped together for routing that include pieces for completing a particular operation or portion of a garment. Bundles are manually moved from one workstation to the next. Factories with a *product layout* (*line layout*) or a *process layout* (*skill center layout*) rely on this method. The two types of progressive bundle systems are the garment bundle and the job bundle.

• *Garment bundle*—All garment component parts for one single garment are contained in a bundle and move from one work station to the next.

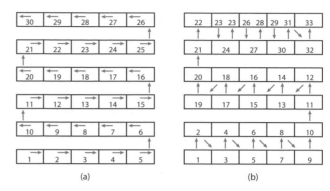

(a)   (b)

Two examples of progressive bundle plant layouts

• *Job bundle*—Component parts bundled according to two or more consecutive assembly operations. As the various garment components are assembled, they are passed through workstations where their pieces are added to the rest of the garment until it is completed.

The progressive bundle system is monitored through

• *Bundle tickets*—Master lists of operations for the bundle, bundle coupons, or identification cards for each assembly operation, routing information, piece rate, and identification regarding style number, size, and shade number.
• *Bundle coupons*—Factory workers are typically compensated according to how many pieces they complete within a given shift. This payment method is called *piece rate*. A worker retains a portion of a bundle coupon and turns it in at the end of the day. The employer calculates pay accordingly.
• *Smart cards* or *electronic bundle tickets*—Sewing operators swipe cards through a card reader connected to a computer system to electronically monitor the work they complete. This method eliminates individual bundle coupons and paper *bundle tickets*. These are accompanied by identification cards providing information contained in the *bundle ticket*.

Progressive bundle system

■ Unit Production System

A production method similar to the progressive bundle system; however, the garment component parts for one single garment are contained in a bundle and moved from one work station to the next by transporters or conveyers connected to an *overhead power rail system* (a track layout supplying electricity and a means for moving garment bundles). A unit production system eliminates the need for manual movement of garment bundles, providing greater efficiency of flow of goods through the plant. Factory workers complete the same operation day after day and become highly efficient. This process is common in factories that use a *product layout* (*line layout*) or a *process layout* (*skill center layout*). The unit production system is monitored by a computer system that

• Controls the routing of bundles
• Monitors work flow
• Records operator production for payroll purposes and inventory control

Unit production plant

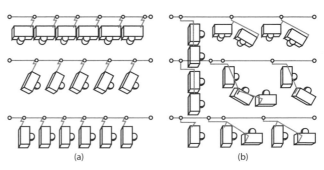

(a)   (b)

Two examples of unit production systems

Direct connection and **tandem methods** are two layouts for *overhead power rail systems* to connect to sewing operators. The *direct connection method* allows for the overhead rail to stop at each sewing operator's station, whereas the *tandem method* connects both single and groups of two or three machines. The method selected depends on the types of garments produced, construction details required for each style, equipment, and factory size.

■ Modular Production System (Modular Manufacturing)

A production method in which teams of individuals work together to complete assembly of a garment. Team members are cross-trained to complete several operations within the group. Employees are compensated as a team rather than as individuals, as it takes all of the members to maintain a consistent work flow and output of completed garments. A modular production system provides flexibility that the other productions systems cannot and works well for manufacturing small quantities of a wide variety of garments and styles. Rather than a line style layout, a horseshoe configuration of equipment is common for this type of production system.

Modular production plant

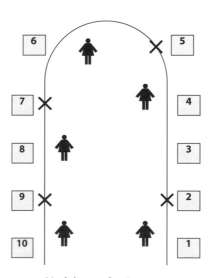

Modular production system

ASSEMBLY OPERATIONS

Garment construction requires a specific sequence of steps to produce the product, known as **assembly operations**. These progressions are very important for manufacturing apparel products based on assembly specifications. No matter which production system a factory utilizes, all processes have efficient planned sequences for the movement of materials and garment parts during manufacturing.

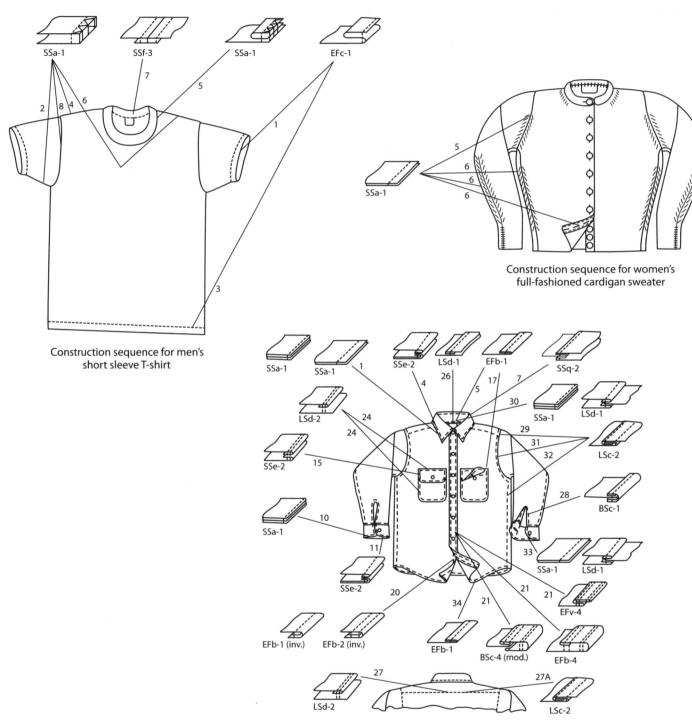

Construction sequence for men's short sleeve T-shirt

Construction sequence for women's full-fashioned cardigan sweater

Construction sequence for men's casual work shirt

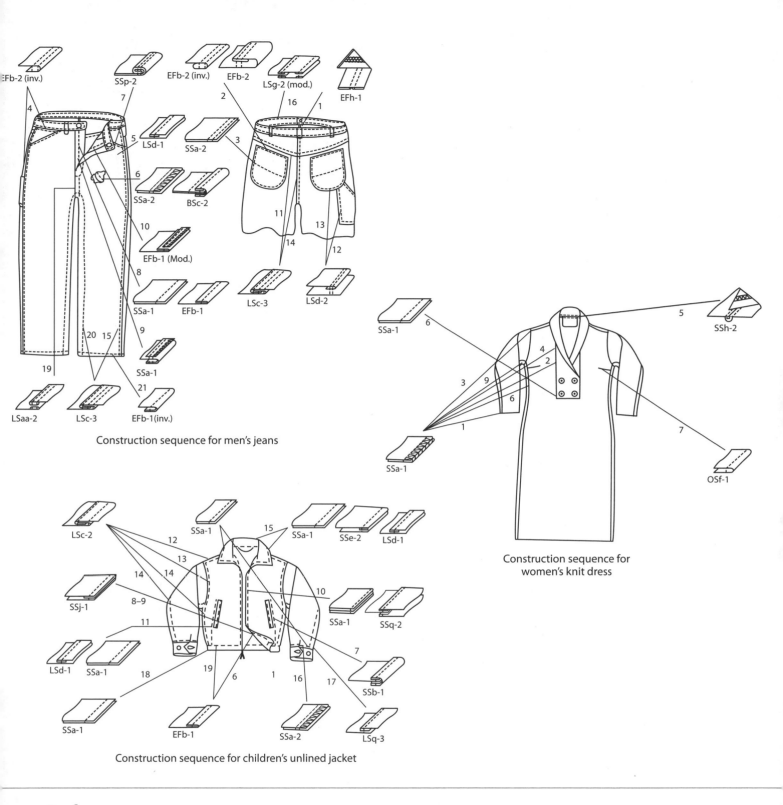

EFb-2 (inv.)

SSp-2

EFb-2 (inv.)

EFb-2

LSg-2 (mod.)

EFh-1

LSd-1

SSa-2

SSa-2

BSc-2

EFb-1 (Mod.)

SSa-1

EFb-1

LSc-3

LSd-2

SSa-1

LSaa-2

LSc-3

EFb-1(inv.)

Construction sequence for men's jeans

SSa-1

SSa-1

SSh-2

OSf-1

Construction sequence for
women's knit dress

LSc-2

SSa-1

SSa-1

SSe-2

LSd-1

SSj-1

SSa-1

SSq-2

LSd-1

SSa-1

SSb-1

SSa-1

EFb-1

SSa-2

LSq-3

Construction sequence for children's unlined jacket

References

Bubonia, J. E. (2014). *Apparel quality: A guide to evaluating sewn products*. New York: Bloomsbury Publishing, Inc.

Glock, R. E., & Kunz, G. I. (2005). *Apparel manufacturing: Sewn product analysis* (4th ed.). Upper Saddle River, NJ: Pearson Education, Inc.

Solinger, J. (1988). *Apparel manufacturing handbook: Analysis, principles, and practice* (2nd ed.). Columbia, SC: Bobbin Blenheim Media Corporation.

CHAPTER 27

Marker Making, Cutting, and Bundling

In preparation for production, graded

patterns and textiles materials must be

prepared for cutting, bundling, and assembly.

The sized production pattern pieces must be

arranged in a layout appropriate for cutting.

There are many considerations when making

a marker.

MARKER LAYOUT CONSIDERATIONS

A **marker** is a layout of pattern pieces and the guide for cutting the garment fabric for production. A marker may be digital or manually drawn, in one or all size ranges for a style. Markers are also used for cutting prototypes in sample sizes. Patternmaking and grading integrated software can create markers to be sent to automated cutting machines to streamline preproduction operations. The **layout of pattern pieces**, also known as **marker layout**, is the arrangement of interlocking (laying in) pattern pieces on paper or virtually on a computer, in preparation for cutting. Pattern layouts help estimate yardage requirements for garments. Pattern pieces are arranged with regard to the structure, design, and width of the fabric. A marker is planned to get the most use of yardage to minimize waste, known as **fabric fallout**, which is the material remaining on the *cutting table* after garment parts are **off-loaded** (removed). To determine fabric yardage needs for production, technical designers must consider width of the fabric as part of the planned arrangement of pattern pieces in the marker.

Grainline marks on individual pattern pieces indicate direction of the lengthwise grain (on-grain, on the bias, or on the cross-grain). Factors of garment design affecting the direction of the grain and placement of pattern pieces on a marker layout include

- Balance
- Direction or pattern in fabric design or construction
- Direction of raised, brushed, or looped nap
- Light refraction quality of weave or knit fabric

When preparing the *marker layout* for cutting, the marker maker places the lengthwise grain, as indicated on the individual pattern pieces, on the length grain of goods. Lengthwise grain of pattern pieces is determined in the initial design and patternmaking stages of development.

When a marker maker creates a digital marker, a **buffer**, or invisible barrier, can protect all or specific pieces from being placed too close to another in the layout. Another option when creating digital markers is blocking. **Blocking** protects pattern pieces and accommodates the width of the knife blade to prevent unintentional cutting. If a paper copy of a digital marker is needed for cutting, it is sent to a printer to be **plotted** on a continuous roll having the same width dimensions as the fabric to be cut and is the length of the marker.

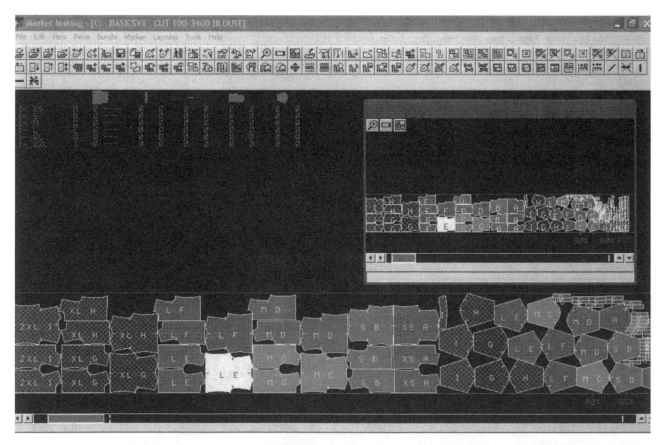

Digital marker layout

MARKER LAYOUTS FOR CUTTING SPECIFIC FABRICS

Marker makers consider layout in relation to how the fabric will be spread on the *cutting table*. **Marker placement** is the position on the piece goods spread to ensure the marker edge is parallel with the selvage so all cuts will be complete. **Fabric spread** indicates how the material will be laid into multiple plies for cutting. When each layer of fabric is laid face up or face down in the spread, it is referred to as a **single-ply spread**. Single-ply spreads are cut at each end of the spread in order to keep all layers facing the same direction. A **face-to-face spread** is laid out like an accordion. Each new ply of fabric is spread and folded back on the previous layer so that the face sides of the fabric lie against each other. Garments are cut from tubes of fabric in a **tubular spread**. Such garments do not have side seams.

Goods with particular weaves, patterns, or finishes, known as **directional fabrics**, need special consideration in planning a marker layout. This group of fabrics includes

- Brushed
- Knitted
- Looped
- Napped
- One-way fabric designs
- Pile
- Satin

One-way or directional fabric when reversed can show a different color tone or design. All pattern pieces to be cut from directional fabrics should be placed on the marker in the same direction. Directional fabrics require more yardage.

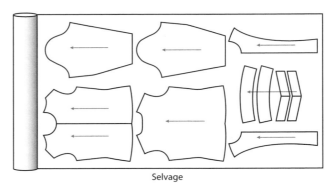

One-way layout for directional fabrics

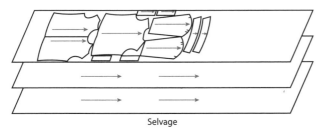

Single-ply fabric spread

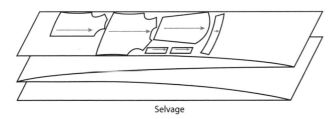

Face-to-face fabric spread

Geometric fabric designs such as plaids, stripes, checks, and border designs require a special layout so that after the fabric is cut and seamed, the pattern matches.

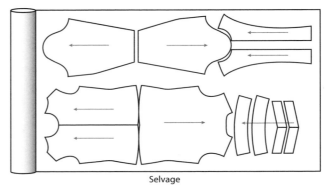

Two-way layout

Tubular fabric spread

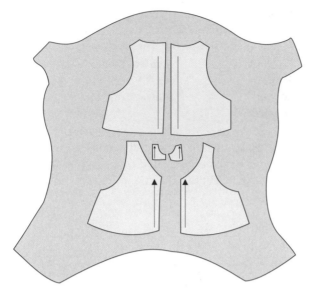

Pattern layout for cutting a garment from an animal skin

Pattern layout for cutting fabric with a border print

Animal Skin Marker Layout Skins are considered napped fabrics and require a one-way marker layout on a single spread. Animal skins are measured in square feet (centimeters squared) and differ individually in shape, size, color, and surface markings. To accommodate large pattern pieces, skins may be enlarged or elongated by piecing.

Border Fabric Design Marker Layout Pattern pieces arranged on the marker on either the length- or cross-grain direction of a *border print* to use or emphasize the border design on the garment.

Finished Border Fabric Marker Layout Pattern pieces arranged on the marker on either the length- or cross-grain direction of a finished *border fabric* to utilize the border design on the garment. These fabrics have a decorative finish, which may be scalloped, on one or both lengthwise grain edges. Finished border fabrics include eyelet and lace.

Diagonal Design Fabric or Diagonal Print Fabric Marker Layout In a marker layout, all pattern pieces are placed in the same direction (one-way) on fabrics printed with stripes, geometric pattern, or a motif pattern that forms diagonal lines from selvage to selvage.

Diagonal Weave Fabric or Twill Type Fabric Marker Layout Pattern pieces are arranged on the marker in a one-way direction with the grainline parallel to the selvage of a *twill weave* to avoid color tone differences caused by light refraction.

Directional Design Fabric or One-Way Design Fabric Marker Layout *One-way designs* require all pattern pieces to be placed in the same direction (one-way) in the marker layout.

Knit Fabric Marker Layout Pattern pieces are arranged on the marker in a one-way direction with the grainline parallel to the selvage for tubular, sweater, and other knit fabrics to avoid color tone differences caused by light refraction.

Light-Reflecting Fabric Marker Layout Pattern pieces are arranged on the marker in a one-way direction with the grainline parallel to the selvage to avoid color tone differences caused by light refraction.

Napped Fabric Marker Layout Pattern pieces are arranged on the marker in a one-way direction with the grainline parallel to the selvage to avoid color tone differences caused by light refraction. Garments are designed to have the brushed surface oriented downward.

Pile Fabric Marker Layout Pattern pieces arranged on the marker in a one-way direction with the grainline parallel to the selvage to avoid color tone differences caused by light refraction. When the marker is laid out for cutting the fabric in the downward direction, the pile of the material in the finished garment possesses a smooth texture and the color tone of the fabric is lighter, with a silver-cast sheen. However, some velvet or velour fabrics are laid out on the marker so they are cut with the pile oriented in an upward direction. This provides a more luxurious appearance to the garment.

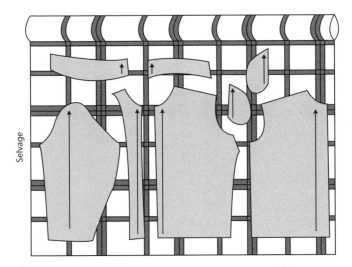

Pattern layout for cutting balanced or even plaid fabrics

Balanced Plaid or Even Plaid Marker Layout Pattern pieces arranged in the marker layout so the geometric pattern design matches or produces chevrons at seam lines. A balanced plaid, a mirror image of a series of colored groups of yarns within the pattern repeat, creates the linear pattern in both the lengthwise and crosswise directions of the fabric.

Unbalanced Plaid Marker Layout Marker layouts are planned in a one-way direction. Unbalanced plaids contain colored groups of yarns that create unsymmetrical geometric designs that vary in the lengthwise, crosswise, or both directions of the fabric. Garments are designed with the geometric pattern positioned on the body in one direction only.

Uneven Plaid Marker Layout Pattern pieces arranged in the marker layout in a one-way direction in order to match the plaid at the seams. Uneven plaids contain colored groups of yarns that create the geometric pattern repeat differently in the lengthwise and crosswise directions.

Balanced Stripe Marker Layout Pattern pieces arranged in the marker layout so the geometric designs correspond or produce a chevron at the seam line. A balanced stripe is a design with the color and width of a line or series of lines in a mirror repeat to the right and left of the center stripe.

Even Stripe Marker Layout Pattern pieces are arranged in the marker layout so the geometric designs correspond or produce a chevron. Even stripes are a two-color design of alternating lines or series of lines, of even width, in either the lengthwise or crosswise direction.

Uneven Stripe or Unbalanced Stripe Marker Layout One-way marker layout is required to continue stripes in consecutive order at a seam line. A stripe design in which lines of mixed width and color are repeated consecutively, forming a one-way directional design. Garments are designed with the geometric pattern positioned on the body in one direction only.

FABRIC SPREADING

Fabric is shipped on rolls to manufacturers and the cloth is measured, inspected, and rewound in preparation for cutting. The wound fabric is placed on a spreading machine that moves back and forth over the cutting table, laying the plies at the desired length, as determined by the marker layout. The spreading machine and cutting table widths are determined by the width of the goods. Table length is determined by the type of marker, plus allowance for the fabric stretch factor, and type of machinery.

A **layup**, also referred to as a **lay**, is the total number of fabric plies, one over the other, in a one-way or face-to-face spread, for cutting multiple garment components when many garments must be cut simultaneously for mass production. The number of plies in the fabric spread is known as **count** or **ply count**. Each layer should be counted at both ends to ensure accuracy. When a fabric defect is found in the lay, a **splice** is made in the fabric to cut the damaged area. **Splice lap** is when the cut edges of the fabric are overlapped and checked to ensure both plies extend past the marked splice by no less than ½ inch (1.27 cm) and no more than 1 inch (2.54 cm). The completed marker is placed on top of the ply on a layup that will be manually cut. When a spread will be cut using a computer-driven machine, the digital marker is sent to the cutting machine, and the cutting tool essentially draws the marker layout on the layup as it is cut. Design elements and fabric type determine how a marker is planned and how the fabric plies are spread.

Spreading should be completed without tension. When material is stretched as it is laid, it is referred to as a **tight spread**. The opposite type is known as a **slack spread**, which possesses ripples or ridges in the layup that are caused by spreading the fabric too loosely in the lengthwise direction between the ends. When fabric layups are created, the selvages of the plies can be aligned at the center or at the edge of the material. A **center-aligned spread** aligns the vertical midpoints of each ply, which

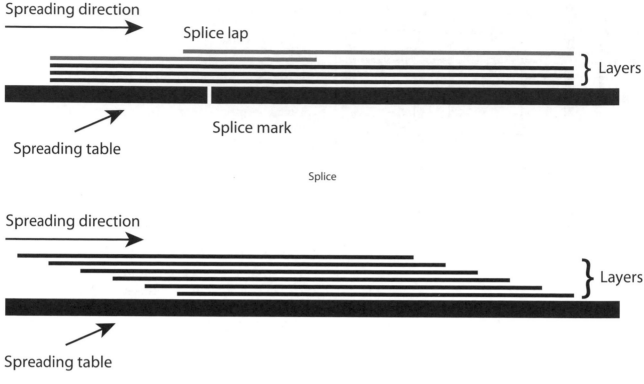

Spreading direction

Splice lap

} Layers

Splice mark

Spreading table

Splice

Spreading direction

} Layers

Spreading table

Leaning

creates a layup having both sides that are equidistant from the lengthwise midpoint of the spread. A **straight-edge-aligned spread** precisely aligns the selvages of the plies on one side of the layup to form a straight edge. Depending on the consistency of the width of the material being spread, the opposite side of the layup may or may not be vertically aligned to form parallel edges. When the fabric edge of the spread is not square to the tabletop, it is called **leaning** and must be corrected to avoid problems when cutting.

Cutting Table Stationary, flat work area at waist height, with a width and length designed according to the plant layout, fabric, spreading machine, or cutting procedures. A cutting table is the base or work surface for layout and cutting operations.

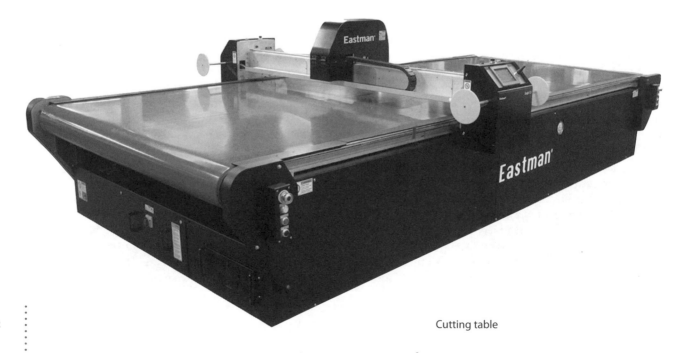

Cutting table

Plies Multiple layers of fabric spread out for the purpose of cutting many garments and their corresponding component parts at the same time.

Spreading Fabric Process of superimposing a predetermined number of fabric plies on the cutting table either manually or by means of a fabric spreading machine. The end result of spreading is referred to as a spread, lay, or layup.

Cut-Off Machine or End Cutter Magnetically guided electric cutter designed with a long handle and equipped with a circular blade that operates in a grooved cross-table track. Machine sizes are available in 48 to 78 inches (1.2 to 2 meters) wide. A cut-off machine is used in conjunction with a spreading machine to spread a one-way layup.

Cutting plies

Spreading fabric

Cut-off machine

Industrial Cutting Procedure Guide for Fabric Spreading

FABRIC		GARMENT		SPREAD
Asymmetrical (directional)	⇐	Asymmetrical		Face One Way – Nap One Way
Symmetrical	⇄	Asymmetrical		Face One Way – Nap Up and Down
Asymmetrical	⇐	Symmetrical		Face One Way – Nap One Way
Symmetrical	⇄	Symmetrical		Face One Way – Nap Up and Down

End catcher/End guide rail

End Catcher or End Guide Rail Weighted crossbar hinged to a clamp-secured base that spans the cutting table. The catcher or end rail can be placed and locked at any position on the spreading table. A serrated rubber facing on the crossbar eliminates teeth and pinholes in the goods. The catcher bar is designed to swing out of the way when cutting. An end catcher or end guide rail is used to

- Secure cloth in position when moving a spreader back and forth
- Fold over goods at ends
- Hold fabric ends securely

Face-to-face spreader

Face-to-Face Spreader Automated spreading machine that lays and aligns a ply of fabric with each pass over the cutting table. A catcher actuates a reversing gear at each end of the layup. The speed of the machine can be set to conform to the type of fabric to be cut. Typical machine widths range from 48 to 84 inches (1.2 to 2.1 meters) wide. A shutoff switch permits the machine to ride back empty for spreading one-way fabric. Each ply is counted as it is spread.

Manual spreader

Manual Spreader Manually operated spreading machine with a rail that permits the operator to maintain alignment of the fabric edges while laying multiple plies of the fabric on the cutting table. This type of spreader can lay face-to-face or one way.

One-Way Spreader Automated spreading machine riding on a geared rail synchronized to work with an end guide rail and cut-off machine at either end of the layup. Speed of the machine can be set to conform to the type of fabric. Typical machine widths range from 48 to 84 inches (1.2 to 2.1 meters) wide. Each ply is counted as it is spread. Use of the cut-off rail eliminates fabric fold buildup at the ends of the spread.

One-way spreader

Tubular Knit Spreader Automated spreading machine with an adjustable electromagnet to hold assorted widths of tubular fabrics in place. The machine is actuated by the catchers to reverse direction of spreading at each end of the layup. The speed of the machine can be set to conform to the type of fabric to be cut. Typical machine widths measure up to 66 inches (1.7 meters) or wider. A shutoff switch permits the machine to ride back empty for spreading one-way fabric. Each ply is counted as it is spread. Tubular knit spreaders can handle different weights and types of tubular knits or flat folds.

Tubular knit spreader

CUTTING FABRIC LAYUPS

In preparation for cutting fabrics, manufacturers employ a variety of machines, including large pieces of stationary equipment and handheld tools. Stationary and portable cutting equipment in a variety of sizes are engineered for heavy-duty and general-purpose cutting of lightweight to heavy-duty fabrics, from work clothes to lingerie. Blades are designed with straight, serrated, wave, or saw-toothed edges, to accommodate various fabric constructions and layup heights. In addition, there are knives engineered to cut through synthetic, foam, and rubber materials.

Knives are sharpened with smooth, medium, or coarse grit stones or belts, depending on the edge needed for the type of fabric to be cut. A knife used for synthetic fabric requires lubrication (a stainless liquid is automatically dispensed along the blade) to reduce heat buildup, which causes fabric fusion.

To ensure the safety of the operator and produce quality cutting along the ends and selvages of the fabric spread, manually operated portable cutting machines, such as a band knife or knife blade, require a minimum of 4 inches (10 cm) of unoccupied space between the edges of the cutting table and all edges of the fabric layup.

Stationary cutting machines controlled by computer software may contain a self-sharpening vertical reciprocating blade, a water jet, or a laser to cut the plies of fabric in a layup. Fabric plies are laid on a table with a bristled surface to be cut by an automated machine with a vertical reciprocating blade. The layup is covered with a film of plastic;

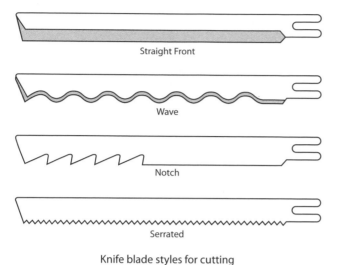

Straight Front

Wave

Notch

Serrated

Knife blade styles for cutting

then a vacuum beneath the bristled surface removes the air to provide a dense, compressed block for cutting. The bristle surface of the cutting table allows the blade to fully penetrate all layers of the spread.

Cloth Measuring and Inspection Machine Stationary, motor-driven unit containing a means for supporting a bolt of fabric and a mandrel for rerolling the fabric after it has passed over an inspection board. The machine is operated by a foot pedal or hand control and is available in widths from 48 to 120 inches (1.2 to 3.25 meters) wide. All units have variable-speed motors. Fabric can be wound face-in or face-out as desired. Fabrics with a lot of give, such as knits, require units designed to unroll and reroll yardage with a minimum of tension. Units are equipped with illuminated inspection boards for ease in visual inspection of fabric flaws. Cloth measuring and inspection machines are used

- To wind and unwind fabric
- To measure and examine goods
- To package and split fabric rolls
- For inventory purposes

Cloth measuring and inspection machine

Clamp Gripping device consisting of two opposing metal arms joined at a central pivot point to form handles and bills. Clamps are operated through the force of a spring that holds the bills in a closed position. Clamps are used to

- Hold fabric layers together
- Hold a marker to a layup

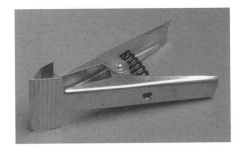

Clamp

Cutting Line Designated lines on a marker indicating the edges of pattern pieces that are used as guides for cutting.

Drill Portable electrically driven metal rod operating with a vertical drilling motion, housed in a frame and base, with a control switch and handle. Two styles of drill points are available—the awl or the hypodermic:

- *Awl drill point*—Solid needle that either cuts a hole in the fabric or severs the yarns at a designated point. Awl drill points create a permanent hole that is visible in the fabric but will be concealed within the finished garment.
- *Hypodermic drill point*—Hollow needle filled with marking fluid that is either removed during pressing or permanently remains in the fabric but is concealed within the finished garment.

Drills are available in lightweight and heavy-duty models to accommodate all types of fabrics. There are even models with lower-speed motors to eliminate synthetic fabrics from fusing.

The type of needle used is dictated by the type of fabric. Thinner needles are used for closely woven fabrics. Thicker needles are used for loosely or coarsely woven fabrics. Machines are available in sizes 6, 8, and 10 inches (15.24, 20.32, and 25.4 cm). Needles range from 1/16 to 1/2 inch (1.6 to 12.7 mm) in diameter. The needle heat can also be adjusted for permanently setting holes in loosely woven fabrics. Drills are used to

- Pierce holes for pattern markings
- Penetrate through multiple fabric plies to facilitate subsequent sewing procedures
- Indicate pattern markings such as diminishing points of darts and dart tucks
- Indicate placement of pockets and trimmings, buttons and buttonholes, and pleats and shirring
- Indicate point or position of design features such as gussets, godets, and bands

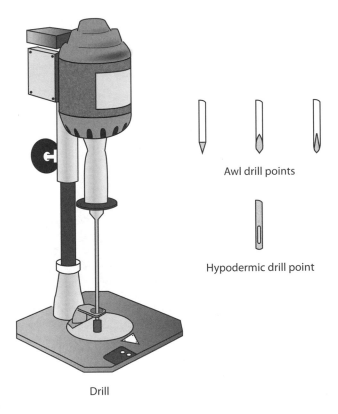

Awl drill points

Hypodermic drill point

Drill

Notching Cutting an incision through all fabric plies to a depth of ³⁄₁₆ of an inch (0.48 cm) on the perimeter of a pattern piece.

Notched fabric

Electrical cloth notcher

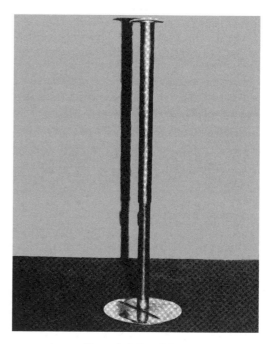

Manual cloth notcher

Electrical Cloth Notcher Strip-resistant wire blade connected to a heating unit housed in a frame with a control switch and handle. The searing action of the blade produces a limited depth notch resembling a burn mark. Models are available for hot and cold notching. Frame sizes are available in 4, 6, and 8 inches (10.16, 15.24, and 2032 cm). Blade sizes are available in ⅛, ¼, ⅜, ½, and ⅝ inch (3.2, 6.4, 9.5, 12.7, and 15.9 mm). Electrical cloth notchers are used to produce a

- Slot notch in lays of knitted, soft wool, loosely woven, and bulky fabrics
- Seared notch limited to the width of the wire blade

Manual Cloth Notcher Straight blade fixed to a spring-action recoil piston and affixed to a base. Frame sizes are available in 4, 6, and 8 inches (10.16, 15.24 and 2032 cm). Blade sizes are available in ⅛, ¼, ⅜, ½, and ⅝ inch (3.2, 6.4, 9.5, 12.7, and 15.9 mm). Manual cloth notchers are used

- To produce slit notches in limited lays of fabric
- On firmly woven materials

Straight Knife Cutter or Knife Blade Cutter Portable electric cutter designed to hold a vertical knife blade, which operates with an up-and-down cutting motion or stroke, with a base plate that rides on the cutting table to prevent it from tipping or swaying while an operator is cutting. A heavy-duty motor is used for difficult cutting. Medium-duty machines are used for high lays of soft fabric. Small motor machines are used for cutting lightweight materials. High plies of coarse fabrics require a special heavy-duty motor with an extra blade length for cutting. Machines are available in 5-, 6-, 8-, 10-, and 14-inch (12.7, 15.24, 20.32, 25.4 and 35.56 cm) sizes with blade lengths that are matched to the machine size. Wheel or belt sharpeners are used to maintain a sharp cutting edge. These cutting machines are equipped with a gear reduction unit to slow the blade to half speed to prevent fusing while cutting synthetic materials. Straight knife cutters are used

- For straight cuts, intricate curves, and sharp corners
- To cut a variety of fabrics, heavy duty to lightweight, according to the blade capacity
- To cut high layups

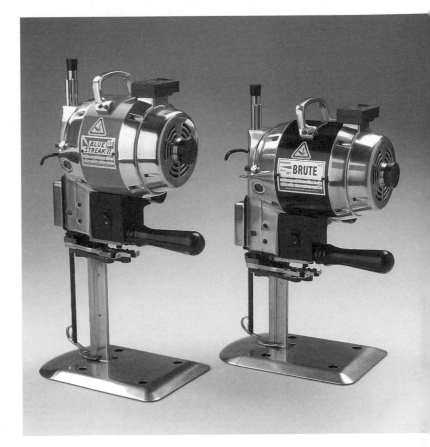

Straight knife cutter/Knife blade cutter

Standup Rotary Cutter Electric cutter designed to hold a circular blade. A heavy-duty motor is used for difficult cutting. Medium-duty machines are used for high lays of soft fabric. Small motor machines are used for cutting lightweight materials. Special feather-weight motors offering a 2½ inch (6.35 cm) blade are used for lays less than ¾ inch (1.905 cm). Machine size ranges from 2½ through 10 inches (6.35 to 25.4 cm) in diameter, with blade diameters matched to the machine size. Machines are equipped with a gear reduction unit to slow the blade to half speed, preventing fusing when cutting synthetic materials. Standup rotary cutters are used

- For straight cuts and wide or gradual curves
- To cut lays of limited height

Standup rotary cutter

CUTTING FABRIC LAYUPS (continued)

Clicker press/Die cutting press

Clicker press die

Clicker Press or Die Cutting Press Stationary single- or double-arm electric or hydraulic press that houses steel cutting dies made to the exact dimensions of a garment section. Die cutting is limited to specific layup heights. A clicker press is used

- To precisely cut collars, cuffs, flaps, and pockets
- To cut small garment parts such as bands, tabs, welts, underlay pieces, and shoulder pads
- When garment parts are duplicated frequently

Computerized Laser Cutting Machine Computer-driven cutting machine utilizing a laser beam to burn or dissolve the fabric along the cutting lines of the marker and through the multiple layers of fabric without fusing the layers together.

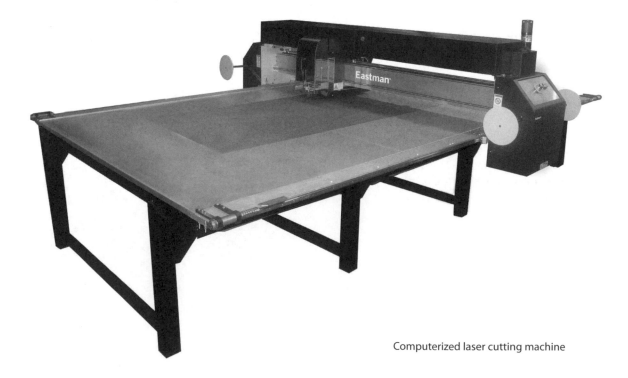

Computerized laser cutting machine

Computerized Water Jet Cutting Machine Computer-driven cutting machine utilizing a high-intensity water jet stream to pierce through the multiple layers of fabric at a high rate of speed that does not wet the fabric plies.

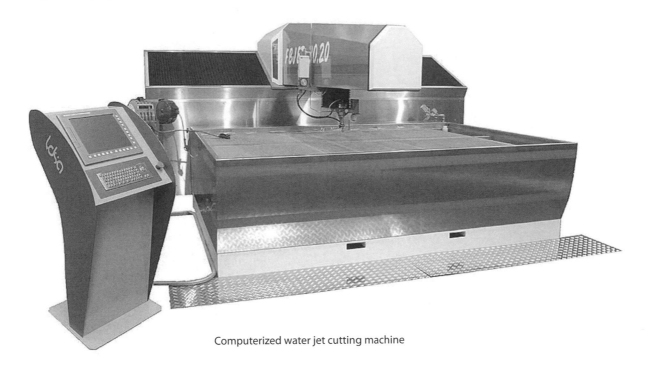

Computerized water jet cutting machine

Computerized Vertical Reciprocating Blade Cutting Machine Computer-driven cutting machine that utilizes a vertical reciprocating blade to shear through the multiple layers of fabric.

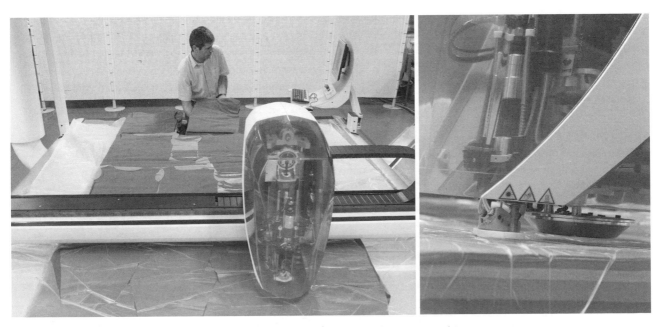

Computerized vertical reciprocating blade cutting machine

BUNDLING

Offloading of pattern pieces

Upon the commencement of cutting, a worker will offload pattern pieces from the cutting table, which are counted, prepped to indicate shade, and grouped and bundled according to the designated production process to be used. A **bundle** is a stack of cut garment sections that have been separated from the layup, and folded or tied. Bundles are sorted and grouped according to pattern size and *shade marking*. If garment parts require fusing of interlinings, this step is typically completed in the cutting room. Some factories may

- Send the garment pieces out for fusing
- Send the specified amount of fabric yardage to be block fused prior to cutting
- Die-cut interlinings to correspond with the pattern pieces they will be fused to
- Roll-to-roll fuse the fabric

See Chapter 26 for additional bundling definitions under the progressive bundle production system such as garment bundle, job bundle, bundle tickets, bundle coupons, and smart cards or electronic bundle tickets.

Shade Marking Ensuring proper shade match by marking each pattern piece, within every ply of the spread. All of a garment's component parts should be cut from the same ply in order to guarantee shade match.

Shade marking ticket

Shade marking machine

Fusing Process of using prescriptive guidelines for application of temperature, time, and pressure in order to properly achieve a secure bond between the *fusible interlining* and the shell fabric.

Block Fusing A relatively small square or rectangular portion of the fabric is fused with an interlining.

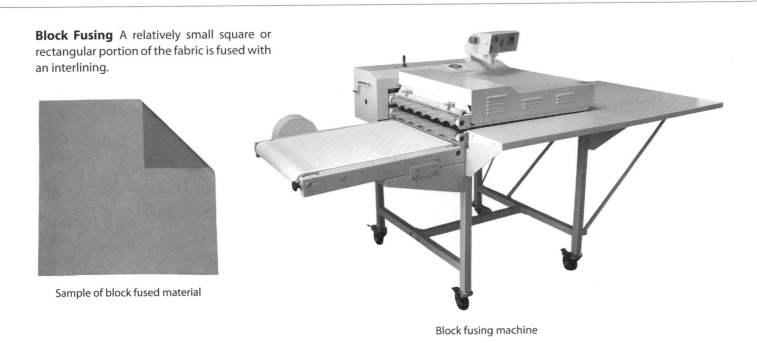

Sample of block fused material

Block fusing machine

Roll-to-Roll Fusing The entire length of the fabric roll is fused with *interlining*. The fabric roll is loaded and fed through a fusing press and is rewound onto the roll and is ready for spreading and cutting.

Roll-to-roll fusing

CHAPTER 28

Finishing

After garments are sewn, loose threads are

trimmed, and garments are inspected and

defects repaired, garments are then pressed,

folded or hung, tagged, and packaged for

shipment. These procedures are all part of the

process known as **finishing**.

FINISHING PROCESSES

Thread Trimming Cutting excess thread ends from garment seams to provide a clean, neat appearance.

Thread Sucking Suctioning or vacuuming loose threads from garments to remove unwanted thread waste.

Some finished garments require wet or dry processing to add performance properties or change their aesthetic appearance. **Wet processing** is used on a variety of casual knitted and woven garments. Wet processing includes

- Washing to soften fabric
- Washing to alter the color by using bleach, pumice stone, enzymes, or acids
- Washing to preshrink garments
- Overdyeing to add color

Dry processing is used on denim garments to create an aged, distressed, worn appearance. Dry processing includes

- Brushing, sanding, or lasering to remove color
- Sanding to abrade the fabric on certain portions of a garment
- Lasering to distress the fabric

Brushing A dry processing technique that abrades the surface of a garment with a brush containing bristles made of aramid, nylon, or wire bristles to create a worn look. Brushing utilizes a hand-held electrical brush or automated brush and is less damaging to the garment and a faster process than sanding. Brush shapes include

- Flat
- Concave
- Convex

Laser Etching A dry processing technique that utilizes a CAD/CAM–driven laser to burn the top layer of the dyestuff to remove color or burn holes in a garment. This technique can be used to create almost any kind of distressed or aged look of a garment and is commonly used to simulate whiskering and sanding effects.

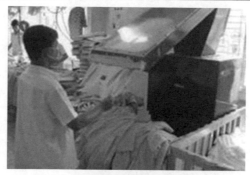
Thread sucking

Brushing

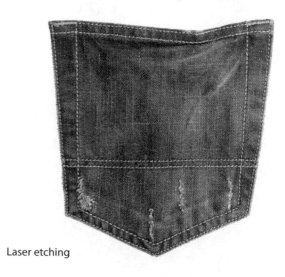
Laser etching

Sanding A dry processing technique that utilizes sand-paper to remove color from the surface of the garment to achieve a distressed appearance. Sandblasting was once very popular but is now banned in many countries due to the health risks associated with workers breathing in particles of fibers and dust produced. Commonly used sanding tools include

- Hand-sanding block
- Dremel tools
- Grinders

Tacking A process for temporarily stitching portions of a garment in an effort to protect specific areas when abrasion techniques are applied. The stitching is removed after the desired level of distressing is achieved.

Whiskers, Hige, or Creases A dry processing technique used for distressing denim garments by creating faded creases or lines in areas of wear such as

- Lap area
- Front of the thighs
- Back of the knees
- Hems
- Bottom of pant legs

Techniques used to create whiskers or crease effects include

- Application of a resin followed by hand iron or hotpress
- Hand sanding or Dremel tool

Sanding

Whiskers

PRESSING

Pressing smoothes the surface, shrinks fullness, and shapes the fabric at darts, curved seams, and cap of sleeves. Fiber content determines the temperature of the pressing tool. Fiber texture determines how the fabric is to be handled. Pressing tools selected depend on

Type of fabric
Type of fabric finish
Type of garment
Construction of garment
Technique of pressing

- *Pressing*—The process of alternatively pressing down and lifting up a heated iron on fabrics or newly stitched seams, darts, and other parts of the garment to set them.
- *Ironing*—The process of sliding a heated iron back and forth over a wrinkled fabric or garment by means of pressing with or without steam.

- *Setting*—The process of flattening or creasing a section of fabric or garment by means of pressing with or without steam.
- *Steaming*—The process by which steam is passed through fabric, usually downward by means of a steam iron, sleeve buck, form finisher, or dampened press cloth. An alternative method is to permit the steam to rise up through the fabric from below.
- *Shrinking*—The steaming process whereby an area of a garment or fabric is caused to draw in or contract in size.
- *Underpressing*—The process of pressing small units of work such as finished collars, cuffs, pockets, yokes, seams, darts, and tucks, as construction of garment proceeds.
- *Finger Pressing*—The process of using one's fingers in place of an iron to open a seam or to crease a fold.
- *Sponging*—The process of dampening the surface of a fabric or garment by means of a wet sponge.

PRODUCTION PRESSING EQUIPMENT

Appropriate pressing equipment is essential to properly finish a garment. Many different types of equipment for pressing exist, some for general use and others for special applications.

Gravity Feed Iron A weighted metal plate, approximately 8 inches (20 cm) long by 5 inches (13 cm) wide, that tapers to a point at one end, furnished with a handle and steam release knob control. The iron produces steam from water that is supplied through a hose from a suspended water tank. The heated steam generated by the iron can be adjusted. Gravity feed irons are used to smooth or crease fabrics and to provide a steady source of steam for sustained operation.

Iron Rest A flat, rectangular-shaped, heat-resistant, flexible rubber- or silicone-coated metal plate where an iron rests when not in use. Industrial irons are designed to lay with the iron surface plate face down. An iron rest is used to prevent the ironing surface from scorching.

Gravity feed iron

Iron rest

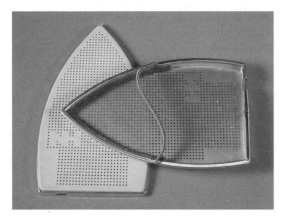

Iron shoe

Iron Shoe A metal fitting with a Teflon sheet laminated to the bottom surface that is perforated and shaped to strap on the sole of a steam iron. An iron shoe is used in place of a pressing cloth to

- Prevent scorching that produces shine on the surface of fabrics
- Evenly distribute steam from the iron over the entire ironing surface
- Press the face of garments made of synthetic fabrics or blends

Industrial Vacuum Ironing Board A flat board, approximately 54 inches (1.4 meters) long by 15 inches (38 cm) wide, that tapers to 6 inches (15 cm) at one end and is supported at table height. The board is perforated, padded, and covered with fabric and is permanently fixed to a stand. When a garment is steam pressed, excess moisture is suctioned from the garment through the surface of the board. Some vacuum ironing boards are equipped to blow air up through the board to create a cushion of air in which to press. Up-air vacuum boards are useful when pressing garment areas that mark easily, such as pockets and fly front closures, and are also used for preventing napped fabric surfaces from being crushed.

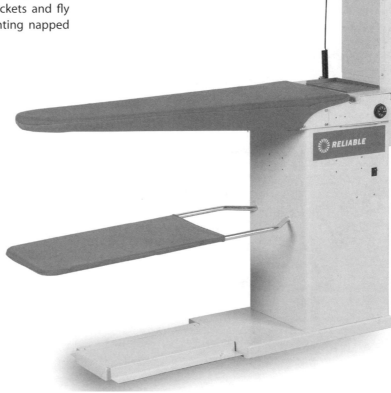

Industrial vacuum ironing board

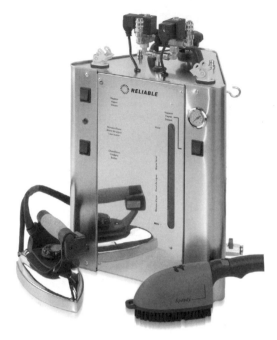

Steam Iron and Boiler A weighted metal plate, approximately 8 inches (20 cm) long by 5 inches (13 cm) wide, that tapers to a point at one end, furnished with a handle and steam release knob control. The iron operates with steam supplied through a hose from a separate chamber that heats water into steam. The heat and pressure of the steam generated from the boiler can be adjusted. Steam irons and boilers are used to smooth or crease fabrics and to provide a steady source of steam for sustained operation.

Steam iron and boiler

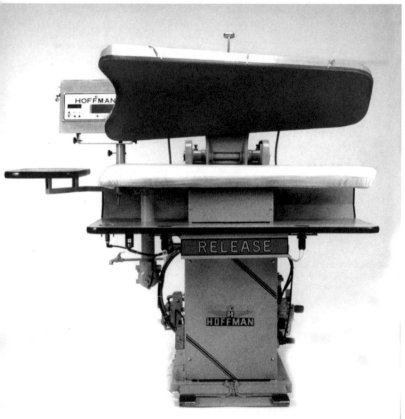

Steam press

Steam Press A two-piece flat or curved padded form that applies heat, moisture, and pressure when the upper and lower opposing beds are activated by a foot pedal or handle. Padded surfaces are covered with silicone-treated fabric, heavy canvas, or drill cloth. Externally generated steam may pass through the top, bottom, or both surfaces. A steam press is used to

- Facilitate the pressing of a particular garment part such as a collar, shoulder, or body of a coat
- Shape and smooth the final garment
- Smooth and shape garment parts, making it possible for a machine operator to perform a variety of subsequent operations of garment assembly
- Shrink fabrics before they are sewn
- Press creases and pleats in garments
- Press the face and underside of garments at the same time

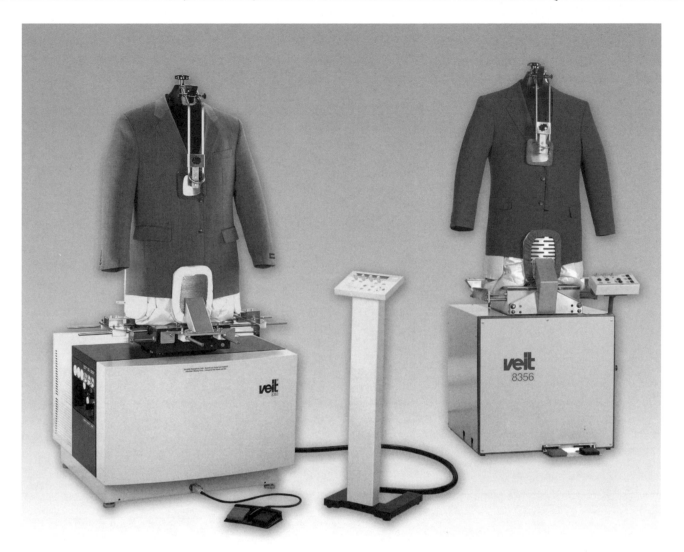

Form finisher

Form Finisher A collapsible fabric structure simulating a garment shape that inflates and applies heat and steam when activated. The shape of the pressing form is planned to conform to a garment category such as shirts, evening gowns, or knit garments. The forms are made of natural or synthetic fabric and are planned with zippers at strategic points for increased or decreased diameters and changing shapes. A form finisher is used to press an entire garment at one time and is chosen because it will not distort the shape of the garment or mar the fabric.

Puff Iron An ovoid metal ironing head, with or without a covered surface, that is fixed to a stand. Padded surfaces are covered with silicone-treated fabric, heavy canvas, or drill cloth. A puff iron is used to

- Press or shape contoured seams
- Press puffed sleeves, ruffles, or pocket details
- Block and shape millinery

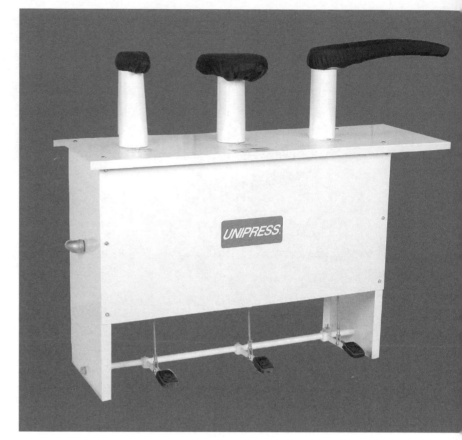

Puff iron

Sleeve Former A flexible hardwood and metal form for shaping sleeves of jackets and coats during pressing on a steam press or form finisher. Sleeve formers are available in sizes from 24 inches (60.9 cm) long with up to 13-inch (33 cm) expansion, 24 inches (60.9 cm) long with up to 11-inch (27.9 cm) expansion, 12 inches (38.4 cm) long with up to 7½-inch (19 cm) expansion. Sleeve formers are sold in pairs.

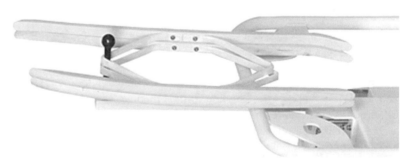

Sleeve former

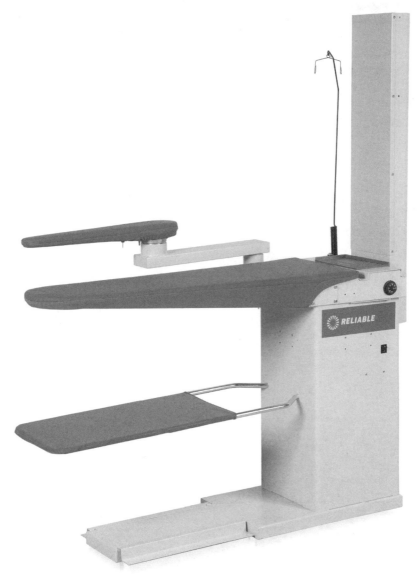

Sleeve buck

Sleeve Buck A rounded metal padded and covered board measuring approximately 21 inches (53 cm) long, tapering from a width of 5 inches to 2½ inches (12.7 to 6.4 cm), that is attached to an ironing board or press. A sleeve buck is used to press sleeves, short seams, and hard-to-reach areas.

Reference

WAWAK, Inc. (2015). *Pressing and spotting*. Retrieved January 28, 2016, from http://www.wawak.com/Pressing-Spotting

CHAPTER 29

Quality Assurance, Product Testing, and Inspection

Testing throughout the development and manufacturing of apparel products ensures quality and compliance with safety regulations. Product testing leads to better quality garments and higher customer satisfaction.

The practice of testing is an integral part of fiber, yarn, fabric, and finished garment production that allows firms to achieve product consistency at expected quality levels. **Testing** involves the methods for evaluating materials and completed products, including

- Preparing specimens
- Performing experiments
- Evaluating and analyzing data to determine if materials or products meet appearance, performance, and quality expectations as they relate to end use

Quality control is the process for ensuring specified quality levels are maintained through continually testing at different phases of production, performing frequent inspections, and ensuring proper use of equipment and established procedures. When materials or products are not meeting quality standards, action must be taken to correct any problems affecting product appearance, performance, and safety, in order to maintain customer satisfaction and protect the brand's reputation. **Vender compliance** is important for ensuring performance standards and product specifications are being met as part of the contractual agreement.

TEST METHOD DEVELOPMENT

Proper procedures for testing must be strictly followed in order to provide reliable, reproducible results. **Reliability** refers to the consistency, dependability, and reproducibility of test methods, procedures, and results from data obtained during testing. When tests are repetitively performed on the same material, consistent data should be collected in order to ensure **reproducibility**. Specific procedures for examination and evaluation, known as **standardized test methods**, have been developed for textile materials and products by international, national, and federal organizations and agencies. The organizations and agencies developing and maintaining standard test methods to ensure consistent quality include

- **International Organization for Standardization (ISO)** Recognized as the largest organization of its kind, this nongovernmental body is composed of members of the national standards institutes from 163 countries.
- **American National Standards Institute (ANSI)** Internationally recognized organization, focused on the U.S. private sector. ANSI also accredits companies utilizing ISO standards.
- **ASTM International** Internationally recognized global organization.
- **Association of Textile, Apparel & Materials Professionals (AATCC)** Internationally recognized global organization specifically focused on dyed or chemically treated materials and products.

- **European Committee for Standardization (CEN)** European organization focused on voluntary national standards.
- **National Institute of Standards and Technology (NIST)** Federal agency that is a nonregulatory division of the U.S. Department of Commerce (DOC).
- **U.S. Consumer Products Safety Commission (CPSC)** U.S. federal regulatory agency focused on protecting customers from flammable and chemical hazards, as well as those that can cause injury to a child.
- **U.S. Department of Defense Single Stock Point (U.S. DODSSP)** U.S. federal agency, appointed by the U.S. Department of Defense, to oversee national standards for military uniforms.
- **Association of the Nonwoven Fabrics Industry (INDA)** American trade association focused on nonwoven materials and products.
- **European Disposables and Nonwovens Association (EDANA)** Internationally recognized organization focused on voluntary standards for nonwoven materials and products. Originally this organization was formed to serve the nonwovens industry in Europe but has expanded internationally with a specific focus on Europe, the Middle East, and Africa.

FRAMEWORK OF A TEST METHOD

Standardized test methods follow specific formats for all types of testing developed. Each test method is catalogued with a name and number. The naming and numbering system as well as format of information varies from organization to organization. The standard format used by ASTM, which may vary slightly depending on the specific method, is as follows.

Scope Purpose of the test method and the materials covered within.

Referenced Documents Other standards possessing information related to the test method. Referenced documents can include other standards for test methods, specifications, or terminology.

Terminology Definitions for terms used within the test method.

Summary of Test Method Brief explanation of how the test method is performed.

Significance and Use Information regarding acceptance testing and how the method and data gathered should be used.

Acceptance Testing Assessment of whether a material or product is meeting specified criteria for approval.

Apparatus Equipment, device, or instrument and materials needed to perform a test.

Hazards Precautions that should be taken to ensure one's safety while performing the test.

Sampling Procedures for taking and preparing test specimens, which include

- Determining dimensions of the specimens
- Determining the number of specimens required
- Methods for preparing specimens for testing

Conditioning Exposing the specimens and materials to standard atmospheric conditions to prepare them for testing. Conditioning is used to control the atmospheric conditions in a testing lab in order to provide reproducible results. Standard atmospheric conditions maintained for testing textiles are 70° Fahrenheit +/– 2 degrees (21° Celsius +/– 1) and 65 percent relative humidity +/– 2 percent.

Conditioning is not always required. Suggested minimum conditioning time periods as specified in ASTM D 1776 Standard Practice for Conditioning and Testing Textiles include

- 8 hours for animal fibers and rayon fibers
- 6 hours for natural cellulose fibers
- 4 hours for acetate fibers
- 2 hours for other manufactured fibers

Procedure Step-by-step instructions indicating how to perform the test.

Preparation of Equipment or Equipment Calibration Instructions for preparing the equipment for testing and verifying accuracy of results.

Standard Calibration Fabric Material used for verifying the performance of equipment for testing. Fiber properties for specific types of fabrics are determined under the International Calibration Standards Program.

Calculation Procedure for obtaining results. Instructions may include formulas or rating scales.

Report Documentation of procedures used for testing, how data was calculated, and statement of results.

Precision and Bias Statistical information regarding accuracy of test results and any factors that may influence results.

Key Words Important terms used in the test method.

Lab Sample Materials or garments selected from a lot sample for use in obtaining specimens for testing.

Lot Sample Individual materials or garments randomly selected as lab samples for acceptance testing.

Specimen Portion used for testing that is taken from a lab sample.

Control Material or garment used as a standard during testing and evaluation for comparison purposes.

TYPES OF TESTING

There are two main categories of tests: destructive and nondestructive. **Destructive tests** require specimens to be cut from the lab sample, **whereas** nondestructive tests allow for measurements to be taken on a material or finished product without causing damage. Testing can be completed in a laboratory setting on individual garment component materials, as well as on the finished garments that are worn to evaluate performance in relation to end use. Wear testing allows a designer, manufacturer, or product developer to evaluate the performance of a product in the environment in which the consumer will use it, also known as wear-service conditions. ASTM D 3181 Standard Guide for Conducting Wear Tests on Textiles provides specific guidelines for this type of testing.

Performance features such as aesthetics and functionality are a critical component of whether a customer is satisfied with a product. **Aesthetic performance features** refer to the appearance or attractiveness of the product. **Functional performance features** target the durability and usefulness of the product with regard to end-use expectations. Common tests performed on apparel products evaluate aesthetic or functional performance features as they relate to abrasion, appearance, colorfastness, dimensional stability, safety, strength, and structural properties. **Characterization testing** is used to verify that structural properties of materials such as fibers, yarns, and fabrics meet required specifications. Commonly used tests for characterizing materials include

- Fiber identification
- Yarn construction
- Fabric count
- Fabric thickness
- Fabric weight

Abrasion

Abrasion is one material rubbing against itself or another surface, and it can affect the appearance and strength of a garment. Two flat fabric surfaces rubbing against each other or against another object cause **flat abrasion**. When a fabric is repeatedly folded and unfolded, the yarns wear against each other in **flex abrasion**. **Edge abrasion** affects the edges of apparel products where the fabric edge rubs against another surface, causing wear. ASTM International and AATCC recommend multiple methods for testing abrasion and wear of textile products.

Abrasion resistance tests:

- Accelerator method
- Flex abrasion method
- Inflated diaphragm method
- Martindale method
- Oscillatory cylinder method
- Hex bar method
- Pile fabric abrasion
- Rotary platform, double head method
- Uniform abrasion method

Pilling resistance and surface change tests:

- Brush pilling tester
- Elastomeric pad
- Martindale method
- Random tumble

Snagging resistance tests:

- Bean bag method
- Mace method

These abrasion test methods and specific procedures can be found in the ASTM International annual book of standards, AATCC technical manual, or ISO standards.

Appearance and Stiffness

The overall look and appeal of a garment describes appearance. **Appearance retention** refers to the ability of a material or garment to maintain its aesthetic look during wear, refurbishment, and storage. Wrinkling is a common problem with textile materials. If a material is **wrinkle resistant**, it possesses the ability to oppose deformations caused by folding or bending. When fabrics are resilient or have elasticity to bounce back from compression or deformation, they are said to have **wrinkle recovery** properties. **Stiffness** is the ability of a fabric to resist bending. Appearance and stiffness tests for textile products are as follows.

Appearance tests:

- Appearance of fabrics after repeated home laundering
- Appearance of apparel after repeated home laundering
- Wrinkle recovery appearance method
- Wrinkle recovery angle method

Stiffness tests:

- Stiffness of fabrics
- Stiffness of nonwoven fabrics cantilever method
- Stiffness of fabric blade slot method
- Stiffness of fabric circular bending method

These appearance test methods and specific procedures can be found in the ASTM International annual book of standards, AATCC technical manual, and ISO standards.

■ Colorfastness

Color plays a significant role in the aesthetic appearance of textile and apparel products. **Colorfastness** is the ability of a textile product to resist color change or loss. Color loss or change can occur by transference from another material during wear, refurbishment, or storage, or by exposure to environmental conditions. Colorfastness and color change tests for textile products are as follows.

Colorfastness tests include colorfastness to

- Acids and alkali
- Chlorine and hydrogen peroxide bleach
- Burnt gas fumes
- *Crocking*
- Dye transfer of fabric-to-fabric in storage
- Drycleaning
- Dry heat excluding pressing
- Heat from hot pressing
- Home laundering with activated oxygen bleach detergent
- Laundering
- Light
- Light at high temperatures
- Light and humidity
- Nonchlorine bleach in home laundering
- Oxides of nitrogen in the atmosphere under high humidity
- Ozone in the atmosphere under low humidity
- Ozone in the atmosphere under high humidity
- Perspiration
- Perspiration and light
- Steam pleating
- Sea water
- Sodium hypochlorite bleach in home laundering
- Perchloroethylene solvent spotting
- Water spotting
- Chlorinated pool water

Color change tests include

- Color change due to flat abrasion
- Color measurement of fibers
- Whiteness of textiles

Colorfastness test methods and specific procedures can be found in the ASTM International annual book of standards, AATCC technical manual, and ISO standards.

Gray Scale for Evaluating Color Change Rating scale used to evaluate changes in color composed of five numerical grades of standard gray chips. Each pair of chips provides a visual comparison showing progressive changes in color or contrast corresponding to colorfastness ratings.

Gray Scale for Staining Rating scale for evaluating inadvertent color transference composed of five numeric grades of standard white and gray chips. Each pair of chips provides a visual comparison showing progressive changes in color or contrast corresponding to colorfastness ratings.

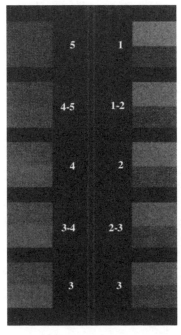

Gray scale for evaluating color change

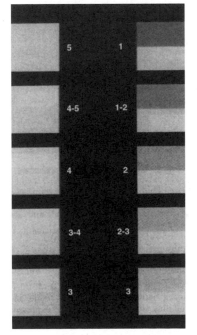

Gray scale for evaluating staining

Chromatic Transfer Scale Rating scale used to evaluate inadvertent color transference composed of five numeric grades consisting of *Munsell®* color chips of red, yellow, green, blue, and purple. Each color is aligned in rows to create vertical gradations (light to dark) to provide a visual comparison for changes in contrast or color that correspond to the rating scale. A *9-Step Chromatic Transference Scale* contains 60 color chips (see Color plate 10).

Crocking Color rub-off due to excess dye on the surface of textile materials.

Frosting White cast that appears on the surface of textile materials caused by loss of color due to abrasion and poor dye penetration. Some dye classes do not penetrate the fiber, so dye remains on the exterior only.

Staining Unwanted color transferred from one material onto another that can occur during wear, refurbishment, or storage.

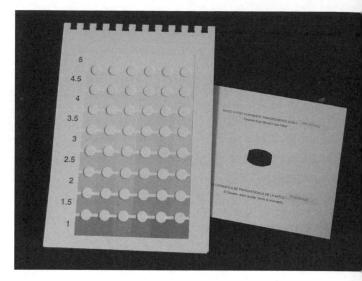

Chromatic transfer scale

Dimensional Stability

When textile products are subjected to specific conditions relating to temperature and humidity, the dimensions can change. When apparel items are refurbished **dimensional change** can occur in the form of shrinkage or growth. **Shrinkage** is a loss in the length or width dimensions of a textile material or product, whereas **growth** is a gain in length or width measurements. **Dimensional stability** of a material or product means the ability to retain its shape and dimensions under specific conditions relating to temperature and humidity. Tests used for determining dimensional stability of textile products include

- Dimensional stability of fabrics to changes in humidity and temperature
- Dimensional changes in commercial laundering of woven and knitted fabrics except wool
- Dimensional changes of fabrics after home laundering
- Dimensional changes on drycleaning in perchloroethylene using the machine method
- Dimensional changes of fabrics using the accelerated method
- Appearance of fabrics after repeated launderings

Dimensional stability test methods and specific procedures can be found in the ASTM International annual book of standards, AATCC technical manuals, and ISO standards.

Safety

Safety is a major concern for the textile and apparel industry. The three main areas of concern are flammability, toxicity, and strangulation from drawstrings in children's apparel. **Flammable** refers to any textile material having the ability to combust and burn with a flame. **Flammability** pertains to properties a textile product possesses that provide ease of ignition and the ability to continue burning. In the United States, the Consumer Products Safety Commission (CPSC) oversees manufacturer's compliance with the Code of Federal Regulations (CFR) pertaining to

flammable products. The CFR outlines three flammability classes for textiles:

- Class 1—Normal Flammability. Materials that take more than 7 seconds to ignite are permitted for use in wearing apparel.
- Class 2—Intermediate Flammability. Materials with a raised fiber surface that take between 4 and 7 seconds to ignite are permitted for use in wearing apparel.

- Class 3—Rapid and Intense Burning. Materials that ignite in less than 4 seconds and are not permitted for use in wearing apparel.

Materials classified with Class 3 flammability cannot be legally sold in the United States due to their highly flammable nature.

Tests used for determining flammability of textile products include

- Flame resistance of textiles
- Flammability of apparel/clothing textiles
- Flammability of children's sleepwear: Sizes 0 to 6x
- Flammability of children's sleepwear: Sizes 7 to 14
- Flammability of textiles used in children's sleepwear

Nonflammable Textile product that burns without a flame.

Noncombustible Textile product that will not burn.

Flame Resistant Ability of a textile product to extinguish itself after ignition.

Flame Retardant Chemical finish applied to textiles to provide flame-resistant properties.

Another safety concern that poses health risks is **toxicity**. Certain dyes, fibers, or finishes may be toxic, and some substances are carcinogenic. Individuals with sensitive skin tend to be more affected by wearing apparel made with certain fibers, dyes, or finishes. Tests used for determining toxicity of textile products for general wearing apparel include

- Identification of textile finishes
- Release of formaldehyde from fabric using the sealed-jar method
- Antibacterial finishes on fabrics
- Transfer of dyes
- Alkali in wet processed textiles

Certain Azo Dyes Nitrogen-based synthetic dyestuffs banned in some countries because under certain conditions they produce cancer-causing allergenic aromatic amines.

Certain Flame Retardants Chemical finishes banned in some countries due to health risks associated with cancer, thyroid problems, and damage to organs.

Fluorinated Organic Compounds Man-made chemical compounds used to provide fabrics with water, oil, and grease resistance are banned in some countries due to health risks associated with absorption into the body where they accumulate in the kidneys, serum, and liver.

Formaldehyde Chemical compound that can be used as a binder for dyes and pigments or as part of a wrinkle-free finish formulation that is banned in some countries due to health risks associated with irritation of mucous membranes and the respiratory tract when released into the air.

Lead Naturally occurring chemical element used in some garment findings made from metal or plastic that is banned in some countries due to health risks associated with cancer and contact dermatitis.

Nickel Naturally occurring chemical element used in some garment findings made from metal that is banned in some countries due to health risks associated with contact dermatitis.

The third major safety risk is strangulation from drawstrings in children's apparel. Some countries have created voluntary standards that prohibit drawstrings from being used in hoods and necklines of children's garments for ages 18 months to 10 years of age.

Safety-related test methods and specific procedures can be found in the ASTM International annual book of standards, AATCC technical manual, and ISO standards. See also Table 29.1.

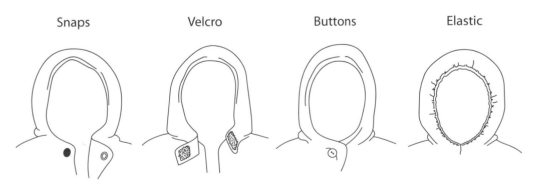

Snaps   Velcro   Buttons   Elastic

CPSC Recommended alternatives for hood and neck closures for children's garments

TABLE 29.1

Summary of Safety Regulations by Country

Regulation	Country			
	Canada	Harmonized EU	Japan	U.S.
Certain Azo Dyes	N	R	N	N
Certain Flame Retardants	R	R	R	R
Flammability:				
General Wearing Apparel	R	R	N	R
Children's Sleepwear	N	N	R	R
Fluorinated Organic Compounds	R	R	N	V, P
Formaldehyde	N	N	R	R
Lead	N	N	N	R
Nickel	N	R	N	N
Drawstrings in Children's Apparel	V	R	N	V

Note:
R = Required Regulation
V = Voluntary Regulation
N = No Regulation
P = Proposed Ban

■ Strength

The strength of garment components in relation to functionality and end use is important to evaluate to avoid fabric or seam failure. A material's **tensile strength** refers to the ability of the fabric to resist tension before rupturing or breaking. Following are the six categories of tensile tests that can be performed on textiles and wearing apparel:

- Breaking strength
- Tearing strength
- Modulus
- Bursting strength
- Seam strength
- Fabric failure
- Seam slippage

Breaking Strength Force required to break multiple yarns in a textile specimen in the warp or filling direction; amount of force required to tear fabric. Breaking strength is performed on woven and nonwoven fabrics.

Tearing Strength Force required for breaking one or a couple of yarns in a textile specimen in the warp or filling direction; amount of force required to continue a tear. Tearing strength is performed on woven fabrics.

Modulus Directional force applied to a textile specimen causing repeated elongation and recovery in order to examine the resistance limit prior to causing permanent distortion or damage. Modulus is performed on low- and high-power knit fabrics.

Bursting Strength Multidirectional force required for rupturing yarns in a textile specimen. Bursting strength is performed on woven, knitted, and nonwoven fabrics.

Seam Strength Force required for rupturing seam stitching. Seam strength test can result in seam failure, fabric failure, or seam slippage.

Fabric Failure When force applied to the seam of a garment causes the fabric to tear. Fabric failure can occur when the construction of the seam is stronger than the material of the apparel product.

Seam Slippage When tension applied to a seam of a garment causes the yarns of the fabric to slide away from the seam.

Testing can provide valuable information regarding the strength of fabrics, seam constructions, and a combination of the two when used in garments. Tests that determine strength of textile products include

- Breaking strength/force and elongation of fabrics
- Elongation of elastic fabrics
- Stretch properties of textile products
- Stretch properties of knitted textiles
- Stretch properties of woven fabrics with stretch yarns
- Strength of seams
- Tension and elongation of fabrics
- Tension and elongation of elastic fabrics
- Tearing strength of fabrics

Strength test methods and specific procedures can be found in the ASTM International annual book of standards, AATCC technical manuals, and ISO standards.

■ Structural Properties

Fibers, yarns, and fabrics play an important role in apparel production and customer satisfaction of end products. Companies conduct testing on fibers, yarns, fabrics, and finished products to ensure consistency of materials throughout development and production, so the end products will meet their customer's performance expectations. Tests to determine structural properties of textile products include

- Bow and skew in woven and knitted fabrics
- Distortion of yarns in woven fabrics
- Fiber analysis
- Fabric density

- Fiber fineness
- Linear density of textile fibers
- Linear density of yarns
- Mass unit area of fabrics
- Thickness of nonwoven fabrics
- Yarn construction
- Yarn number
- Yarn twist

Structural property test methods and specific procedures can be found in the ASTM International annual book of standards, AATCC technical manuals, and ISO standards.

PERFORMANCE SPECIFICATIONS

Standard performance specifications are established by many organizations developing standard test methods as well as individual companies or agencies wishing to set performance ratings above minimum industry expectations. These performance specifications are used to determine requirements for acceptability of materials or finished products based on test results gathered. Specifications for performance follow specific formats, like test methods. Each performance specification is catalogued with a name and number. The naming and numbering system as well as format of information varies from organization to organization. The standard format used by ASTM International, which may vary slightly depending on the performance specification, includes

- Scope
- Referenced documents
- Terminology

- Specification requirements
- Significance and use
- Sampling
- Test methods
- Key words

Specification Requirements List or table of minimum or maximum ratings, percentages, and numbers to determine acceptable performance levels for specific tests performed with regard to end use.

Product performance specifications for apparel products are grouped by

- Men's and boys; or women's and girls; or men's, women's, and children's
- Woven or knitted (if applicable)
- Type of fabric or type of garment
- Fabric finish (if applicable)

INSPECTION

Inspection is the process of visually examining component parts, and apparel products at various stages of completion, as well as measuring garment dimensions in relation to required standards and tolerances, to determine if they meet established requirements or to identify defects and take corrective action. It is at the discretion of individual companies to determine which stages of development, manufacturing, and distribution products will be evaluated and inspected for compliance.

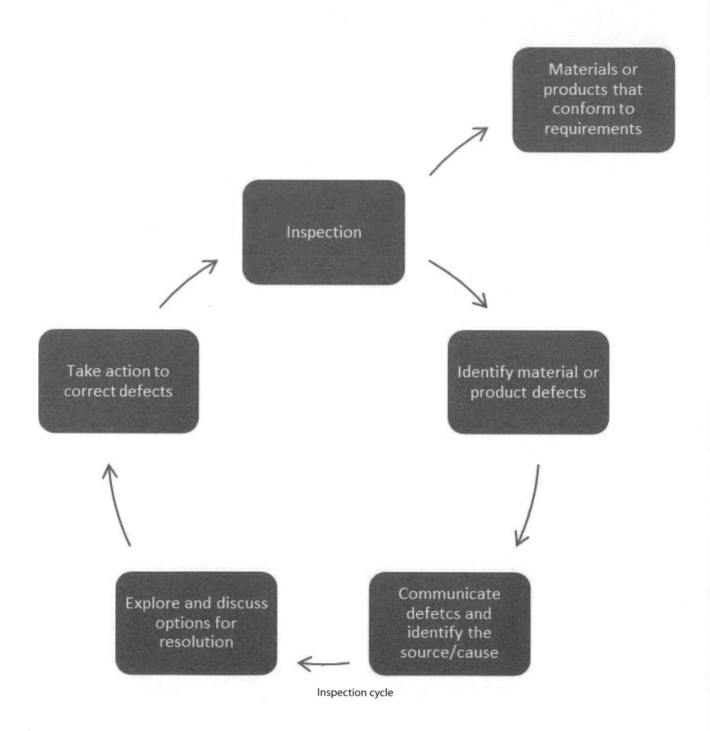

Inspection cycle

Measurement Instructions

1. Bust/ Chest*
- With front of garment facing up, measure straight across bust/chest from side to side at armholes seam.
- On garments with pleats, fully extend pleats without stretching fabric.

2. Across Chest
- With front of garment facing up, measure 5 in. down from high shoulder point parallel to center front.
- Measure straight across 5 in. from armhole.
- On garments with pleats, fully extend pleats without stretching fabric.

3. Sweep* - Garments with Vents or Shirttail Hems
- Lay garment flat in closed position.
- Measure straight across from side to side at top of vent or shirttail hem.

4. Sweep* - Garments with Straight Hems
- Lay garment flat in closed position.
- Measure from side to side along bottom of garment.

6. Across Shoulder
- With back of garment facing up, locate shoulder points (where shoulder seam meets top of armhole, or where natural fold of shoulder meets top of armhole) on each side of garment.
- Measure straight across shoulders from point to point.
- If garment is sleeveless, measure excluding any trim at armhole.

7. Across Back
- With back of garment facing up, measure 4 in. down from high shoulder point parallel to center back.
- Measure across at 4 in. mark from armhole to armhole.

8. Center Back Length
- Measure from center of back neck seam, down center of the back, to bottom of garment.

9. Shoulder Slope
- Draw an imaginary line parallel with hem from high shoulder point out to shoulder width.
- From that point, measure straight down to shoulder point.

12. Sleeve Length - Garments with Raglan Sleeves
- Lay garment with back facing up,
- Measure from center back neck at base of neck, in a straight line down sleeve, to sleeve edge.

13. Armseye - Raglan Back
- Lay back of garment facing up, with body panel lying flat (without wrinkles at armhole seam).
- Measure from base of neck following contour of seam to armhole/side seam intersection point.

15. Armseye - Sleeved & Sleeveless*
- Lay front of garment facing up with body panel lying flat (without wrinkles at armhole seam).
- Following armhole seam contour, measure from bottom of armhole to top of armhole keeping tape on body side of seam.
- Care must be taken to rotate tape measure so that measuring edge is absolutely flat along armhole seam.

16. Upper Arm*
- Measure 1 in. down from underarm, then from that point measure straight across sleeve perpendicular to center fold of sleeve.

5. Front Length
- Measure from high shoulder point, down front body, to bottom of garment

Take measurements with:
- *a dressmaker's or fiberglass coated tape measure (checked periodically against a metal ruler to assure accuracy).*
- *garments laid on a flat surface in a relaxed position.*
- *all wrinkles gently smoothed out.*
- *buttons and/or zippers fully closed (unless otherwise stated).*

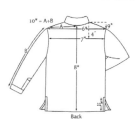

Back

10. Sleeve Length - Garments with Set-In-Sleeves
- With back of garment facing up, measure half of shoulder width starting at center back neck, to shoulder point at top of armhole, then along center fold of sleeve to cuff edge.

11. Vent Height
- Measure from bottom edge of garment to top of vent opening.

14. Armseye - Raglan Front
- Lay garment with front facing up and body panel lying flat (without wrinkles at armhole seam).
- Measure from base of neck following contour of seam to armhole/side seam intersection point.

Front

17. Elbow*
- Fold sleeve in half, so edge of cuff is positioned at bottom of armhole.
- Measure straight across this fold from underarm to center fold.

18. Cuff Opening*
- Measure straight across bottom of sleeve from underarm side of cuff to center fold side of cuff.
- For button cuff, cuff should be measured closed and buttoned on first button.

19. Cuff Height
- Measure from cuff/sleeve seam down to edge of cuff.

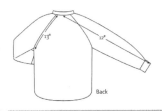

Back

Front

20. Neck Width
- Lay garment flat.
- Measure straight across from high shoulder point to high shoulder point at base of ribbing or collar.
- If there is no collar or trim, measure from edge to edge at high shoulder point.

Front

21. Front Neck Depth
- Lay garment flat with front facing up.
- Draw an imaginary line at base of neck from high shoulder point to high shoulder point.
- From that center point, measure straight down to base of ribbing or collar at center front.

Front

22. Back Neck Depth
- Lay garment flat with back facing up.
- Draw an imaginary line at base of neck from high shoulder point to high shoulder point.
- From that center point, measure straight down to base of ribbing or collar at center back.

Front

23. Collar Height
- Measure at center back from base of collar to top outer edge of collar.

Back

24. Collar Length at Outer Edge
- Undo all the buttons and lay collar flat so that inside of garment is facing up.
- Measure along collar edge from collar point to collar point

Back

25. Collar Point
- Lay collar flat.
- Measure from base of collar to outer edge of collar point.
- If there is no collar band, measure from neck seam to collar point.

26. Collar Band Height
- Measure at center back from neck line seam to top of band.

27. Collar Base Edge - With or Without Band
- Undo all buttons and lay collar flat with inside of garment facing up.
- Measure along collar base from edge to edge.
- If garment has a zipper exclude the zipper from the measurement.

28. Neck Circumference
- Undo all buttons and lay collar flat so that inside of garment is facing up.
- Measure from center of button to farthest end of buttonhole along inside of collar band.

29. Placket Width
- Measure placket on exterior of garment from seam or stitched edge to finished edge.

30. Placket Length
- Measure placket on exterior of garment from top edge to bottom seam or stitched edge.

31. Pocket Width - Exterior
- Measure the pocket across the top opening edge to edge.

32. Pocket Length - Exterior
- Measure at longest point from top opening edge to bottom finished edge.

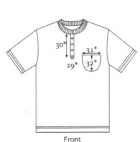

Front

Directions for inspecting a shirt to verify garment size and dimensions

A **defect** is a flaw or imperfection in material or a garment that does not meet the level of quality specified. Sometimes a product will be labeled as **nonconforming**, which means the product does not meet the specified quality requirements but may not be defective. For a product to be judged as **defective**, it must contain enough flaws for it to no longer satisfy the desired appearance and functional characteristic for the product's end use. Three rating categories for classifying defects include

Critical Defects—Level one, severe flaws, can injure the wearer and in worst-case scenarios cause death. Critical defects can include

- Broken needle or straight pin stitched into a garment that can cut or puncture the skin of the wearer
- Missing label or noncompliance with labeling regulations where burns or contact dermatitis may result in injury to the wearer
- Improperly attached snap or grommet where the prong ends are exposed and can cut or puncture the skin of the wearer

Major Defects—Level two flaws impact the functional performance of the garment and will likely cause product failure during usage. Major defects can include

- Broken zipper
- Missed stitches
- Open seam

Minor Defects—Level three flaws affect only the appearance of the garment, not performance or function. Minor defects can include

- Shading
- Soil
- Wavy seam

These levels of defects are further subdivided into two groups:

- Material defects
- Garment defects

■ Material Defects

Defects found in apparel fabrics impact the visual appearance and structure of knitted and woven materials. These defects can occur due to flaws in yarns, broken needles, or malfunctions of knitting or weaving equipment. Fabric finishing can also result in defects that affect the visual appearance and performance and in certain situations the structure of the material during application of color, as well as mechanical or chemical processing. Fabric inspection machines allow for fabric defects to be detected and marked accordingly. This allows for fabric defects and flaws to be detected to avoid them from being incorporated into finished products.

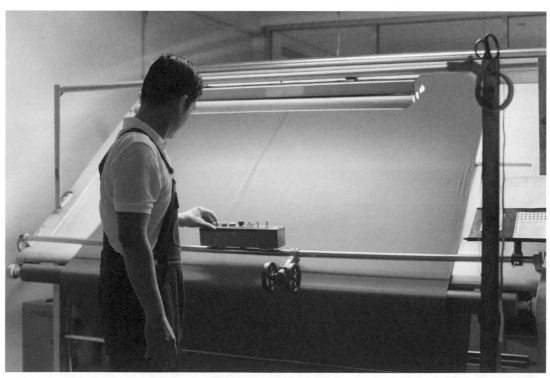

Fabric inspection machine

Barre Unwanted streaks across the width of knitted fabric caused by differences in the yarns, fabric structure, or dyes.

Barre

Birdseye The unplanned formation of two consecutive tuck stitches in a knitted fabric.

Broken Pick A gap in woven fabric caused by a yarn break in the filling direction of the material.

Broken pick

Bow Arcs formed across the width of a knitted or woven fabric because the filling or course yarns have become displaced during finishing.

Color Out Areas of a knitted or woven fabric that are missing color due to a color running low or a blocked screen during the printing process.

Color Smear Smudged color on a fabric as a result of a problem with the printing paste or machine.

Course Yarn or Thick Yarn A yarn woven into fabric that is significantly larger in size than surrounding yarns.

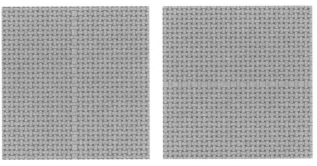

Course yarn or thick yarn

Crease Mark Portion of the fabric that has been unintentionally folded and set or that was not removed properly during finishing and cannot be pressed out.

Crease mark

Double Pick Two filling yarns inserted in the same shed (temporary space between the upper and lower warp yarns) during weaving.

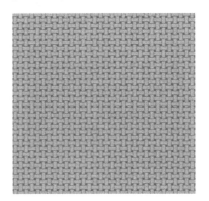

Double pick

INSPECTION (continued)

End out Space created in woven fabric caused by a yarn break or a yarn running out.

End out

Fine Yarn or Thin Yarn Yarn woven into fabric that is significantly smaller in size than surrounding yarns.

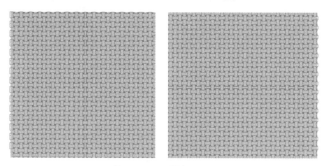

Fine yarn or Thin yarn

Float Skip in the interlacing of yarns in the warp or filling direction where the yarn passes over several yarns rather than interlacing with each one.

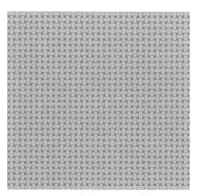

Float

Hole An unwanted opening in knitted or woven fabric caused by damaged or broken yarns.

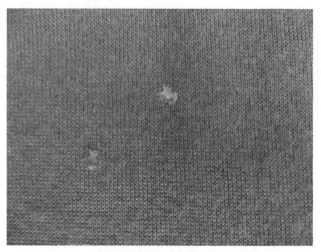

Holes in knitted fabric

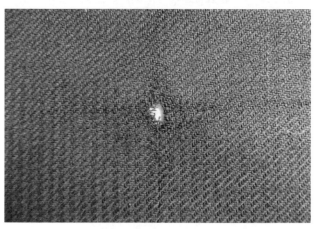

Hole in woven fabric

Jerk-in An extra filling yarn mistakenly pulled into the fabric by the shuttle during weaving that does not extend across the width of the woven material.

Jerk-in

Ladder or Run Vertical line of unformed knit stitches resulting from a dropped stitch or a broken yarn that has caused the unravel.

Ladder or Run

Misregister Misalignment of colors during printing caused by print rollers that are out of sync with each other.

Needle Line Vertical line of distorted stitches in a knitted fabric caused by a bent needle.

Pinholes Punctures along the selvedge of fabric resulting from how the material was held taut during finishing.

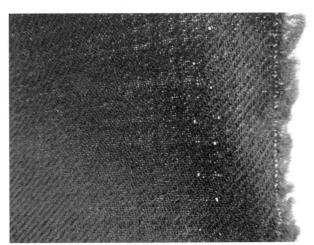

Pinholes

Scrimp Undyed portion of material resulting from a crease that was formed during printing.

Shaded Unplanned visible difference in color across the fabric from selvedge to selvedge.

Slub Section of a yarn that is significantly thicker than the surrounding yarns and appears as an unintended lump.

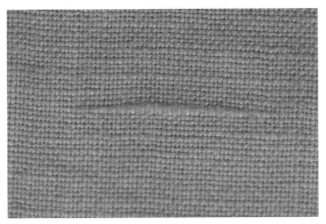

Slub in woven fabric

Skew Diagonal appearance in a knitted or woven fabric caused by displacement of courses or filling yarns. The courses and wales or warp and filling yarns are not perpendicular to each other.

Skew in knitted fabric

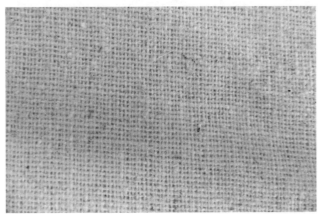

Skew in woven fabric

Soiled Yarn Portion of a yarn that is dirty or stained.

Thin Place Unplanned area in a woven fabric that contains thinner yarns, which causes the spacing to be looser in comparison to the rest of the material.

Water Spots Fabric discolorations resulting from improper dying or use of contaminated water during dying.

■ Garment Defects

Defects can also occur at various stages of manufacturing such as cutting, fusing, and assembly. Garment defects can impact the appearance, fit, function, and performance of end products. Cutting defects occur when fabric is cut into garment pieces for assembly, and these typically cannot be repaired. Fusible interlinings can be problematic as well if they are not properly adhered. Fusing defects impact the appearance of the end product and can be rejected during end inspections or may not appear until the customer has worn and refurbished the item several times, resulting in customer dissatisfaction. During construction, sewing defects can impact the appearance, fit, function, and performance of the end product. Some assembly defects can be repaired, whereas others cannot.

Blistering or Bubbling Pebbled surface on a garment area caused by improper fusing. This can result from one of the following:

- Over-fusing
- Under-fusing
- Uneven pressure during fusing
- Uneven temperature during fusing

Broken Stitch Thread of a stitch that has been cut during wet processing or severed by a needle stitching across an existing seam.

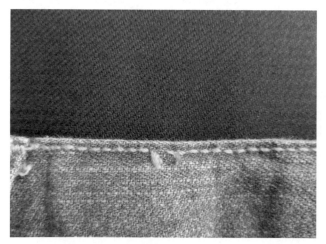

Broken stitch

Burst Seam Ruptured seam in a woven garment caused by tension or as a result of improperly joined materials.

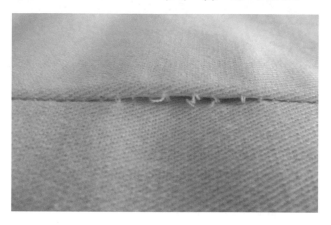

Burst seam

Cracked Seam or Cracked Stitches Broken stitches or a ruptured seam in a knitted garment caused by stretching the fabric beyond the capacity of the elasticity of the stitching or seam.

Cracked seam or cracked stitches

Drill Hole Visible puncture in the garment fabric from a misplaced drill mark during cutting. Drill marks indicate dart ends and help sewers stitch darts and position pockets on garments.

Deep Notch Visible cut in the finished garment where a notch was cut too long.

Faulty Zipper Nonfunctional zipper that is broken or missing a component part preventing it from performing properly.

Frayed edges Displaced yarns on garment panel edges due to a dull knife blade during cutting.

Fused Edges Edges of garment panels that have melted due to a knife blade cutting thorough synthetic fabrics too quickly, causing the fabric plies in a layup to bond together.

Delamination Breakdown of the adhesive bonding between a shell fabric and an interlining, causing the layers to separate.

Incorrect Ply Tension Fabric in a layup that is spread too loosely, causing unwanted folds or creases, or too tightly, resulting in distorted garment panels during cutting.

Incorrect SPI or Incorrect SPC The number of stitches per inch (SPI) or stitches per centimeter (SPC) does not match the amount specified and is not within tolerance. When the number of stitches is too few, seam failure can occur. When the number of stitches is too many for the type of material selected, the fabric can tear at the seam line while the seam stays intact; this is called fabric failure.

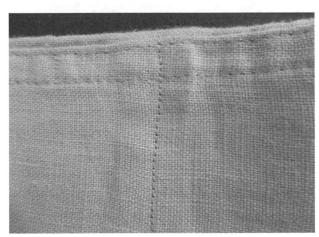

Incorrect SPI or incorrect SPC

Irregular Stitching Stitching that is not sewn straight during garment assembly due to poor craftsmanship of a machine operator.

Irregular stitching

Loose Buttons Improperly attached buttons due to insufficient thread or failure of the operator to properly secure the thread end, causing the stitching to pull out.

Loose button

Loose Thread End Tail of thread at the end of a seam, stitch line, or embroidered area that has not been properly trimmed.

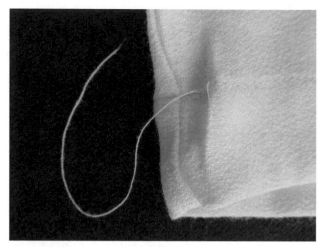

Loose thread end

Misaligned Plies The edges of a fabric spread where each layer is not properly aligned, causing small portions of garment panels to be trimmed off during the cutting process.

Mismatched Fabric Design A check, plaid, or stripe patterned fabric that should be matched at the seams in a finished garment but is not due to misalignment of the plies during fabric spreading.

Mismatched fabric design

Missing Component Garment element, such as a finding or trim piece, that is inadvertently omitted during assembly.

Moiré Effect Appearance of watermarks or a wavy striped pattern on the surface of a garment caused by the alignment of the interlining's adhesive dots and the weave structure of the shell fabric.

Needle Damage Hole in the fabric caused by a needle during assembly.

Needle damage

Open Seam When fabric plies are not entirely caught in a seam during assembly, resulting in a hole due to operator error.

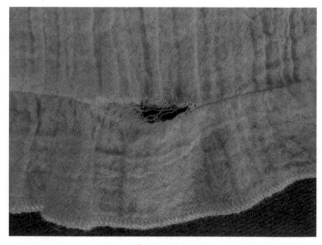

Open seam

Over-fusing Improper bonding of an interlining to the shell fabric (due to excess heat, pressure, or time during fusing) that causes a weak bond because the adhesive is absorbed or transferred into the garment fabric.

Raw Edges Unplanned frayed ends of fabric at the hemline or seams within a garment due to operator error. The material is not adequately stitched to cover the fabric edge, or the fabric is improperly folded at the seam, causing it to get caught in the stitching.

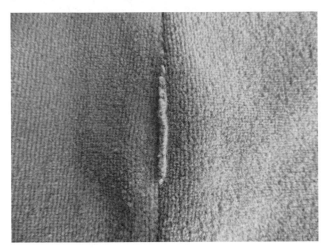

Raw edges

Ropy Hem Skewing or twisting of the fabric at the hem of a garment that prevents it from lying flat and is caused by operator error.

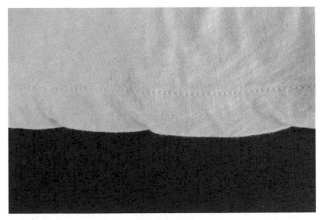

Ropy hem

Run-off or Over-run Stitching Edge stitching or top-stitching continued beyond the designated end point as a result of operator error.

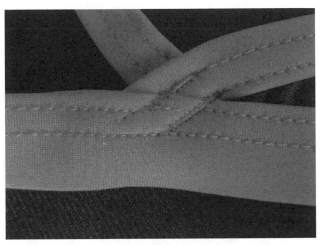

Run-off or over-run stitching

Seam Grin Visible stitching at the seam line on the face of the garment caused by unbalanced thread tension.

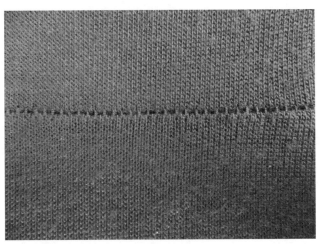

Seam grin

Seam Pucker Rippling of the fabric along the seam line due to unbalanced tension or improper distribution along the seam line during assembly.

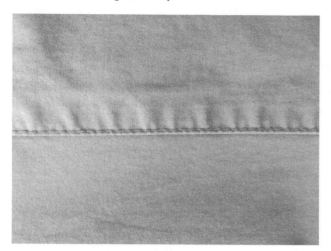

Seam pucker

Seam Repair Restitching an area of a garment to correct broken stiches or an open seam.

Seam repair

Shading Garment components or panels from different dye lots are assembled into a garment as a result of poor shade marking. The color is noticeably different and appears mismatched.

Size Defects Problems with the gradation of sizes or differences in the measurement of one garment part to another. This type of defect can result from improper grading or a bundling of garment parts from different sizes.

Skipped Stitch During stitch formation, the needle misses the bobbin or looped thread, preventing a stitch from forming. A skipped stitch is sometimes found at the thickest part of an intersection where two seams cross each other.

Skipped stitch

Soil Dirt, chalk, ink, grease, or oil stain on a garment from markings that have not been removed or from equipment during assembly.

Soil on knitted garment

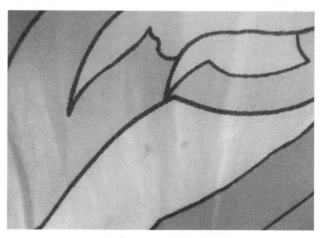

Soil on woven garment

Strike Back or Back-bleed Over-liquefied adhesive resin visible on the inside of a garment interlining caused by too high a fusing temperature, too much pressure, or too long of a fusing time.

Strike Through or Bleed-through Over-liquefied adhesive resin visible on surface the garment caused by too high a fusing temperature, too much pressure, or too long of a fusing time.

Thread Discoloration Change in thread color caused by excess dye pickup from the fabric during wet processing that can give the thread a dirty appearance.

Twisted Garment The side seam of a garment wraps to the front or back creating a distorted appearance. This defect can happen for a few reasons, which include using a skewed fabric, improperly matching the front and back panels when the side seam is sewn, or the sewing machine failing to feed the top and bottom layers of material uniformly, which results in one side being longer than the other. Sewing operators will sometimes trim off the longer edge rather than restitch the seam. In this case, if the fabric is cut, the seam cannot be repaired.

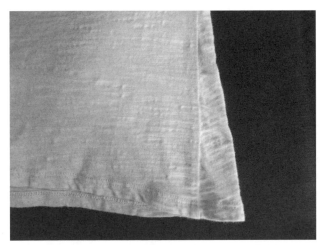

Twisted garment

Unbalanced Stitch Tension Formation of stitches along a seam line that is too loose or too tight, causing seam grin or puckering.

Uneven Seams Difference in the measured length of seams that are planned to be identical. This is caused by operator error during sewing.

Under-fusing Interlining adhesive is not fully activated due to insufficient heat, time, or pressure during fusing, which causes an improper bond between the interlining and the shell fabric.

Unraveling Buttonhole The end of the stitching of a buttonhole is not properly secured, or the stitching is severed when the buttonhole opening is cut, causing the thread to pull out.

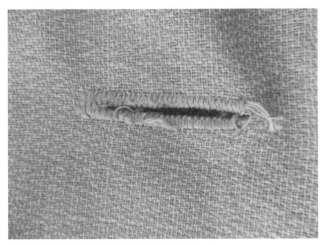

Unraveling button

Unrelated Seam Area of a garment that is inadvertently caught in the seam due to operator error.

Visible Stay Stitch Stitching used to temporarily stabilize the fabric to prevent stretching or distortion from occurring during assembly that has not been removed or concealed within the garment.

Visible stay stitch

Wavy Seam Seam that does not lie flat as a result of the fabric being stretched during assembly.

Wavy seam

Wrong Grain Garment panels that are not cut on the designated grain (i.e., straight grain or bias grain) or are cut off-grain.

Wrong Thread Color Thread color that is mismatched and does not meet the specified color standard.

Wrong Thread Type and Size Improper thread construction used in the assembly of a garment that does not meet specifications.

Wrong thread type and size

References

AATCC. (2008). *About AATCC*. Retrieved January 31, 2016, from http://www.aatcc.org/abt/

AATCC. (2016). *2016 Technical manual of the American Association of Textile Chemists and Colorists*. (Vol. 91). Research Triangle Park, NC: Author.

ANSI. (2016). *Introduction to ANSI*. Retrieved January 31, 2016, from http://www.ansi.org/about_ansi/introduction/introduction.aspx?menuid=1

ASTM International. (2016a). *About ASTM International*. Retrieved January 29, 2016, from http://www.astm.org/ABOUT/aboutASTM.html

ASTM International. (2016b). *2016 ASTM international standards*. (Vol. 07.01). West Conshohocken, PA: Author.

Bubonia, J. E. (2014) *Apparel quality: A guide to evaluating sewn products*. New York: Bloomsbury Publishing Inc.

Cobb, D. (2015, December 4*). Safety first: A closer look at environmentally-preferred DWRs*. IFAI Advanced Textiles Source. Retrieved January 29, 2016 from, http://advancedtextilessource.com/2015/12/safety-first-a-closer-look-at-environmentally-preferred-dwrs/

EDNANA. (2016). *EDNANA at a glance*. Retrieved January 29, 2016, from http://www.edana.org/industry-support/about-edana/edana-at-a-glance

European Committee for Standardization (CEN). (2016) *Who we are*. Retrieved January 29, 2016, from http://www.cen.eu/cenorm/aboutus/index.asp

INDA. (2015). *About INDA*. Retrieved January 29, 2016, from http://www.inda.org/about/index.html

ISO. (2016). *About ISO*. Retrieved January 29, 2016, from http://www.iso.org/iso/about.htm

NIST. (2016). *NIST general information*. Retrieved January 29, 2016, from http://www.nist.gov/index.html

U.S. Consumer Products Safety Commission. (2016). *About CPSC*. Retrieved January 29, 2016, from http://www.cpsc.gov/en/About-CPSC/

U.S. DODSSP. (2016). *About DODSSP*. Retrieved January 29, 2016, from http://www.defense.gov/About-DoD

U.S. Government Printing Office. (2016a). *Electronic code of federal regulations (e-CFR) Title 16 commercial practices, Part 1610 standard for the flammability of clothing textiles*. Retrieved January 29, 2016, from http://www.ecfr.gov/cgi-bin/text-idx?SID=d439c72a4dfcbb816fb6eb7b1be87512&mc=true&node=pt16.2.1610&rgn=div5

U.S. Government Printing Office. (2016b). *Electronic code of federal regulations (e-CFR) Title 16 commercial practices, Part 1615 Standard for the flammability of children's sleepwear: sizes 0 to 6x*. Retrieved January 29, 2016, from http://www.ecfr.gov/cgi-bin/text-idx?SID=d439c72a4dfcbb816fb6eb7b1be87512&mc=true&node=pt16.2.1615&rgn=div5

U.S. Government Printing Office. (2016c). *Electronic code of federal regulations (e-CFR) Title 16 commercial practices, Part 1616 Standard for the flammability of children's sleepwear: sizes 7 to 14*. Retrieved January 29, 2016, from http://www.ecfr.gov/cgi-bin/text-idx?SID=d439c72a4dfcbb816fb6eb7b1be87512&mc=true&node=pt16.2.1616&rgn=div5

CHAPTER 30

Packaging

Packaging can be defined as the process of

packing goods, or it can refer to the actual

container and component materials that hold

and protect apparel products. Packaging

is not only an important part of preparing

goods for shipment and distribution; it can

also be used for merchandising products.

Packaging is available in a variety of forms, materials, sizes, and quantities. Some important functions of packaging include

- Maintaining shape and support for the product
- Providing information to the consumer such as brand, size, price, style, and color
- Aiding with merchandising on the sales floor
- Attracting consumers to products

- Protecting against damage due to dirt, dust, light, moisture, soil, creasing, crushing, tearing, pressure, and wrinkling

SHIPPING PACKAGING

After merchandise is produced, it is packed and shipped to retailers in bulk. The end consumer does not see the outer containment packaging used for shipping from the factory. **Shipping packaging** includes the crate, box, or bag and packing materials used during shipment of bulk goods from the factory to the retail venue. This category of packaging includes:

| Bags | Cartons |
| Boxes | Crates |

Shipping packaging does not include the covering or wrapping used for individual items within a shipment.

Carton—Rigid, one-piece container, made of paper or plastic, used to hold items shipped in bulk that are folded, hung, or bundled together for transport.
Crate—Sturdy wooden container that holds cartons during shipping.
Hanger Box—Carton equipped with a rack for holding garments hung on hangers.

Shipping Box—Corrugated cardboard or rigid plastic container for transporting goods. Shipping boxes are formed or folded into a shape, which may or may not require glue, staples, or tape to hold. Boxes may be constructed as one piece or two. Bases and lids are available in a variety of sizes, weights, and volume capacities.
Packaging Tape (Sealing Tape)—Paper or plastic film with adhesive applied to one side that may contain filament threads to reinforce and secure boxes during shipment. Some tape is self-adhesive, whereas others require moisture to activate the gummed surface. Colored or transparent tape is available in 1-inch (2.54 cm), 2-inch (5.08 cm), and 3-inch (7.62 cm) widths. Tape is put up in 110-yard (100.58 m) rolls.
Strapping—Band of steel, polyester, nylon, or plastic (polypropylene) material manually or mechanically wrapped around a shipping box and heat sealed to provide strength and stability during shipping. Strapping can help prevent a box from breaking open during shipment and is available in widths ranging from (3⁄16 inch) to (5⁄8 inch).

MERCHANDISE PACKAGING

The materials used to pack individual product units for shipping or sale to the end user are known as **merchandise packaging**. Many products are packaged to ease the transition between shipment and placement on the sales floor. **Floor-ready merchandise** is packed and shipped from the factory, essentially as it will be stocked and displayed in the retail store. Individual product units are prepared with the required hangtags, bar code and price stickers or tickets, security tags or devices (if applicable), and hung on hangers, folded, or packed with the appropriate means for making the merchandise ready for placement on store fixtures.

■ Packaging for Flat Folded or Rolled Merchandise

Some products are best merchandised in a folded or rolled format, whether they are displayed in bags or boxes, or void of outer packaging. Folded items may require fasteners to secure the product to another packaging component to maintain the shape and aesthetic appeal. Some apparel items are folded and secured with pins or clips to retain the shape of the item within the packaging. Pins and clips in several different types and sizes are made of metal or plastic. Pins and clips are used for

- Attaching a hangtag to a garment
- Securing the arms of a hung garment during shipping
- Securing folded garments within the packaging

Apparel items packaged in flat folded or rolled forms include

Fleece sweatshirts and sweatpants	Men's and children's undergarments and thermals	Sweaters
Jeans	Pajamas	Ties
Knit tops	Scarves	T-shirts
Men's dress shirts	Socks and hosiery	Turtlenecks

Box Heavy paper, cardboard, or plastic container formed or folded into shape and glued together. Boxes may be constructed as one piece or two, a bottom and lid. Some boxes may include see-through portions and inserts to secure and display merchandise. Boxes are available in a variety of shapes, sizes, and finishes that are used for shipping and merchandise packaging.

Tape Strong, clear, semitransparent, or tan-colored strip of material having an adhesive surface on one or both sides. Tape is available in rolls of different widths and strengths and is used to secure rolled merchandise as well as to seal flat bags. Types of packaging tape include

Cellophane or transparent
Double-sided
Masking

Flat Bag Flexible polyethylene film sack sealed at the bottom, with an open top that can be secured with a heat seal, tied, stapled, or taped with double-sided adhesive. Flat bags may contain air holes. These bags are available in a variety of gauge thicknesses ranging from 1.0 to 1.5 mil. *Mil* is a unit of measurement used for indicating thickness. One mil is equal to 0.001 inch (0.0254 millimeter). Flat bag sizes include

10 × 13 inches (25.4 × 33.02 cm)
11 × 14 inches (27.94 × 35.56 cm)
12 × 18 inches (30.48 × 45.72 cm)
14 × 18.5 inches (35.56 × 46.99 cm)
14 × 20 inches (35.56 × 50.80 cm)
18 × 24 inches (30.48 × 60.96 cm)
20 × 30 inches (50.8 × 76.2 cm)
24 × 38 inches (60.96 × 96.52 cm)

Jet Clip Clear or white plastic fastener ranging in size from 1¼ to 2 inches (31.75 to 50.8 mm) in length with or without teeth. Jet clips are used to secure folded blouses, shirts, slacks, or jeans and commonly put up in boxes of 1,000.

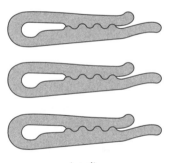

Jet clip

Pinch Clip Matte or shiny aluminum C-shaped bendable clip used to secure woven or knitted garments that are folded or socks that are folded or hung.

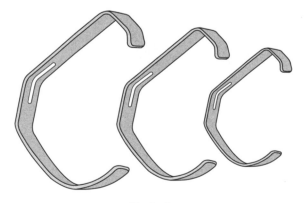

Pinch clip

Flat bag

Ball Point Pin (Satin Pin) Pin with a very fine diameter having a rounded tip and a flat or round head used on fine or delicate fabrics. Pins are available in ½- to 1½-inch (12.7 to 38.1 mm) lengths. This type of pin separates the yarns and slips through the weave instead of penetrating and cutting the yarns. Satin pins are put up in boxes by weight or by number of units, which vary depending on the pin size or supplier.

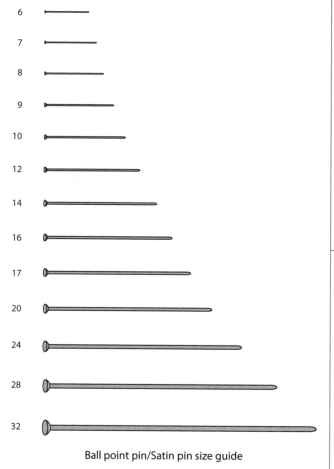

Ball point pin/Satin pin size guide

Straight Pin Pin with a very fine tapered sharp tip and a flat or round head. Pins are available in ½- to 1½-inch (12.7 to 38.1 mm) lengths. Straight pins are put up in boxes by weight or by number of units, which varies depending on the pin size or supplier.

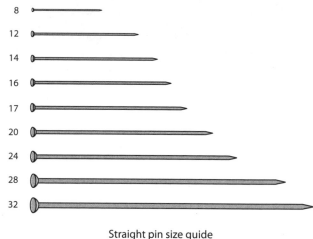

Straight pin size guide

T Pin (T-Head Pin) Rigid metal wire, from 1 to 2 inches (25.4 to 50.8 mm) in length, with a sharply pointed tip and a T-bar-shaped head formed from the wire. The size and shape of the head allows for high visibility and easy removal from folded shirts.

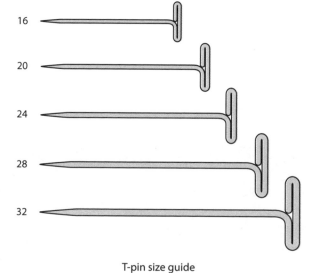

T-pin size guide

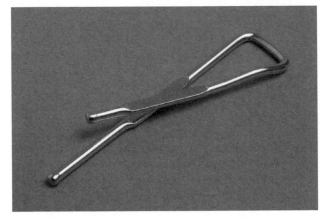

X clip/Metal clip/Crossover shirt clip

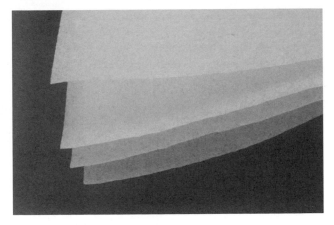

Tissue paper

X Clip, Metal Clip (Crossover Shirt Clip) Rigid metal wire with rounded smooth ends that is formed into an × shape with one closed end and one open end. This clip is used in place of a pin to avoid damage to the garment fabric. The × clip does not penetrate the material like a pin; it slides onto the fabric to provide security much like a paperclip is used to secure papers.

Tissue Paper Lightweight, translucent paper. Tissue paper is used to pack folded shirts, blouses, and sweaters.

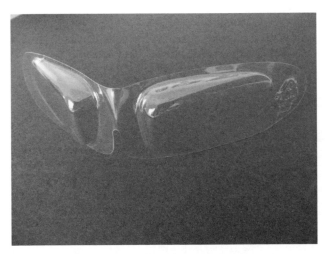

Butterfly

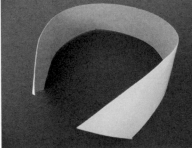

Neck band insert/Collar strip

Butterfly Small plastic or paperboard form available in a variety of shapes and sizes to support the front collar portion of a folded dress shirt. A butterfly is slid onto the top collar button to provide support and maintain the shape of the collar when packaged in a folded configuration.

Neck Band Insert (Collar Strips) Plastic or paperboard band available in widths varying from 1⅛ to 1¹¹⁄₁₆ inches (28.57 to 42.86 mm) and lengths from 15⅞ to 22½ inches (40.32 to 57.15 cm). The neck band is inserted between the shirt neck band and collar to provide support and maintain the shape of the collar when packaged in a folded configuration. Some neck band inserts have a tab on one end that is inserted into slats along the band to provide a firm adjustable ring to fit a wider range of sizes.

MERCHANDISE PACKAGING (continued)

Rubber Band Flexible, extendable ring made from natural or synthetic rubber latex and fillers. Rubber bands are measured by thickness, inner diameter, lay-flat length, and cut width. Rubber bands are used for bundling merchandise and securing boxes and bags. According to Central Elastic Corporation

- Thickness is measured in a relaxed state and ranges from ¹⁄₃₂ inch (0.8 mm) to ⅛ inch (3.0 mm)
- Inner diameter is measured in a relaxed state and ranges from ⁷⁄₁₆ inch (11 mm) to 12 inches (306 mm)
- Lay-flat length is measured with the band pressed flat and ranges from ¹¹⁄₁₆ inch (18 mm) to 18⅞ inch (480 mm)
- Cut widths range from ¹⁄₂₄ inch (1 mm) to 4 inches (10 mm)

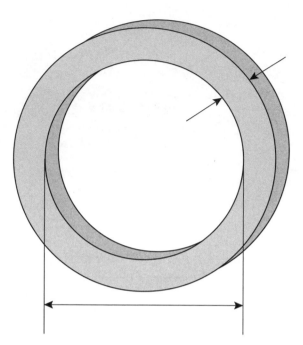

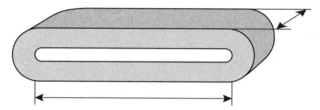

Rubber band lay-flat length and cut width

Rubber band thickness and inner diameter

Shirt Board (Shirt Liner) Paperboard stiffener that forms and supports folded shirts, which are pinned or clipped onto the board. Shirt boards are available in a variety of styles such as

I-boards	Square boards
T-boards	Window boards
Rectangle boards	

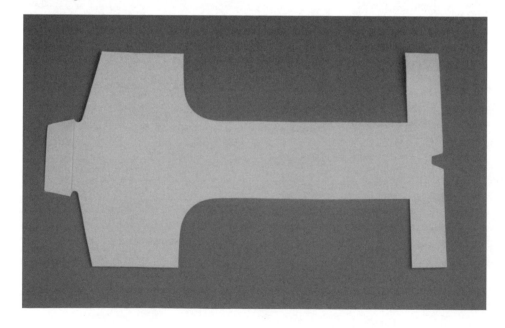

■ Packaging for Hung Merchandise

Some products are best merchandised and displayed hung. Apparel items that are packaged on hangers include

Suits	Coats	Shorts
Dresses	Jackets	Socks
Shirts	Pajamas	Tights
Blouses	Trousers	
Sweaters	Skirts	

Duo Jet Clip Tie Back Fastener Two clear or white plastic clips 1½ inches (38.1 mm) in length with or without teeth tied together with elastic thread. Duo jet clip tie back fasteners secure blouses, shirts, and sweaters that are hung.

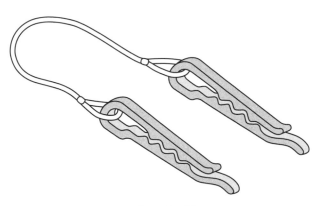

Duo jet clip tie back fastener

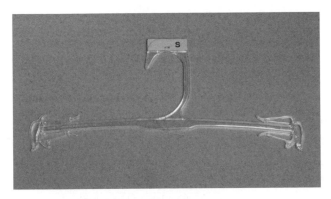

Bra and panty hanger

Bra and Panty Hanger Clear plastic 10-inch (25.4 cm) bar with stationary hook and end clips. Bra and panty hangers have end clips to which merchandise is secured so as not to slip off the hanger. These hangers are packed in cartons of 500 units.

Bottom Hanger, Pant Hanger, or Skirt Hanger Clear, white, or black plastic or wooden hanger with a swivel chrome hook and a rod with metal clips and vinyl cushions, or one with metal clamps or clips that slide to hold a garment in place. Economy bottom hangers may be fully molded from plastic with two loops and tabs to secure a garment. Pant hangers are available in 8 inches (20.32 cm) for children's apparel and 10, 11, 12, and 14 inches (25.4, 27.94, 30.48, and 35.56 cm) for men's and women's bottoms. Heavy-duty hangers are packaged 100 per carton, whereas economy hangers are packed in cartons of 200 or 250 units.

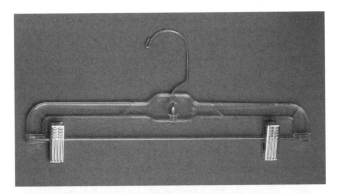

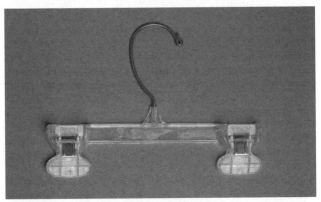

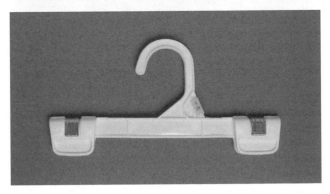

Bottom hanger/Pant hanger/Skirt hanger

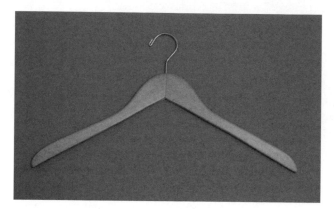

Coat hanger

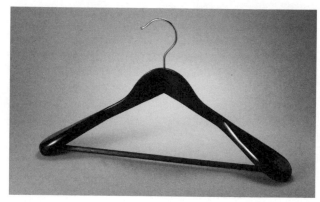

Suit hanger with bar

Coat Hanger Clear, white, or black plastic or wooden hanger with wide, smooth, sloped shoulders with a standard or long swivel chrome hook. Coat hangers are available in 17 and 19 inches (43.18 and 48.26 cm) for men's and women's garments. Hangers are packaged 100 per carton.

Suit Hanger with Bar Black plastic 17- or 19-inch (43.18 or 48.26 cm) long smooth, contoured, sloped shoulder hanger with a swivel chrome hook and molded plastic bar to hang trousers. Hangers are packaged 100 per carton.

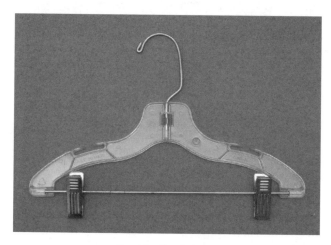

Combination hanger

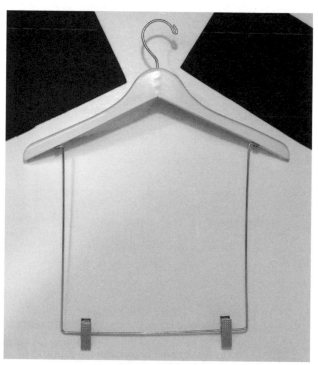

Suit hanger with dropped hook bar

Combination Hanger Clear, white, or black plastic or wooden sloped shoulder hanger with a swivel chrome hook and a metal rod with plastic or metal clips with vinyl cushions. Some combination hangers have notches at the shoulders to allow for a garment with straps to be hung. Economy combination hangers may be fully molded from plastic having a stationary hook and pant bar without clips. Combination hangers are available in 12 inches (30.48 cm) for children's apparel and 12, 16, 17, and 18 inches (30.48, 40.64, 43.18, 45.72 cm) for men's and women's garments. Heavy-duty hangers are packaged 100 per carton, whereas economy hangers are packed in cartons of 500 units.

Suit Hanger with Dropped Hook Bar White or black plastic hanger with wide rounded smooth shoulders, a swivel hook, and metal wire rod dropped 10 inches (25.4 cm) from the shoulders that is equipped with plastic or metal clips with vinyl cushions. Suit hangers with dropped hook bars are used for women's suits. Hangers are packed in cartons of 100 units.

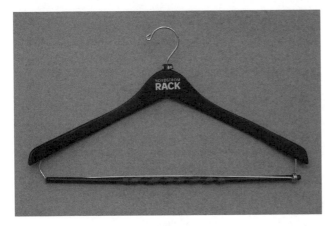

Suit hanger with locking bar

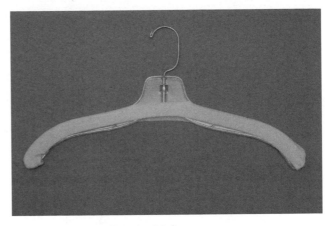

Hanger with foam cover

Suit Hanger with Locking Bar Black plastic or wooden 17-inch-long (43.18 cm) curved, sloped shoulder hanger with a swivel chrome hook and a wooden or plastic round rod with a thick metal wire that hooks onto the rod. Trousers are hung on the rod; then the wire is fastened in place to prevent the garment from slipping off the hanger. Suit hangers with locking bars are packaged 100 per carton.

Hanger Foam Cover A cover stretched over the hanger to prevent garments from slipping off. Hanger covers are sold in bundles of 1,000 units.

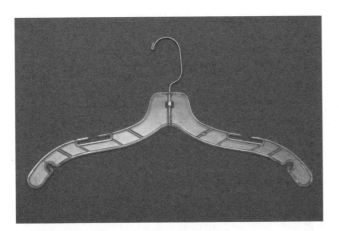

Top hanger

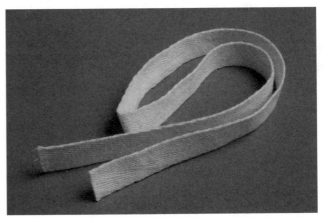

Hanger tape

Top Hanger, Shirt Hanger, or Dress Hanger Clear, white, or black plastic or wooden hanger with sloped shoulders with a swivel chrome hook or fully molded in plastic with a stationary hook. Some hangers have notches at the shoulder for hanging garments with straps. Shirt hangers are available in 12 and 14 inches (30.48 and 35.56 cm) for children's apparel and 17 and 18 inches (43.18 and 45.72 cm) for men's and women's garments. Hangers are packaged 100 or 200 units per carton.

Hanger Tape Black or white, cotton or polyester, ¼-inch (6.35 mm) woven tape sewn into garments to allow them to be hung safely and securely. Hanger tape is also available in clear ¼-inch (6.35 mm) film that varies in thickness. Hanger tape is put up in 800-yard (731.52 m) rolls.

Poly Bag Flexible polyethylene film sack, like those used by drycleaners, having one open end and one closed with a 3-inch (7.62 cm) hanger hole. These bags are available in a variety of gauge thicknesses ranging from 0.43 to 1.25 mil. Poly bags are available with or without sloped shoulders and gussets. Poly bag sizes include

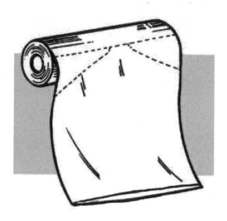

Poly Bags with Gussets

20 × 3 × 36 inches (50.8 × 7.62 × 91.44 cm)
20 × 3 × 54 inches (50.8 × 7.62 × 137.16 cm)
21 × 4 × 30 inches (53.34 × 10.16 × 76.2 cm)
21 × 4 × 36 inches (53.34 × 10.16 × 91.44 cm)
21 × 4 × 38 inches (53.34 × 10.16 × 96.52 cm)
21 × 4 × 54 inches (53.34 × 10.16 × 137.16 cm)
21 × 4 × 66 inches (53.34 × 10.16 × 167.64 cm)
21 × 4 × 72 inches (53.34 × 10.16 × 182.88 cm)
24 × 8 × 72 inches (60.96 × 20.32 × 182.88 cm)

Poly Bags without Gussets

20 × 24 inches (50.8 × 60.96 cm)
20 × 30 inches (50.8 × 76.2 cm)
20 × 36 inches (50.8 × 91.44 cm)
20 × 42 inches (50.8 × 106.68 cm)
20 × 48 inches (50.8 × 121.92 cm)
20 × 54 inches (50.8 × 137.16 cm)
20 × 60 inches (50.8 × 152.4 cm)
20 × 64 inches (50.8 × 162.56 cm)
20 × 72 inches (50.8 × 182.88 cm)

PACKAGING TAGS AND FASTENERS

An important aspect of merchandise packaging is the hangtag. A **hangtag** is a cardstock, paperboard, plastic, fabric, wooden, metal, or other material in the form of a square, rectangle, or die-cut shaped tag that is attached to an apparel item by means of a plastic fastener, braided cord, or safety pin with a ribbon. **Fasteners** secure hangtags to garments or product packaging. Hangtags range from basic one-color graphics and text to full-color graphic images and text.

Information provided on hangtags can include

Brand	Style number
Size	Care information
Style or fit	Fiber information
Price	Distributor
Country of origin	Garment properties such as
Color	shrink-resistant, prewashed
SKU number	for softness, pill-resistant,
Bar code	and water-repellant

When the bar code and price are included on one hangtag, it is known as an **integrated tag**.

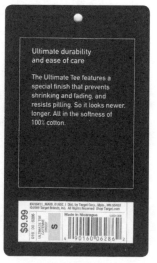

Bar Code Ticket or Bar Code Sticker Cardstock paper tag or self-adhesive sticker printed with a bar code and price. Bar code stickers are affixed to a hangtag, whereas bar code tickets are fastened to the garment alongside the hangtag.

Joker Tag Cardstock or paperboard tab stitched or attached with a plastic fastener to the waistband of casual pants and jeans. Joker tags are easily removed before the garment is worn and include information such as

Size	Price
Brand	Bar code
Color	Country of origin

Pocket Flasher Cardstock or paperboard pocket-shaped tag stitched or attached with a plastic fastener to the back pocket of casual pants and jeans. Pocket flashers can be basic or with multicolor graphics and are easily removed before the garment is worn. Information found on pocket flashers includes

Size	Price
Brand	Bar code
Color	Country of origin

Sock Band Paper or cardstock band with or without an adhesive back to attach to socks and hosiery sold by the pair or in bundles. Sock bands provide information such as

Size	Price
Brand	Bar code
Color	Country of origin

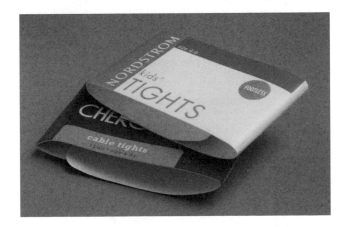

Pressure-Sensitive Size Wrapper Paper or plastic film with a self-adhesive back that is affixed to tops to convey size or fit. Some pressure-sensitive size wrappers or stickers also include brand identification.

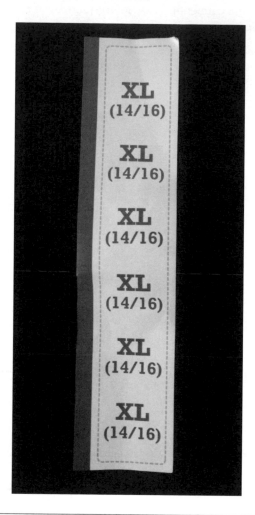

Bar Loc Fastener Opaque white plastic fastener having molded beads along the length with one end that is pointed and one shaped like a barrel. The pointed head is inserted into the barrel portion to close or lock the fastener into a loop shape that can be adjusted to size and is used to attach tags to accessories and shoes. This style fastener will not release once it is locked. Security lock loops are available in 3-, 5-, 7-, and 9-inch (7.62, 12.7, 17.78, and 22.86 cm) lengths and put up in 1,000- or 5,000-piece boxes.

Bar loc fastener

Plastic Fasteners (Tagging Barb) Clear, white, or black plastic fasteners with a smooth filament body and T-shaped ends used to attach tags to garments by means of a tagging gun. Plastic fasteners are available in 1-, 2-, 3-, and 5-inch (2.54, 5.08, 7.62, and 12.7 cm) lengths and put up in 5,000-piece boxes. Each piece or strip holds 50 fasteners.

Plastic fastener/Tagging barb

J-Hook (Hook-Tach Fastener) White fasteners with a hook-shaped top, smooth filament body, and T bottom are used to attach tags to accessories such as socks and gloves. Hook-tach fasteners are attached with a tagging gun. Plastic fasteners are available in 1.5- and 2-inch (3.81 and 5.08 cm) lengths and put up in 5,000-piece boxes. Each piece or strip holds 50 fasteners.

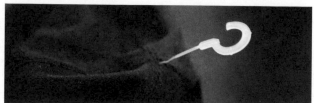

J-hook/Hook-tach fastener

Security Loop Lock White plastic fastener with one end shaped like an arrowhead and one shaped like a barrel. The portion between the connectors is a smooth filament. The pointed head is inserted into the barrel portion to close or lock the fastener into a loop shape and is used to attach tags to accessories and shoes. Security lock loops are available in 5-, 7-, and 9-inch (12.7, 17.78, and 22.86 cm) lengths and put up in 1,000- or 5,000-piece boxes.

Safety Pin Brass- or nickel-plated steel closed wire pin that is bent to form a loop on one end with a secure cap on the other end in which the sharp pin point is clipped. Safety pins are available in ¾- to 2-inch (19.05 to 50.8 mm) lengths.

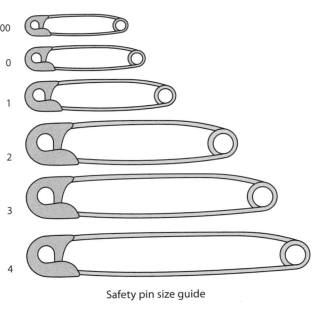

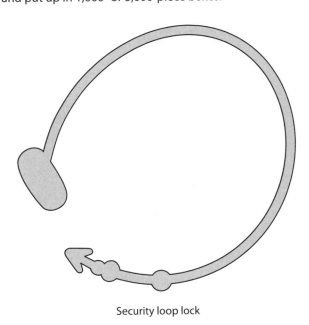

Security loop lock

Safety pin size guide

References

California Thread & Supply (CTS), Inc. (2015). *Poly bags/Garment bags/Cutwork bags.* Retrieved January 20, 2016, from http://www.ctsusa.com/_e/dept/05/Poly_Bags_Garment_Bags_Cutwork_Bags.htm

Central Elastic Corporation. (2016a). *CEC Standard size chart.* Retrieved January 20, 2016, from http://www.cec.com.my/technical-information

Central Elastic Corporation. (2016b). *Secret of rubber band.* Retrieved January 20, 2016, from http://www.cec.com.my/faq

Doran Manufacturing Corporation. (2016). *Shirt boards.* Retrieved January 20, 2016, from http://www.collarstays.com/page11.html

Focus Technology Co., Ltd. (2016). *Drycleaning poly bag.* Retrieved January 20, 2016, from http://www.made-in-china.com/showroom/pemaker/product-detailQqjmrfMvJgVp/China-Dry-Cleaning-Poly-Bag.html

Mulcahy, D. E. (1994). *Warehouse distribution and operations handbook.* New York: McGraw-Hill.

Palay Display Store Fixtures and Supplies. (2015–2016). *Poly bags.* Retrieved January 20, 2016, from http://www.palaydisplay.com/search.php?mode=search&page=1

Surendra Komar & Company. (n.d.). *Box strapping machine.* Retrieved January 20, 2016, from http://www.stitchingpackaging.com/box-strapping-machine.html

CREDITS

All uncredited photos courtesy of Janace Bubonia. All uncredited illustrations courtesy of Fairchild Books.

ASTM STITCH AND SEAM CLASSIFICATIONS